rary wars

8

─ Love & War ─

STORY & ART BY Kiiro Yumi   ORIGINAL CONCEPT BY Hiro Arikawa

Library Wars
Love & War

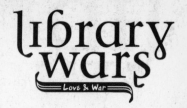

Contents

The Library Freedom Act

Libraries have the freedom to acquire their collections.

Libraries have the freedom to circulate
materials in their collections.

Libraries guarantee the privacy of their patrons.

Libraries oppose any type of censorship.

When libraries are imperiled,
librarians will join together
to secure their freedom.

library wars
Love & War

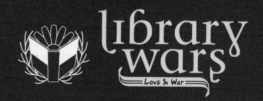

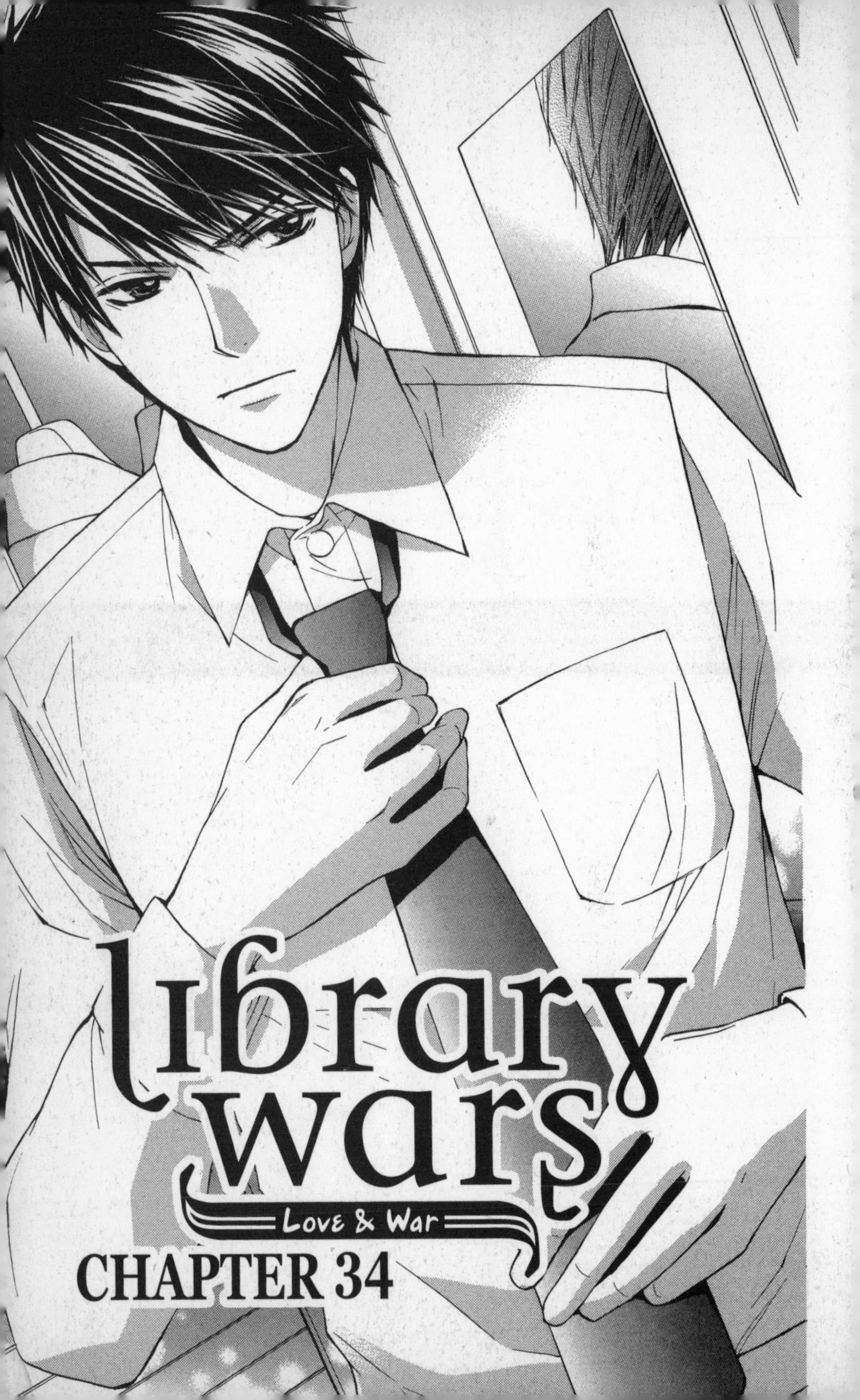
library wars
Love & War
CHAPTER 34

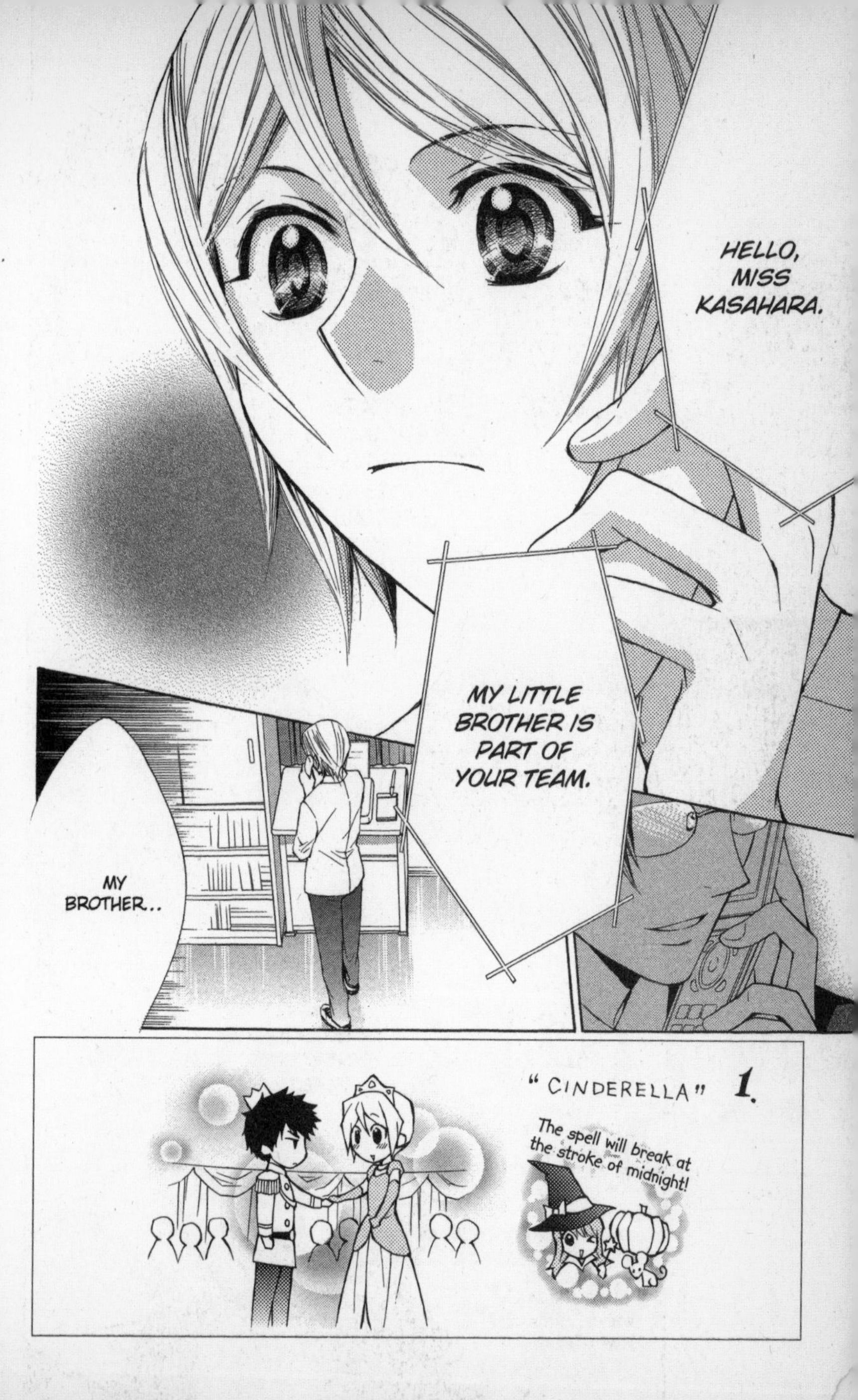
HELLO, MISS KASAHARA.
MY LITTLE BROTHER IS PART OF YOUR TEAM.
MY BROTHER...
"CINDERELLA" 1.
The spell will break at the stroke of midnight!

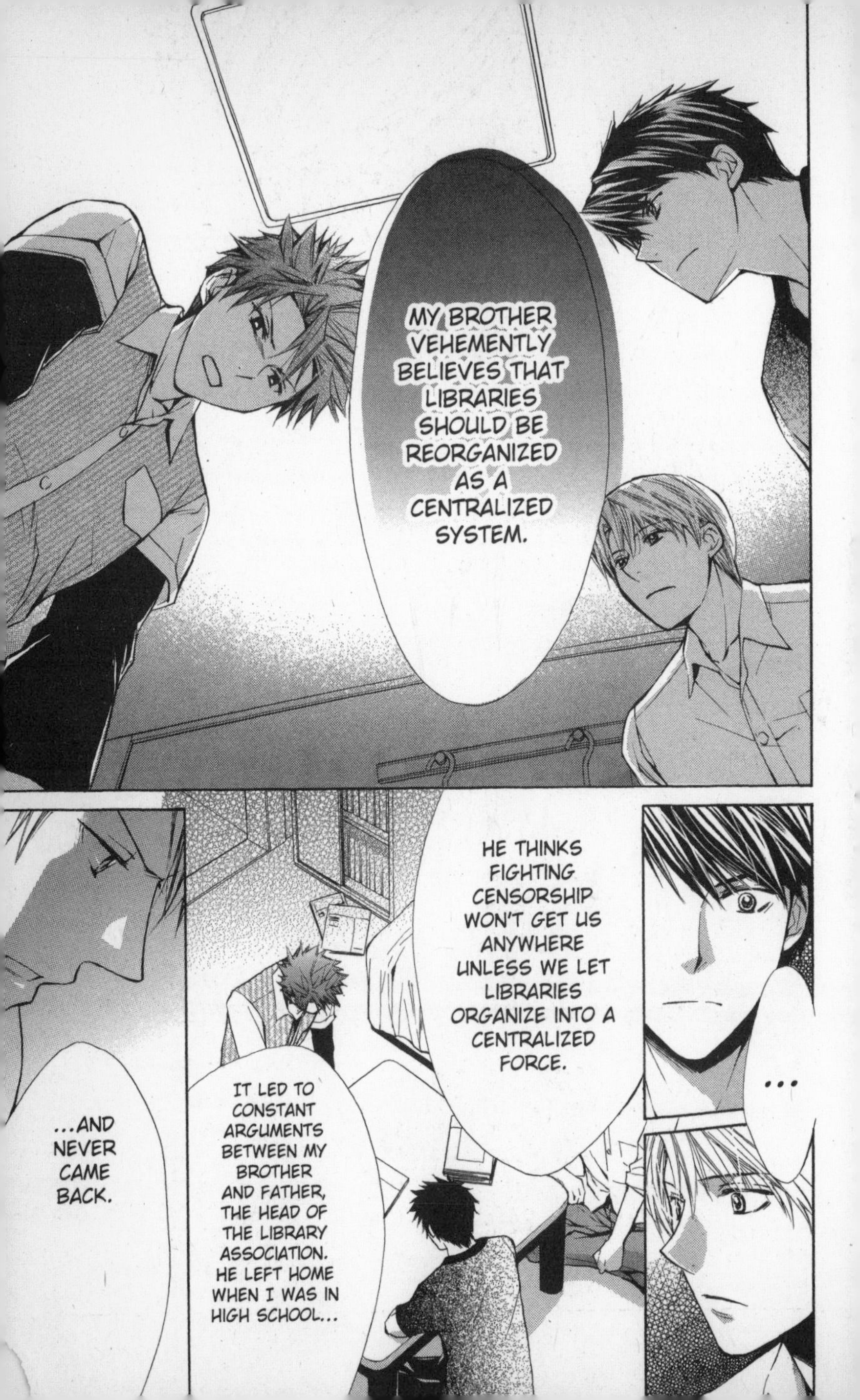
MY BROTHER VEHEMENTLY BELIEVES THAT LIBRARIES SHOULD BE REORGANIZED AS A CENTRALIZED SYSTEM.
...
HE THINKS FIGHTING CENSORSHIP WON'T GET US ANYWHERE UNLESS WE LET LIBRARIES ORGANIZE INTO A CENTRALIZED FORCE.
IT LED TO CONSTANT ARGUMENTS BETWEEN MY BROTHER AND FATHER, THE HEAD OF THE LIBRARY ASSOCIATION. HE LEFT HOME WHEN I WAS IN HIGH SCHOOL...
...AND NEVER CAME BACK.

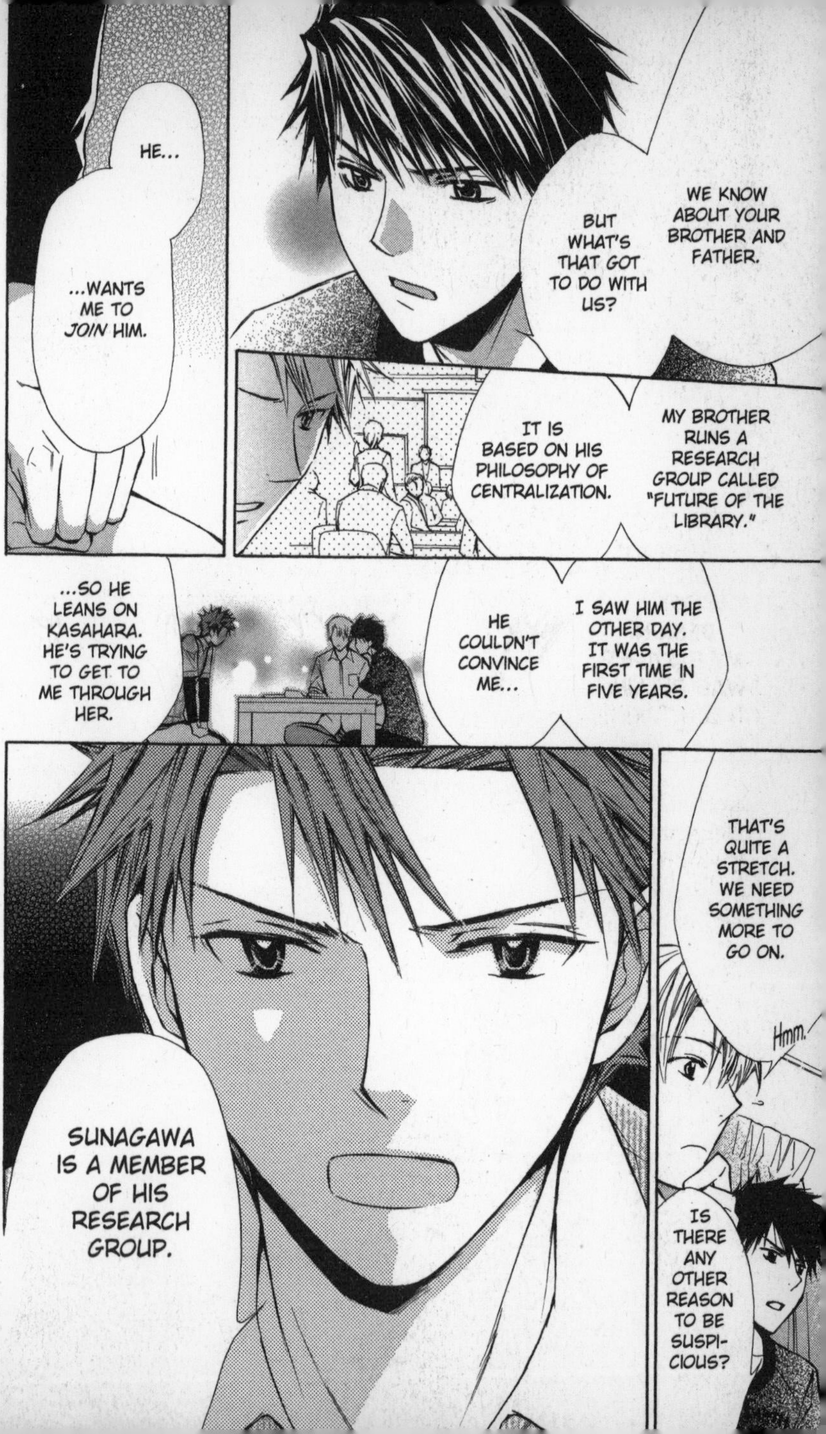
WE KNOW ABOUT YOUR BROTHER AND FATHER.
BUT WHAT'S THAT GOT TO DO WITH US?
MY BROTHER RUNS A RESEARCH GROUP CALLED "FUTURE OF THE LIBRARY."
IT IS BASED ON HIS PHILOSOPHY OF CENTRALIZATION.
HE...
...WANTS ME TO *JOIN* HIM.
I SAW HIM THE OTHER DAY. IT WAS THE FIRST TIME IN FIVE YEARS.
HE COULDN'T CONVINCE ME...
...SO HE LEANS ON KASAHARA. HE'S TRYING TO GET TO ME THROUGH HER.
THAT'S QUITE A STRETCH. WE NEED SOMETHING MORE TO GO ON.
Hmm.
IS THERE ANY OTHER REASON TO BE SUSPICIOUS?
SUNAGAWA IS A MEMBER OF HIS RESEARCH GROUP.

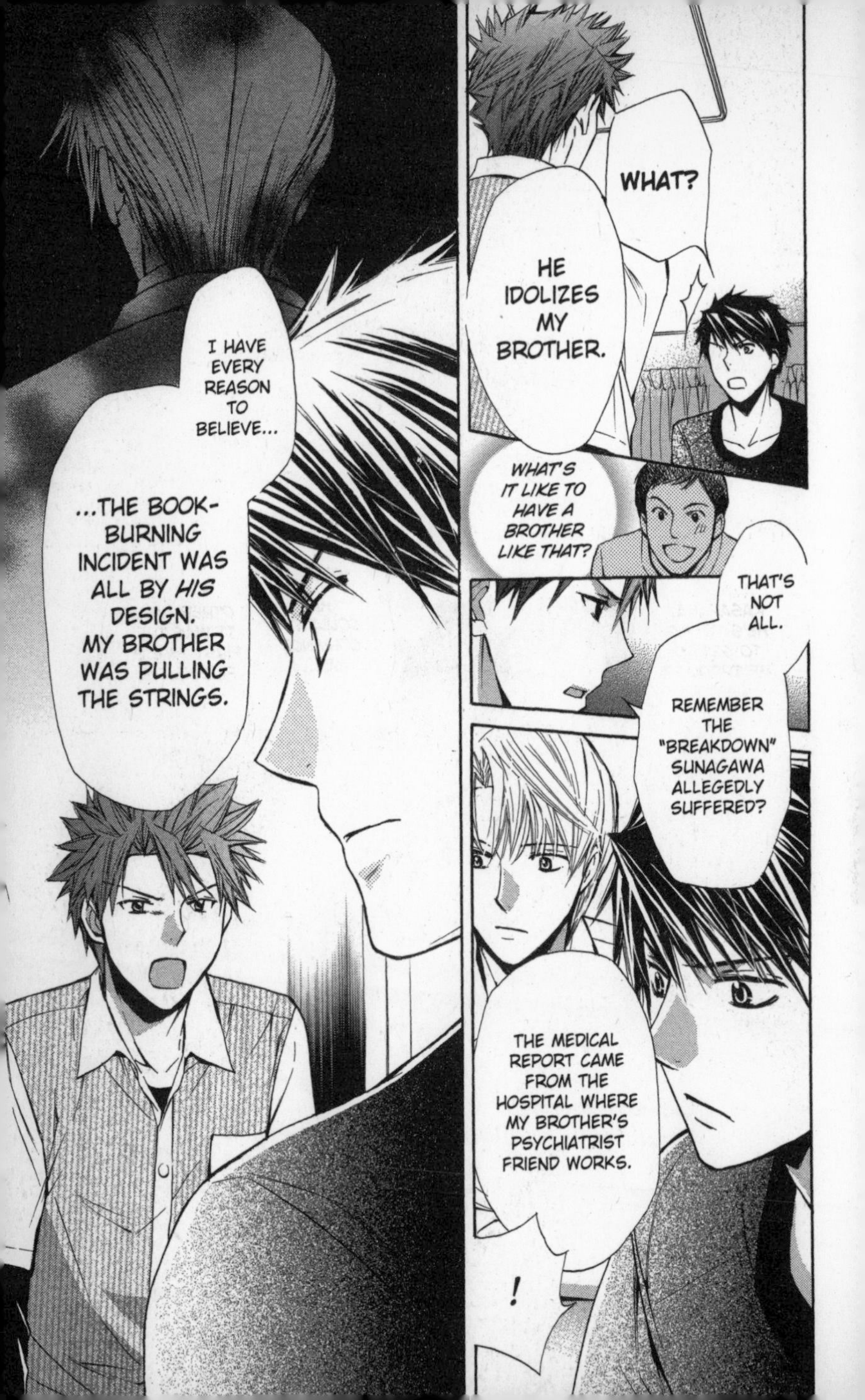
WHAT?
HE IDOLIZES MY BROTHER.
WHAT'S IT LIKE TO HAVE A BROTHER LIKE THAT?
THAT'S NOT ALL.
REMEMBER THE "BREAKDOWN" SUNAGAWA ALLEGEDLY SUFFERED?
THE MEDICAL REPORT CAME FROM THE HOSPITAL WHERE MY BROTHER'S PSYCHIATRIST FRIEND WORKS.
!
I HAVE EVERY REASON TO BELIEVE...
...THE BOOK-BURNING INCIDENT WAS ALL BY *HIS* DESIGN. MY BROTHER WAS PULLING THE STRINGS.

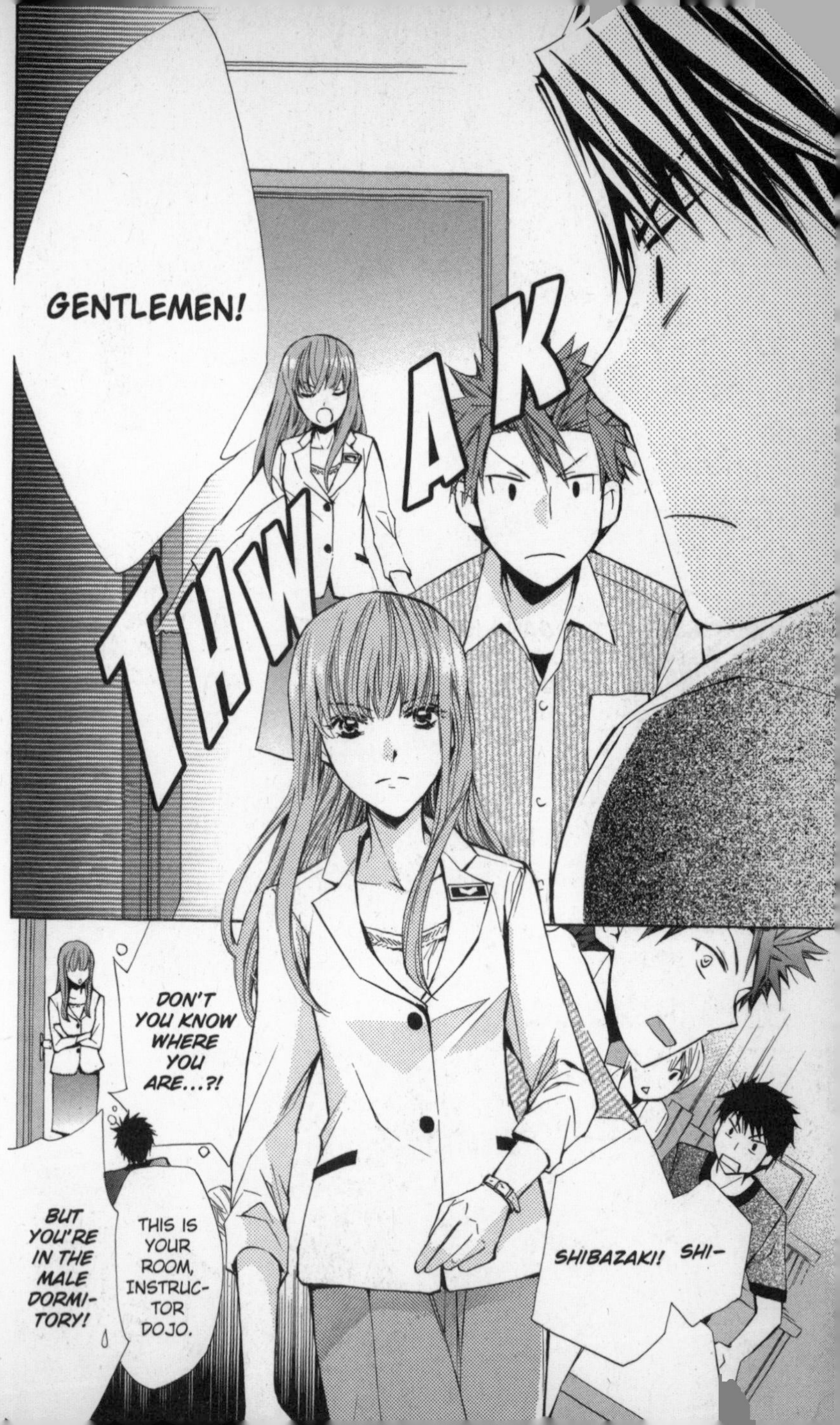
THWAK
GENTLEMEN!
SHI-
SHIBAZAKI!
DON'T YOU KNOW WHERE YOU ARE...?!
THIS IS YOUR ROOM, INSTRUCTOR DOJO.
BUT YOU'RE IN THE MALE DORMITORY!

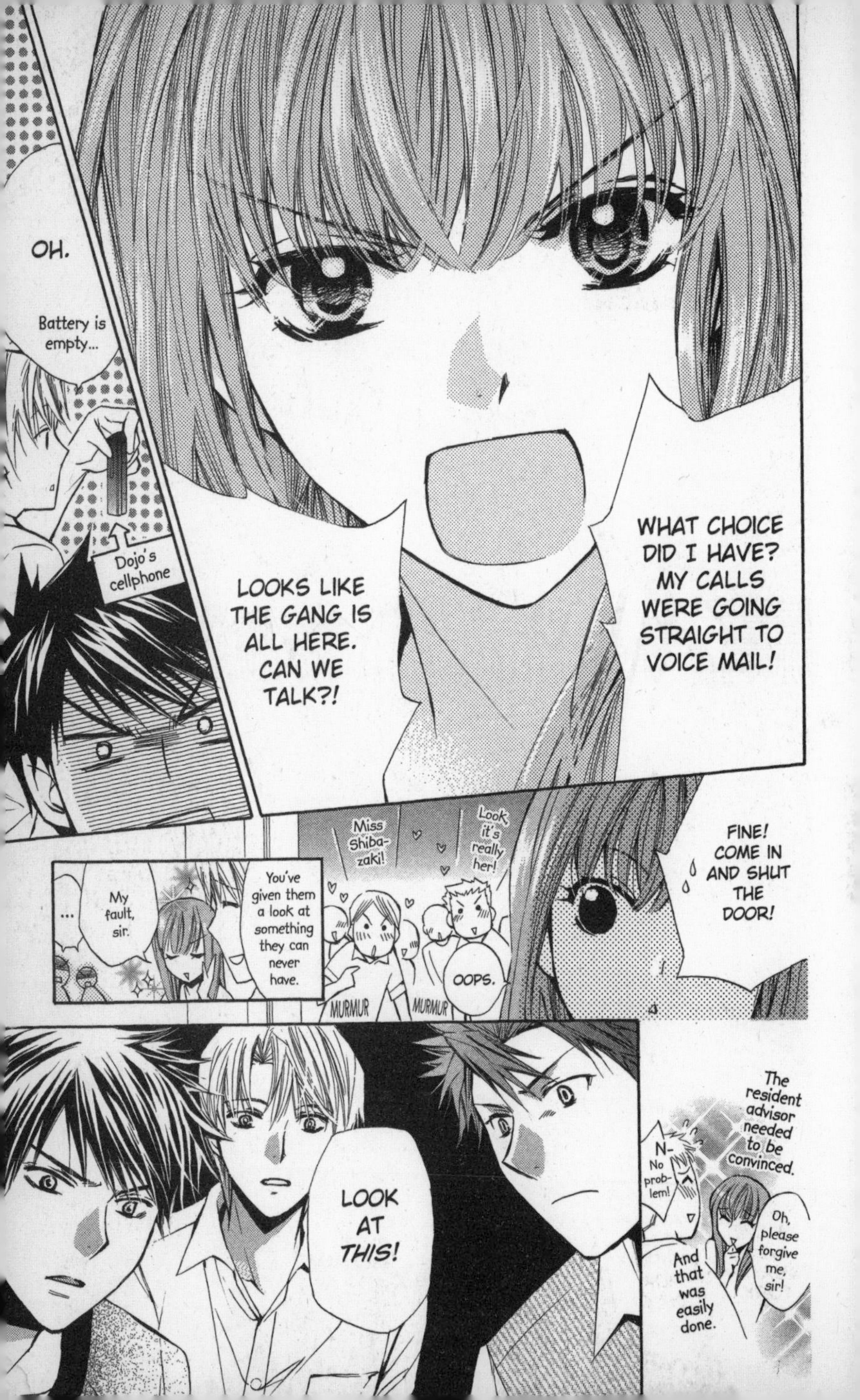
WHAT CHOICE DID I HAVE? MY CALLS WERE GOING STRAIGHT TO VOICE MAIL!
LOOKS LIKE THE GANG IS ALL HERE. CAN WE TALK?!
OH.
Battery is empty...
Dojo's cellphone
FINE! COME IN AND SHUT THE DOOR!
Look, it's really her!
Miss Shibazaki!
OOPS.
MURMUR
MURMUR
You've given them a look at something they can never have.
My fault, sir.
...
The resident advisor needed to be convinced.
N- No problem!
Oh, please forgive me, sir!
And that was easily done.
LOOK AT THIS!

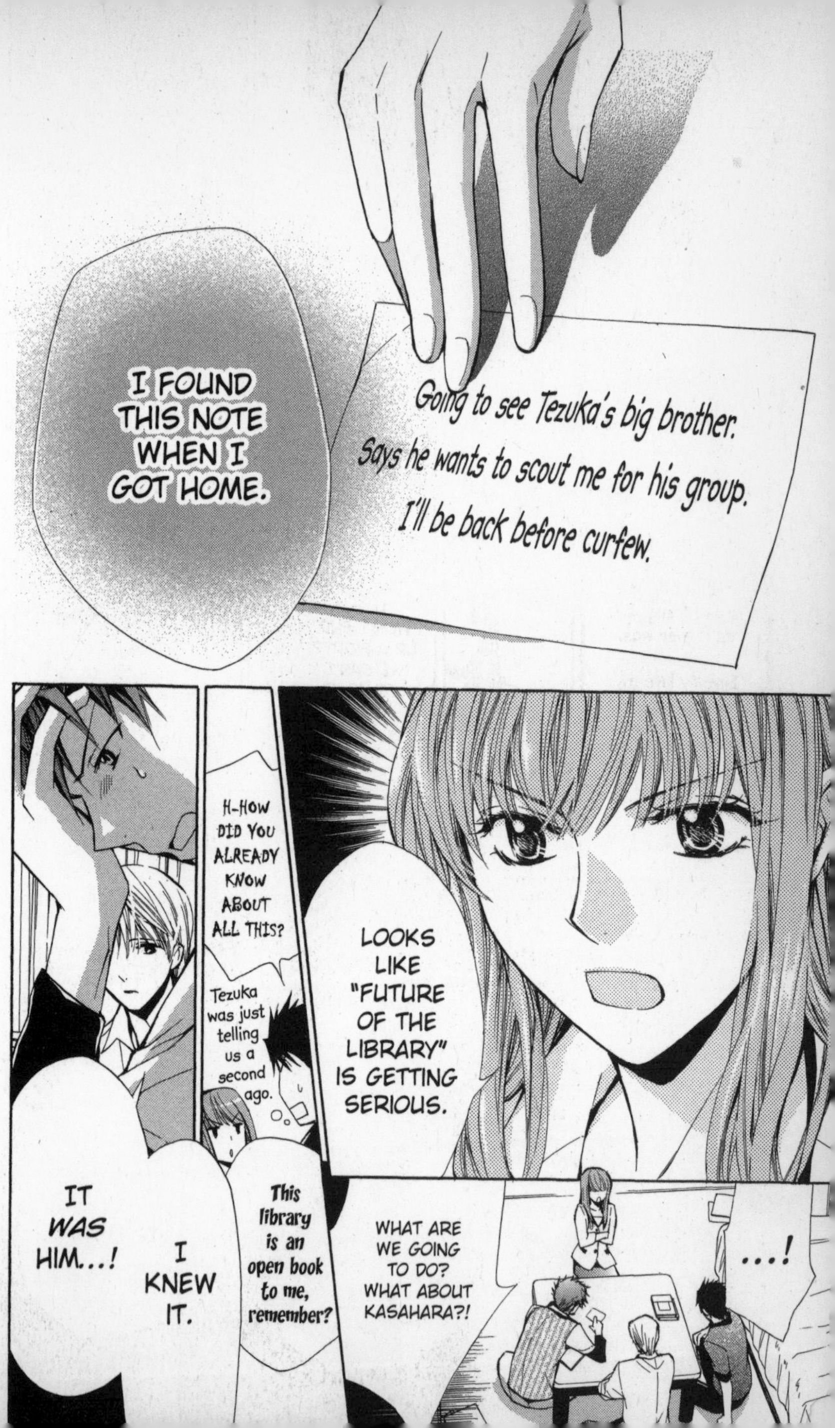
I FOUND THIS NOTE WHEN I GOT HOME.
Going to see Tezuka's big brother. Says he wants to scout me for his group. I'll be back before curfew.
LOOKS LIKE "FUTURE OF THE LIBRARY" IS GETTING SERIOUS.
H-HOW DID YOU ALREADY KNOW ABOUT ALL THIS?
Tezuka was just telling us a second ago.
...!
WHAT ARE WE GOING TO DO? WHAT ABOUT KASAHARA?!
This library is an open book to me, remember?
I KNEW IT.
IT WAS HIM...!

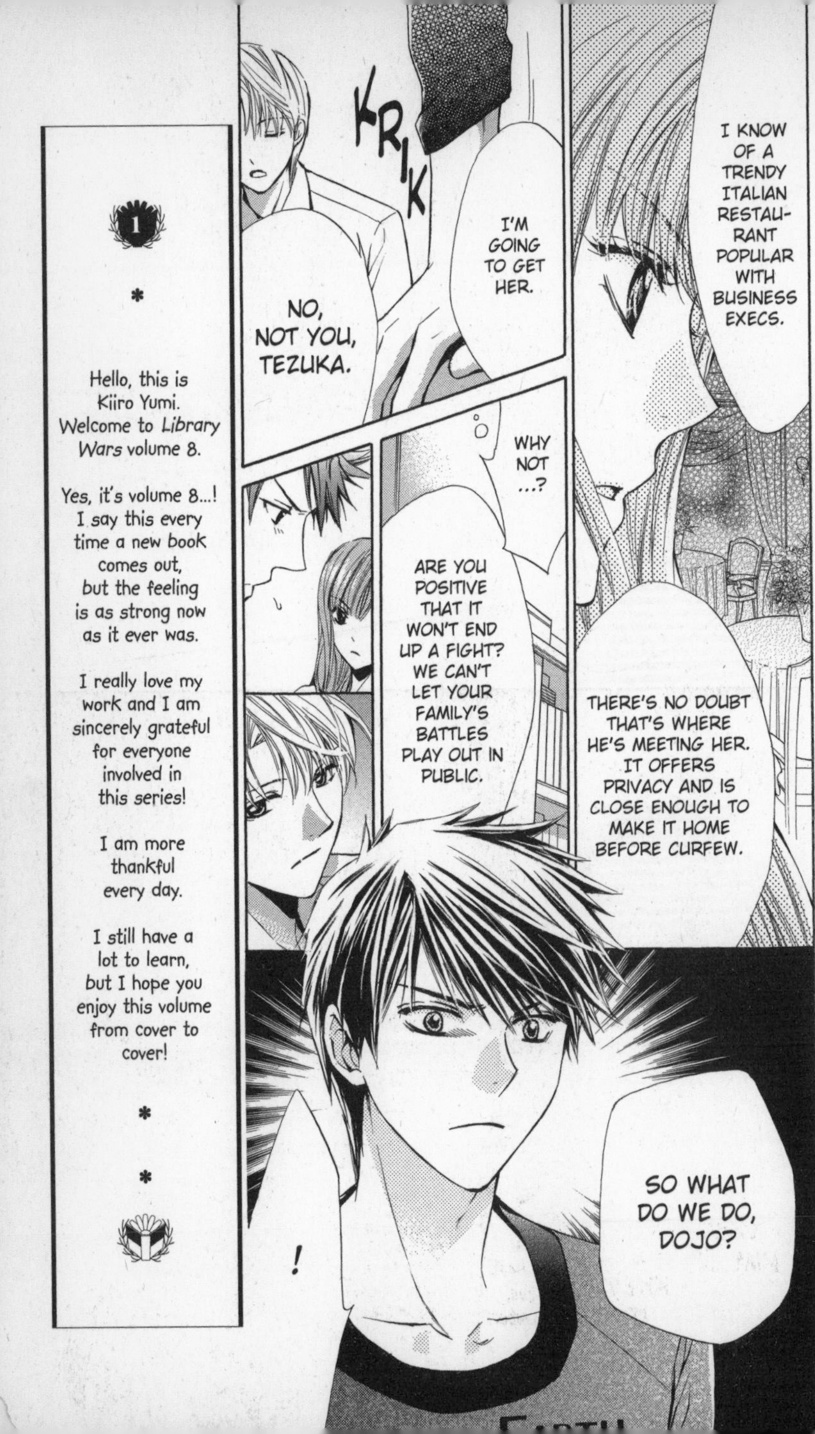
I KNOW OF A TRENDY ITALIAN RESTAURANT POPULAR WITH BUSINESS EXECS.
THERE'S NO DOUBT THAT'S WHERE HE'S MEETING HER. IT OFFERS PRIVACY AND IS CLOSE ENOUGH TO MAKE IT HOME BEFORE CURFEW.
KRIK
I'M GOING TO GET HER.
NO, NOT YOU, TEZUKA.
WHY NOT ...?
ARE YOU POSITIVE THAT IT WON'T END UP A FIGHT? WE CAN'T LET YOUR FAMILY'S BATTLES PLAY OUT IN PUBLIC.
SO WHAT DO WE DO, DOJO?
!

1

*

Hello, this is Kiiro Yumi. Welcome to *Library Wars* volume 8.

Yes, it's volume 8...! I say this every time a new book comes out, but the feeling is as strong now as it ever was.

I really love my work and I am sincerely grateful for everyone involved in this series!

I am more thankful every day.

I still have a lot to learn, but I hope you enjoy this volume from cover to cover!

*

*

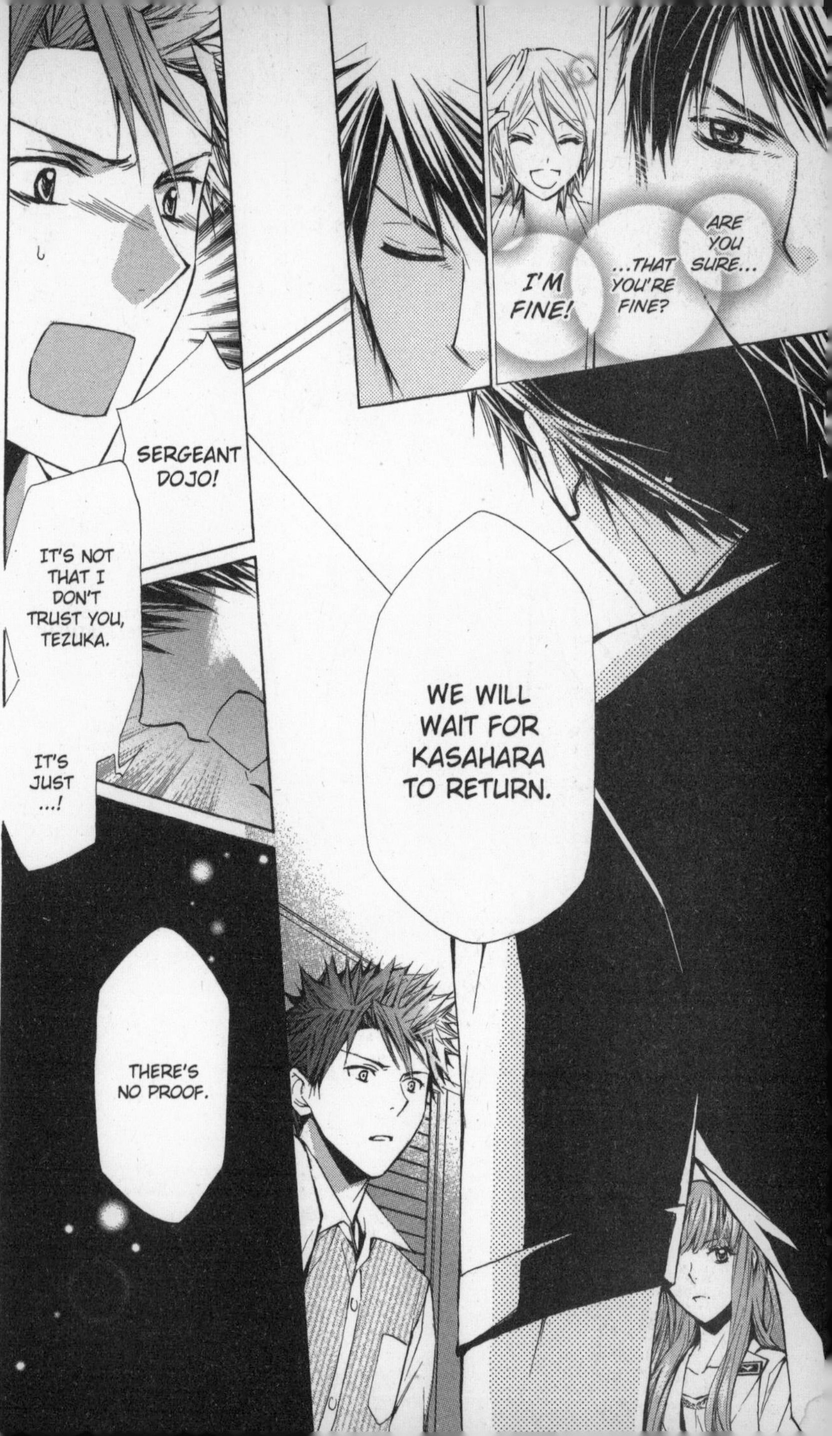
ARE YOU SURE...
...THAT YOU'RE FINE?
I'M FINE!
SERGEANT DOJO!
WE WILL WAIT FOR KASAHARA TO RETURN.
IT'S NOT THAT I DON'T TRUST YOU, TEZUKA.
IT'S JUST ...!
THERE'S NO PROOF.

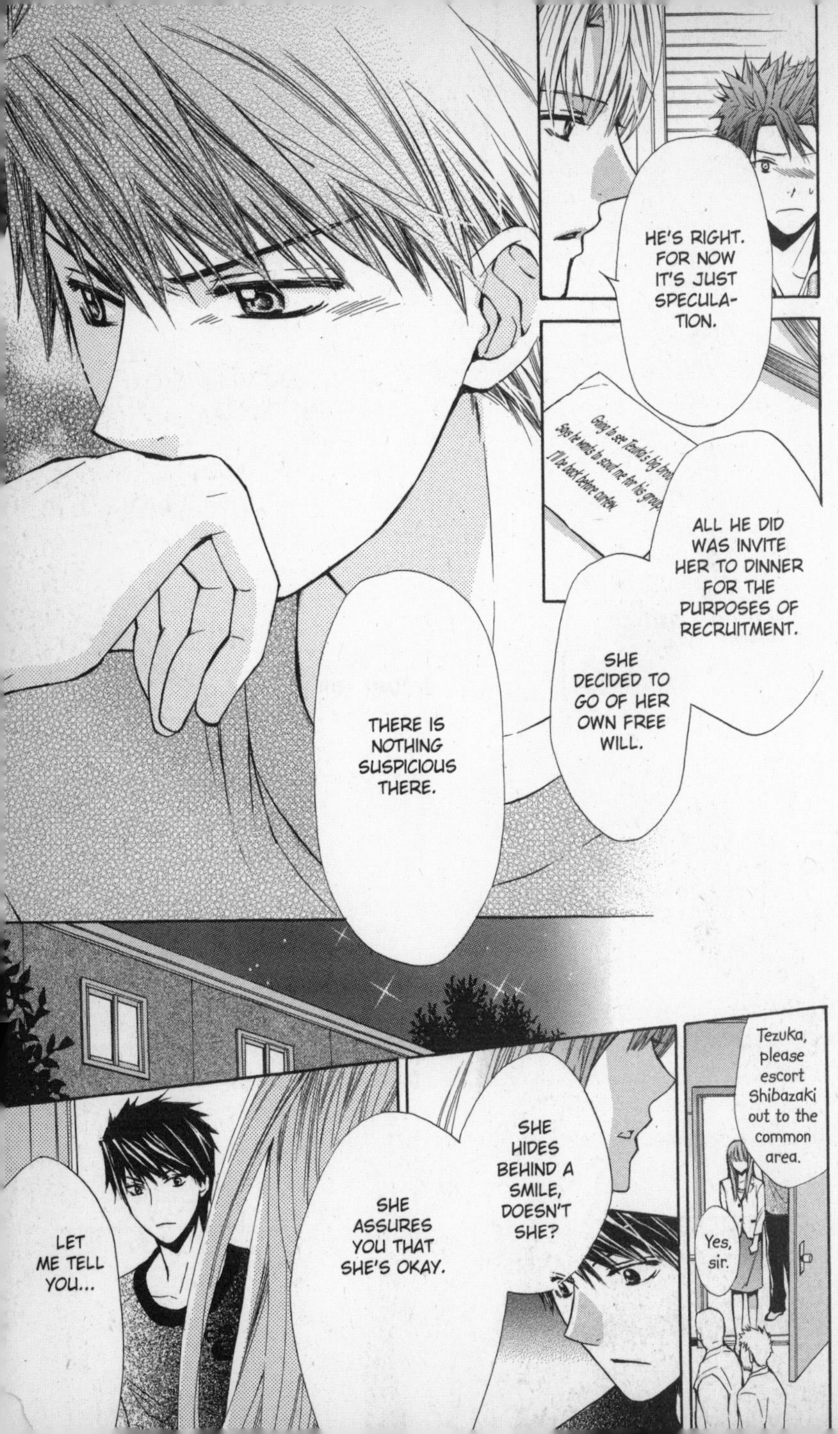
HE'S RIGHT. FOR NOW IT'S JUST SPECULATION.
Going to see Tezuka's big bro
Says he wants to scout me for his group
I'll be back before curfew
ALL HE DID WAS INVITE HER TO DINNER FOR THE PURPOSES OF RECRUITMENT.
SHE DECIDED TO GO OF HER OWN FREE WILL.
THERE IS NOTHING SUSPICIOUS THERE.
Tezuka, please escort Shibazaki out to the common area.
Yes, sir.
SHE HIDES BEHIND A SMILE, DOESN'T SHE?
SHE ASSURES YOU THAT SHE'S OKAY.
LET ME TELL YOU...

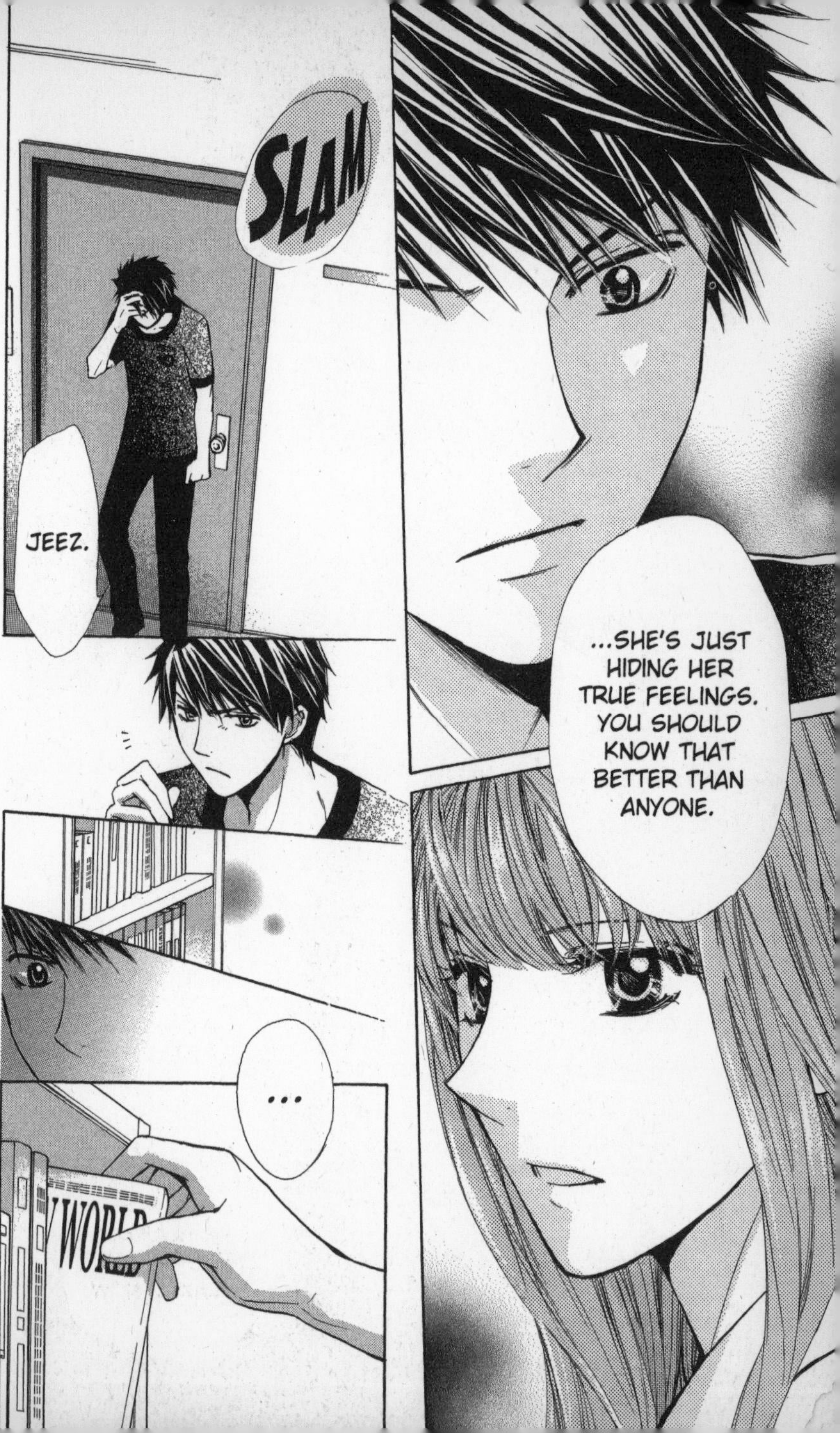
...SHE'S JUST HIDING HER TRUE FEELINGS. YOU SHOULD KNOW THAT BETTER THAN ANYONE.
SLAM
JEEZ.
...
WORLD

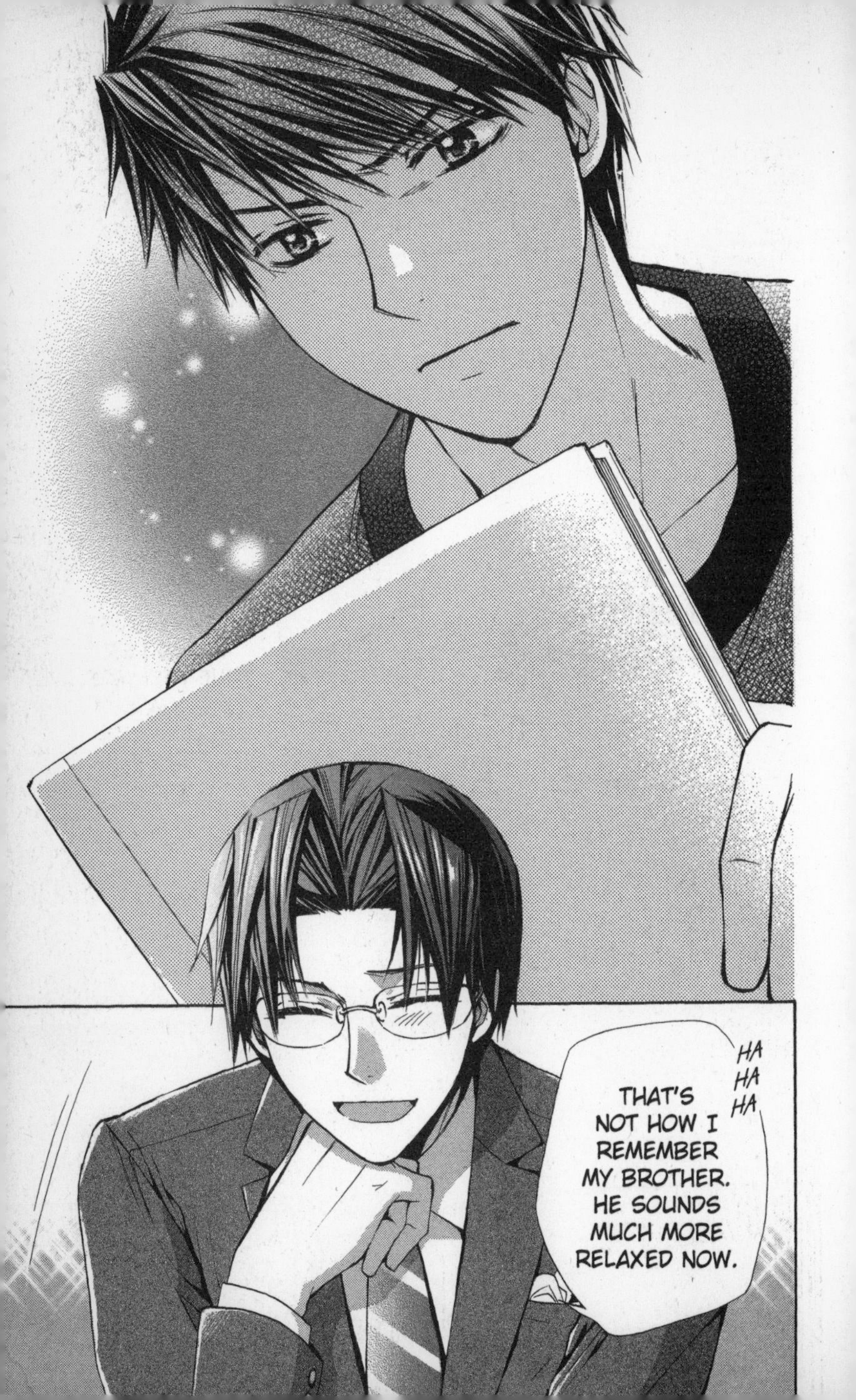
HA HA HA
THAT'S NOT HOW I REMEMBER MY BROTHER. HE SOUNDS MUCH MORE RELAXED NOW.

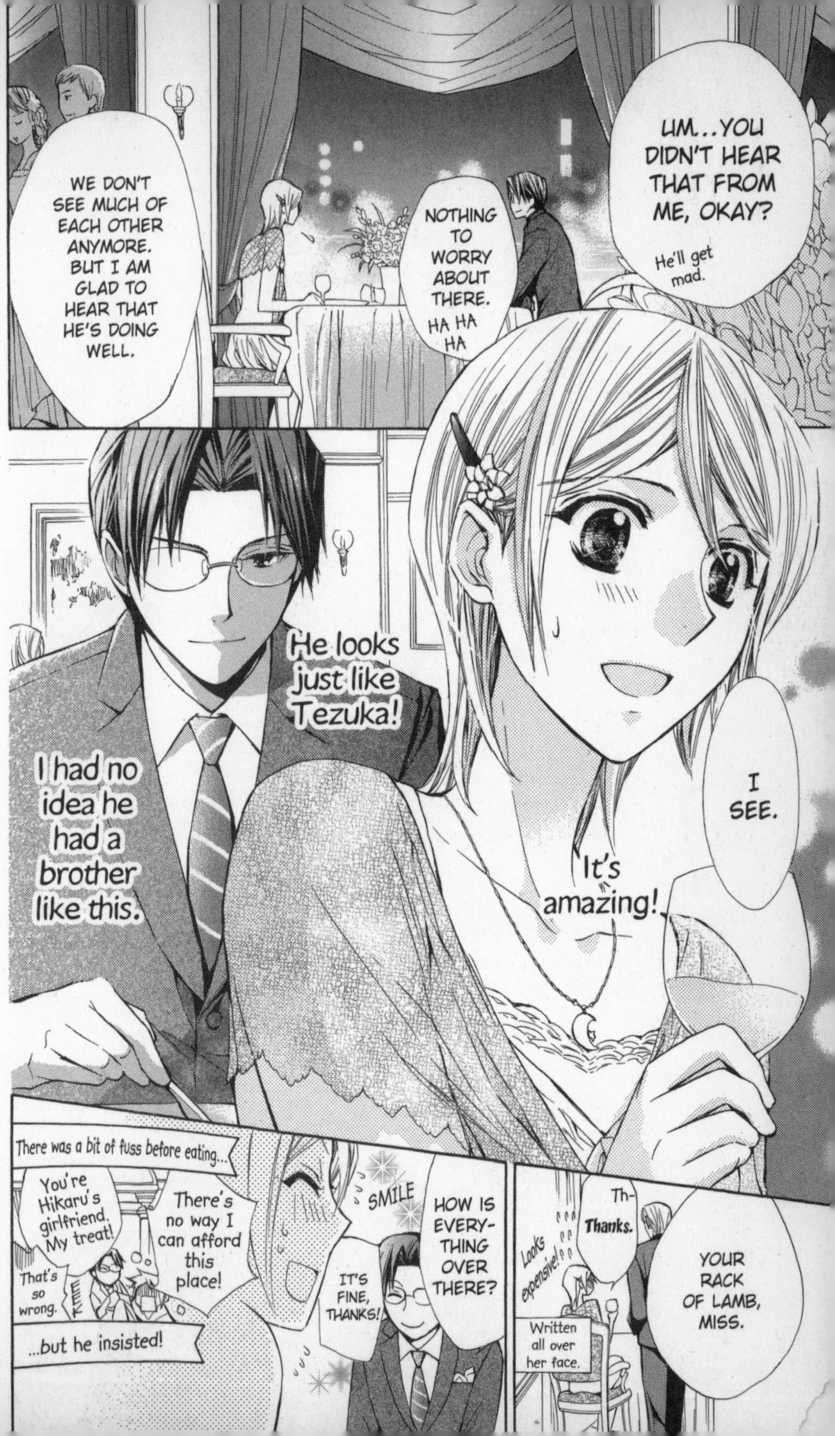
UM...YOU DIDN'T HEAR THAT FROM ME, OKAY?
He'll get mad.
NOTHING TO WORRY ABOUT THERE.
HA HA HA
WE DON'T SEE MUCH OF EACH OTHER ANYMORE. BUT I AM GLAD TO HEAR THAT HE'S DOING WELL.
I SEE.
It's amazing!
He looks just like Tezuka!
I had no idea he had a brother like this.
Th-
Thanks.
YOUR RACK OF LAMB, MISS.
Looks expensive!
Written all over her face.
SMILE
HOW IS EVERYTHING OVER THERE?
IT'S FINE, THANKS!
There was a bit of fuss before eating...
You're Hikaru's girlfriend. My treat!
There's no way I can afford this place!
That's so wrong.
EEK
...but he insisted!

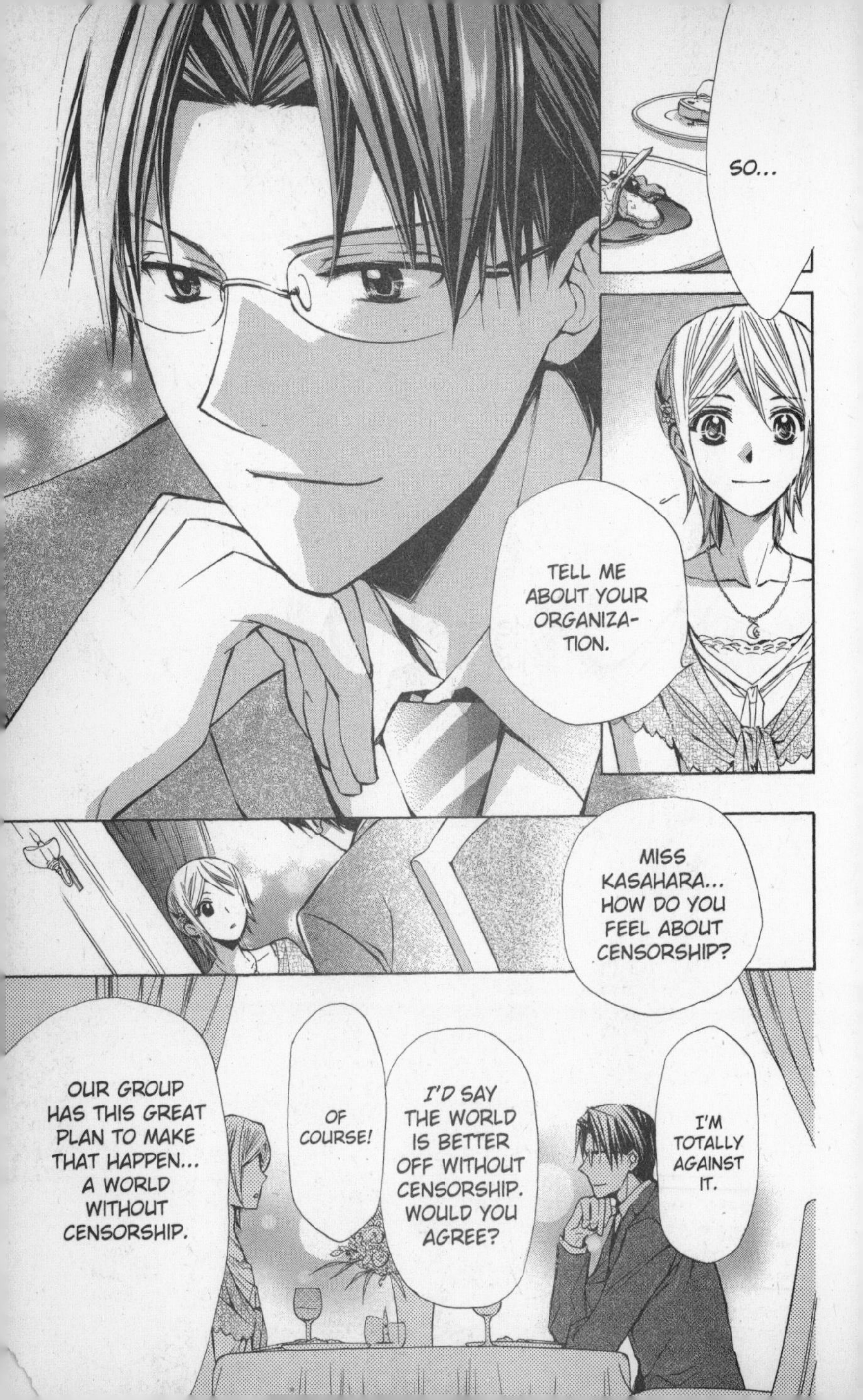
SO...
TELL ME ABOUT YOUR ORGANIZATION.
MISS KASAHARA... HOW DO YOU FEEL ABOUT CENSORSHIP?
I'M TOTALLY AGAINST IT.
I'D SAY THE WORLD IS BETTER OFF WITHOUT CENSORSHIP. WOULD YOU AGREE?
OF COURSE!
OUR GROUP HAS THIS GREAT PLAN TO MAKE THAT HAPPEN... A WORLD WITHOUT CENSORSHIP.

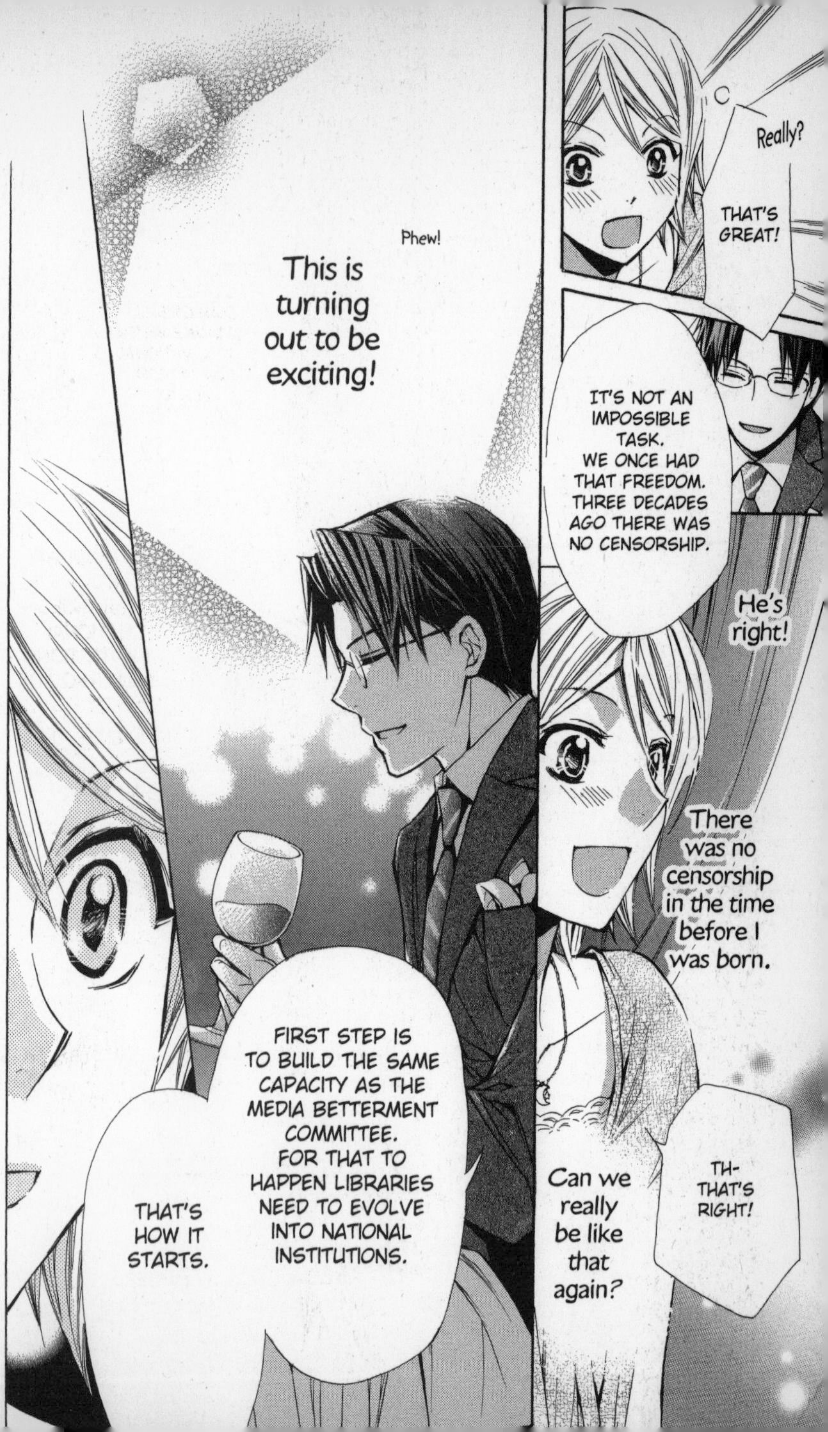
Really?
THAT'S GREAT!
IT'S NOT AN IMPOSSIBLE TASK. WE ONCE HAD THAT FREEDOM. THREE DECADES AGO THERE WAS NO CENSORSHIP.
He's right!
There was no censorship in the time before I was born.
TH- THAT'S RIGHT!
Can we really be like that again?
Phew!
This is turning out to be exciting!
FIRST STEP IS TO BUILD THE SAME CAPACITY AS THE MEDIA BETTERMENT COMMITTEE. FOR THAT TO HAPPEN LIBRARIES NEED TO EVOLVE INTO NATIONAL INSTITUTIONS.
THAT'S HOW IT STARTS.

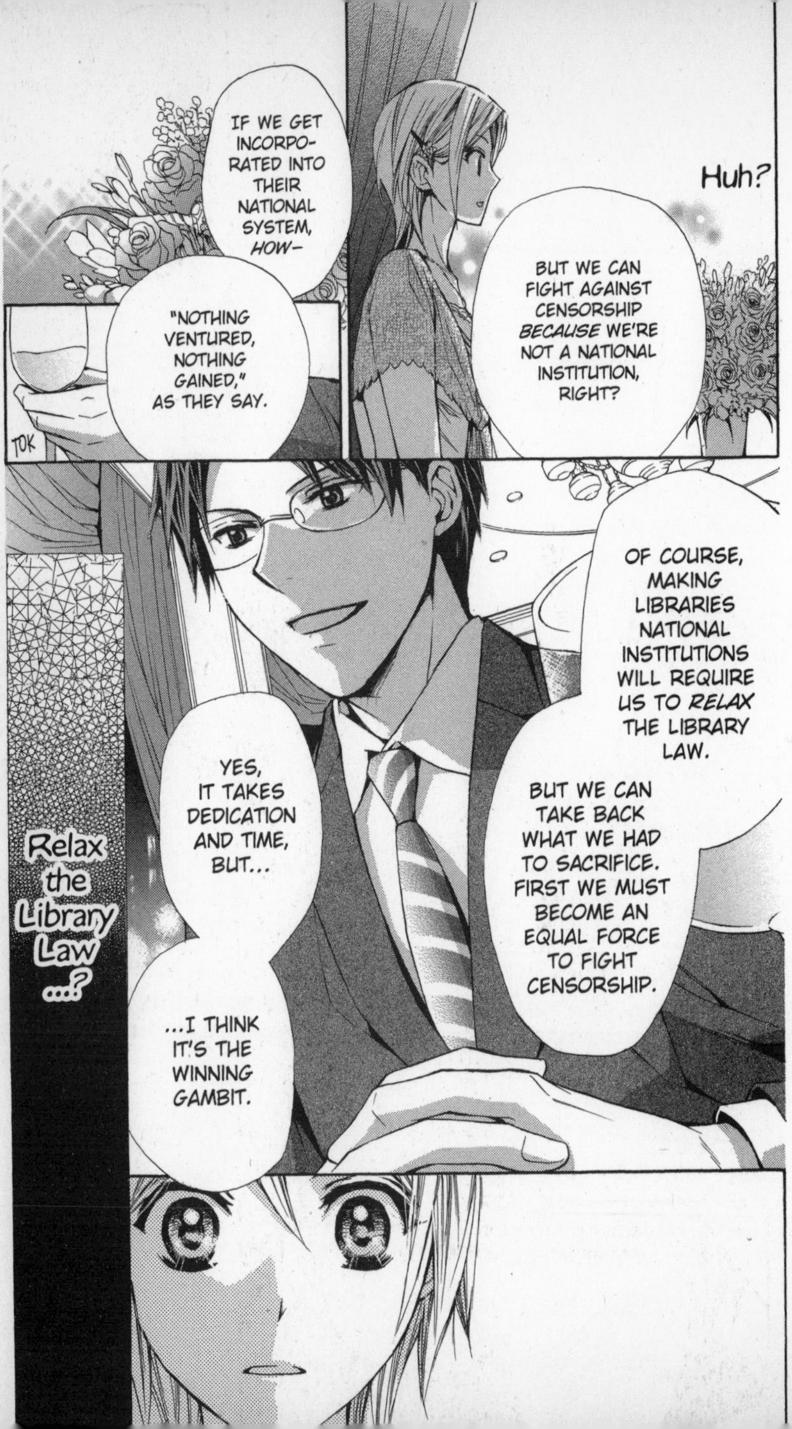

Huh?
BUT WE CAN FIGHT AGAINST CENSORSHIP *BECAUSE* WE'RE NOT A NATIONAL INSTITUTION, RIGHT?
IF WE GET INCORPORATED INTO THEIR NATIONAL SYSTEM, *HOW*–
TOK
"NOTHING VENTURED, NOTHING GAINED," AS THEY SAY.
OF COURSE, MAKING LIBRARIES NATIONAL INSTITUTIONS WILL REQUIRE US TO *RELAX* THE LIBRARY LAW.
BUT WE CAN TAKE BACK WHAT WE HAD TO SACRIFICE. FIRST WE MUST BECOME AN EQUAL FORCE TO FIGHT CENSORSHIP.
YES, IT TAKES DEDICATION AND TIME, BUT...
...I THINK IT'S THE WINNING GAMBIT.
Relax the Library Law ...?

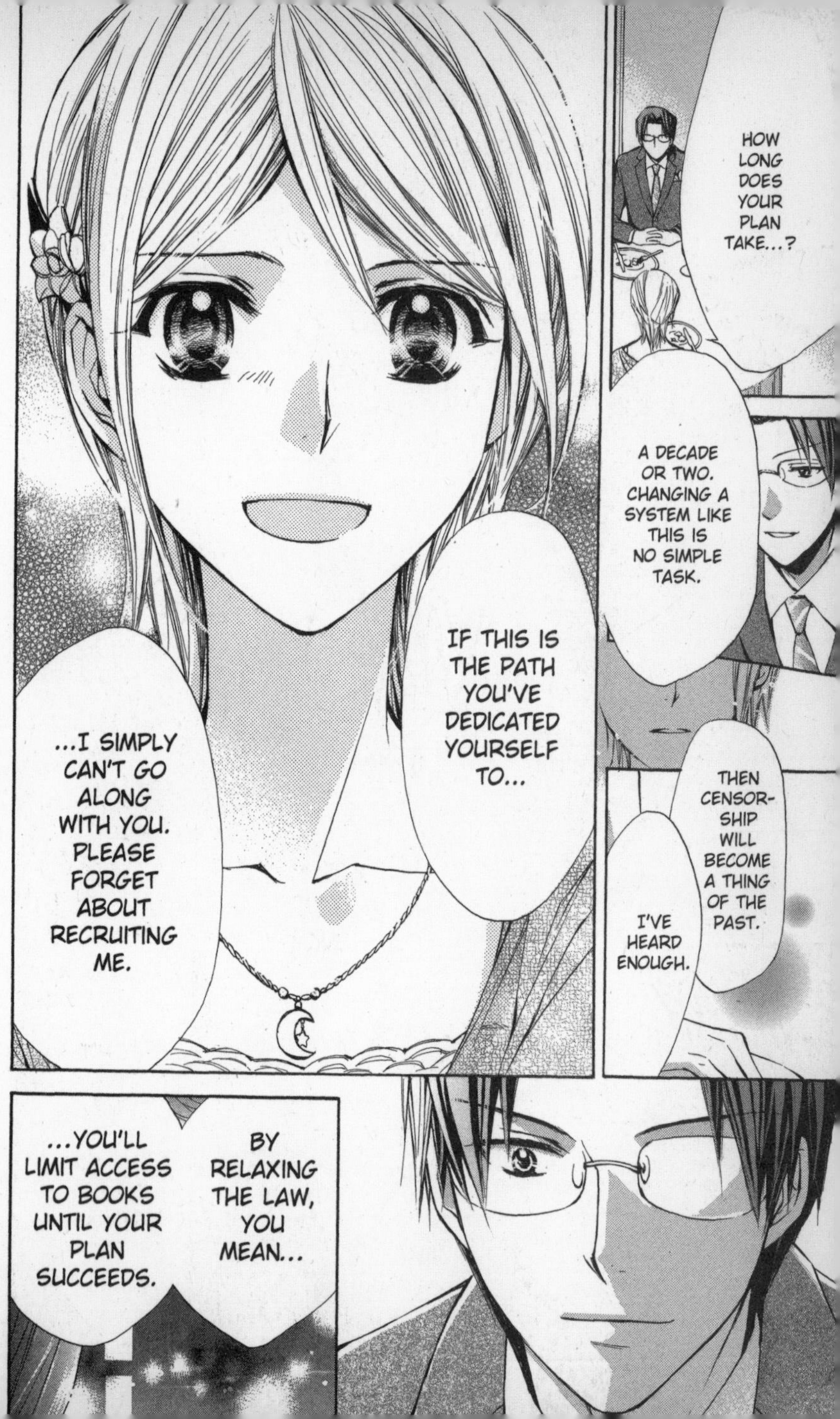
HOW LONG DOES YOUR PLAN TAKE...?
A DECADE OR TWO. CHANGING A SYSTEM LIKE THIS IS NO SIMPLE TASK.
THEN CENSORSHIP WILL BECOME A THING OF THE PAST.
I'VE HEARD ENOUGH.
IF THIS IS THE PATH YOU'VE DEDICATED YOURSELF TO...
...I SIMPLY CAN'T GO ALONG WITH YOU. PLEASE FORGET ABOUT RECRUITING ME.
BY RELAXING THE LAW, YOU MEAN...
...YOU'LL LIMIT ACCESS TO BOOKS UNTIL YOUR PLAN SUCCEEDS.

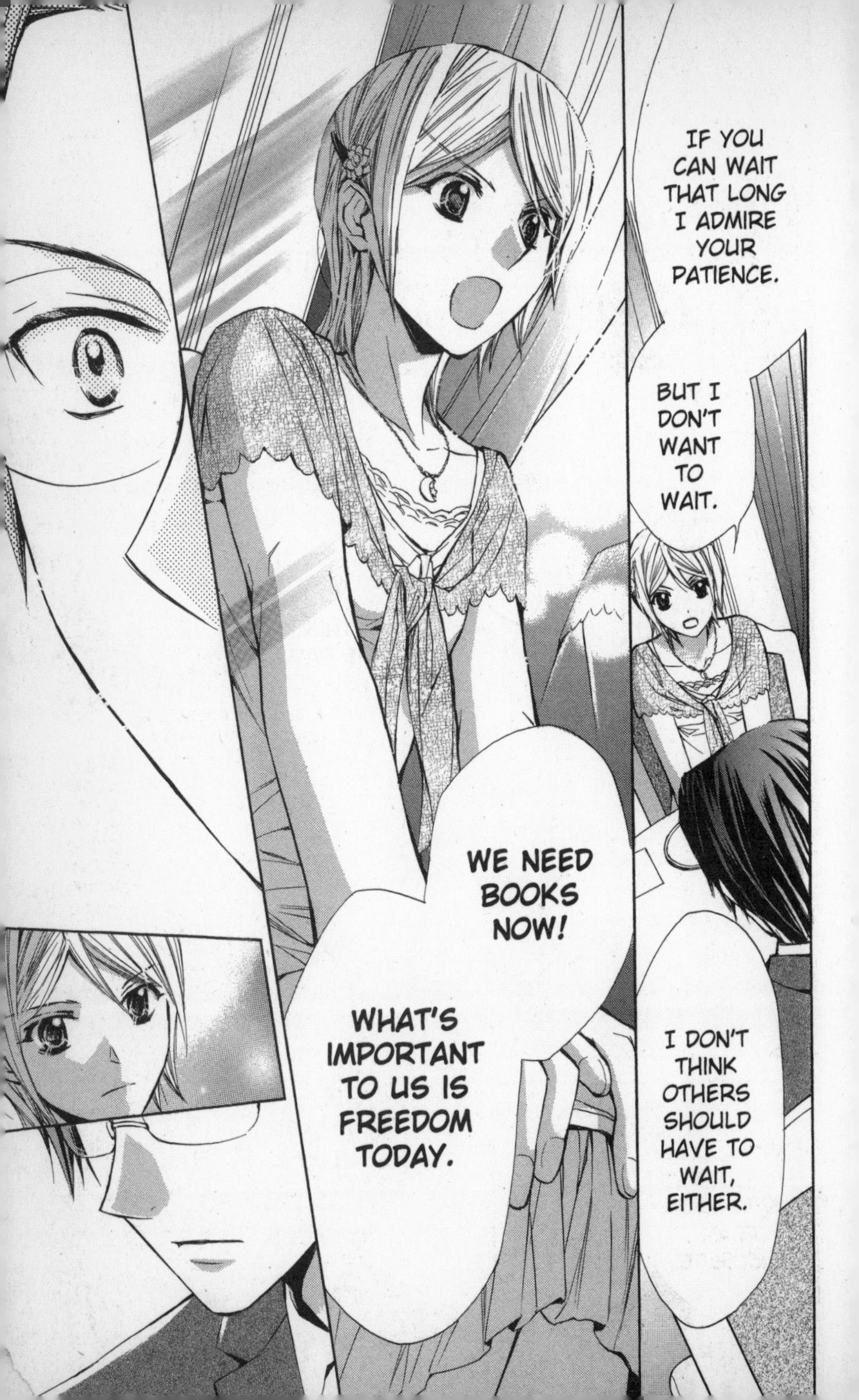
IF YOU CAN WAIT THAT LONG I ADMIRE YOUR PATIENCE.
BUT I DON'T WANT TO WAIT.
I DON'T THINK OTHERS SHOULD HAVE TO WAIT, EITHER.
WE NEED BOOKS NOW!
WHAT'S IMPORTANT TO US IS FREEDOM TODAY.

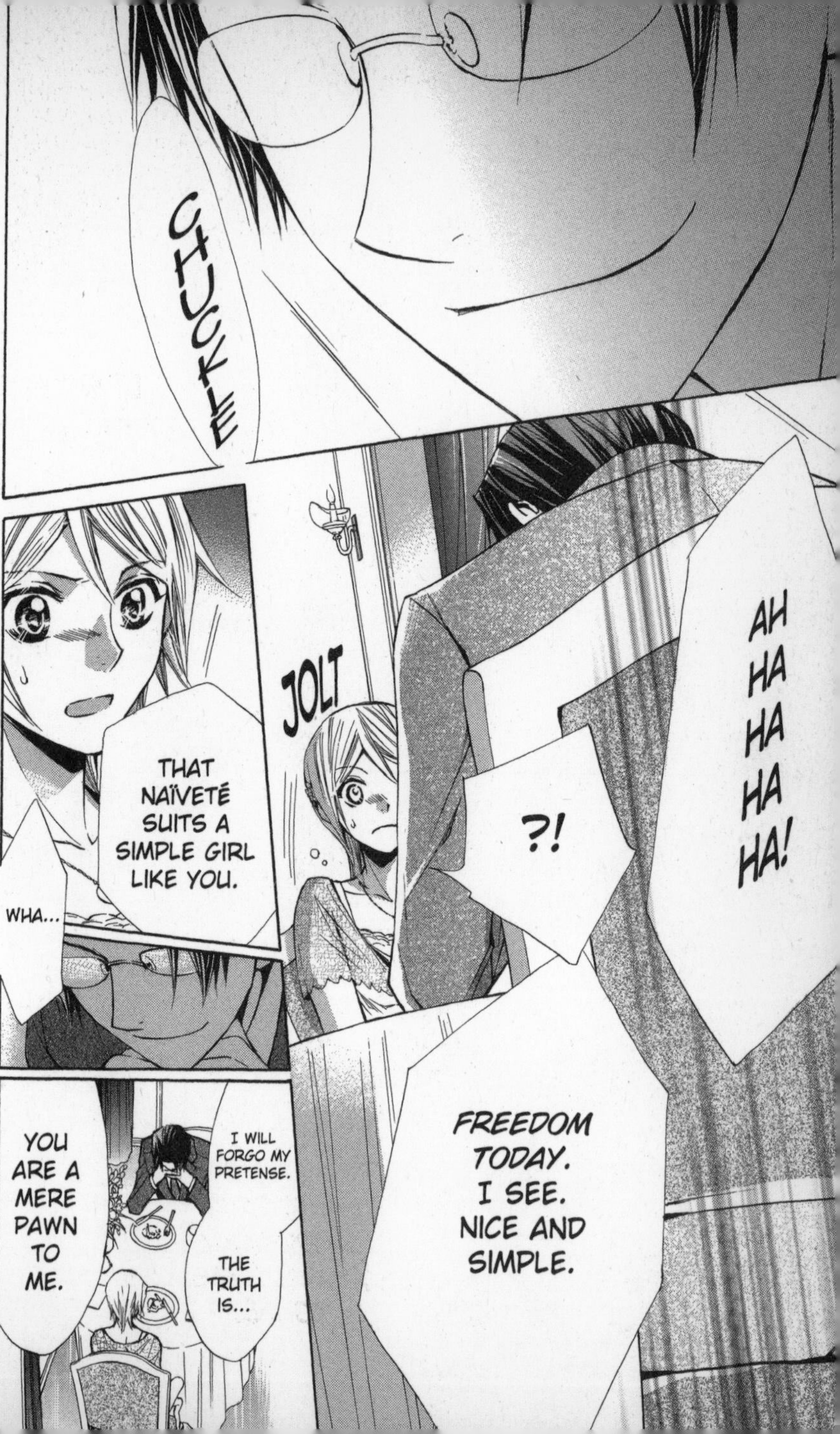
CHUCKLE
AH HA HA HA HA HA!
?!
JOLT
FREEDOM TODAY. I SEE. NICE AND SIMPLE.
THAT NAÏVETÉ SUITS A SIMPLE GIRL LIKE YOU.
WHA...
I WILL FORGO MY PRETENSE.
THE TRUTH IS...
YOU ARE A MERE PAWN TO ME.

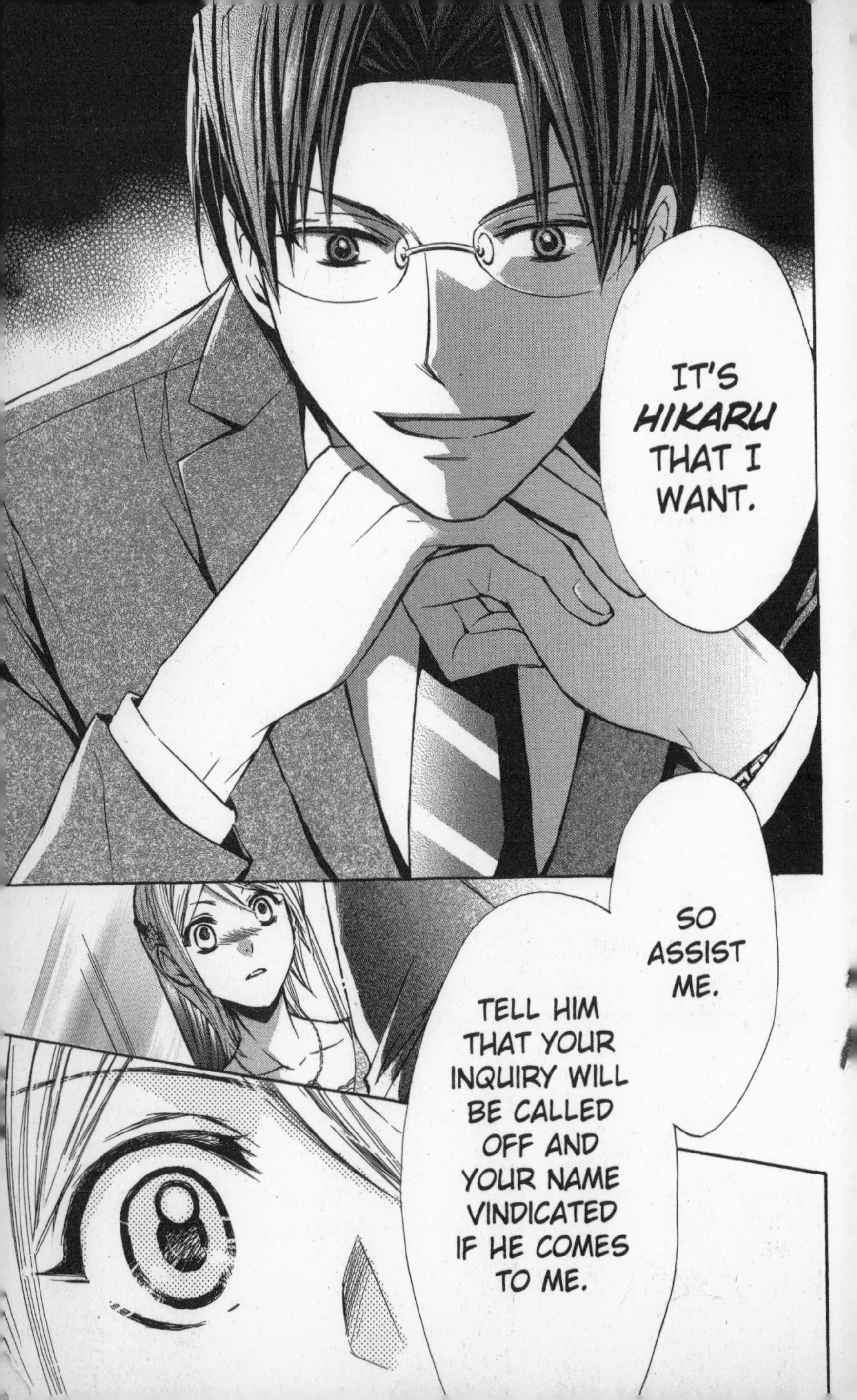
IT'S *HIKARU* THAT I WANT.
SO ASSIST ME.
TELL HIM THAT YOUR INQUIRY WILL BE CALLED OFF AND YOUR NAME VINDICATED IF HE COMES TO ME.

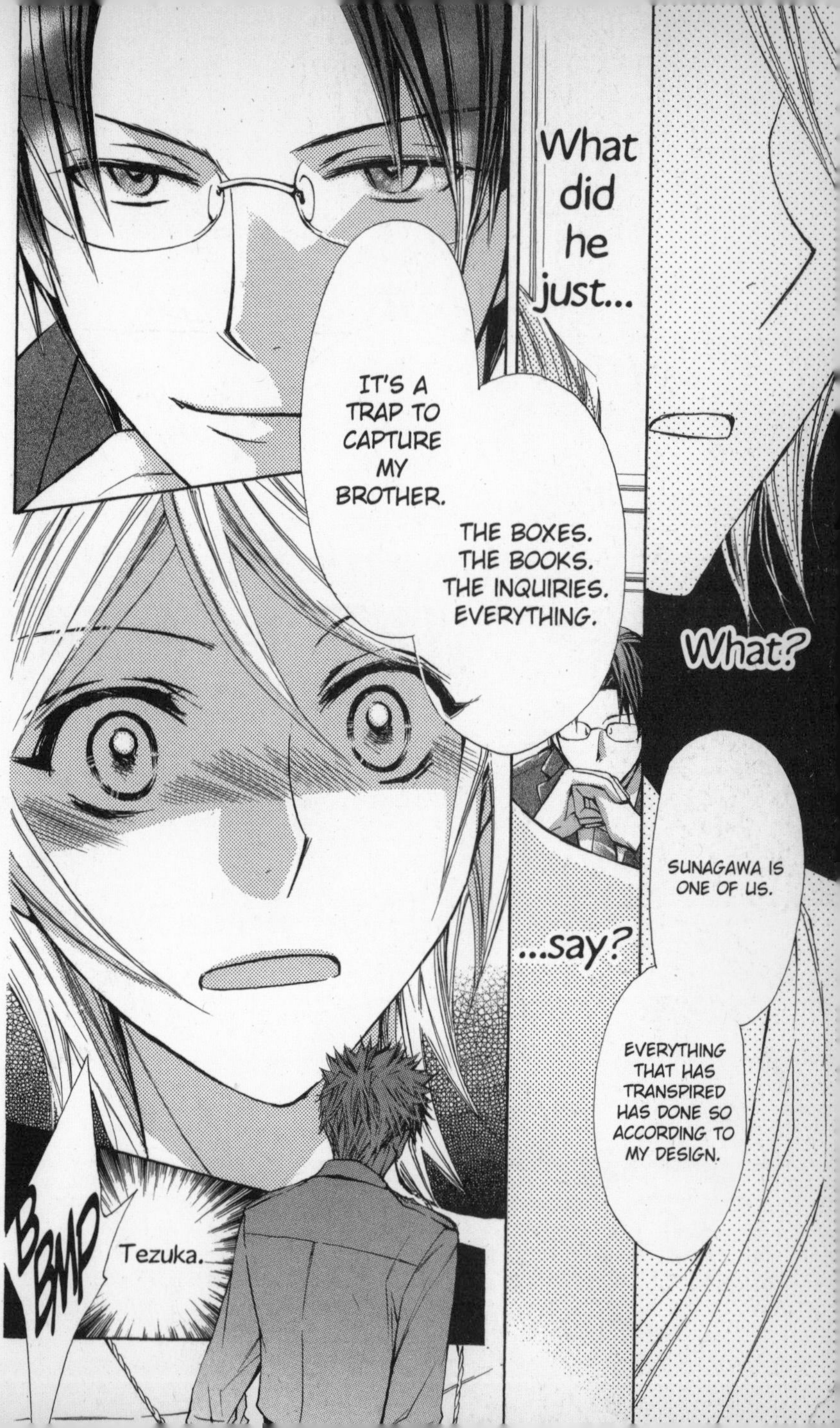
What did he just...
What?
SUNAGAWA IS ONE OF US.
...say?
EVERYTHING THAT HAS TRANSPIRED HAS DONE SO ACCORDING TO MY DESIGN.
IT'S A TRAP TO CAPTURE MY BROTHER.
THE BOXES. THE BOOKS. THE INQUIRIES. EVERYTHING.
BMP
Tezuka.

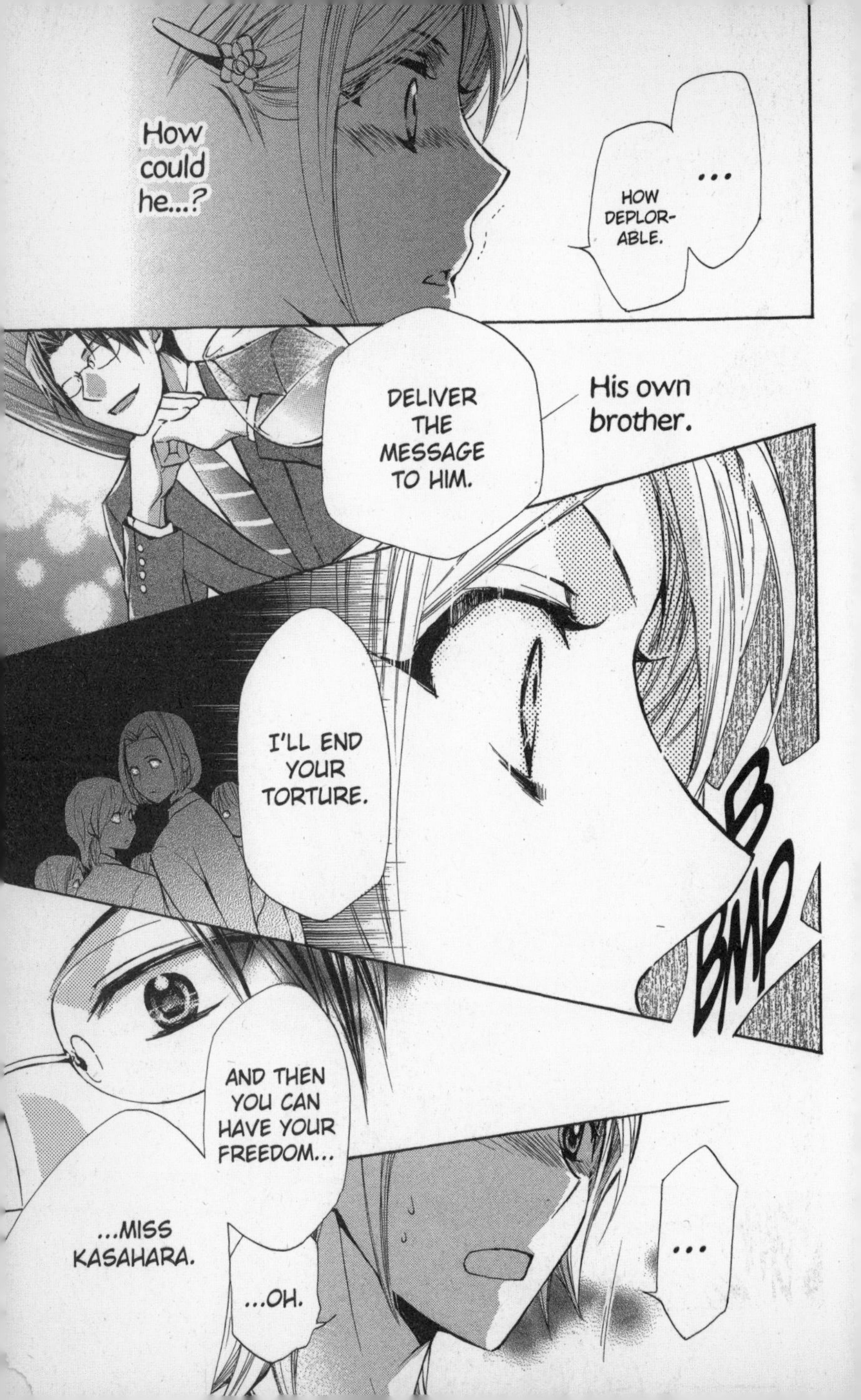

... HOW DEPLORABLE.
How could he...?
His own brother.
DELIVER THE MESSAGE TO HIM.
BMP
I'LL END YOUR TORTURE.
AND THEN YOU CAN HAVE YOUR FREEDOM...
...MISS KASAHARA.
...
...OH.

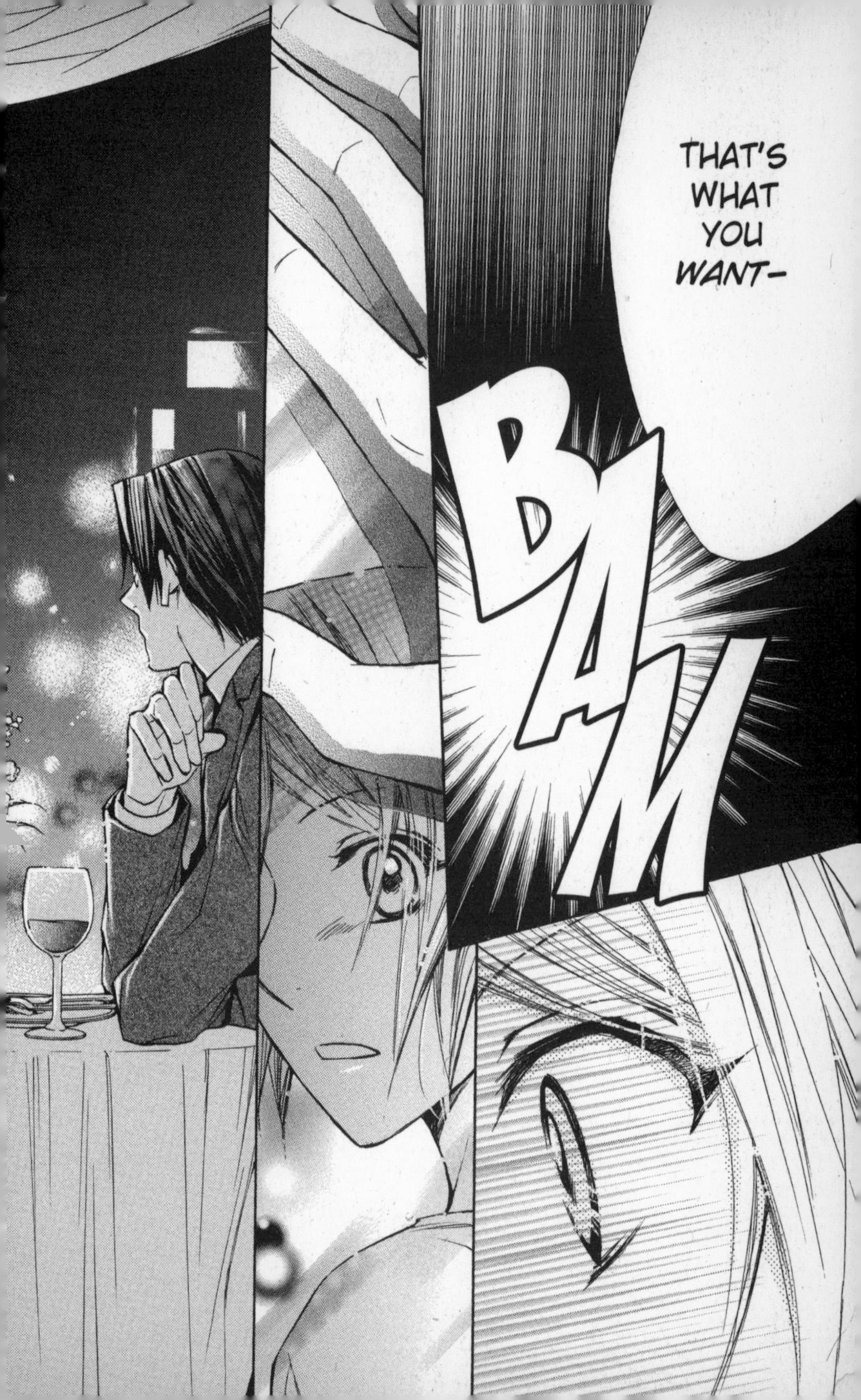
THAT'S WHAT YOU WANT–
BAM

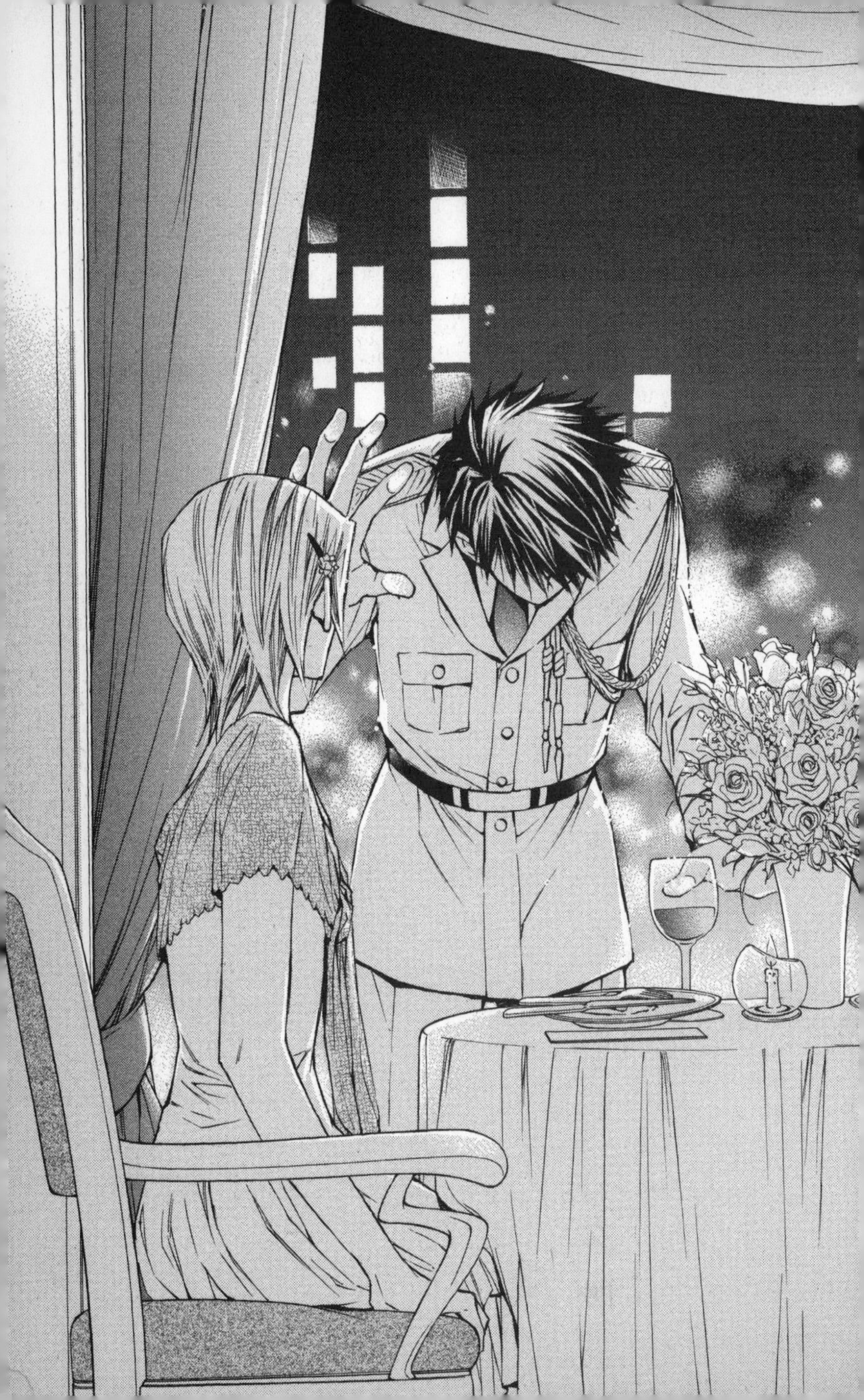

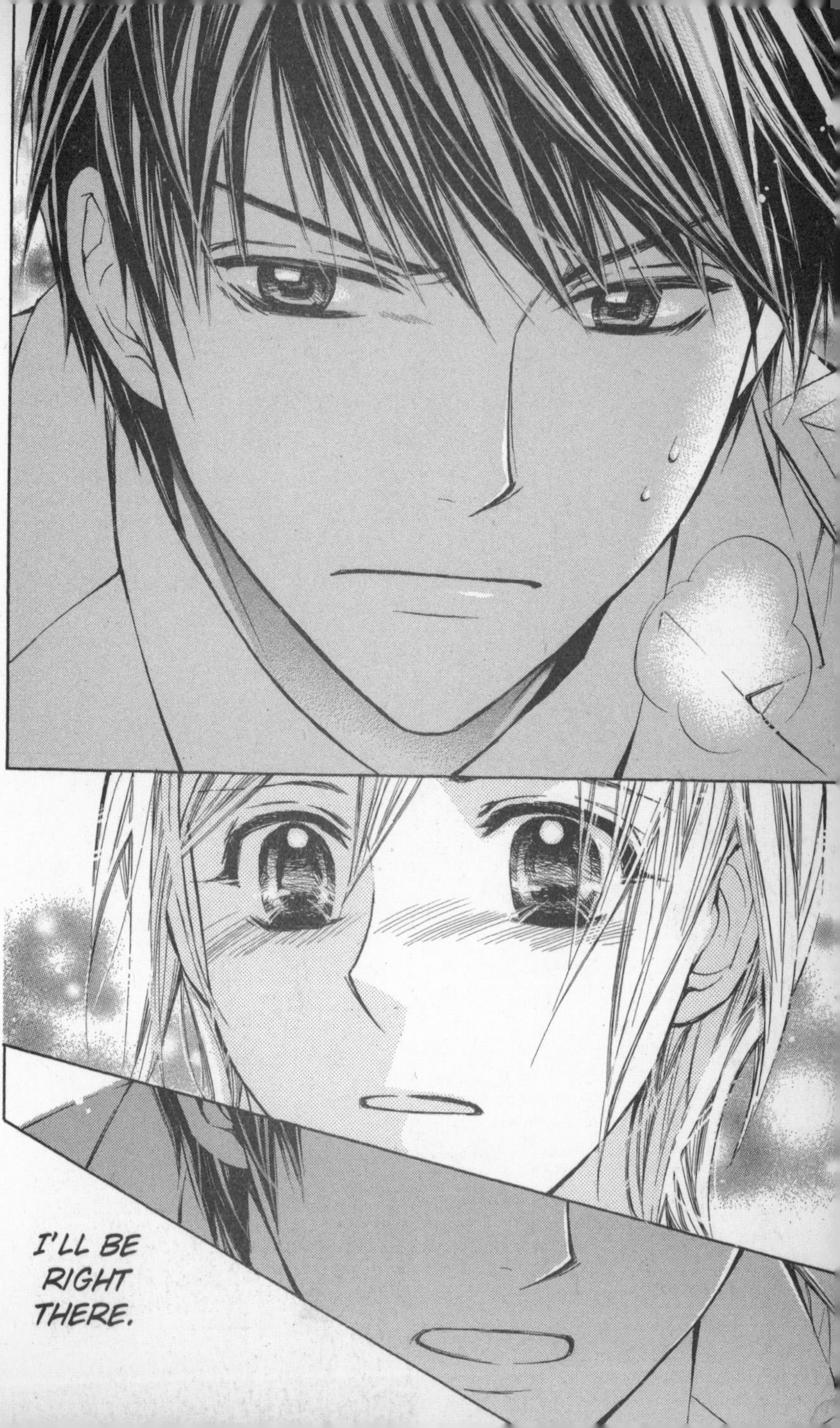
I'LL BE RIGHT THERE.

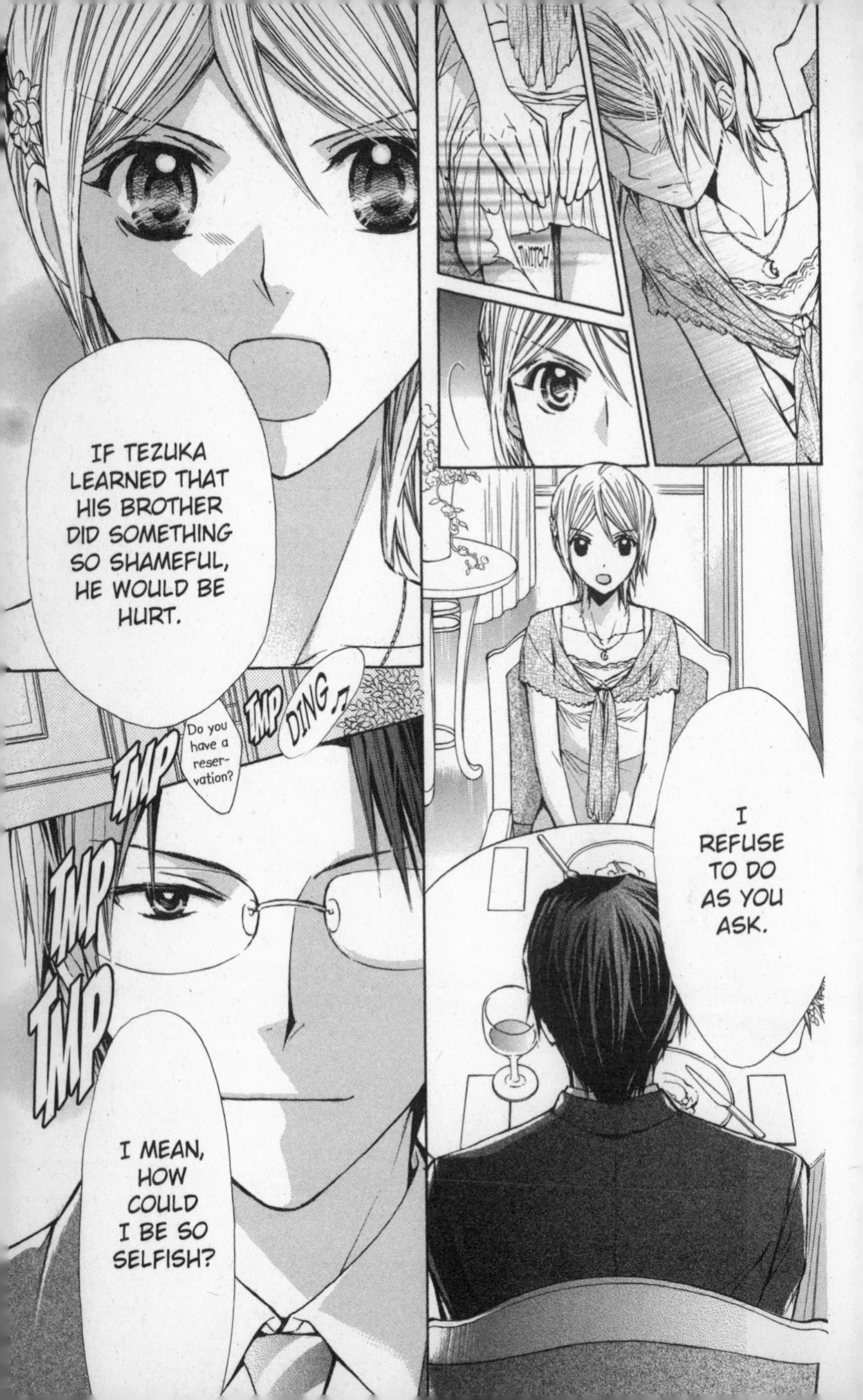

TWITCH
IF TEZUKA LEARNED THAT HIS BROTHER DID SOMETHING SO SHAMEFUL, HE WOULD BE HURT.
I REFUSE TO DO AS YOU ASK.
DING ♫
TMP
Do you have a reser-vation?
TMP
TMP
TMP
I MEAN, HOW COULD I BE SO SELFISH?

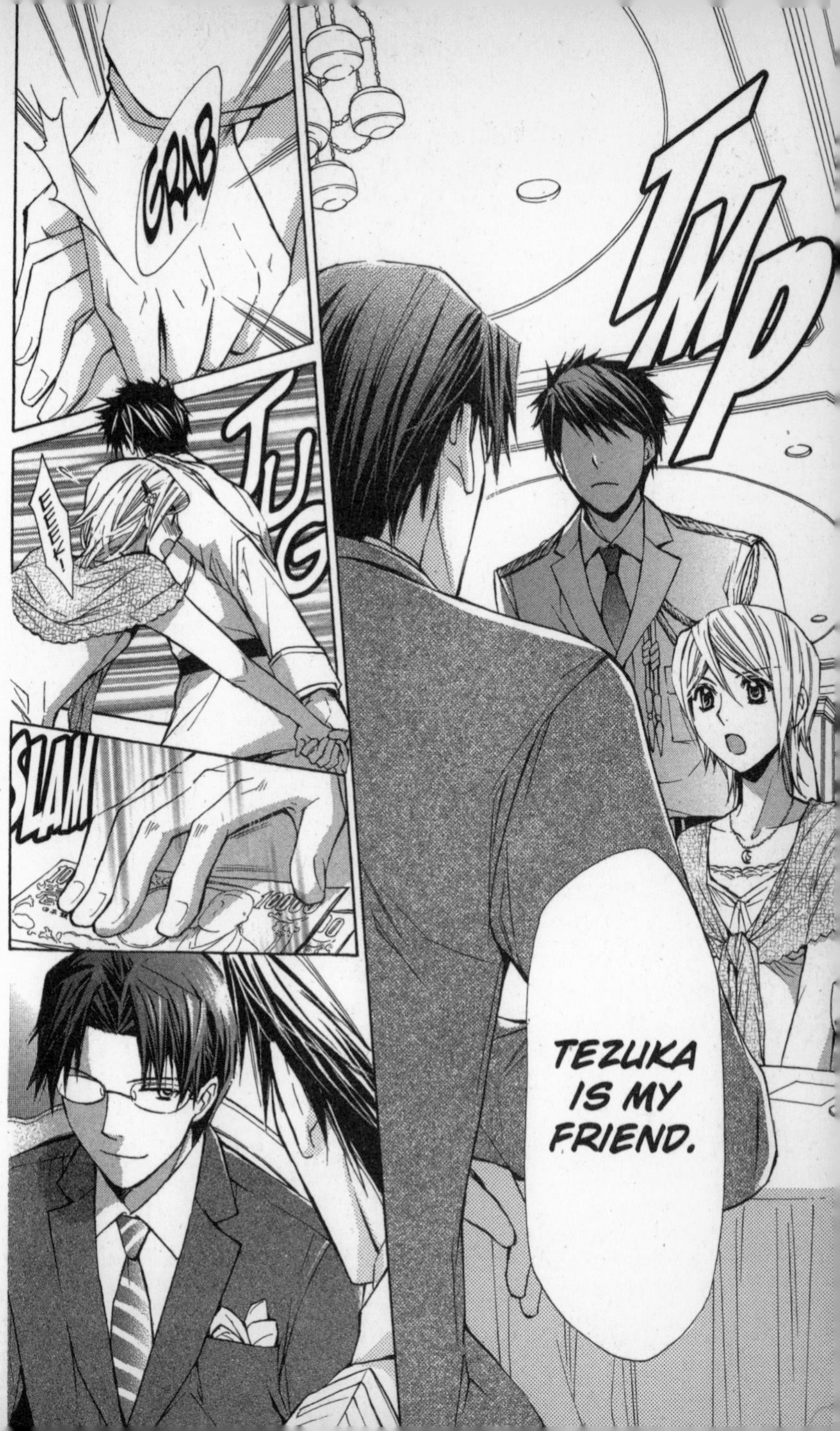
TMP
TEZUKA IS MY FRIEND.
GRAB
TUG
EEEK!
SLAM

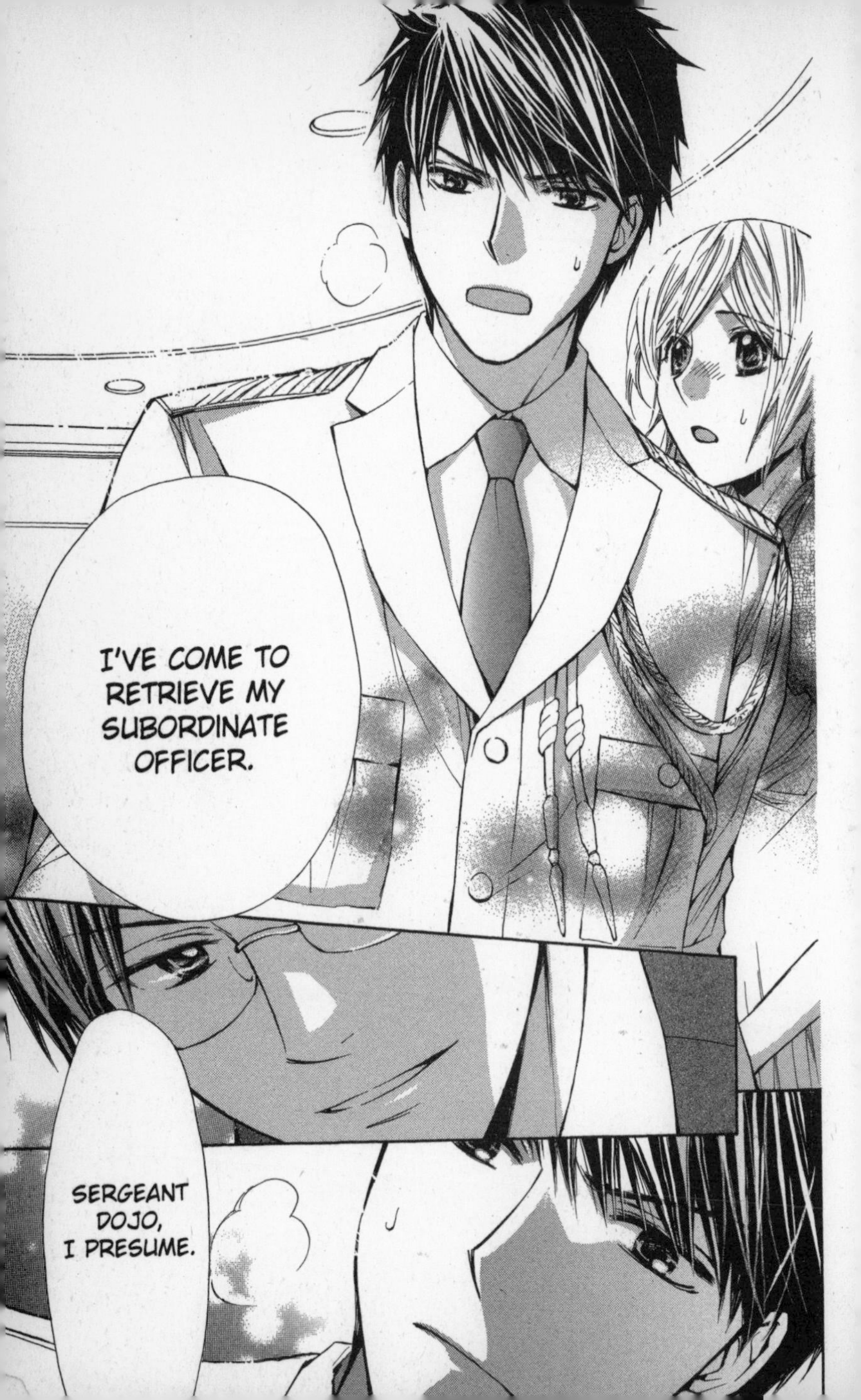
I'VE COME TO RETRIEVE MY SUBORDINATE OFFICER.
SERGEANT DOJO, I PRESUME.

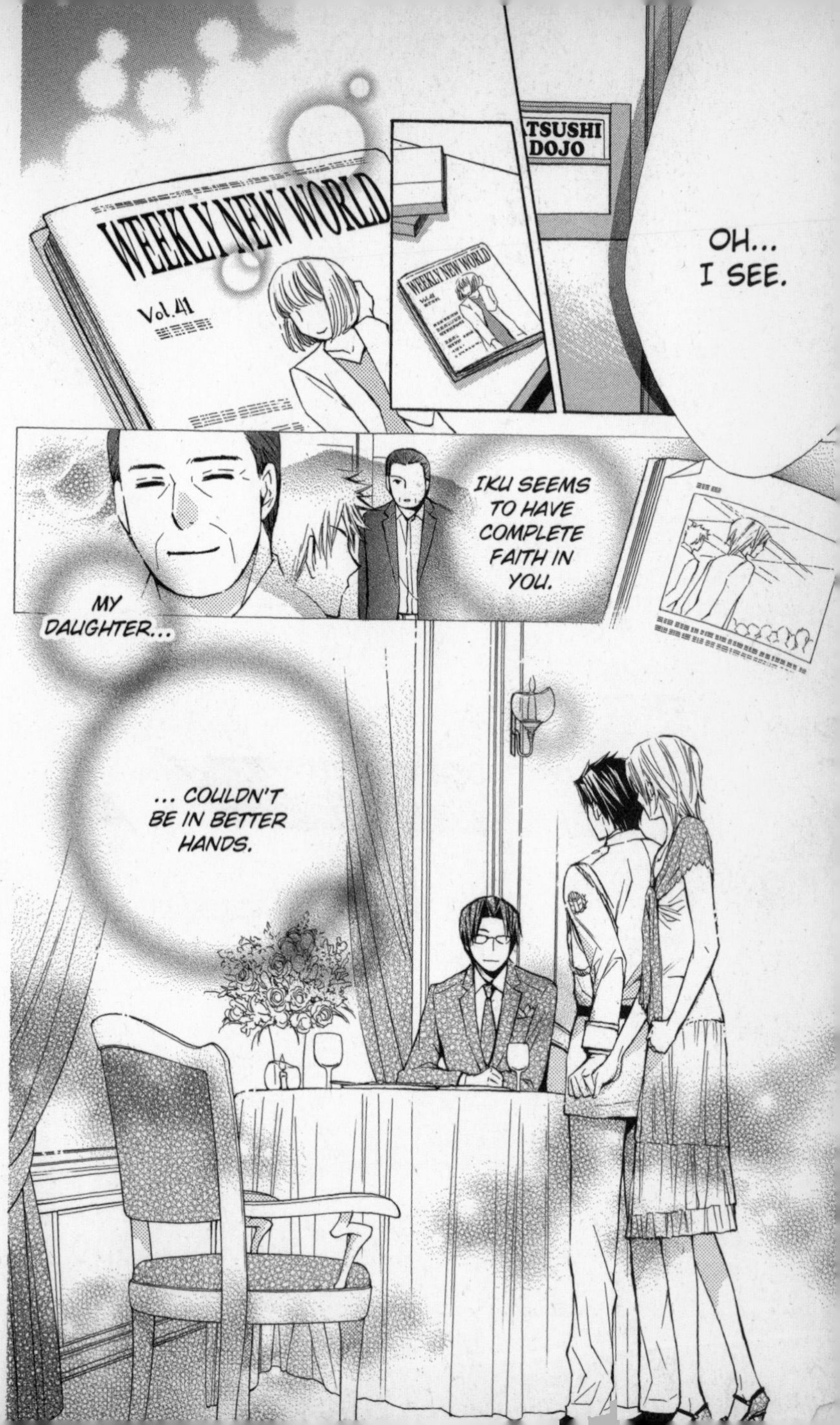
OH... I SEE.
ATSUSHI DOJO
WEEKLY NEW WORLD
WEEKLY NEW WORLD
Vol.41
IKU SEEMS TO HAVE COMPLETE FAITH IN YOU.
MY DAUGHTER...
... COULDN'T BE IN BETTER HANDS.

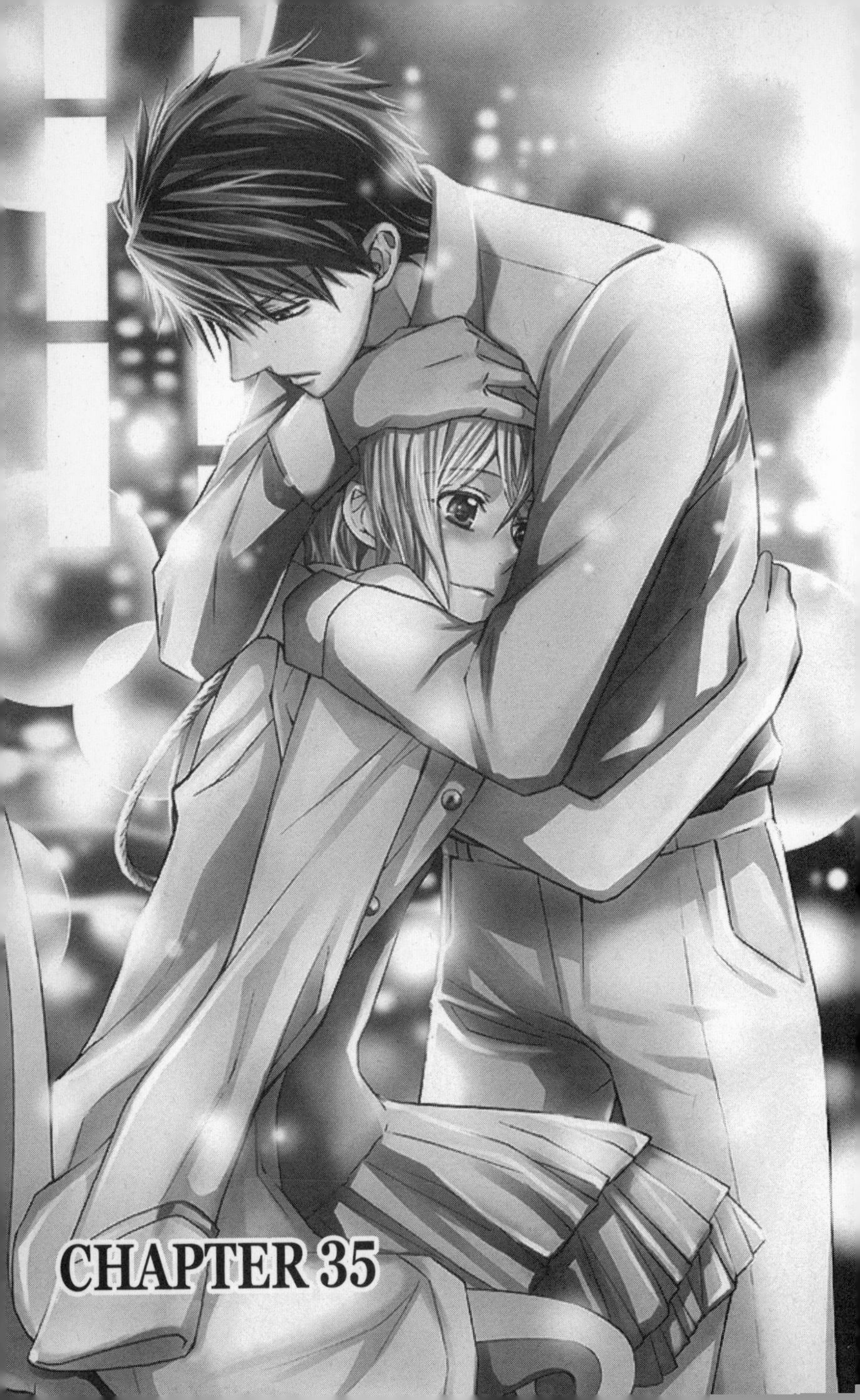
CHAPTER 35

SCARY PHONE CALL

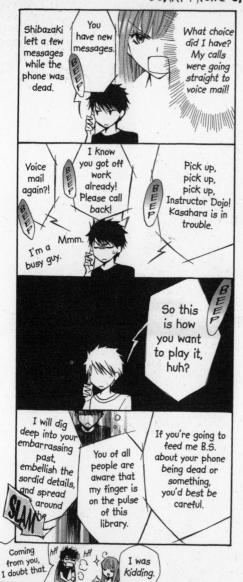

What choice did I have? My calls were going straight to voice mail!
You have new messages.
BEEP
Shibazaki left a few messages while the phone was dead.
Pick up, pick up, pick up, Instructor Dojo! Kasahara is in trouble.
BEEP
I know you got off work already! Please call back!
BEEP
Voice mail again?!
BEEP
Mmm.
I'm a busy guy.
BEEP
So this is how you want to play it, huh?
If you're going to feed me B.S. about your phone being dead or something, you'd best be careful.
You of all people are aware that my finger is on the pulse of this library.
I will dig deep into your embarrassing past, embellish the sordid details, and spread
around
SLAM
I was kidding.
hff
hff
Coming from you, I doubt that.

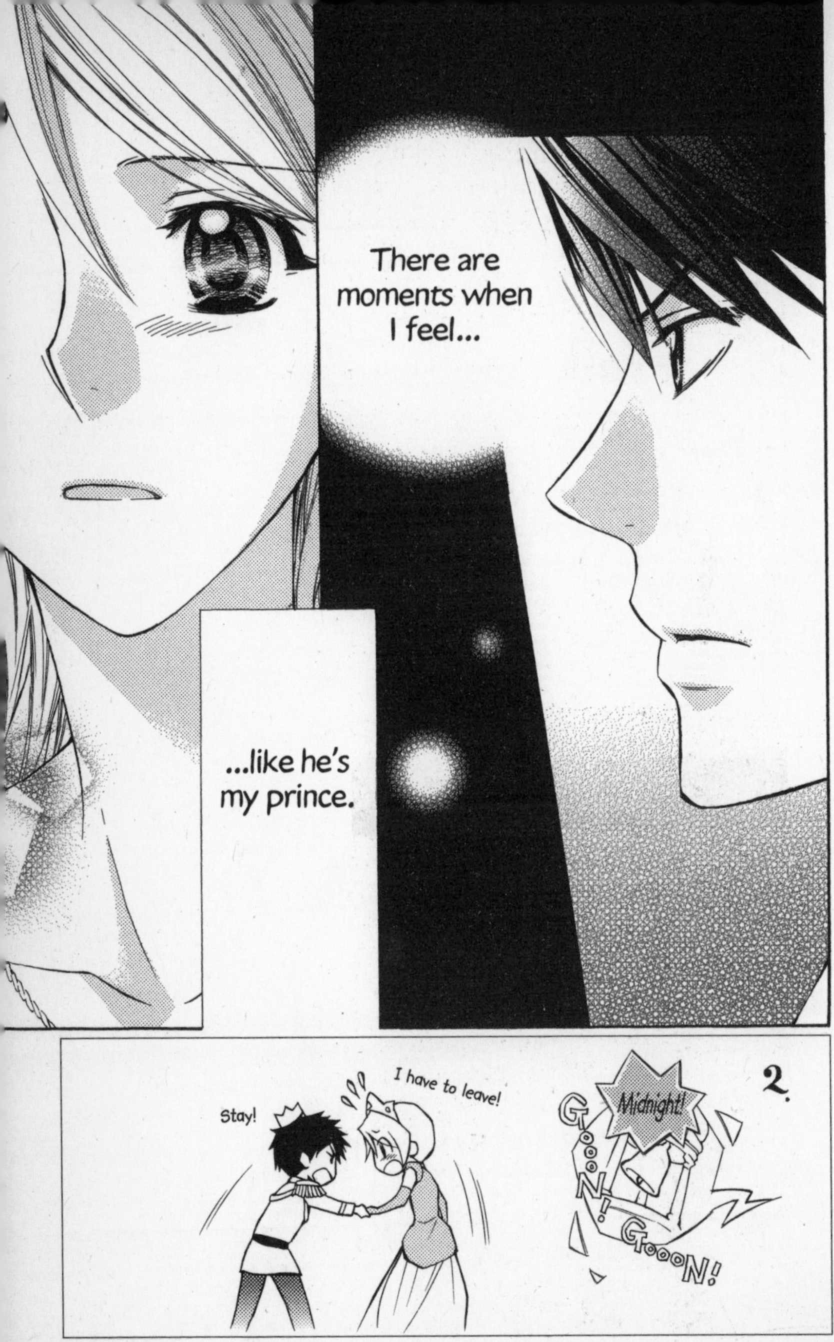

There are moments when I feel...
...like he's my prince.
2.
Midnight!
GOOON! GOOON!
I have to leave!
Stay!

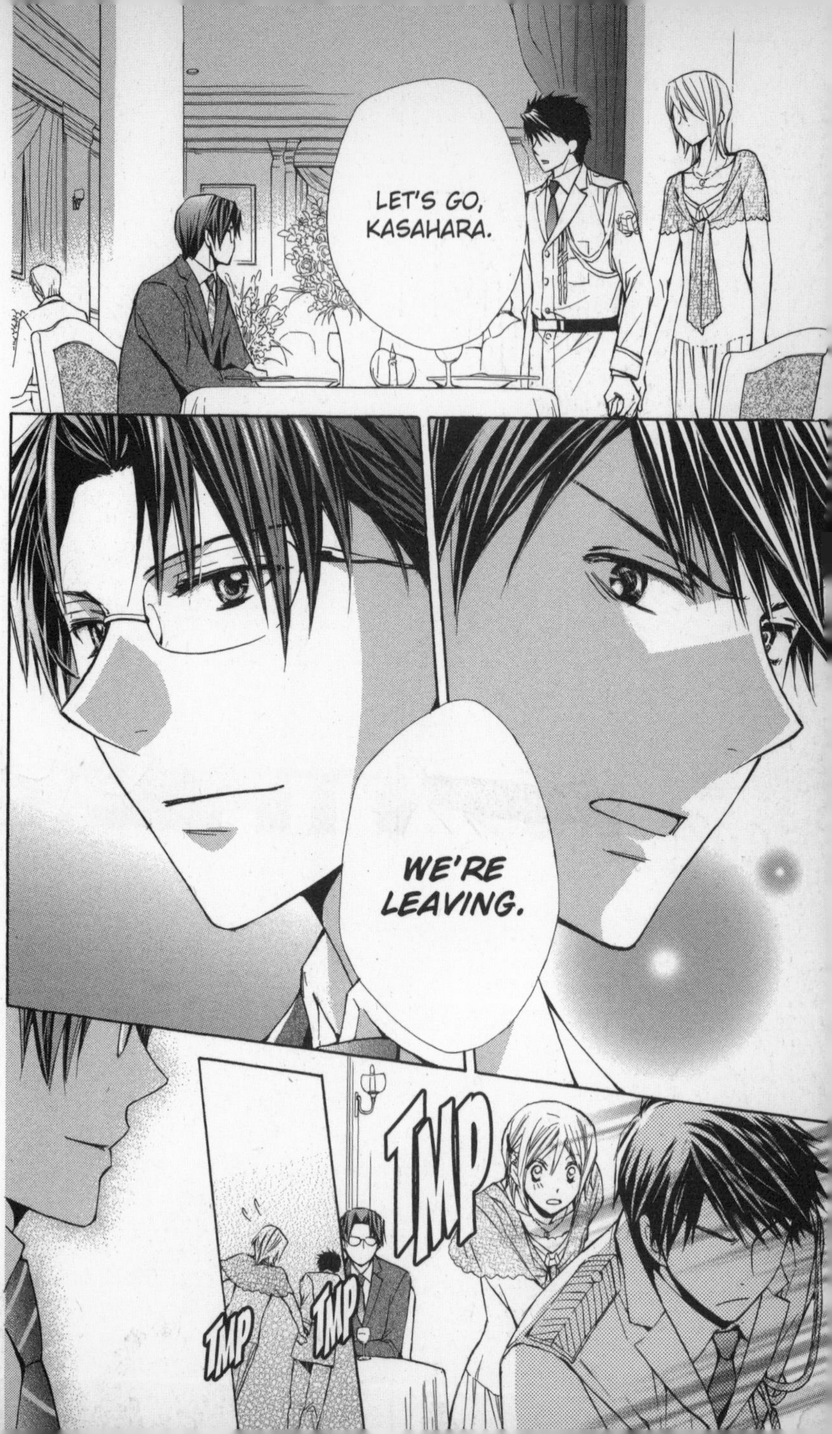
LET'S GO, KASAHARA.
WE'RE LEAVING.
TMP
TMP
TMP

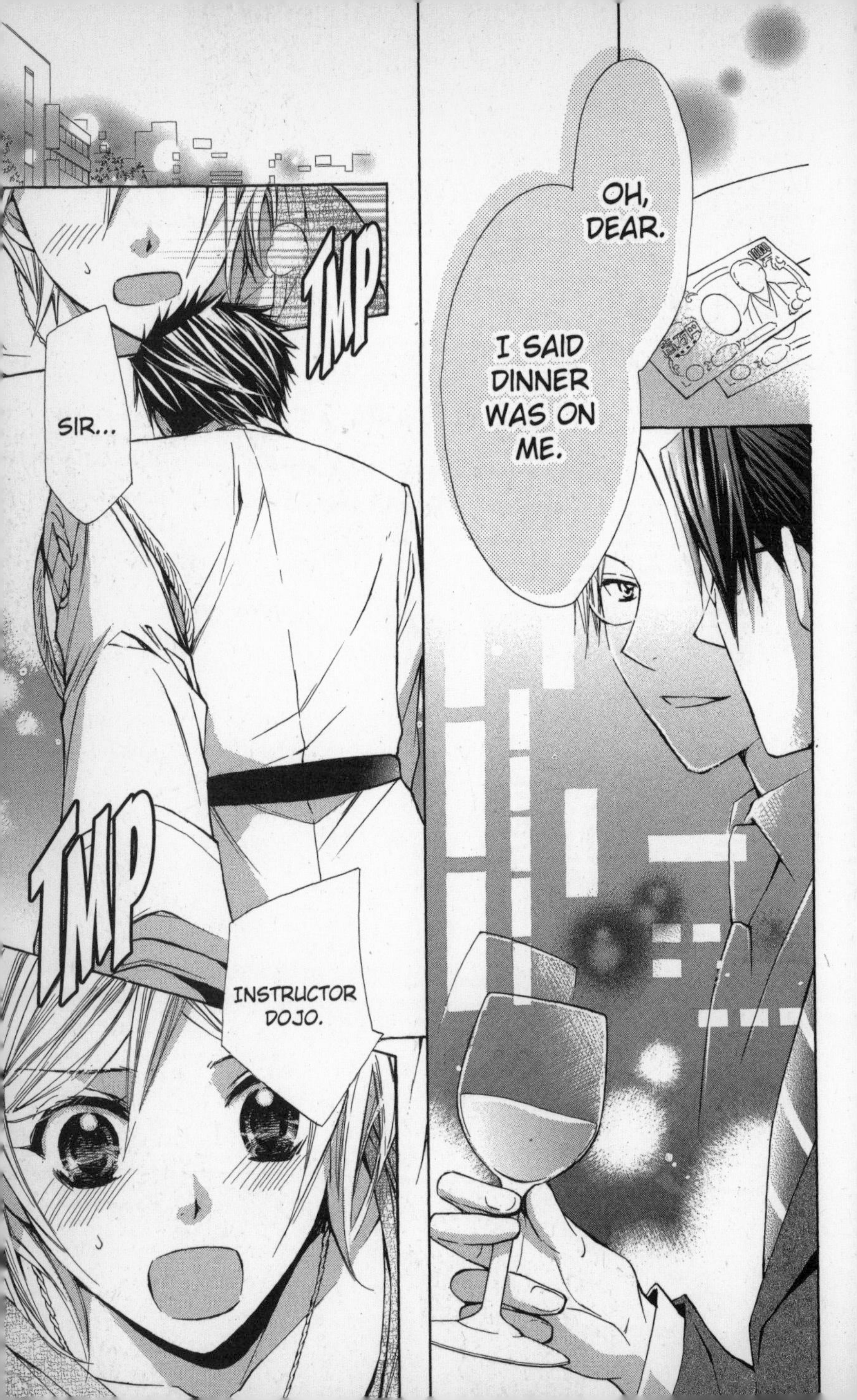
OH, DEAR.
I SAID DINNER WAS ON ME.
TMP
SIR...
TMP
INSTRUCTOR DOJO.

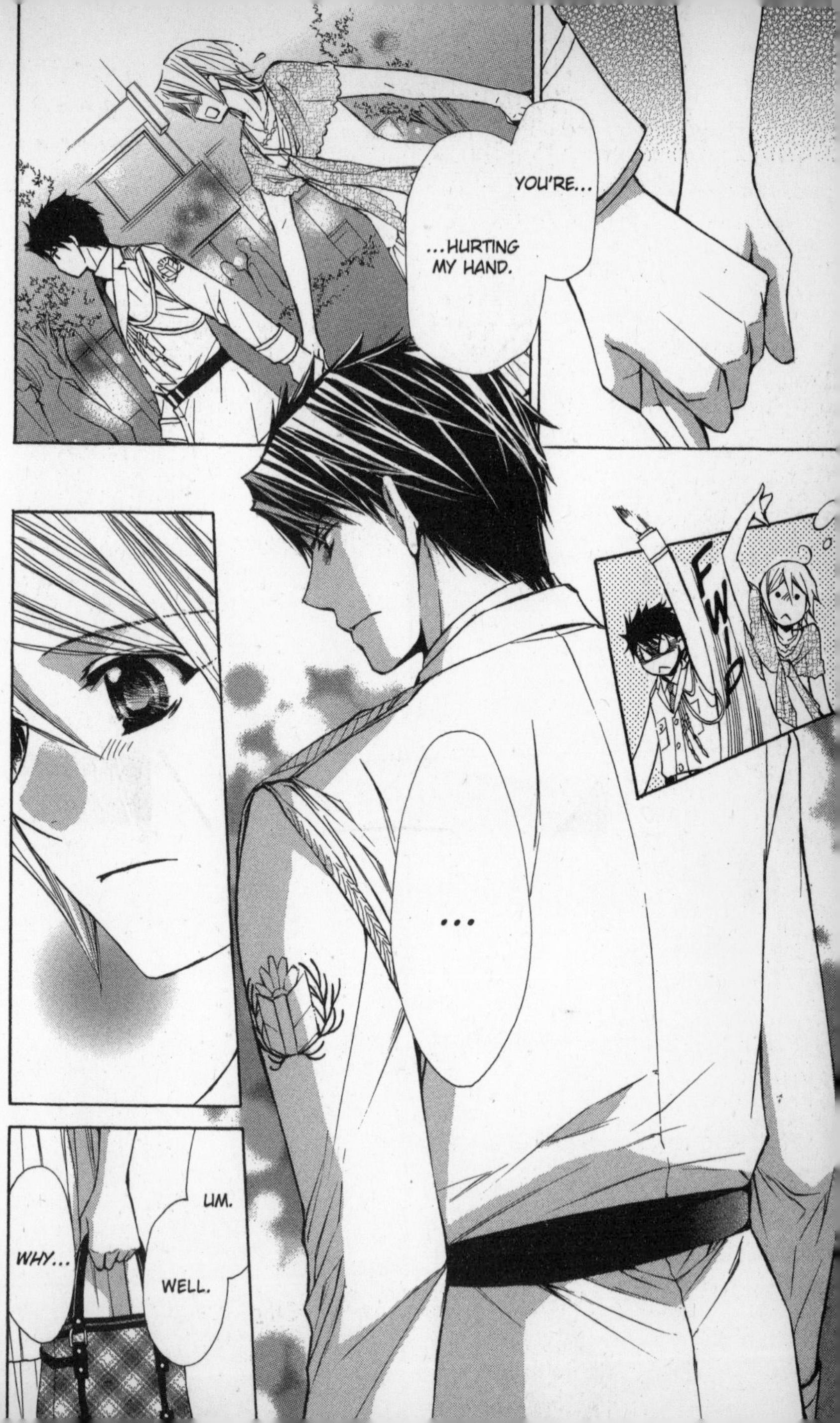
YOU'RE...
...HURTING MY HAND.
FWIP
...
UM.
WELL.
WHY...

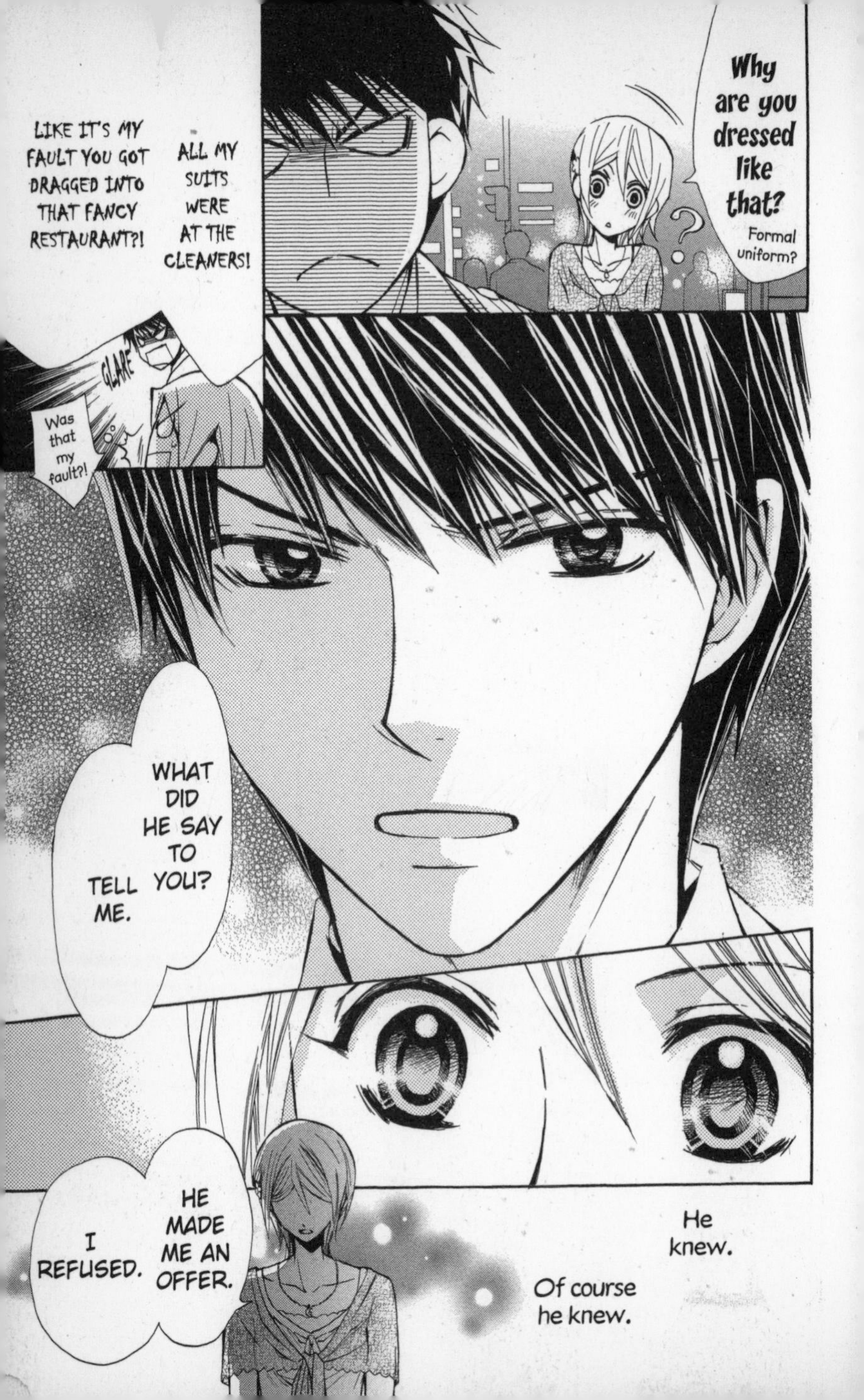
Why are you dressed like that?
Formal uniform?
ALL MY SUITS WERE AT THE CLEANERS!
LIKE IT'S MY FAULT YOU GOT DRAGGED INTO THAT FANCY RESTAURANT?!
GLARE
Was that my fault?!
WHAT DID HE SAY TO YOU?
TELL ME.
He knew.
Of course he knew.
HE MADE ME AN OFFER.
I REFUSED.

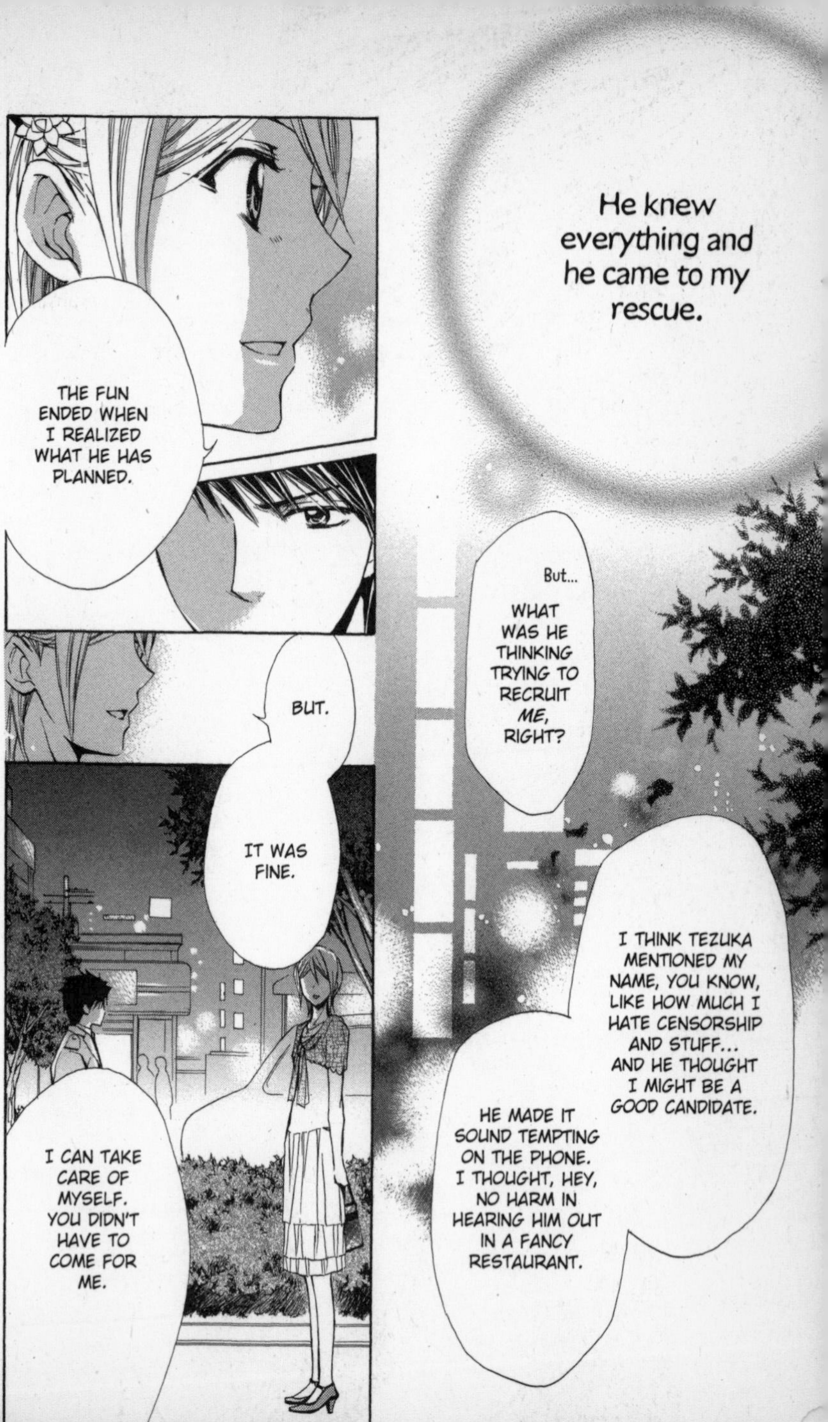
He knew everything and he came to my rescue.
But...
WHAT WAS HE THINKING TRYING TO RECRUIT *ME*, RIGHT?
I THINK TEZUKA MENTIONED MY NAME, YOU KNOW, LIKE HOW MUCH I HATE CENSORSHIP AND STUFF... AND HE THOUGHT I MIGHT BE A GOOD CANDIDATE.
HE MADE IT SOUND TEMPTING ON THE PHONE. I THOUGHT, HEY, NO HARM IN HEARING HIM OUT IN A FANCY RESTAURANT.
THE FUN ENDED WHEN I REALIZED WHAT HE HAS PLANNED.
BUT.
IT WAS FINE.
I CAN TAKE CARE OF MYSELF. YOU DIDN'T HAVE TO COME FOR ME.

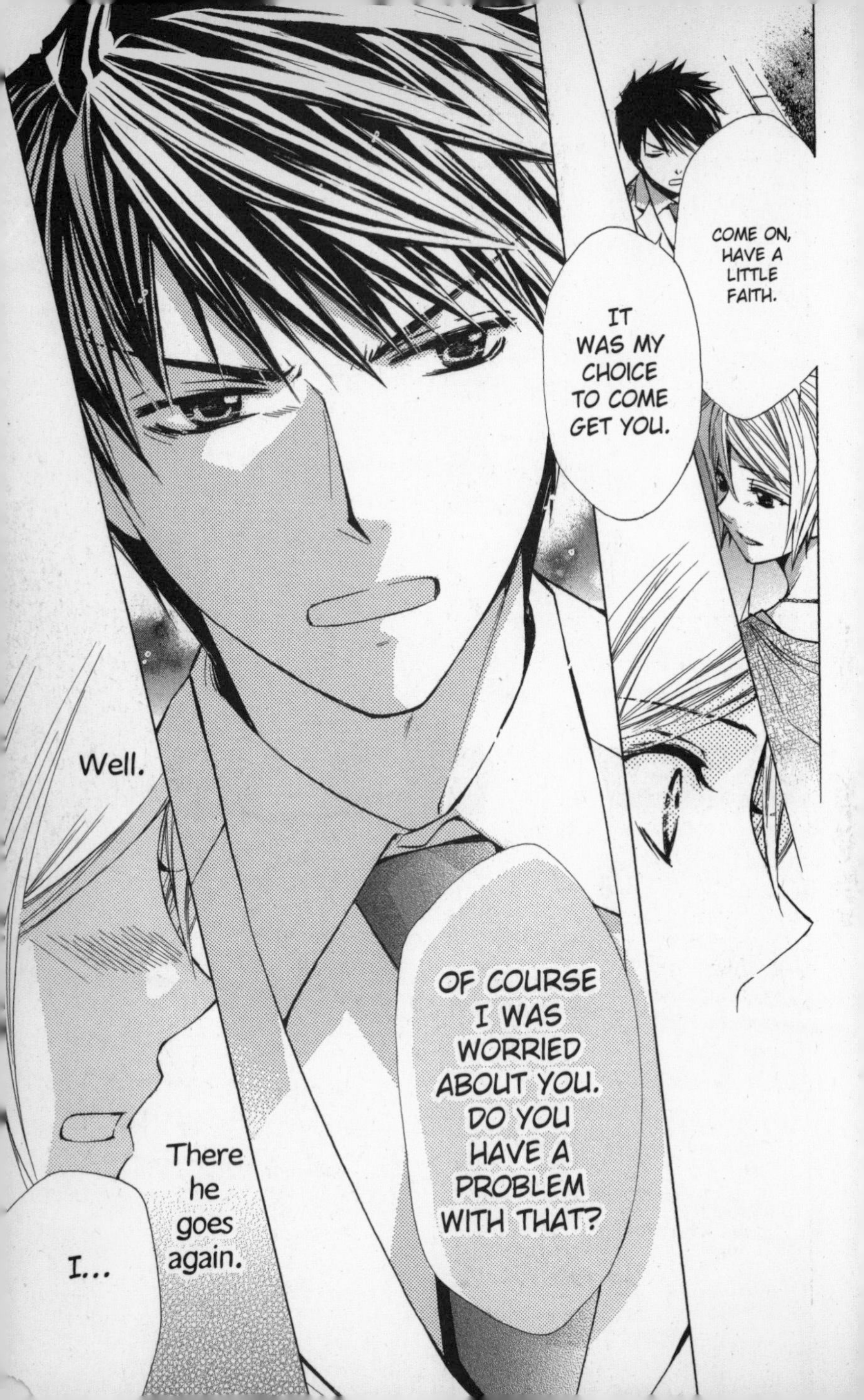
COME ON, HAVE A LITTLE FAITH.
IT WAS MY CHOICE TO COME GET YOU.
OF COURSE I WAS WORRIED ABOUT YOU. DO YOU HAVE A PROBLEM WITH THAT?
Well.
There he goes again.
I...

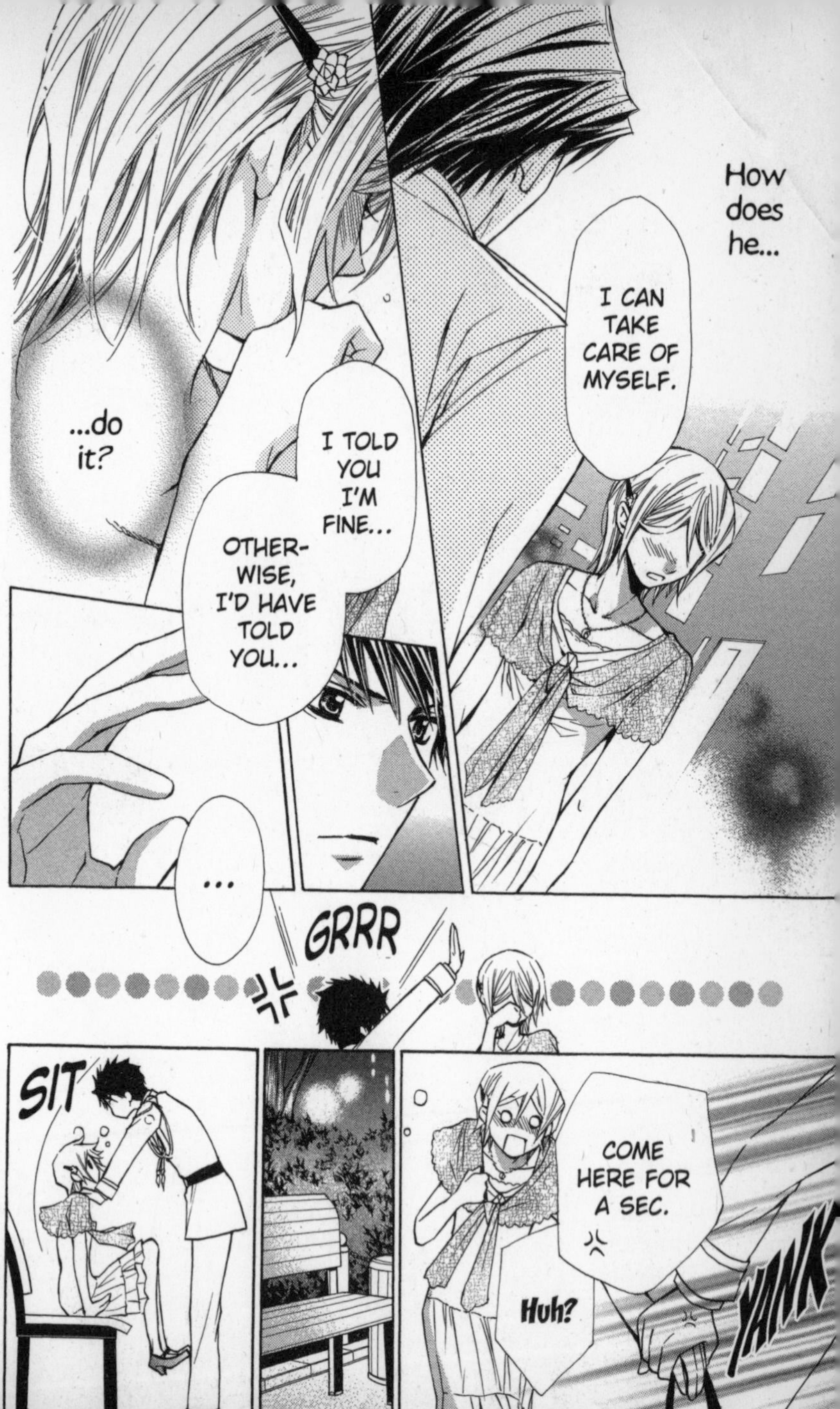
How does he...
I CAN TAKE CARE OF MYSELF.
I TOLD YOU I'M FINE...
OTHER-WISE, I'D HAVE TOLD YOU...
...
...do it?
GRRR
COME HERE FOR A SEC.
Huh?
YANK
SIT

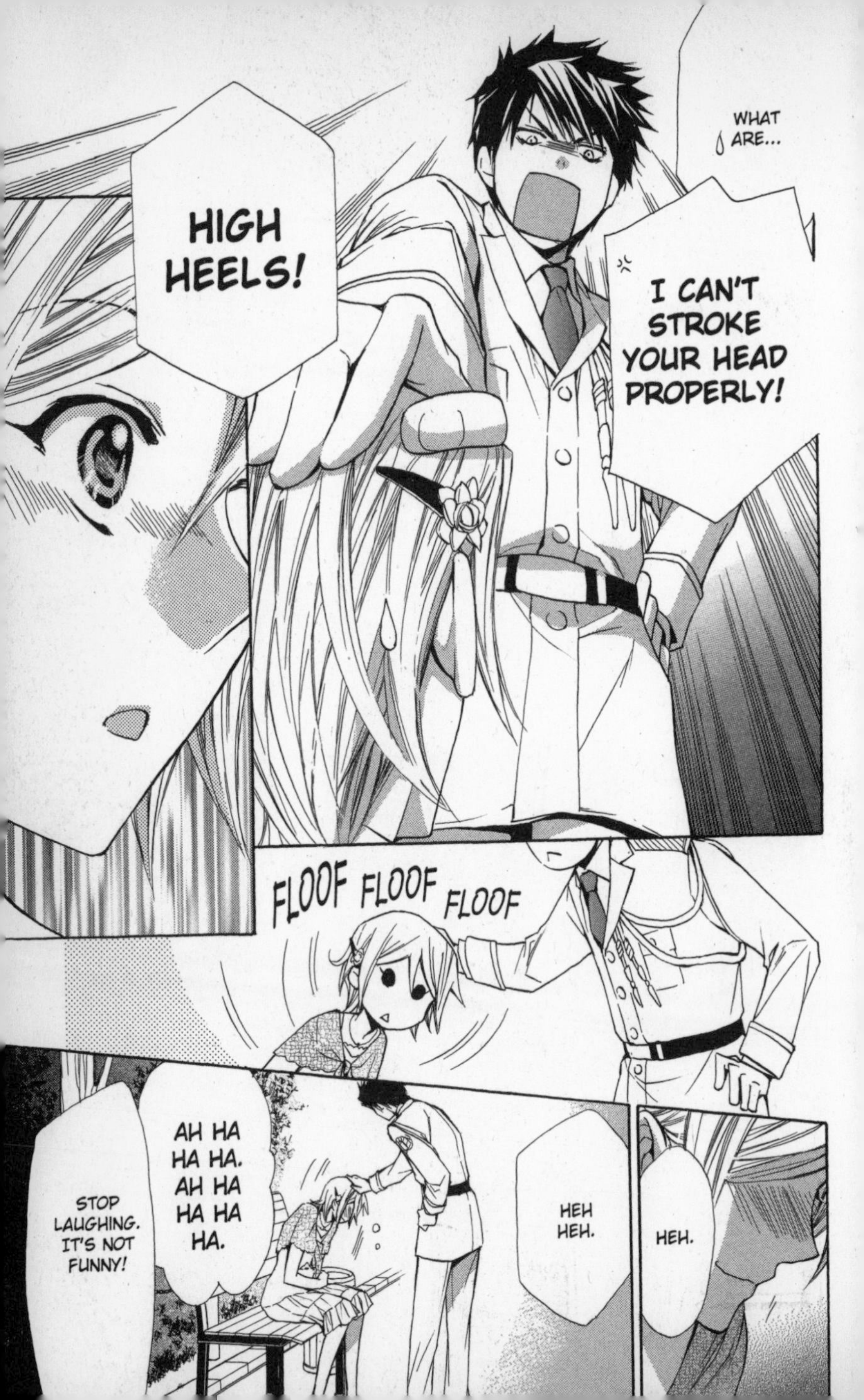
WHAT ARE...
I CAN'T STROKE YOUR HEAD PROPERLY!
HIGH HEELS!
FLOOF FLOOF FLOOF
HEH.
HEH HEH.
AH HA HA HA. AH HA HA HA HA.
STOP LAUGHING. IT'S NOT FUNNY!

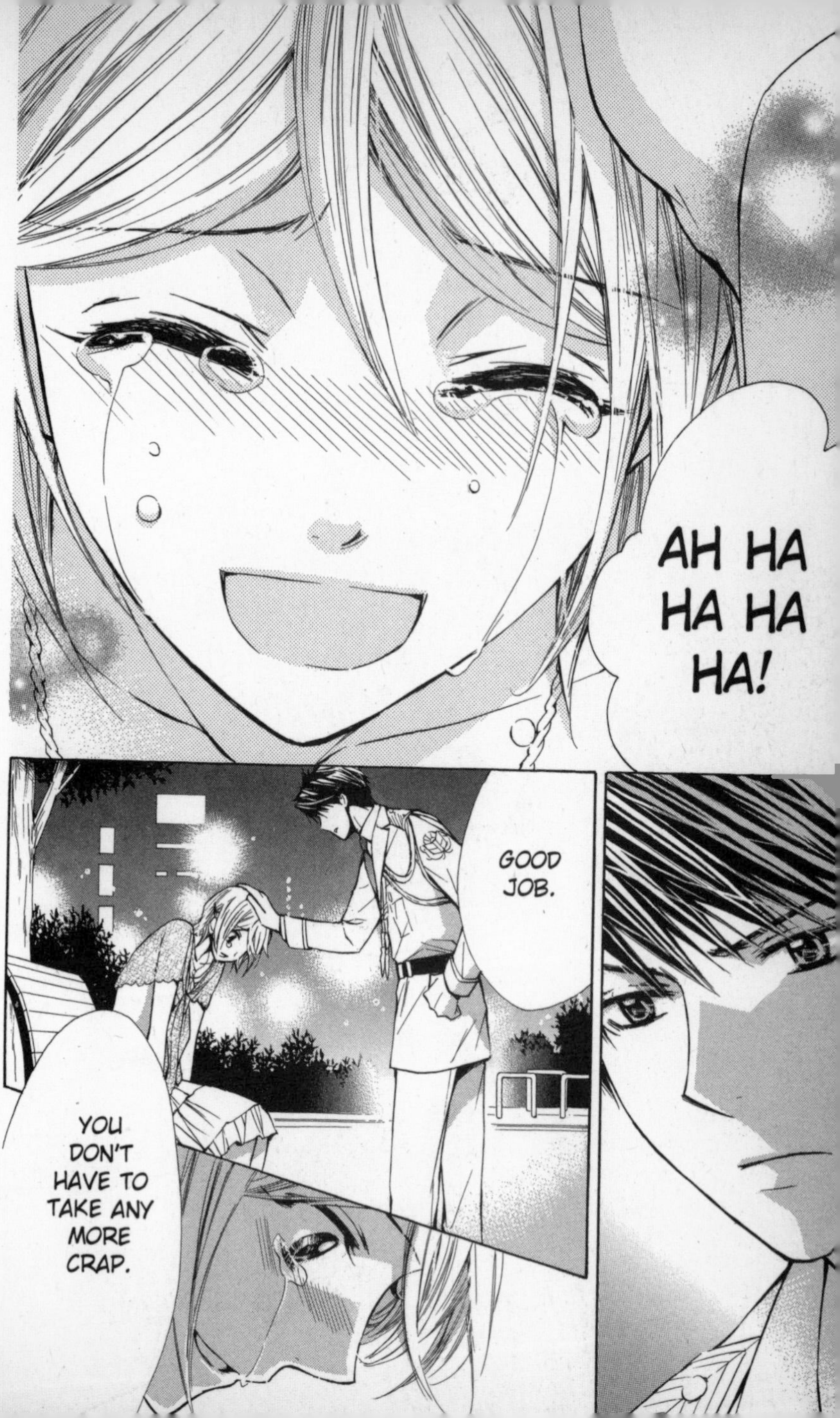
AH HA HA HA HA!
GOOD JOB.
YOU DON'T HAVE TO TAKE ANY MORE CRAP.

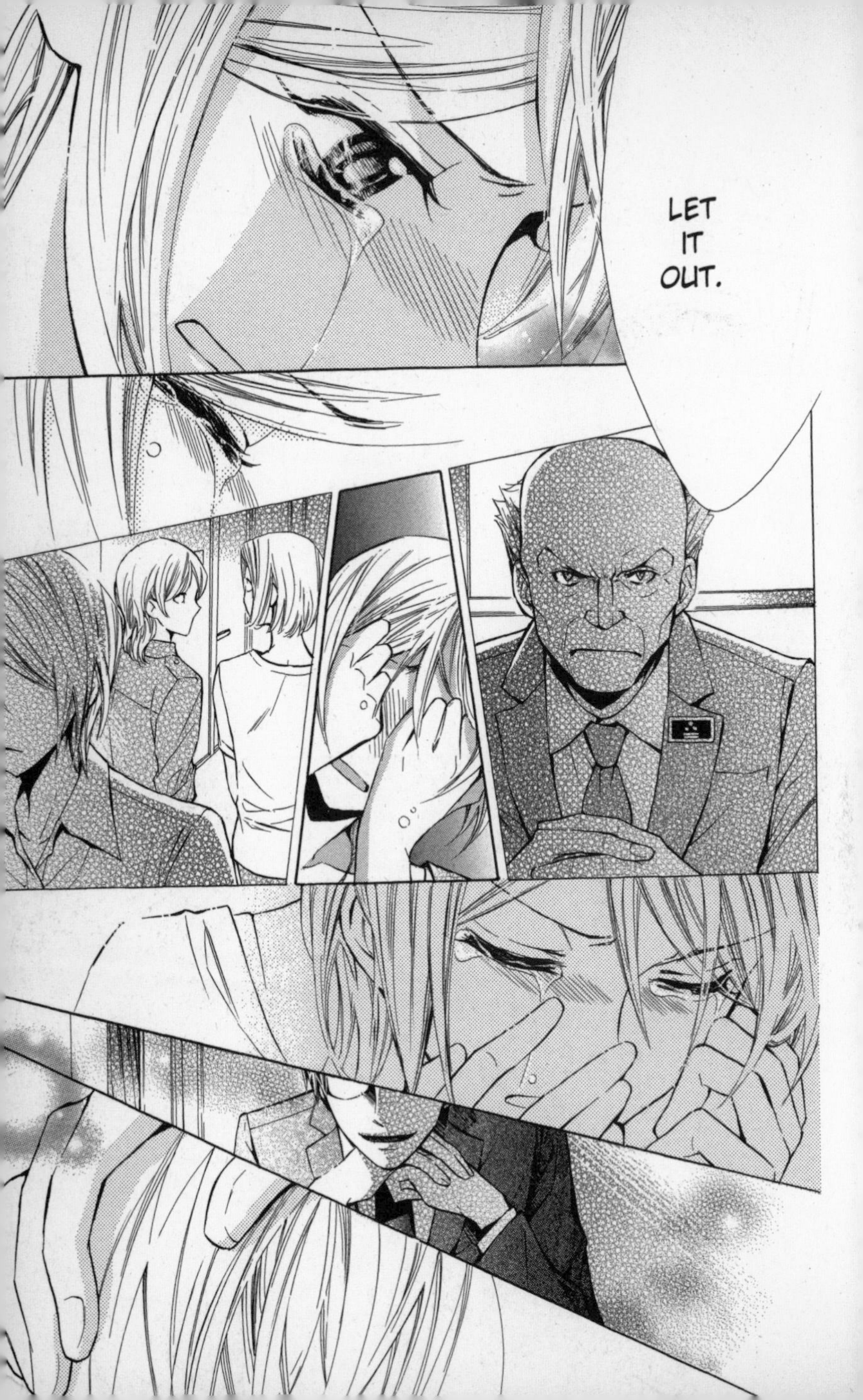
LET IT OUT.

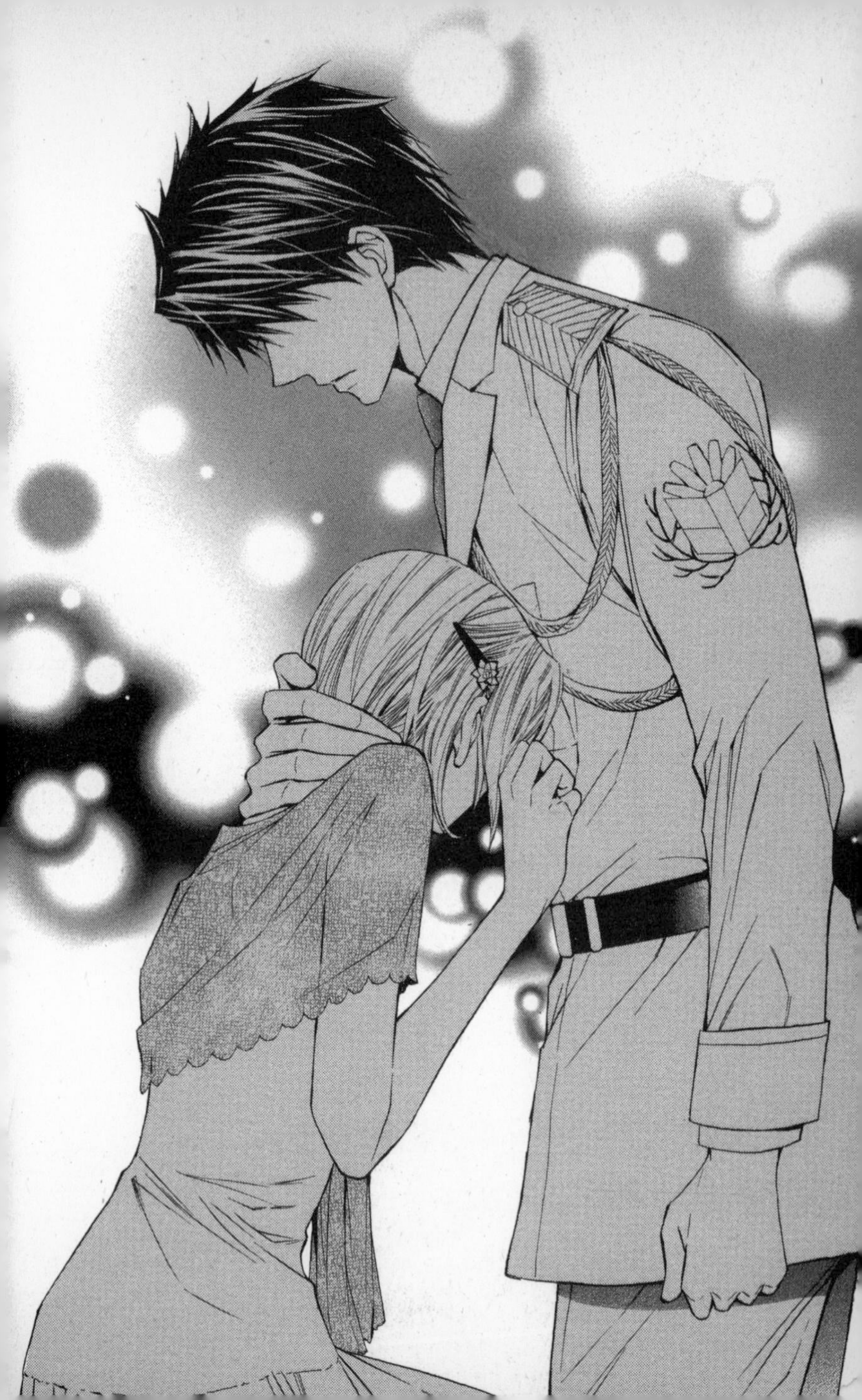

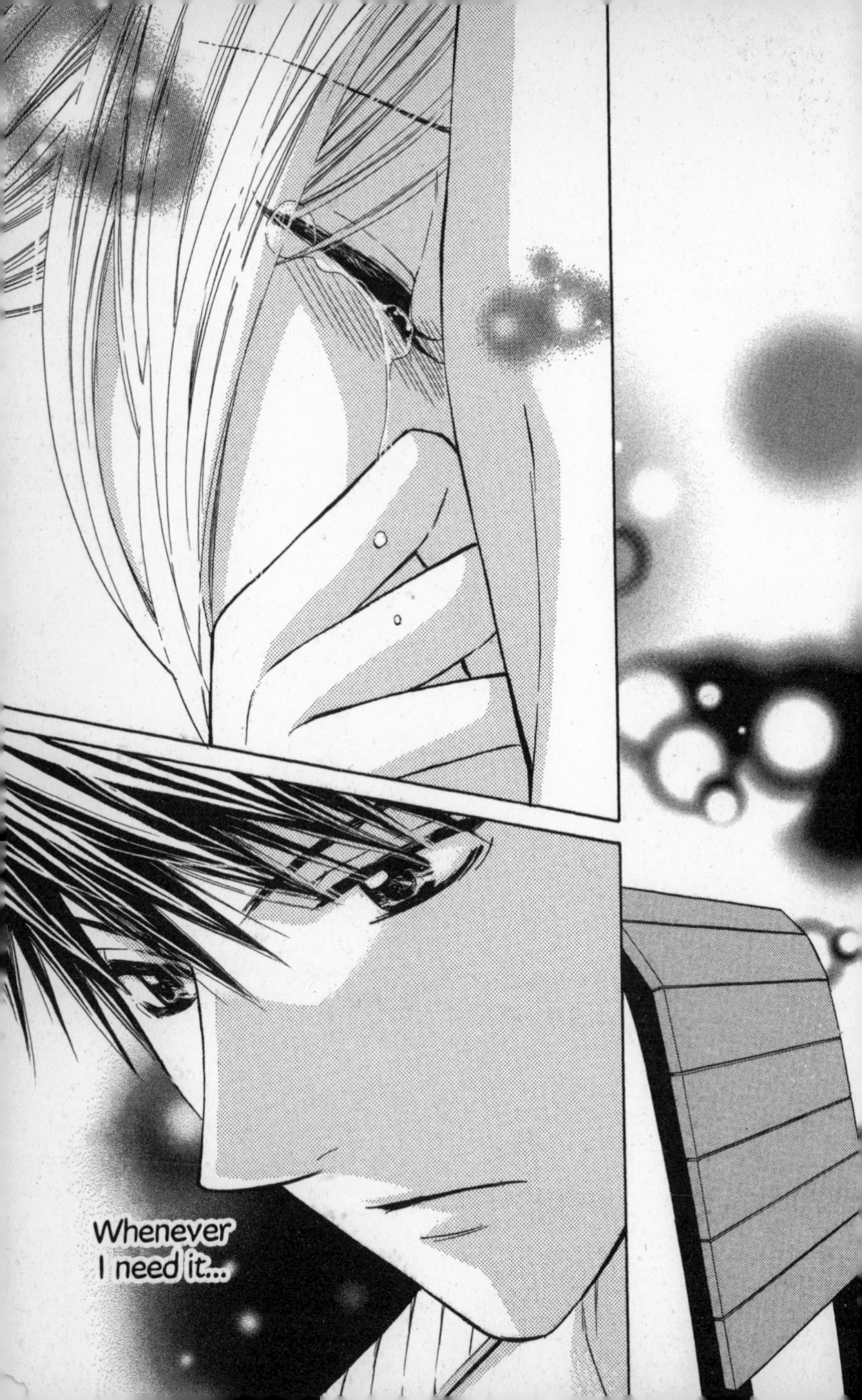
Whenever I need it...

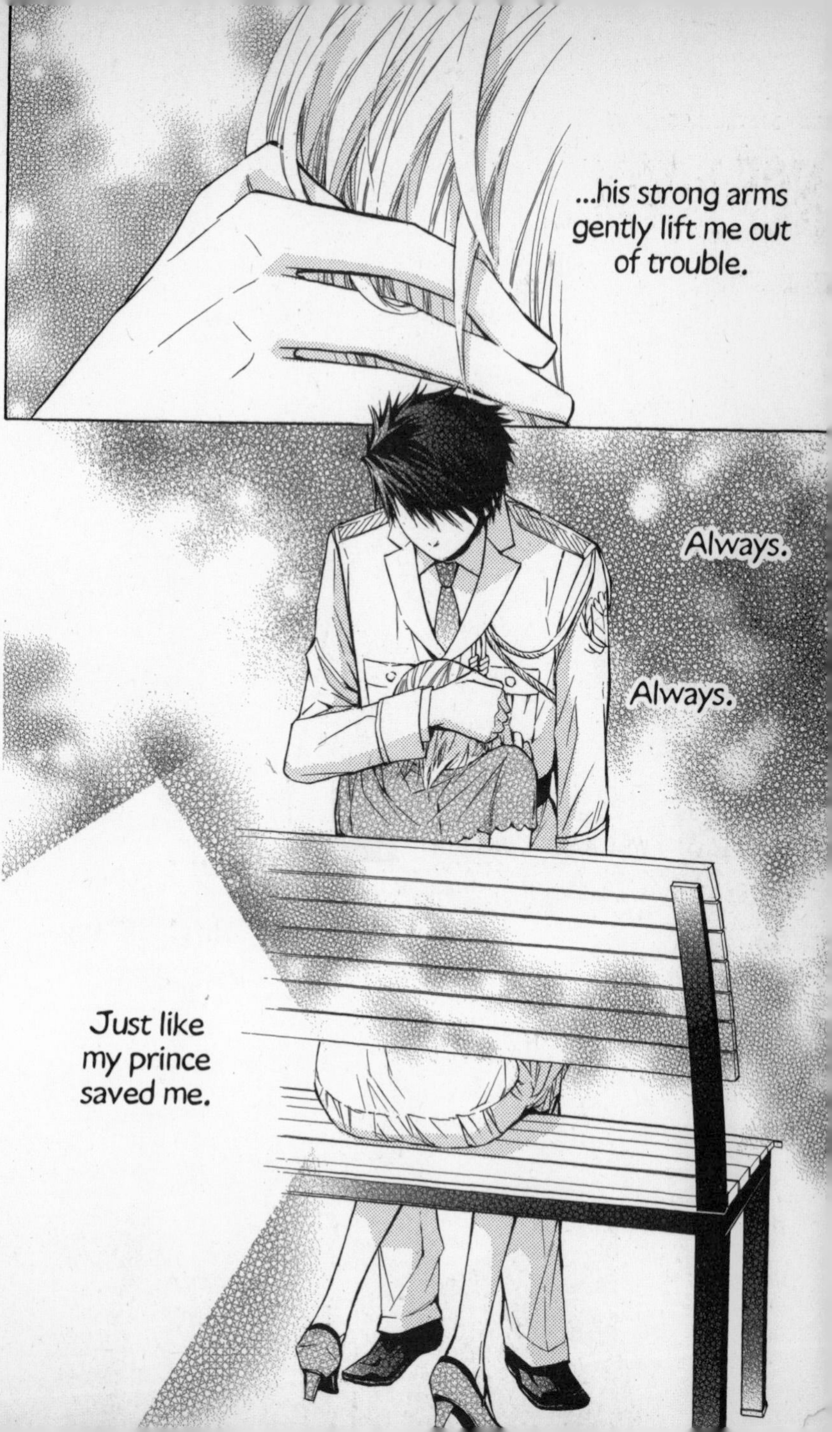
...his strong arms gently lift me out of trouble.
Always.
Always.
Just like my prince saved me.

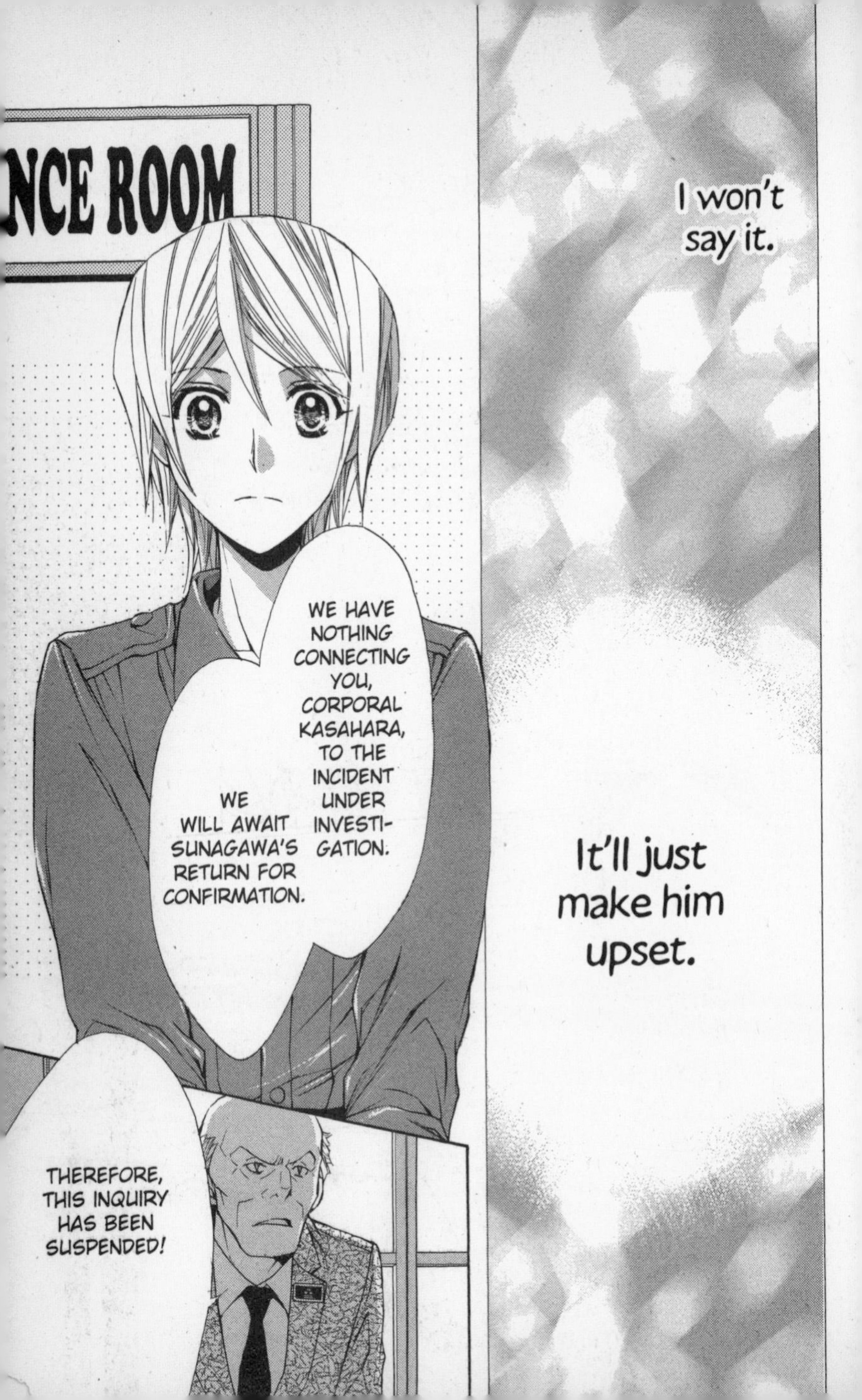
I won't say it.
It'll just make him upset.
NCE ROOM
WE HAVE NOTHING CONNECTING YOU, CORPORAL KASAHARA, TO THE INCIDENT UNDER INVESTIGATION.
WE WILL AWAIT SUNAGAWA'S RETURN FOR CONFIRMATION.
THEREFORE, THIS INQUIRY HAS BEEN SUSPENDED!

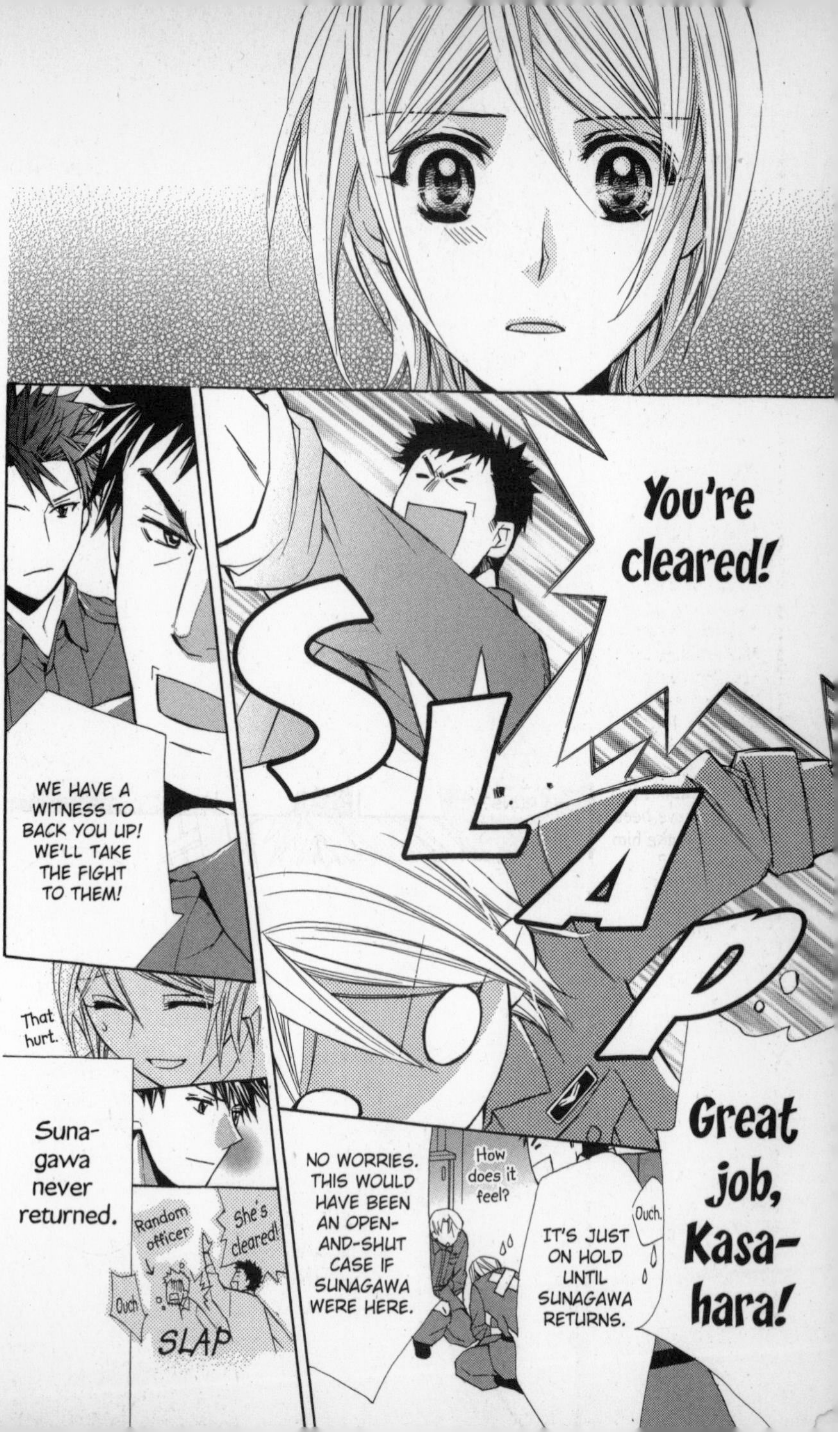
You're cleared!
SLAP
WE HAVE A WITNESS TO BACK YOU UP! WE'LL TAKE THE FIGHT TO THEM!
That hurt.
Great job, Kasahara!
Ouch.
How does it feel?
IT'S JUST ON HOLD UNTIL SUNAGAWA RETURNS.
NO WORRIES. THIS WOULD HAVE BEEN AN OPEN-AND-SHUT CASE IF SUNAGAWA WERE HERE.
Sunagawa never returned.
She's cleared!
Random officer
Ouch
SLAP

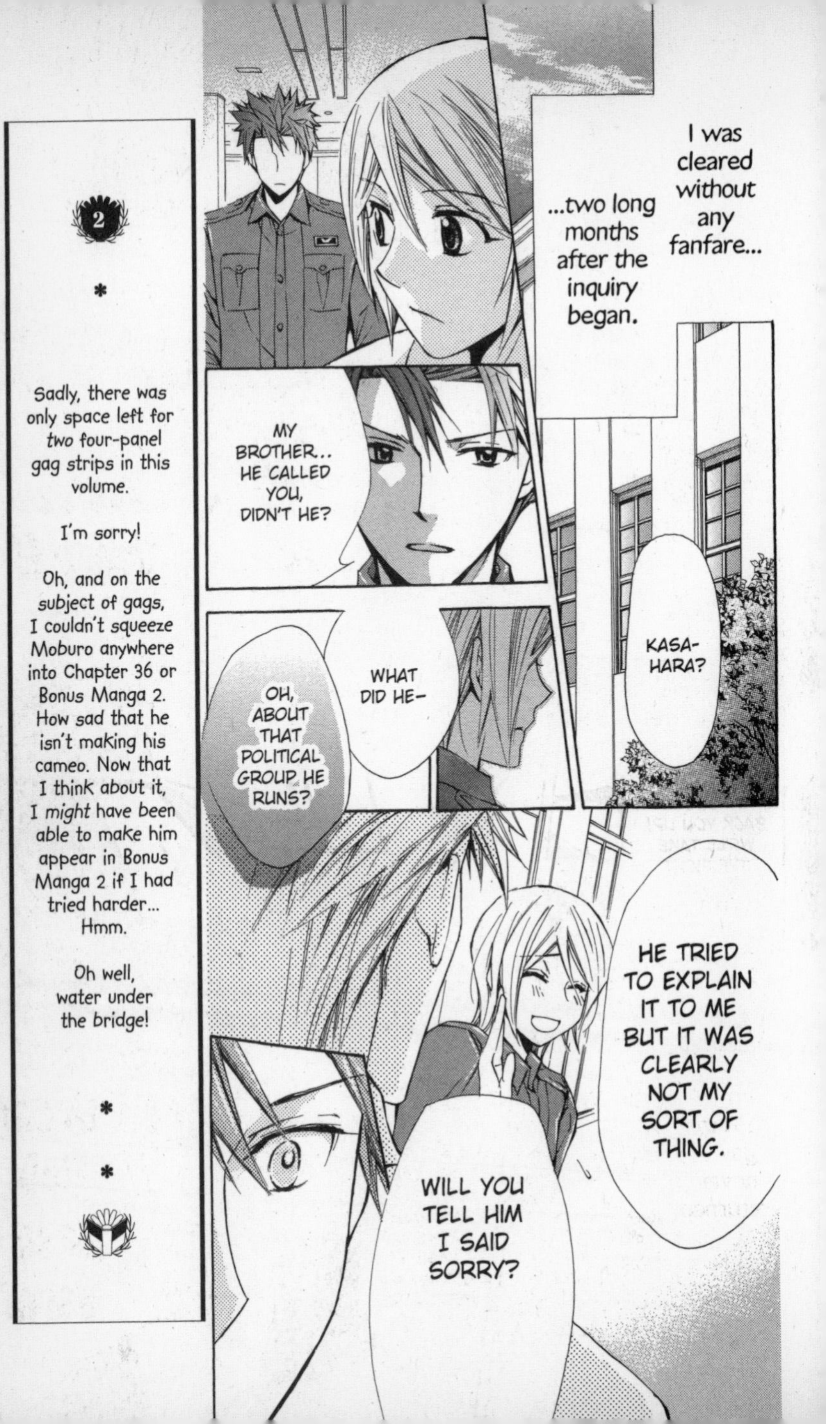
I was cleared without any fanfare...
...two long months after the inquiry began.
KASA-HARA?
MY BROTHER... HE CALLED YOU, DIDN'T HE?
WHAT DID HE-
OH, ABOUT THAT POLITICAL GROUP HE RUNS?
HE TRIED TO EXPLAIN IT TO ME BUT IT WAS CLEARLY NOT MY SORT OF THING.
WILL YOU TELL HIM I SAID SORRY?

2

*

Sadly, there was only space left for *two* four-panel gag strips in this volume.

I'm sorry!

Oh, and on the subject of gags, I couldn't *squeeze* Moburo anywhere into Chapter 36 or Bonus Manga 2. How sad that he isn't making his cameo. Now that I think *about* it, I *might* have been able to make him appear in Bonus Manga 2 if I had tried harder... Hmm.

Oh well, water under the bridge!

*

*

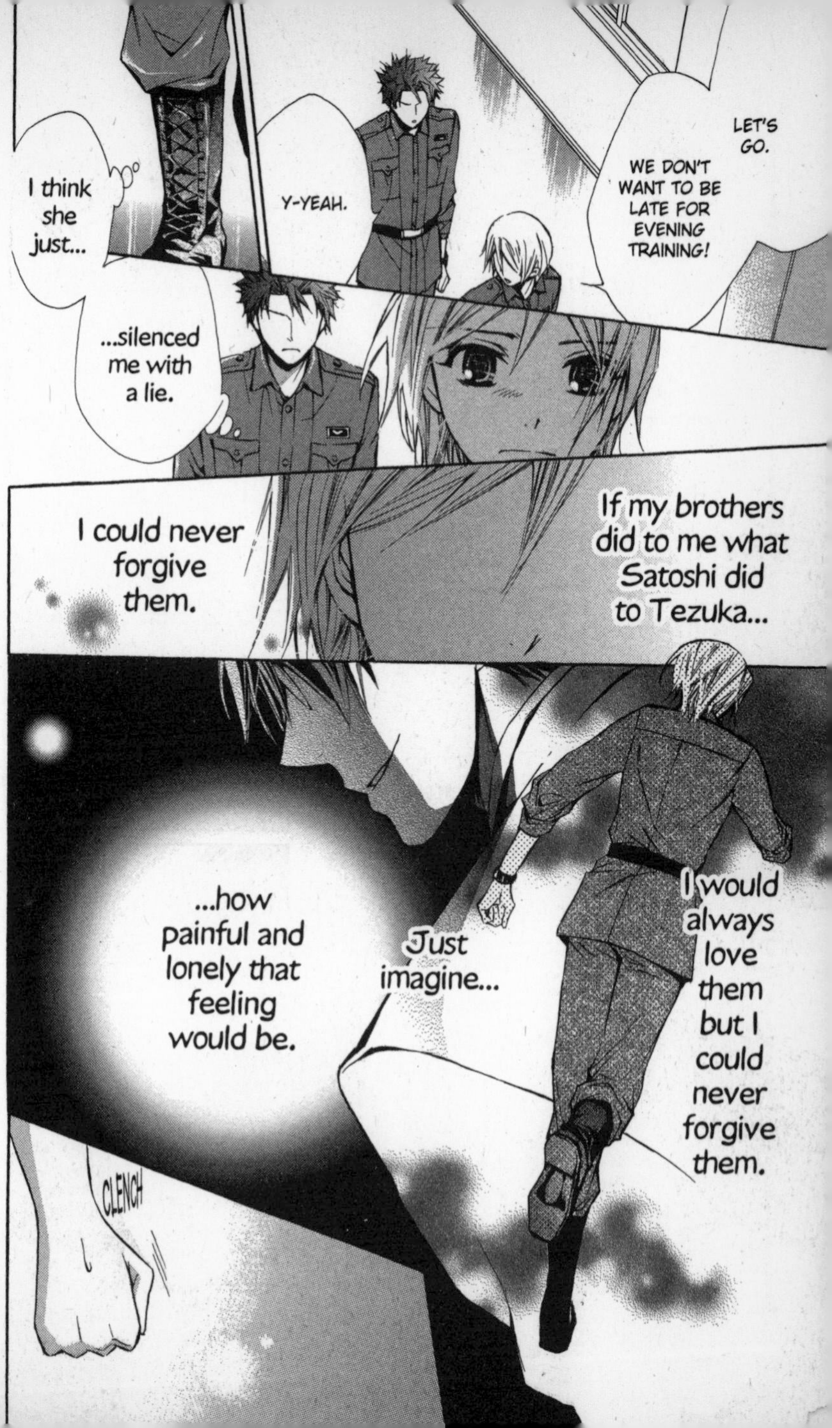
LET'S GO.
WE DON'T WANT TO BE LATE FOR EVENING TRAINING!
Y-YEAH.
I think she just...
...silenced me with a lie.
If my brothers did to me what Satoshi did to Tezuka...
I could never forgive them.
I would always love them but I could never forgive them.
Just imagine...
...how painful and lonely that feeling would be.
CLENCH

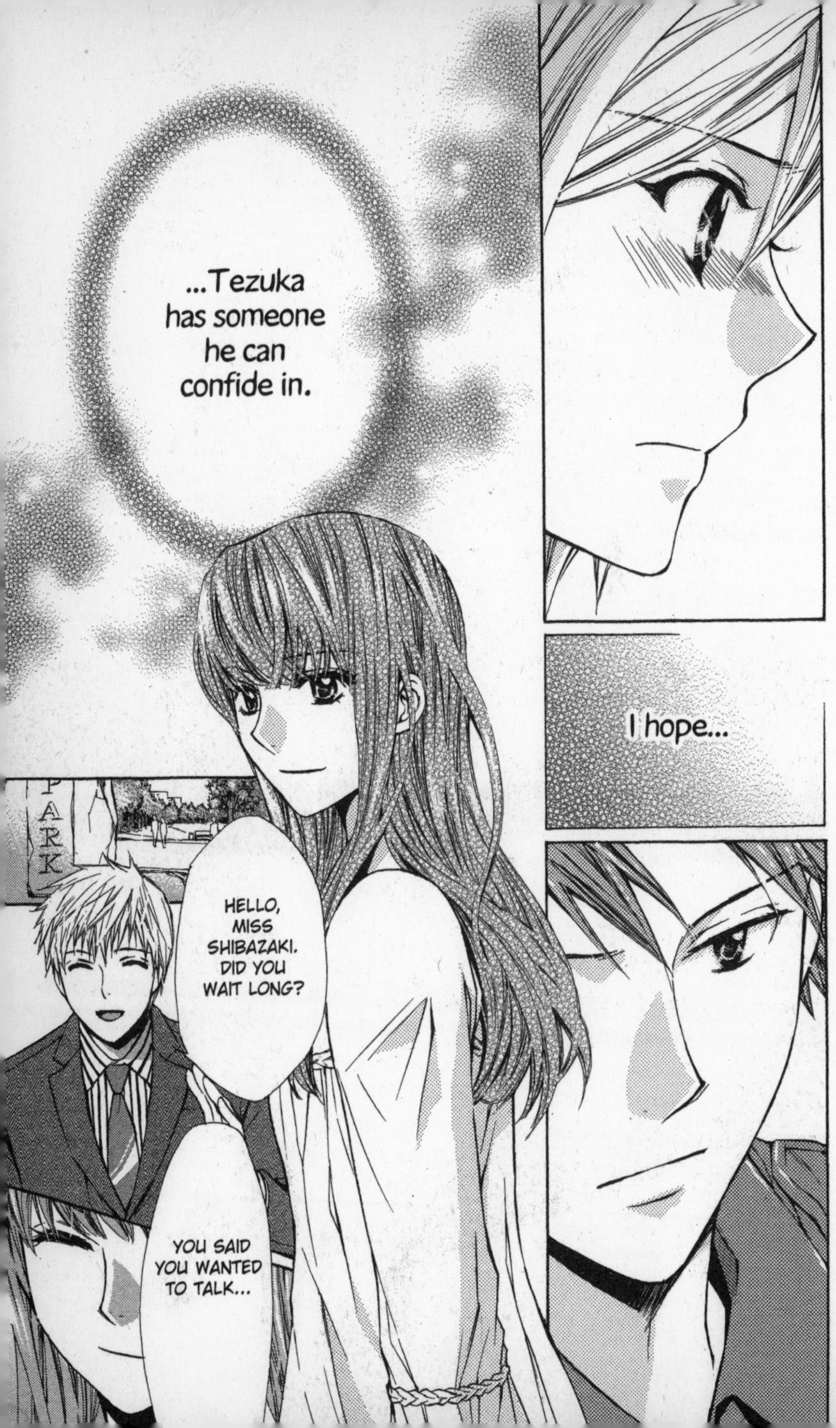
I hope...
...Tezuka has someone he can confide in.
PARK
HELLO, MISS SHIBAZAKI. DID YOU WAIT LONG?
YOU SAID YOU WANTED TO TALK...

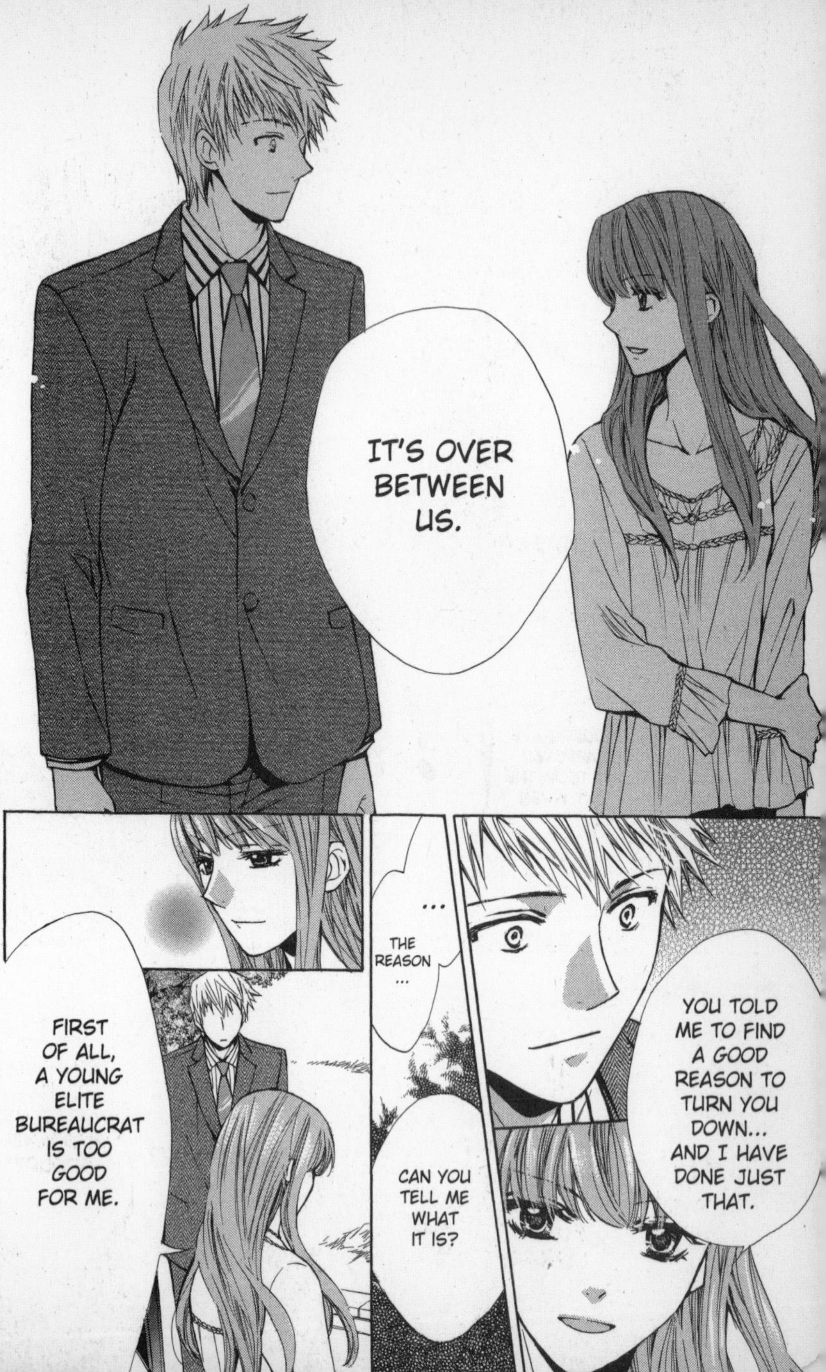
IT'S OVER BETWEEN US.
YOU TOLD ME TO FIND A GOOD REASON TO TURN YOU DOWN... AND I HAVE DONE JUST THAT.
...
THE REASON ...
CAN YOU TELL ME WHAT IT IS?
FIRST OF ALL, A YOUNG ELITE BUREAUCRAT IS TOO GOOD FOR ME.

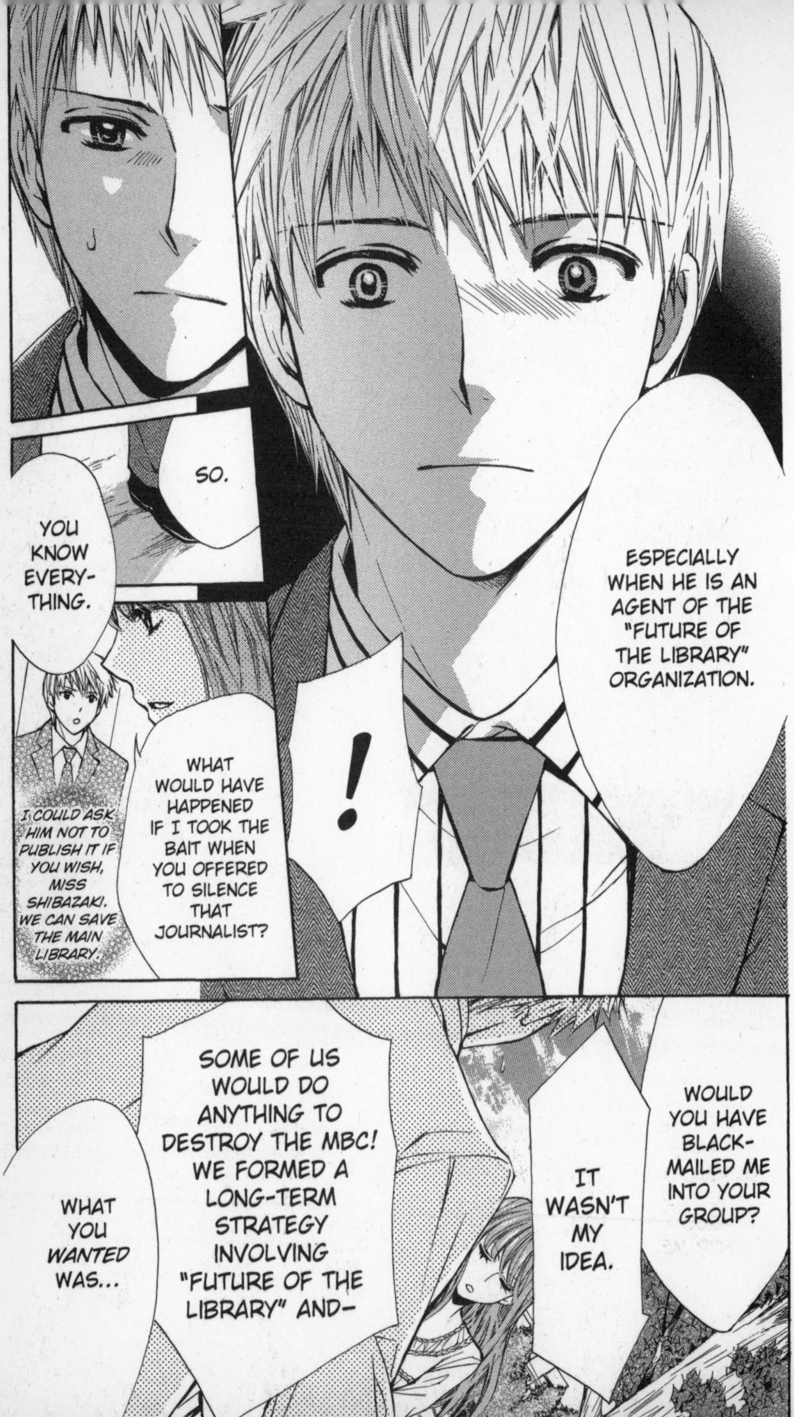
ESPECIALLY WHEN HE IS AN AGENT OF THE "FUTURE OF THE LIBRARY" ORGANIZATION.
!
SO.
YOU KNOW EVERY-THING.
WHAT WOULD HAVE HAPPENED IF I TOOK THE BAIT WHEN YOU OFFERED TO SILENCE THAT JOURNALIST?
I COULD ASK HIM NOT TO PUBLISH IT IF YOU WISH, MISS SHIBAZAKI. WE CAN SAVE THE MAIN LIBRARY.
WOULD YOU HAVE BLACK-MAILED ME INTO YOUR GROUP?
IT WASN'T MY IDEA.
SOME OF US WOULD DO ANYTHING TO DESTROY THE MBC! WE FORMED A LONG-TERM STRATEGY INVOLVING "FUTURE OF THE LIBRARY" AND-
WHAT YOU WANTED WAS...

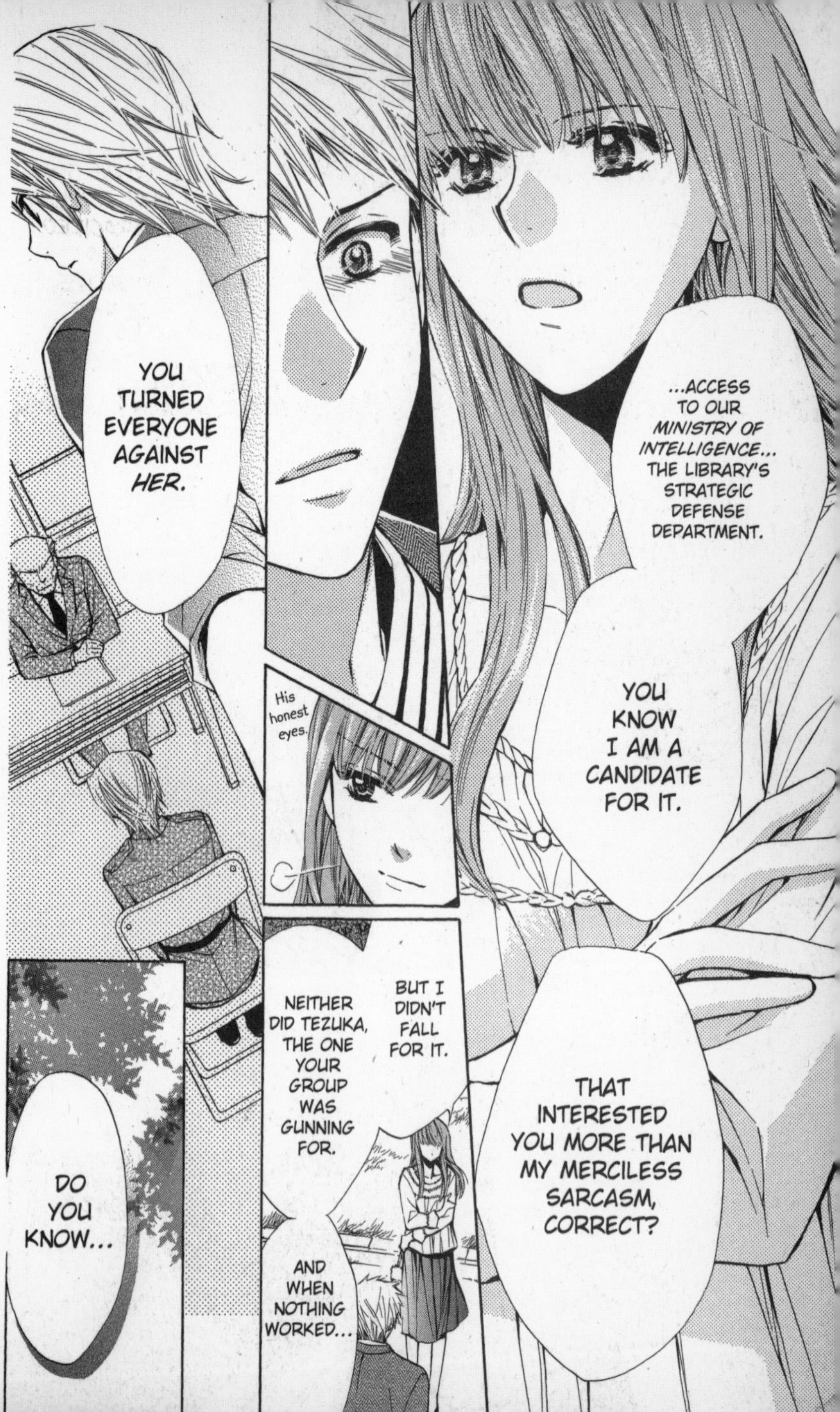
...ACCESS TO OUR MINISTRY OF INTELLIGENCE... THE LIBRARY'S STRATEGIC DEFENSE DEPARTMENT.
YOU KNOW I AM A CANDIDATE FOR IT.
THAT INTERESTED YOU MORE THAN MY MERCILESS SARCASM, CORRECT?
His honest eyes.
BUT I DIDN'T FALL FOR IT.
NEITHER DID TEZUKA, THE ONE YOUR GROUP WAS GUNNING FOR.
AND WHEN NOTHING WORKED...
YOU TURNED EVERYONE AGAINST HER.
DO YOU KNOW...

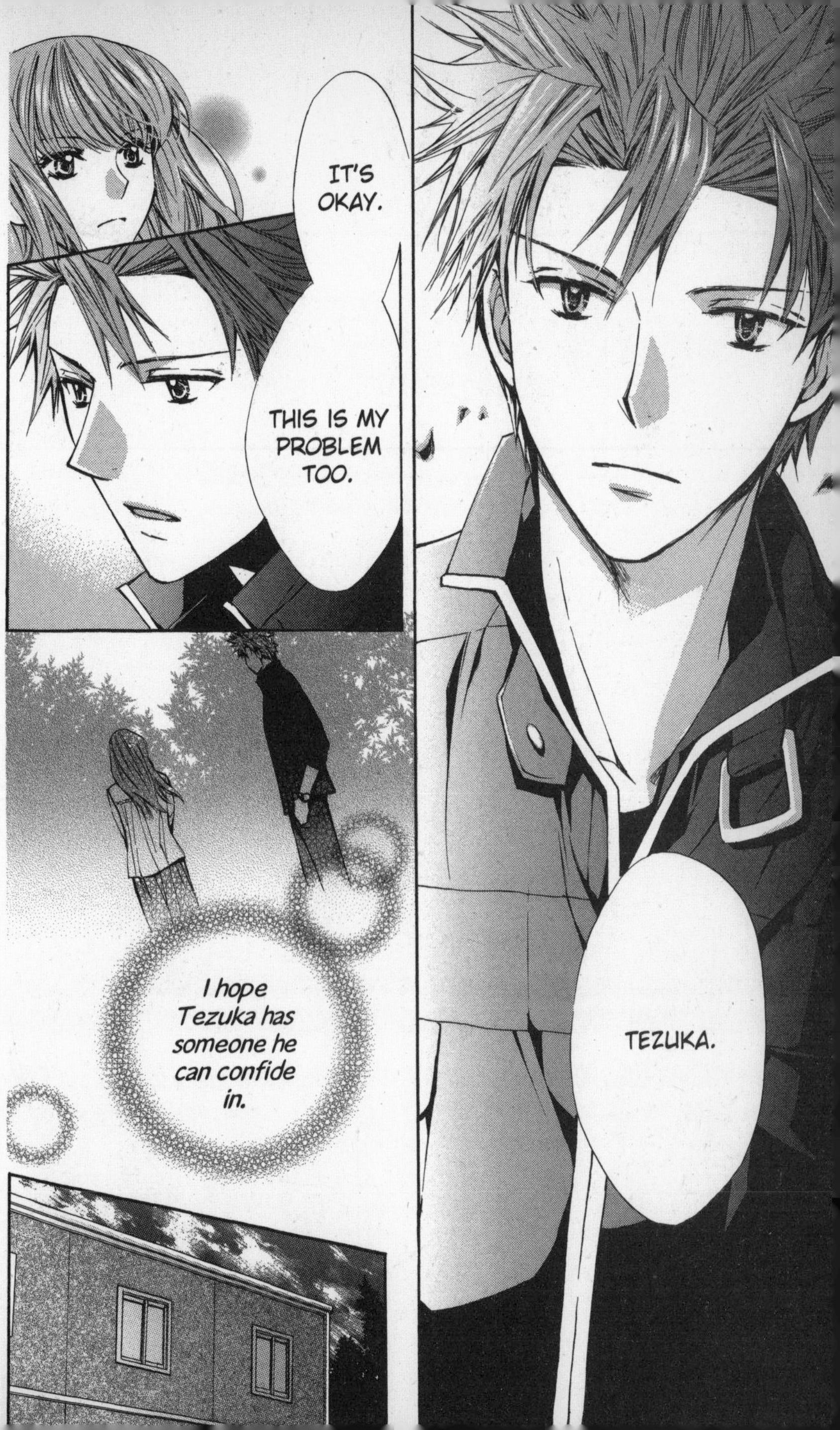
TEZUKA.
IT'S OKAY.
THIS IS MY PROBLEM TOO.
I hope Tezuka has someone he can confide in.

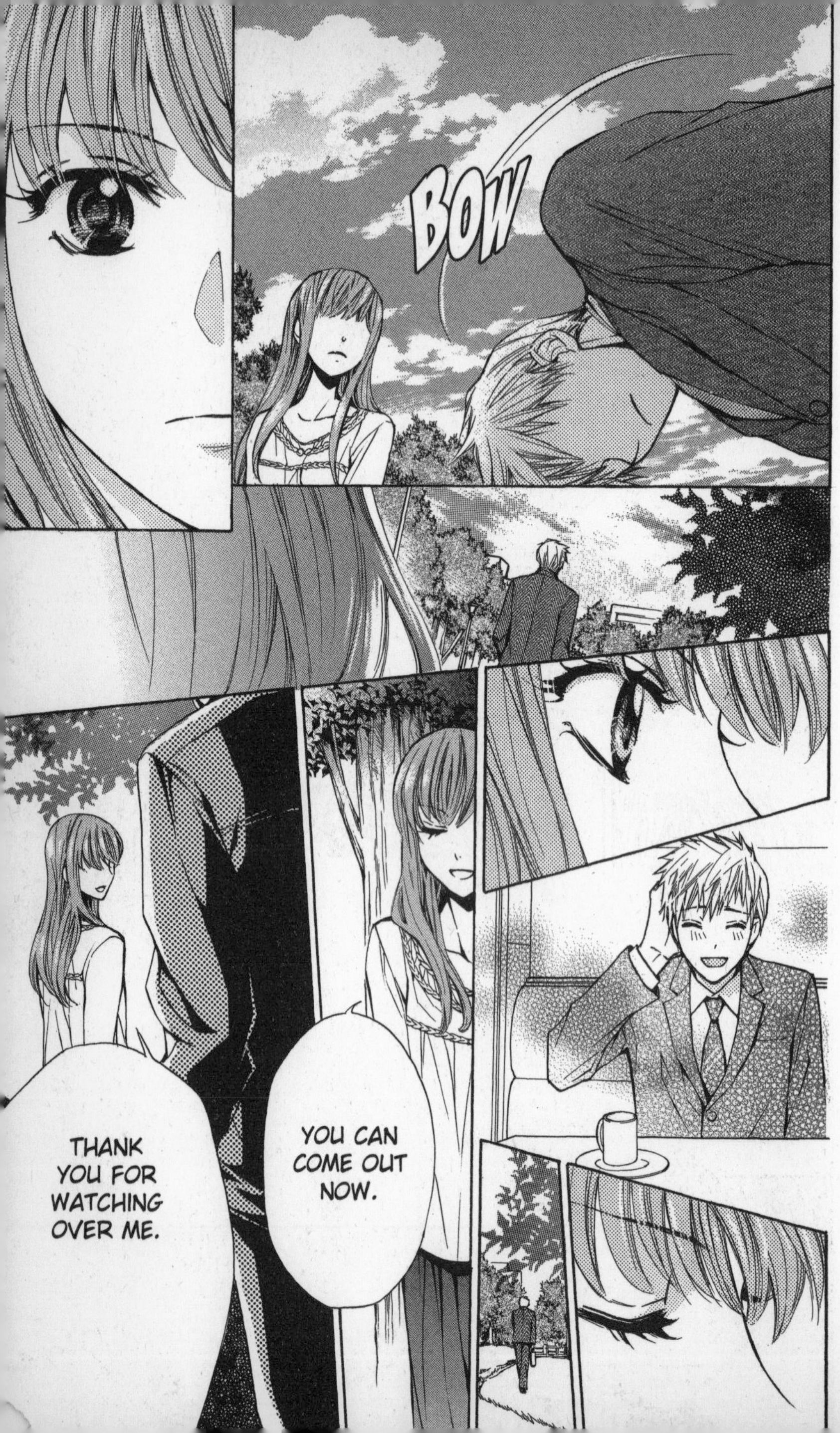
BOW
YOU CAN COME OUT NOW.
THANK YOU FOR WATCHING OVER ME.

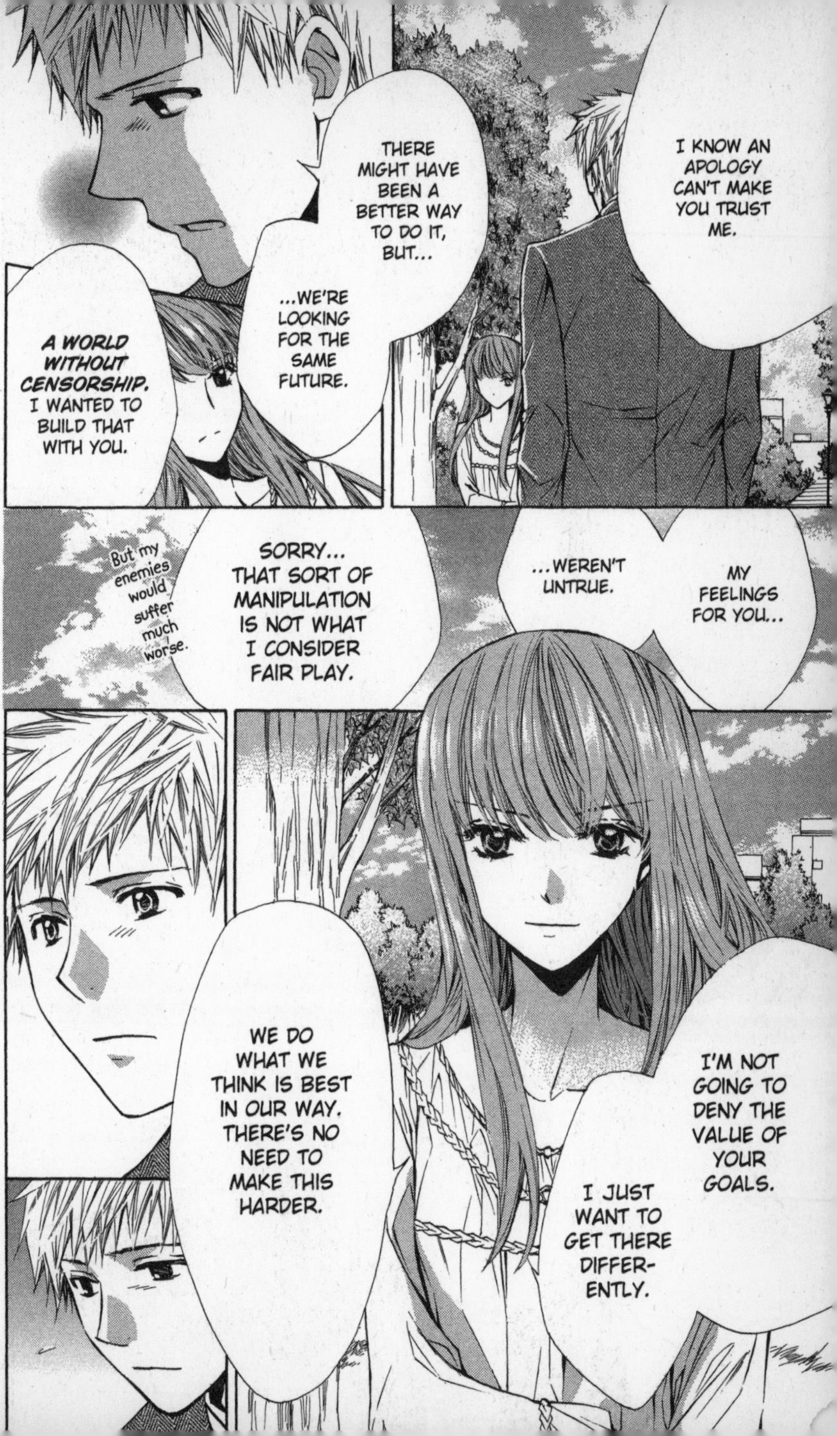
I KNOW AN APOLOGY CAN'T MAKE YOU TRUST ME.
THERE MIGHT HAVE BEEN A BETTER WAY TO DO IT, BUT...
...WE'RE LOOKING FOR THE SAME FUTURE.
A WORLD WITHOUT CENSORSHIP. I WANTED TO BUILD THAT WITH YOU.
MY FEELINGS FOR YOU...
...WEREN'T UNTRUE.
SORRY... THAT SORT OF MANIPULATION IS NOT WHAT I CONSIDER FAIR PLAY.
But my enemies would suffer much worse.
I'M NOT GOING TO DENY THE VALUE OF YOUR GOALS.
I JUST WANT TO GET THERE DIFFER-ENTLY.
WE DO WHAT WE THINK IS BEST IN OUR WAY. THERE'S NO NEED TO MAKE THIS HARDER.

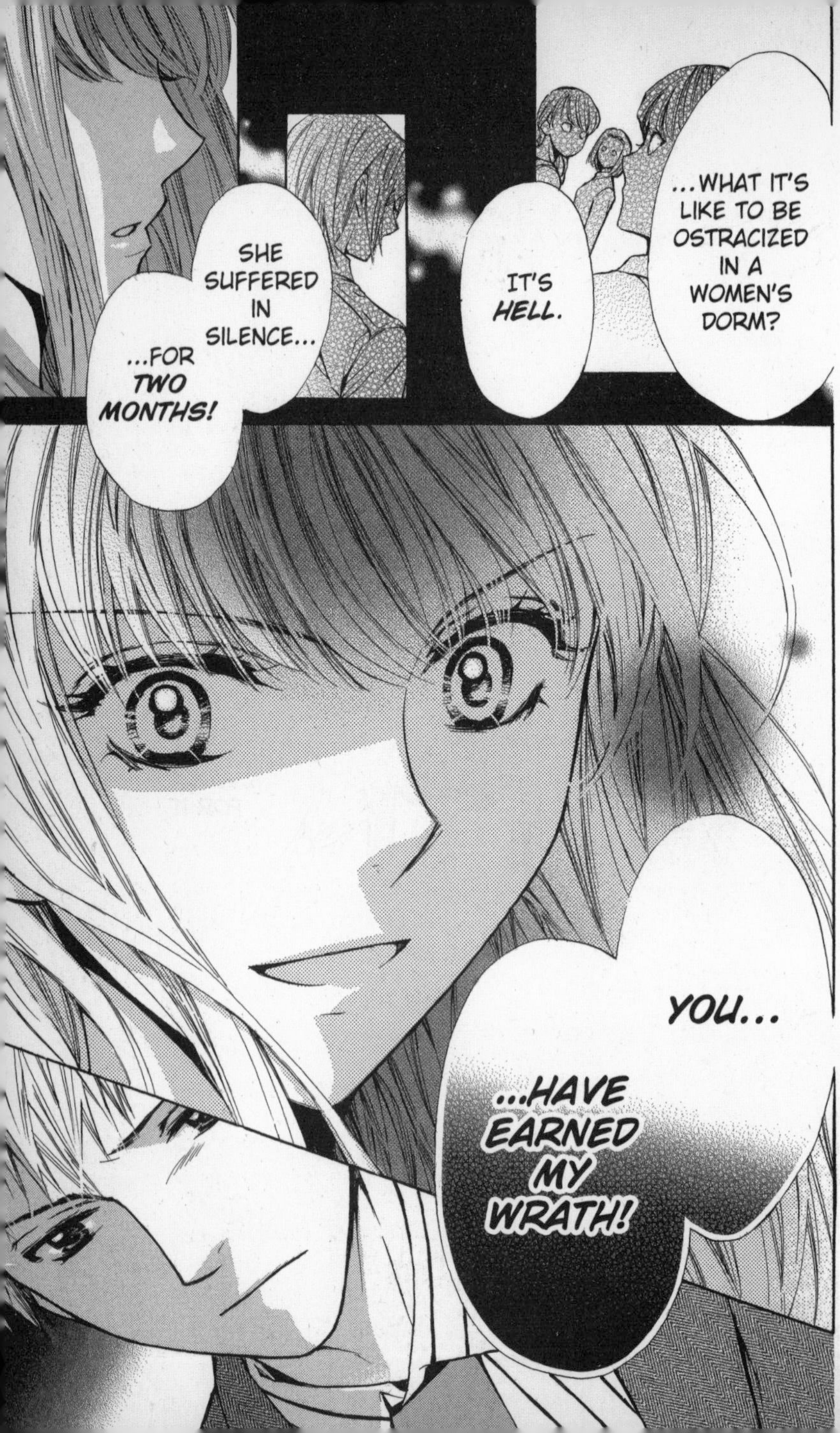
...WHAT IT'S LIKE TO BE OSTRACIZED IN A WOMEN'S DORM?
IT'S HELL.
SHE SUFFERED IN SILENCE...
...FOR TWO MONTHS!
YOU...
...HAVE EARNED MY WRATH!

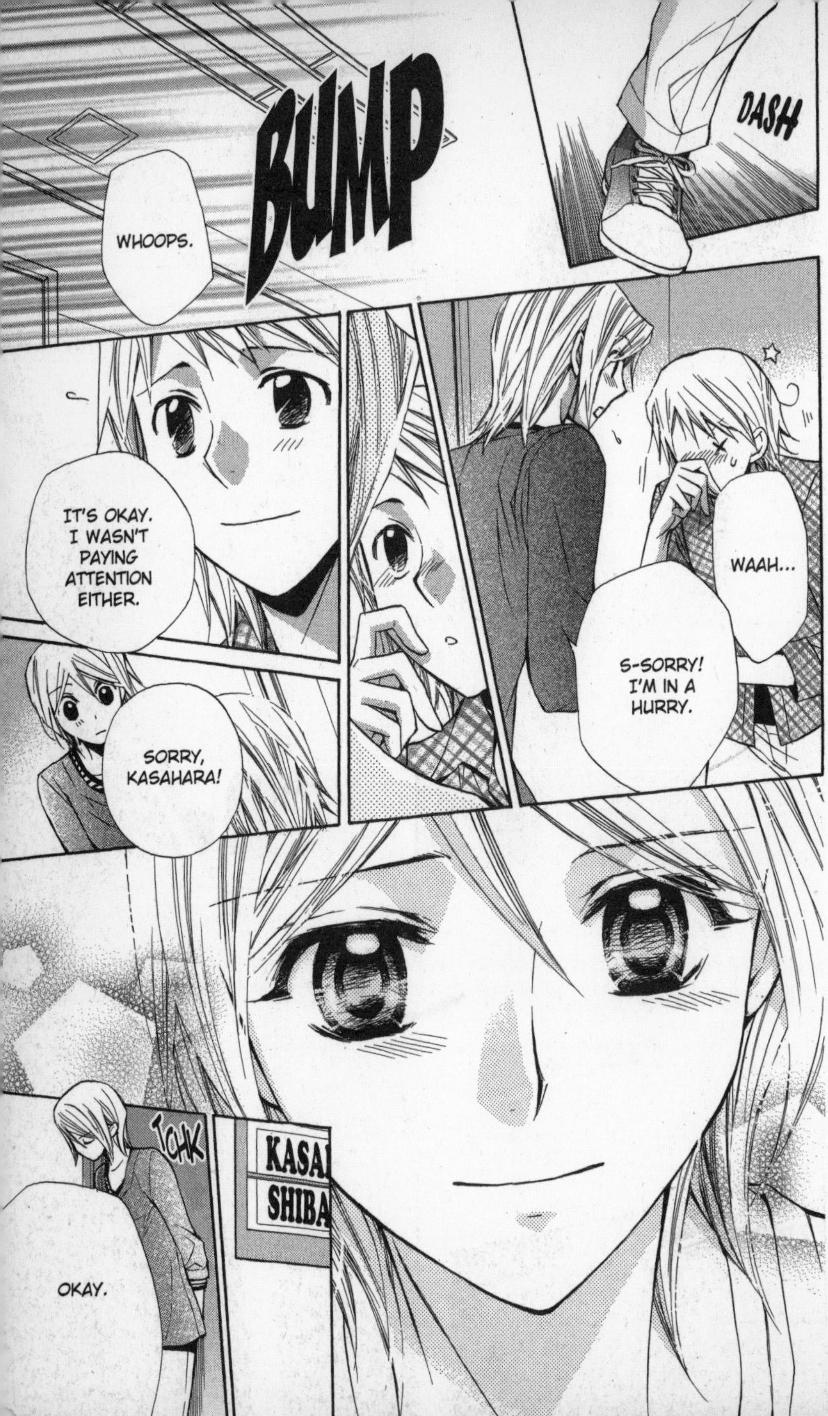
DASH
BUMP
WHOOPS.
WAAH...
S-SORRY! I'M IN A HURRY.
IT'S OKAY. I WASN'T PAYING ATTENTION EITHER.
SORRY, KASAHARA!
TCHK
KASA
SHIBA
OKAY.

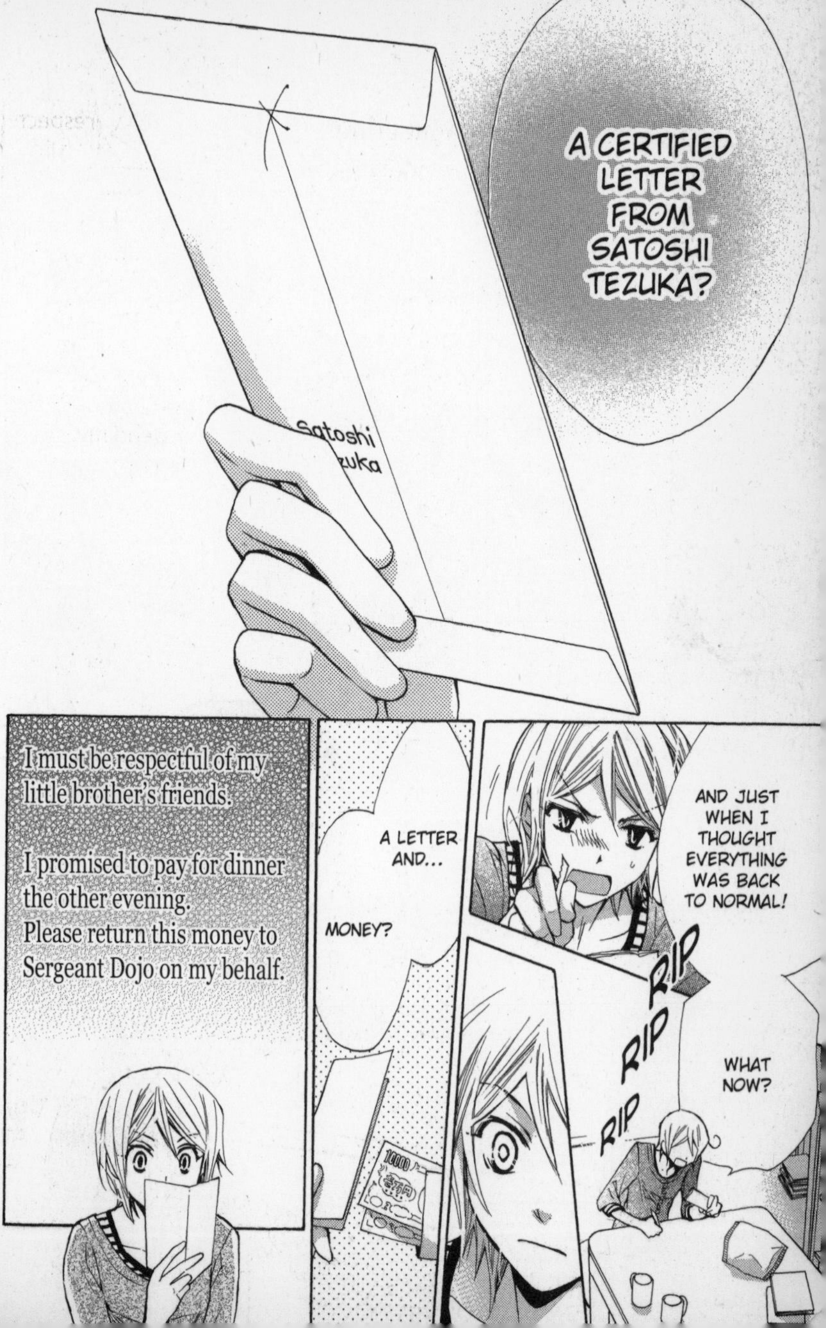
A CERTIFIED LETTER FROM SATOSHI TEZUKA?
Satoshi
AND JUST WHEN I THOUGHT EVERYTHING WAS BACK TO NORMAL!
RIP
RIP
RIP
WHAT NOW?
A LETTER AND...
MONEY?
I must be respectful of my little brother's friends.
I promised to pay for dinner the other evening.
Please return this money to Sergeant Dojo on my behalf.

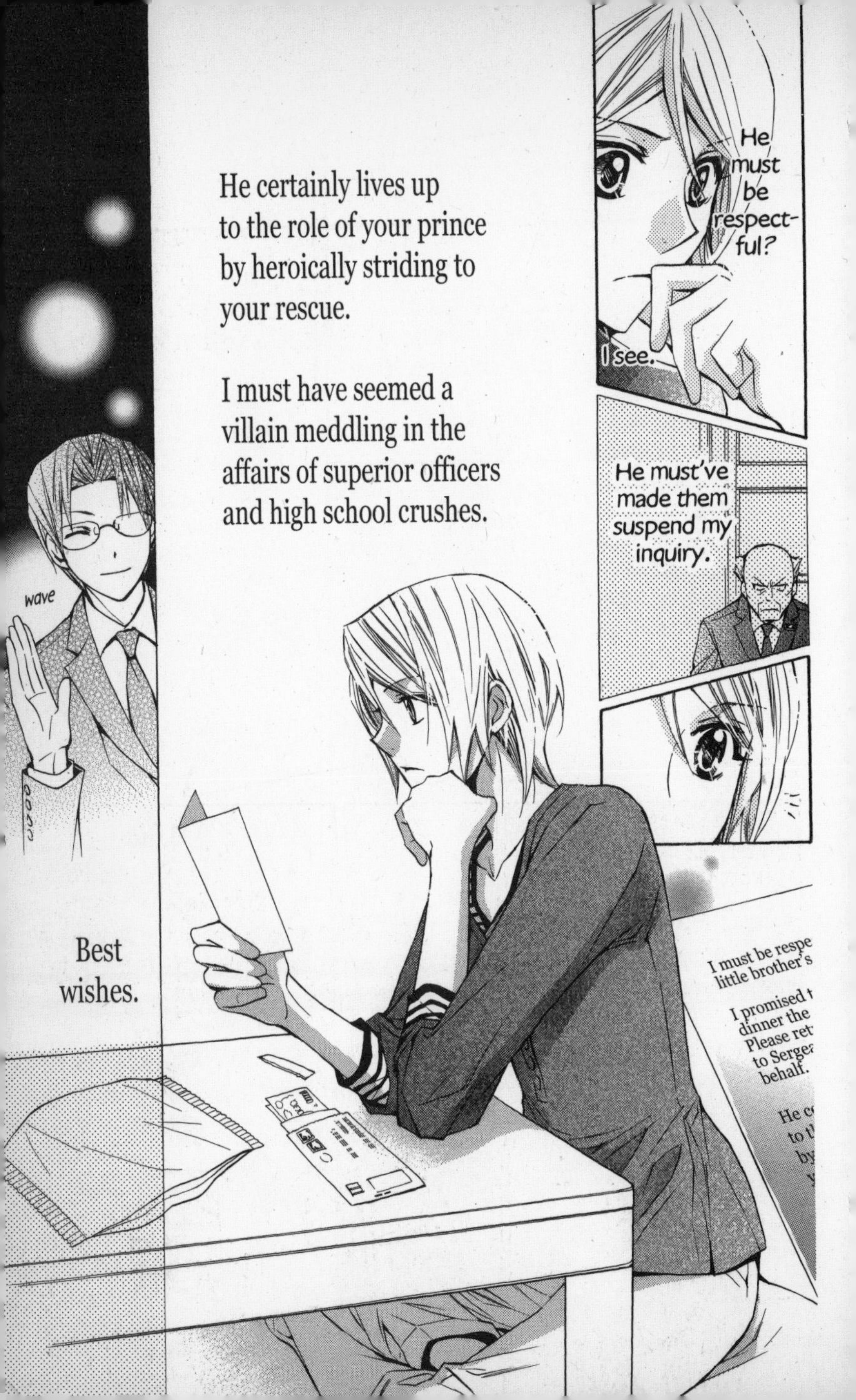
He must be respectful?
I see.
He must've made them suspend my inquiry.
He certainly lives up to the role of your prince by heroically striding to your rescue.
I must have seemed a villain meddling in the affairs of superior officers and high school crushes.
I must be respe
little brother's
I promised
dinner the
Please ret
to Serge
behalf.
He c
to t
by
wave
Best wishes.

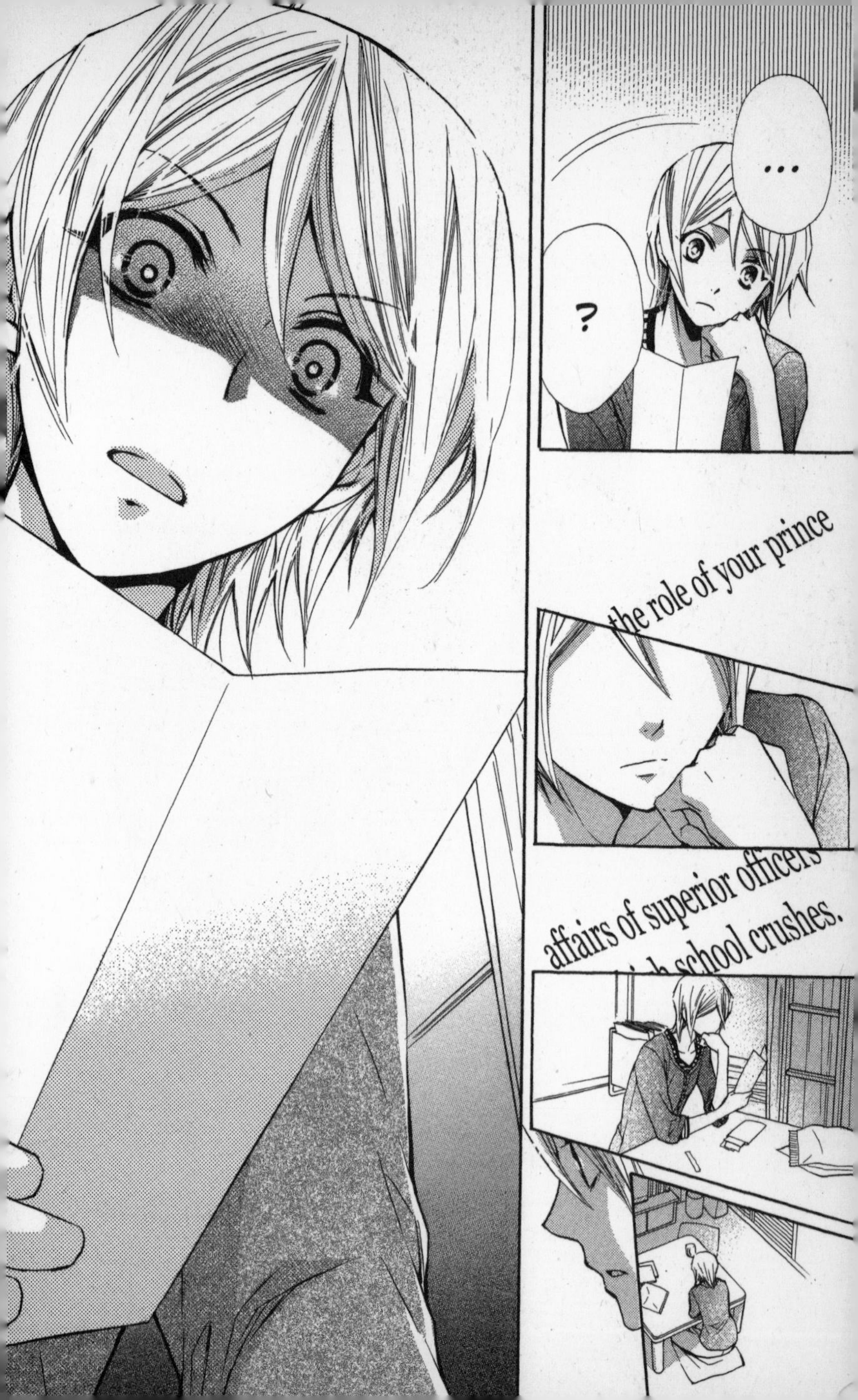
...
?
the role of your prince
affairs of superior officers
school crushes.

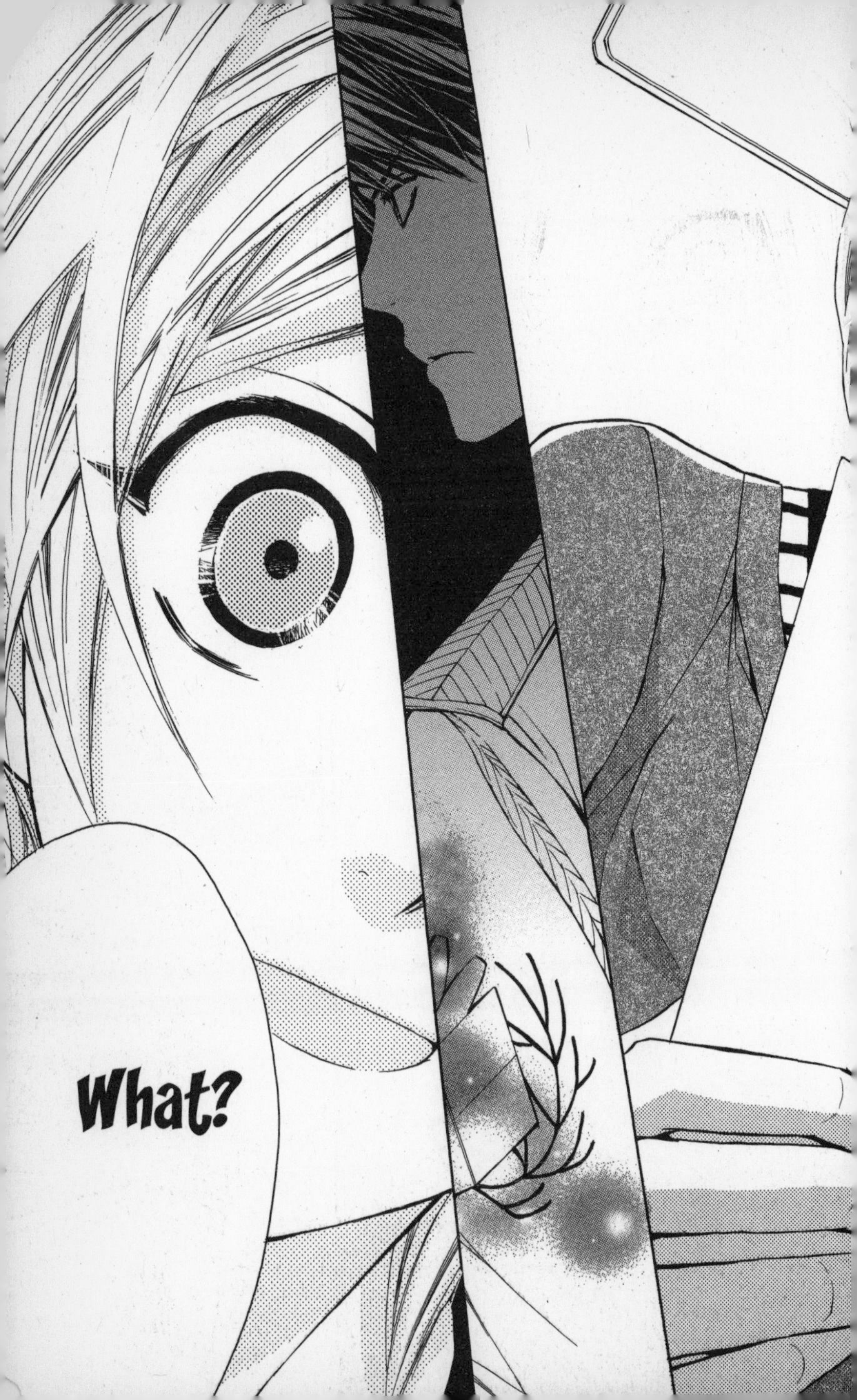
What?

Secret Admirer part 7

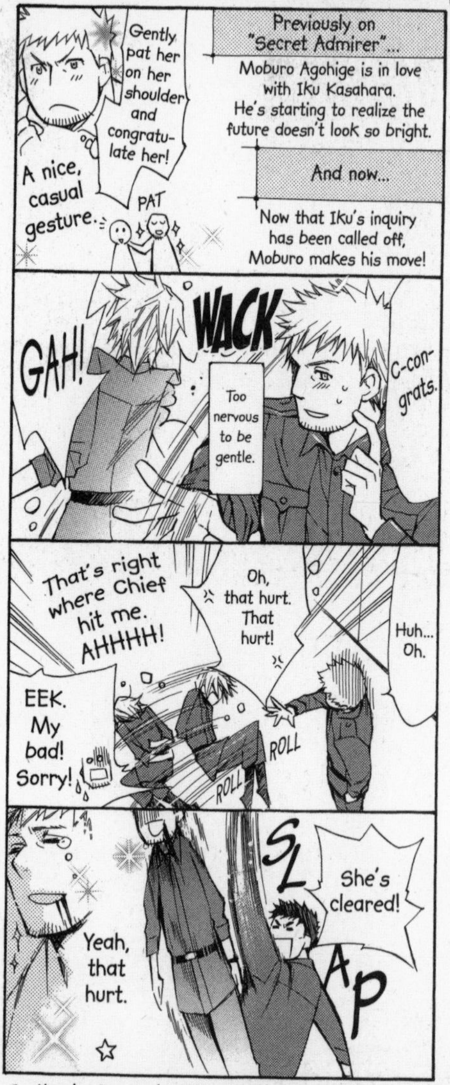
Previously on "Secret Admirer"...
Moburo Agohige is in love with Iku Kasahara. He's starting to realize the future doesn't look so bright.
And now...
Now that Iku's inquiry has been called off, Moburo makes his move!
Gently pat her on her shoulder and congratulate her!
A nice, casual gesture.
PAT
C-congrats.
WACK
Too nervous to be gentle.
GAH!
Huh... Oh.
Oh, that hurt. That hurt!
That's right where Chief hit me. AHHHH!
ROLL
ROLL
EEK. My bad! Sorry!
SLAP
She's cleared!
Yeah, that hurt.

In the last panel of the gag strip in volume 7,
I unwittingly let Moburo appear beard-less!
What a sad mistake...

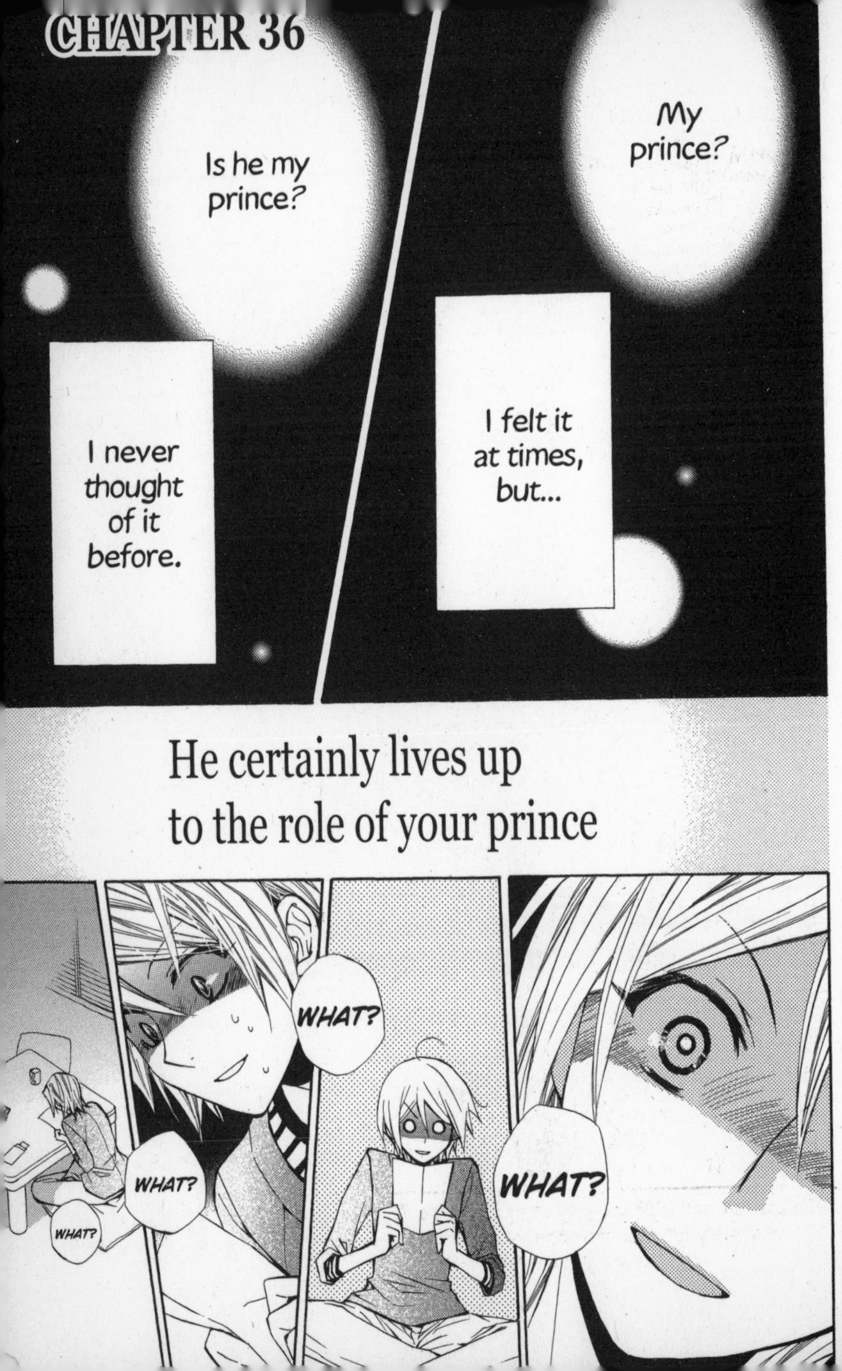
CHAPTER 36
My prince?
I felt it at times, but...
Is he my prince?
I never thought of it before.
He certainly lives up to the role of your prince
WHAT?
WHAT?
WHAT?
WHAT?

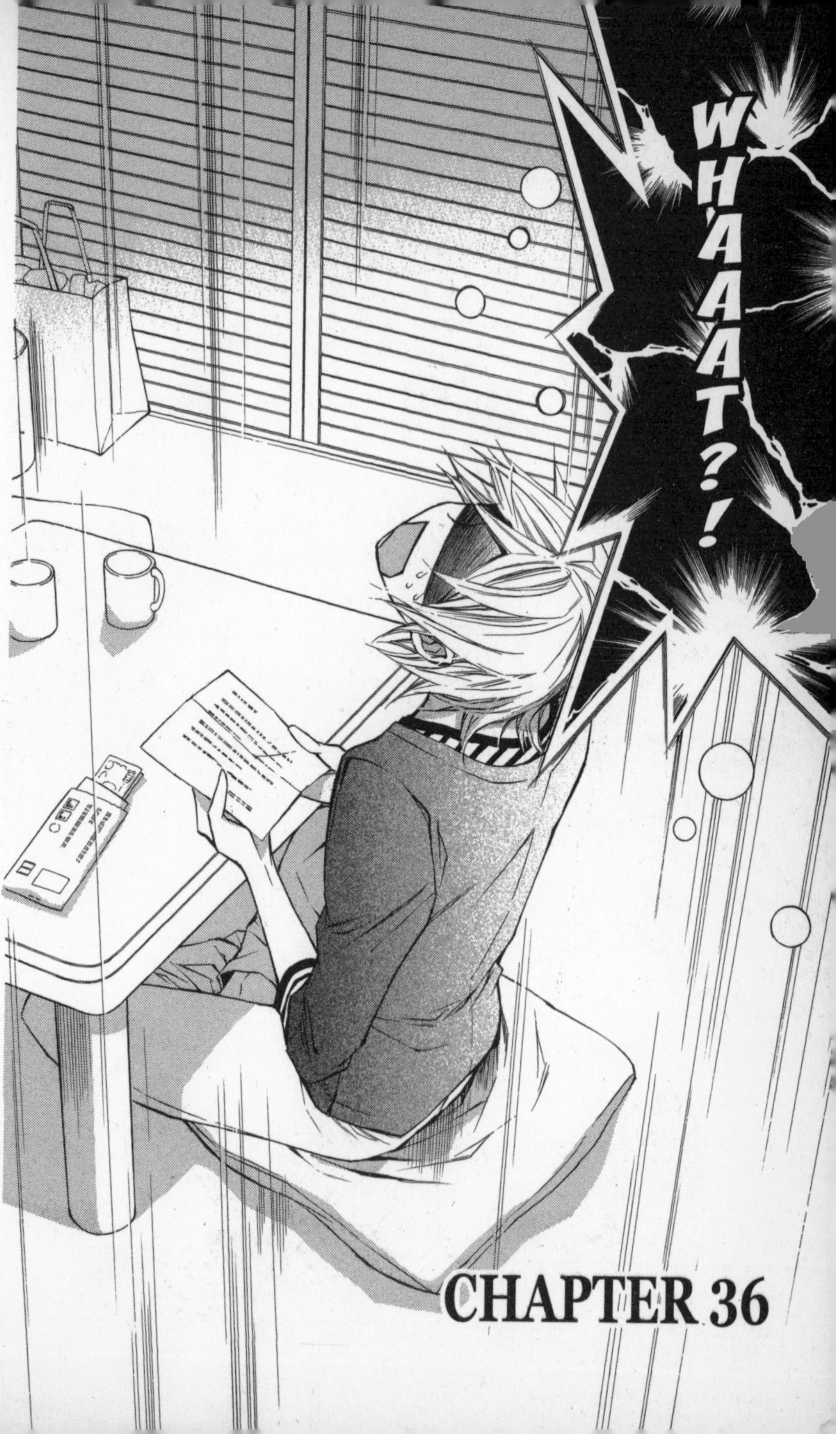
WHAAAT?!

CHAPTER 36

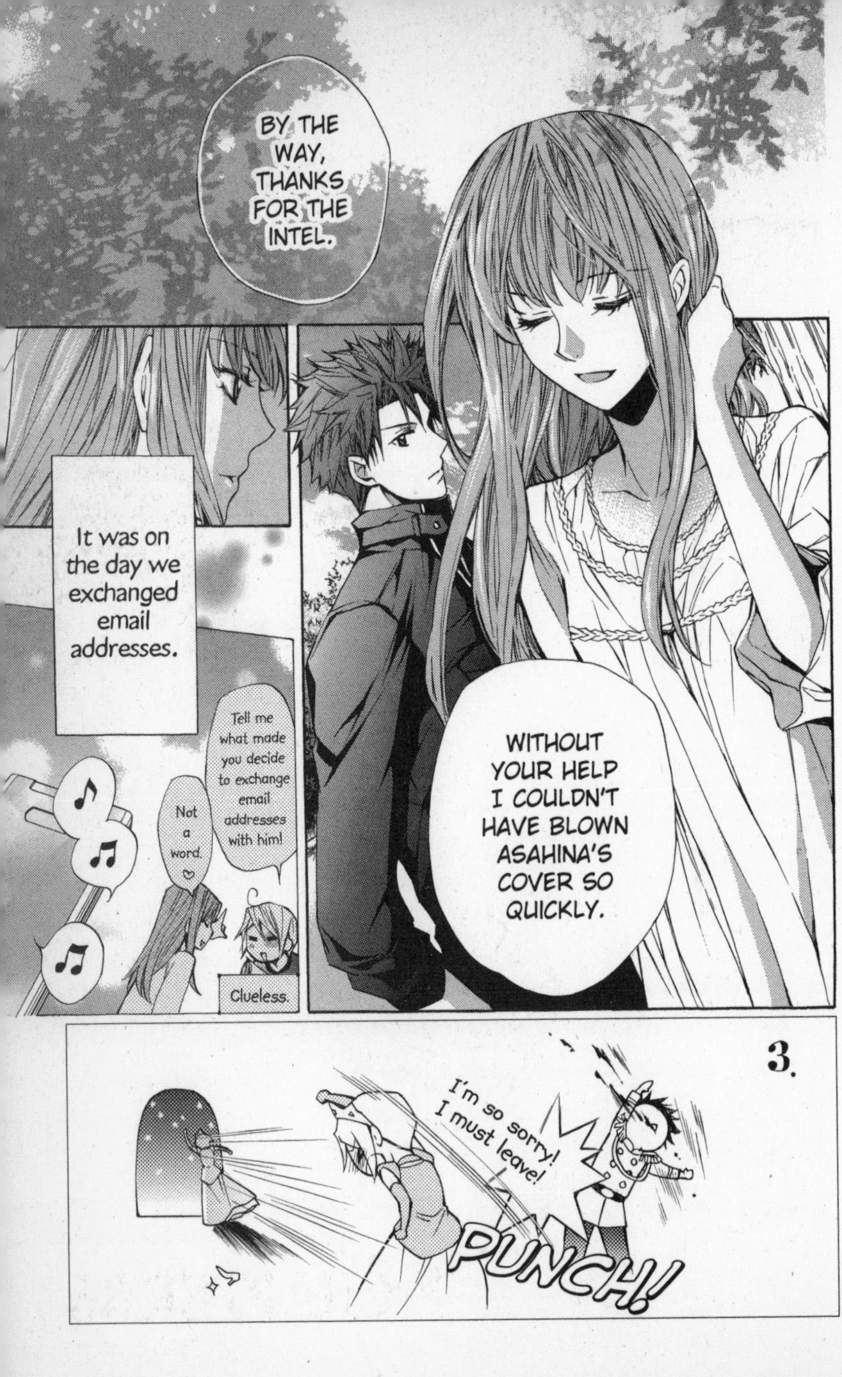
BY THE WAY, THANKS FOR THE INTEL.
WITHOUT YOUR HELP I COULDN'T HAVE BLOWN ASAHINA'S COVER SO QUICKLY.
It was on the day we exchanged email addresses.
Tell me what made you decide to exchange email addresses with him!
Not a word. ♡
Clueless.
3.
I'm so sorry! I must leave!
PUNCH!

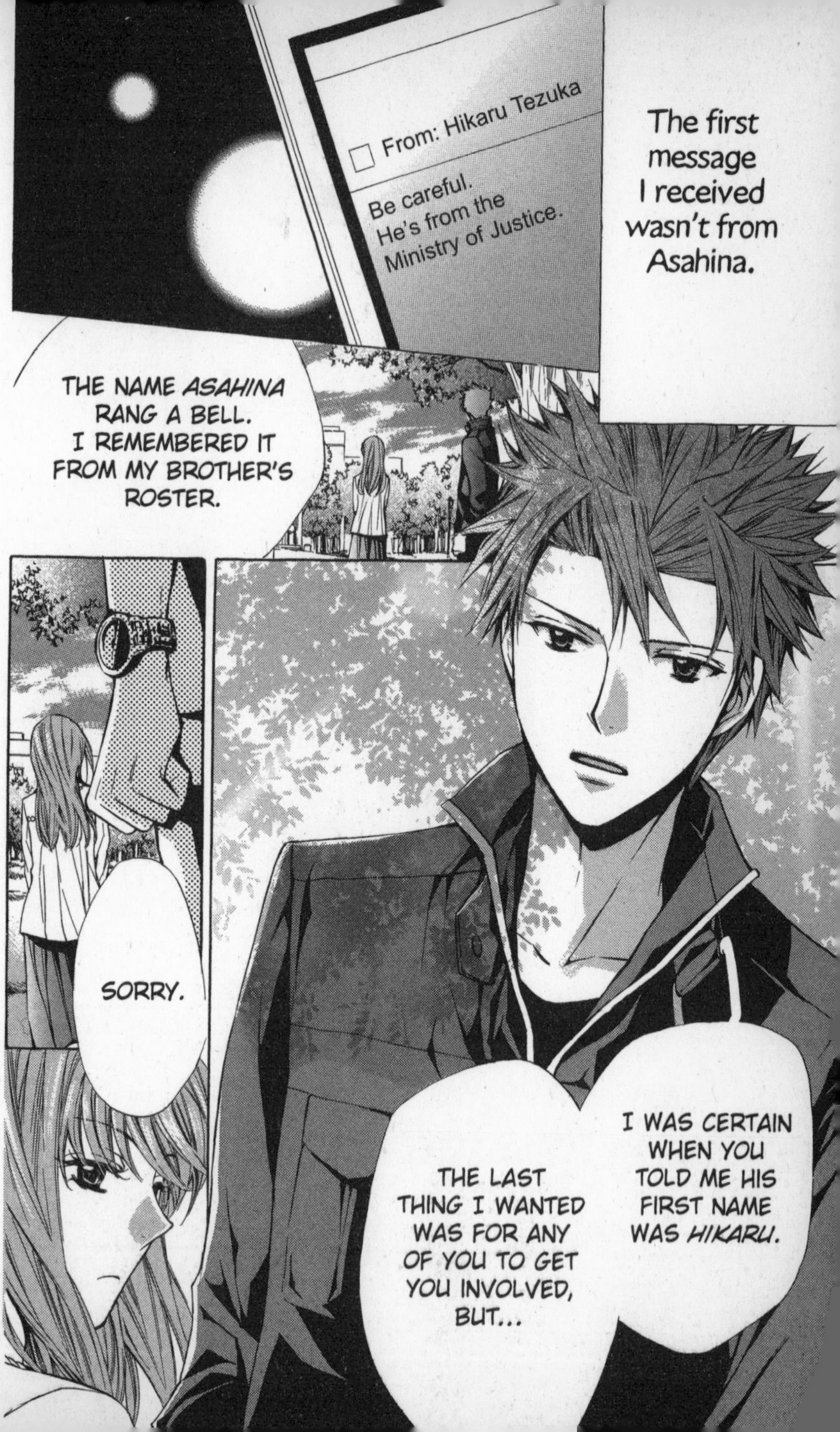
The first message I received wasn't from Asahina.
From: Hikaru Tezuka
Be careful. He's from the Ministry of Justice.
THE NAME *ASAHINA* RANG A BELL. I REMEMBERED IT FROM MY BROTHER'S ROSTER.
I WAS CERTAIN WHEN YOU TOLD ME HIS FIRST NAME WAS *HIKARU*.
THE LAST THING I WANTED WAS FOR ANY OF YOU TO GET YOU INVOLVED, BUT...
SORRY.

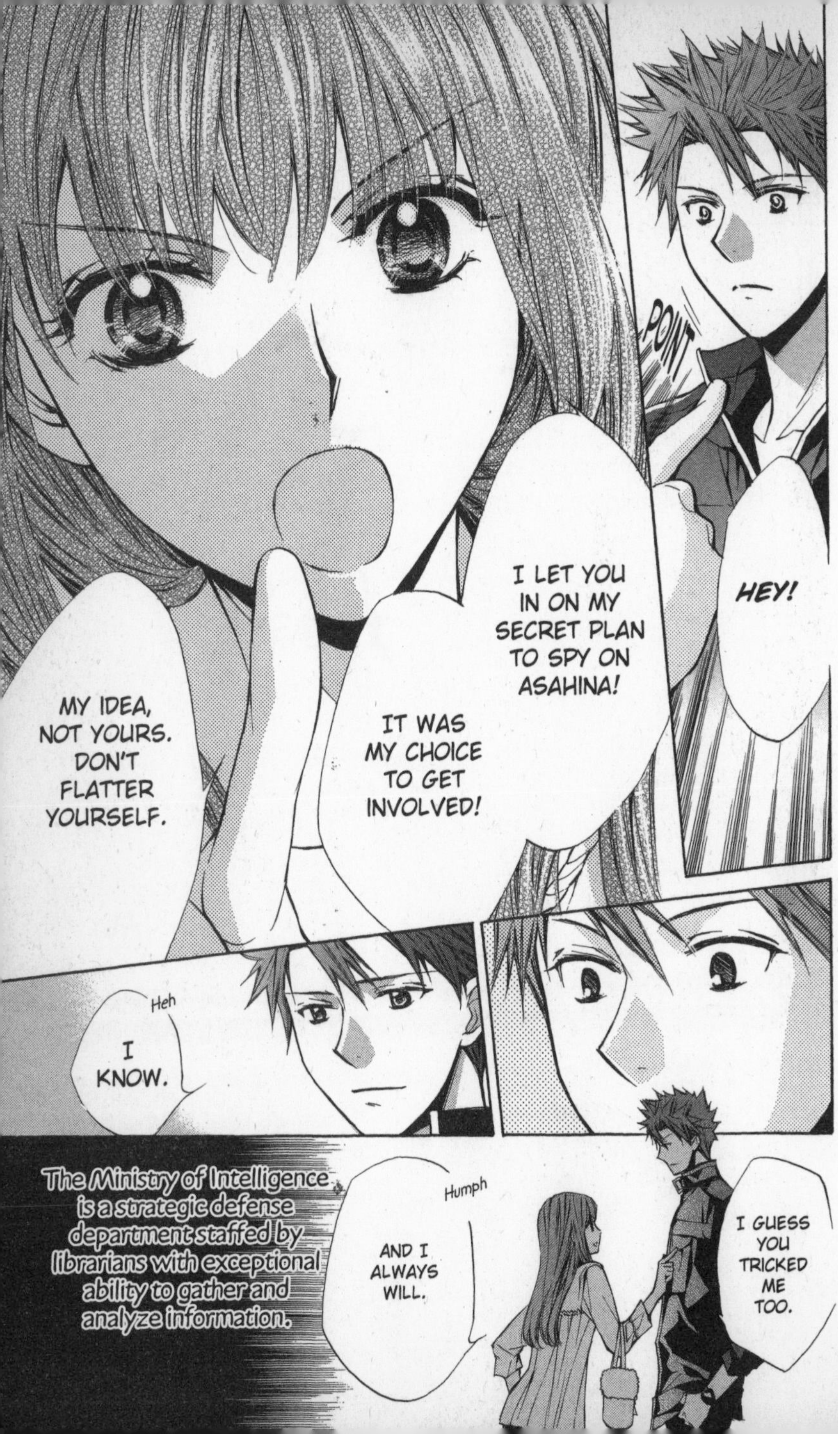
POINT
HEY!
I LET YOU IN ON MY SECRET PLAN TO SPY ON ASAHINA!
IT WAS MY CHOICE TO GET INVOLVED!
MY IDEA, NOT YOURS. DON'T FLATTER YOURSELF.
Heh
I KNOW.
I GUESS YOU TRICKED ME TOO.
Humph
AND I ALWAYS WILL.
The Ministry of Intelligence is a strategic defense department staffed by librarians with exceptional ability to gather and analyze information.

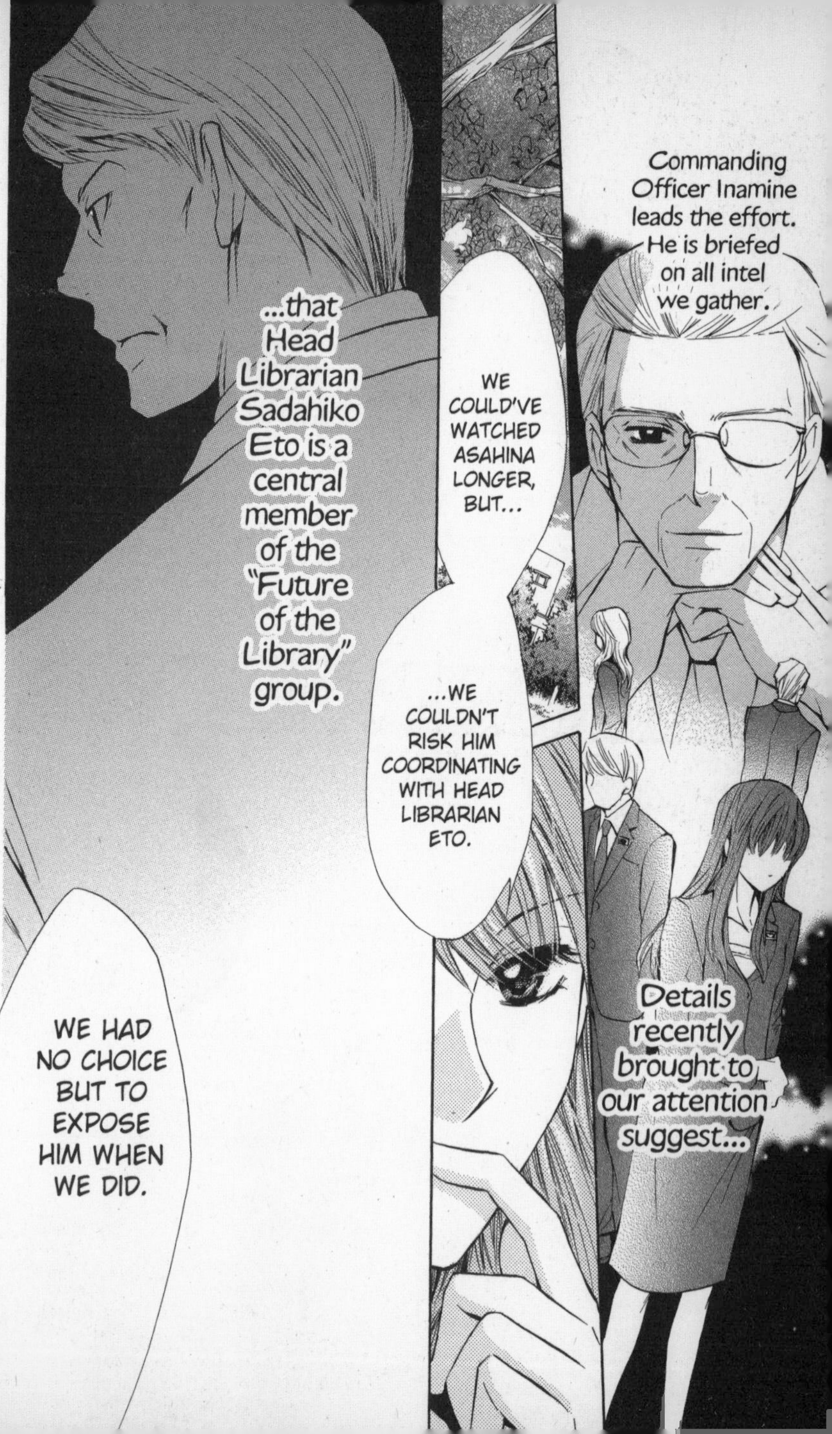

Commanding Officer Inamine leads the effort. He is briefed on all intel we gather.
Details recently brought to our attention suggest...
WE COULD'VE WATCHED ASAHINA LONGER, BUT...
...WE COULDN'T RISK HIM COORDINATING WITH HEAD LIBRARIAN ETO.
...that Head Librarian Sadahiko Eto is a central member of the "Future of the Library" group.
WE HAD NO CHOICE BUT TO EXPOSE HIM WHEN WE DID.

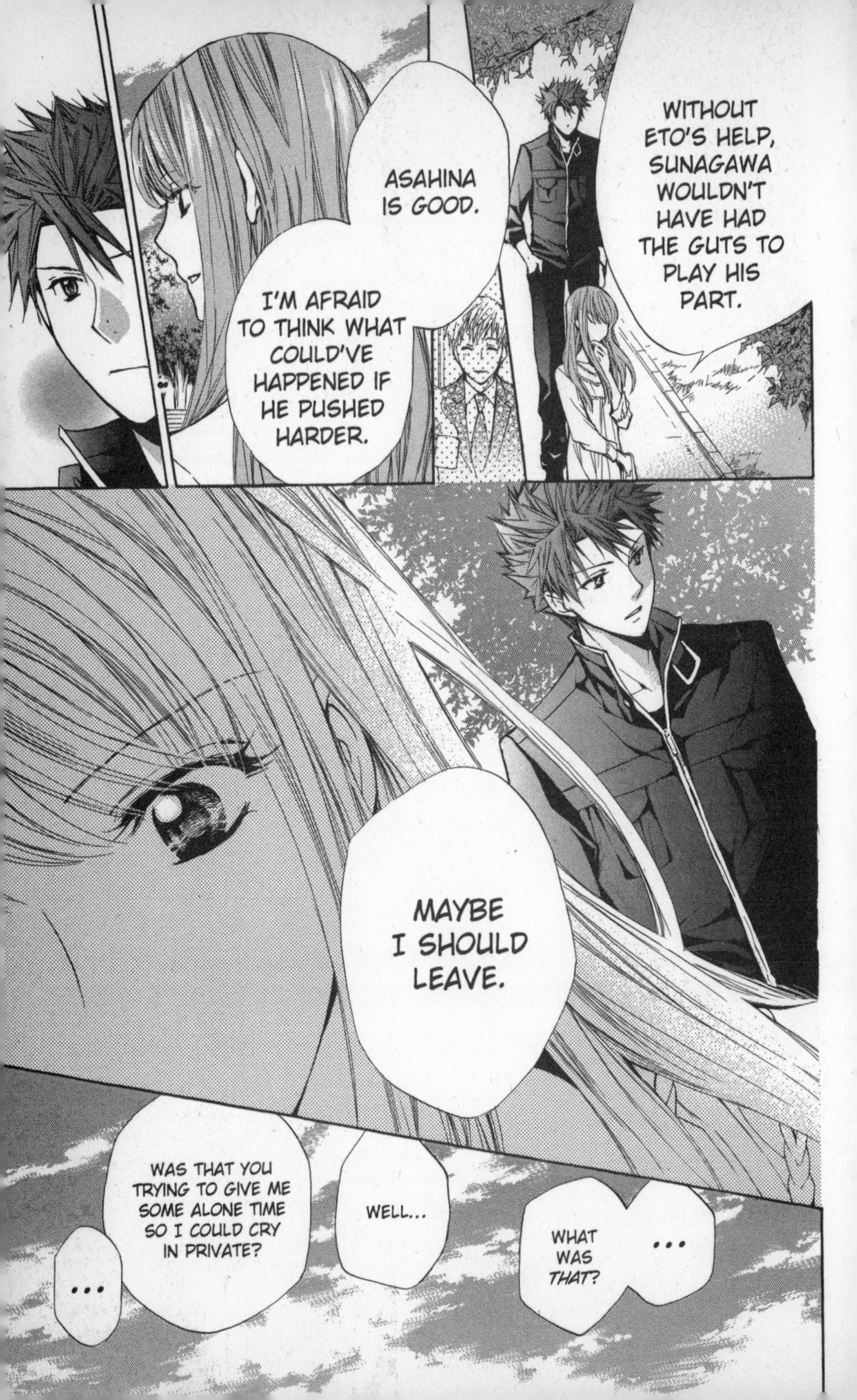
WITHOUT ETO'S HELP, SUNAGAWA WOULDN'T HAVE HAD THE GUTS TO PLAY HIS PART.
ASAHINA IS GOOD.
I'M AFRAID TO THINK WHAT COULD'VE HAPPENED IF HE PUSHED HARDER.
MAYBE I SHOULD LEAVE.
...
WHAT WAS *THAT*?
WELL...
WAS THAT YOU TRYING TO GIVE ME SOME ALONE TIME SO I COULD CRY IN PRIVATE?
...

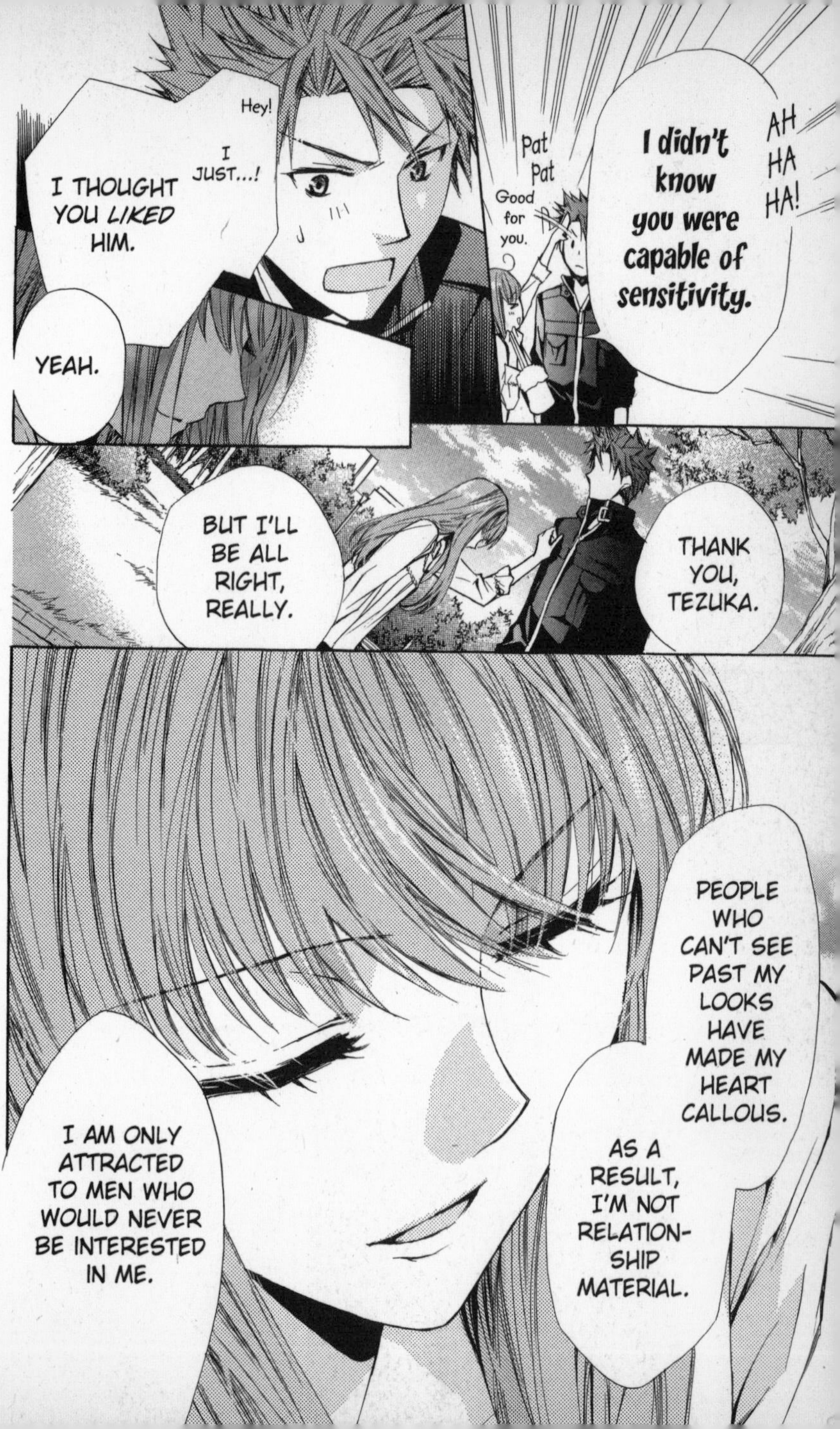
AH HA HA!
I didn't know you were capable of sensitivity.
Pat Pat
Good for you.
Hey!
I JUST...!
I THOUGHT YOU *LIKED* HIM.
YEAH.
THANK YOU, TEZUKA.
BUT I'LL BE ALL RIGHT, REALLY.
PEOPLE WHO CAN'T SEE PAST MY LOOKS HAVE MADE MY HEART CALLOUS.
AS A RESULT, I'M NOT RELATION-SHIP MATERIAL.
I AM ONLY ATTRACTED TO MEN WHO WOULD NEVER BE INTERESTED IN ME.

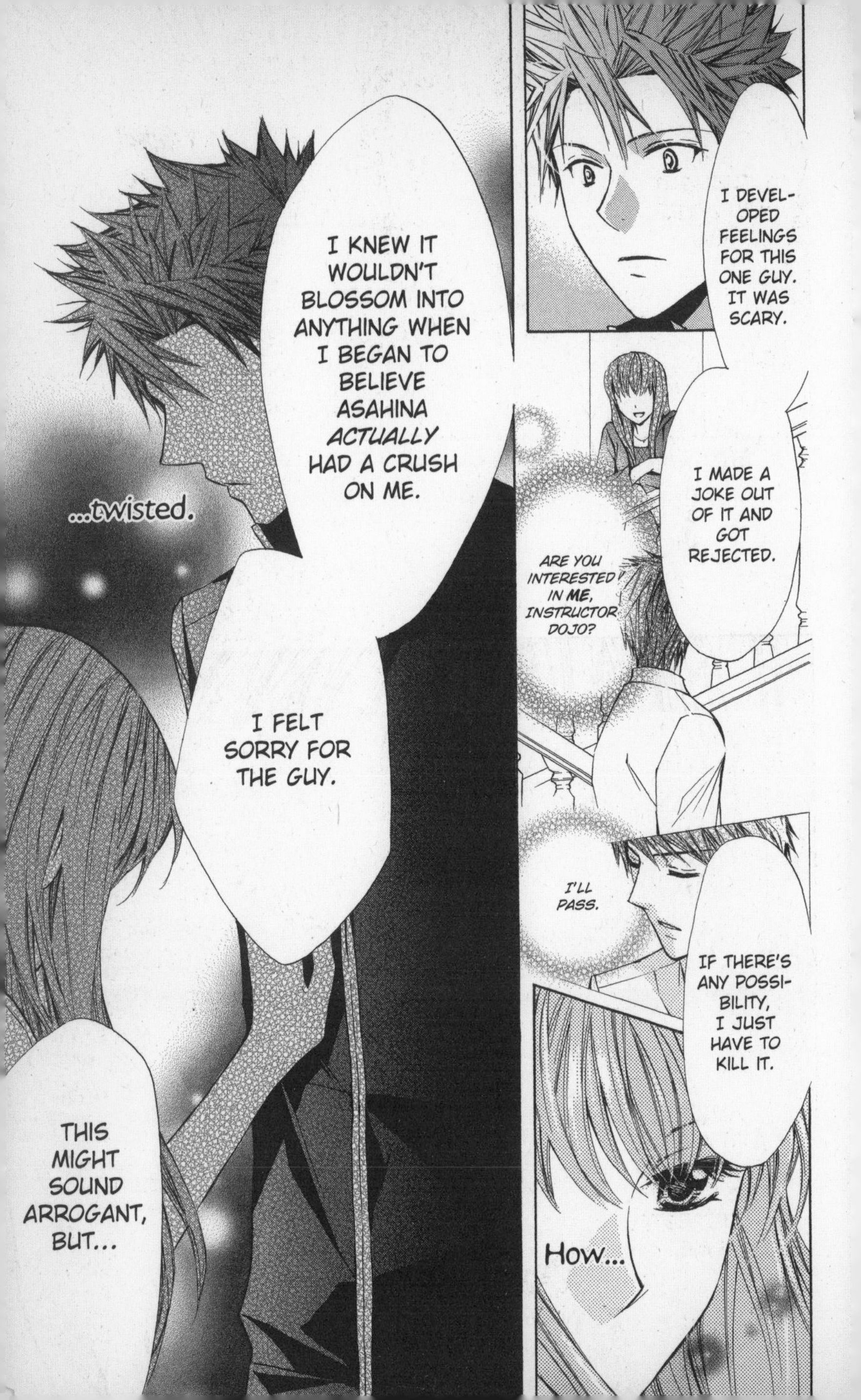
I DEVEL-OPED FEELINGS FOR THIS ONE GUY. IT WAS SCARY.
I MADE A JOKE OUT OF IT AND GOT REJECTED.
ARE YOU INTERESTED IN *ME*, INSTRUCTOR DOJO?
IF THERE'S ANY POSSI-BILITY, I JUST HAVE TO KILL IT.
I'LL PASS.
How...
I KNEW IT WOULDN'T BLOSSOM INTO ANYTHING WHEN I BEGAN TO BELIEVE ASAHINA *ACTUALLY* HAD A CRUSH ON ME.
...twisted.
I FELT SORRY FOR THE GUY.
THIS MIGHT SOUND ARROGANT, BUT...

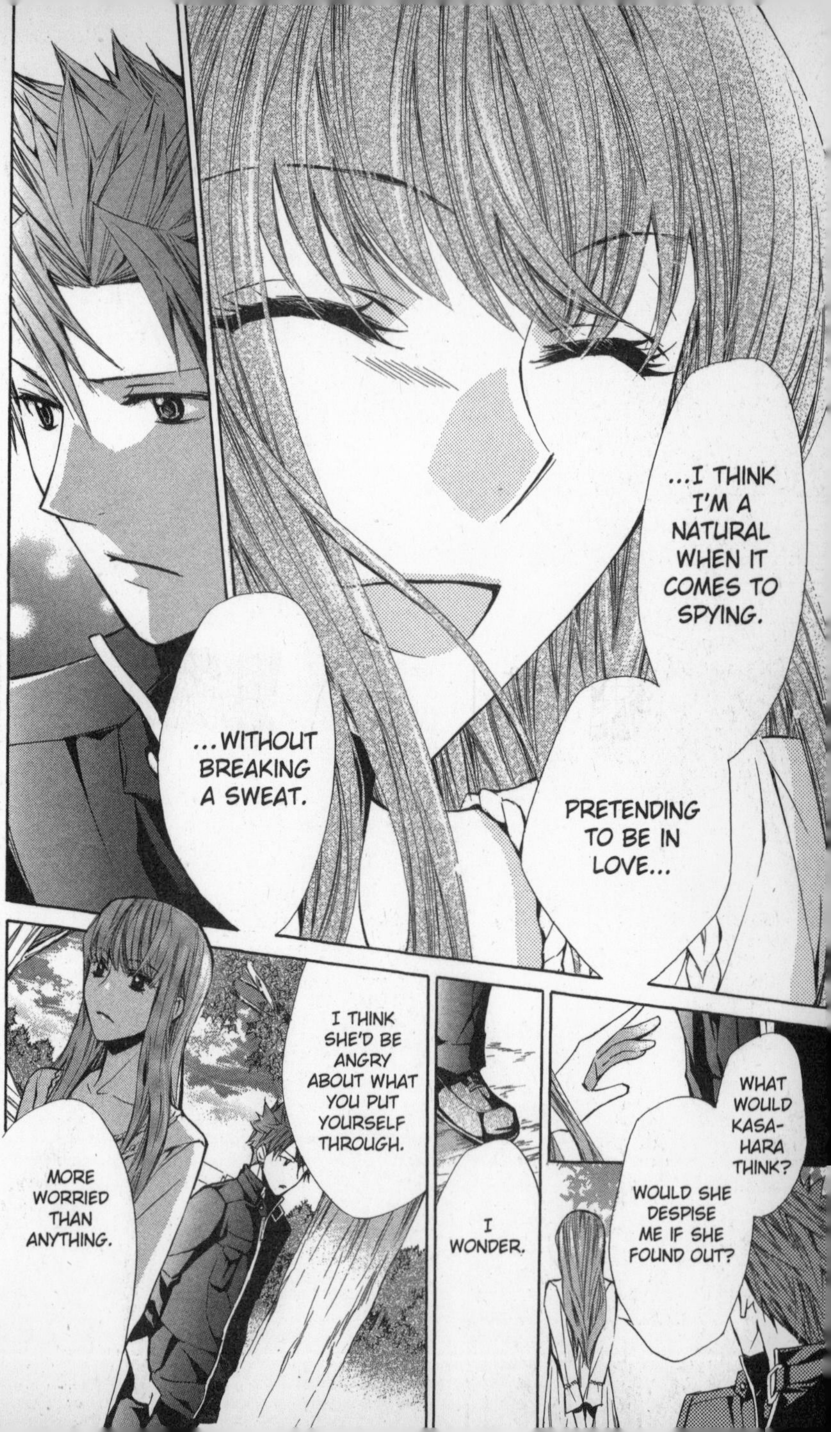
...I THINK I'M A NATURAL WHEN IT COMES TO SPYING.
PRETENDING TO BE IN LOVE...
...WITHOUT BREAKING A SWEAT.
WHAT WOULD KASA-HARA THINK?
WOULD SHE DESPISE ME IF SHE FOUND OUT?
I WONDER.
I THINK SHE'D BE ANGRY ABOUT WHAT YOU PUT YOURSELF THROUGH.
MORE WORRIED THAN ANYTHING.

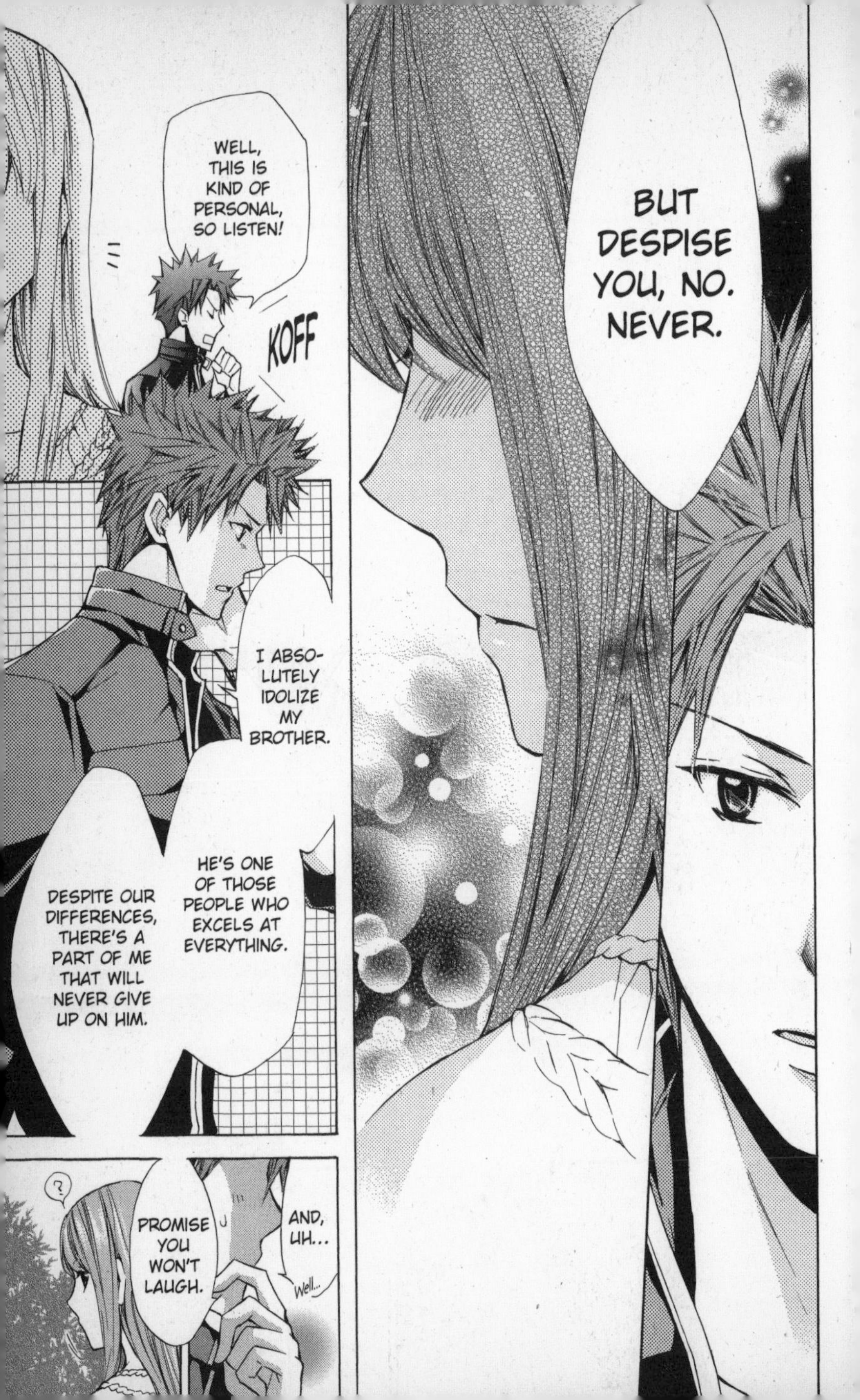
BUT DESPISE YOU, NO. NEVER.
WELL, THIS IS KIND OF PERSONAL, SO LISTEN!
KOFF
I ABSOLUTELY IDOLIZE MY BROTHER.
HE'S ONE OF THOSE PEOPLE WHO EXCELS AT EVERYTHING.
DESPITE OUR DIFFERENCES, THERE'S A PART OF ME THAT WILL NEVER GIVE UP ON HIM.
AND, UH...
Well...
PROMISE YOU WON'T LAUGH.

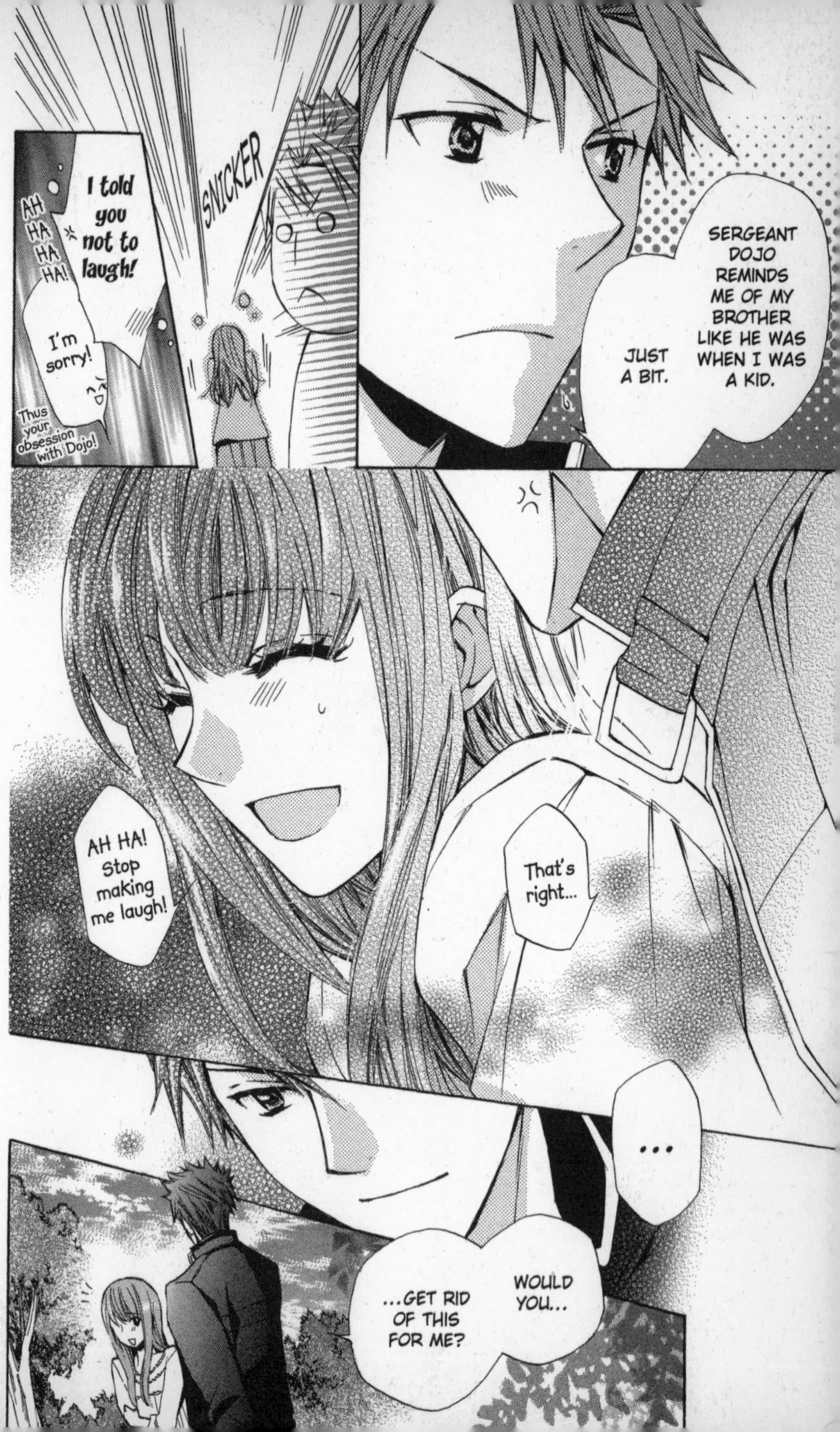
SERGEANT DOJO REMINDS ME OF MY BROTHER LIKE HE WAS WHEN I WAS A KID.
JUST A BIT.
SNICKER
I told you not to laugh!
AH HA HA HA!
I'm sorry!
Thus your obsession with Dojo!
That's right...
AH HA! Stop making me laugh!
...
WOULD YOU...
...GET RID OF THIS FOR ME?

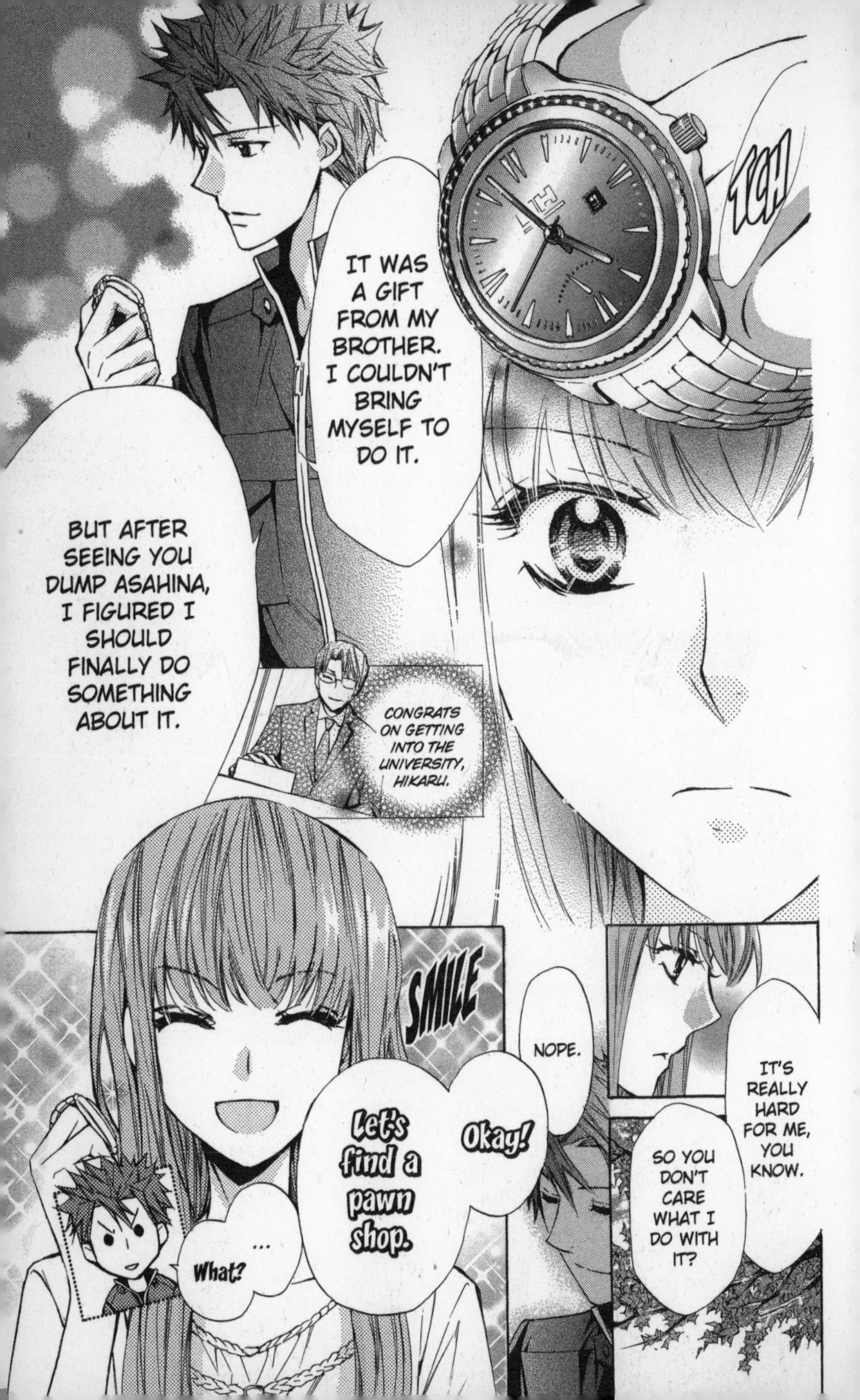
TCH
IT WAS A GIFT FROM MY BROTHER. I COULDN'T BRING MYSELF TO DO IT.
BUT AFTER SEEING YOU DUMP ASAHINA, I FIGURED I SHOULD FINALLY DO SOMETHING ABOUT IT.
CONGRATS ON GETTING INTO THE UNIVERSITY, HIKARU.
IT'S REALLY HARD FOR ME, YOU KNOW.
SO YOU DON'T CARE WHAT I DO WITH IT?
NOPE.
SMILE
Okay!
Let's find a pawn shop.
...
What?

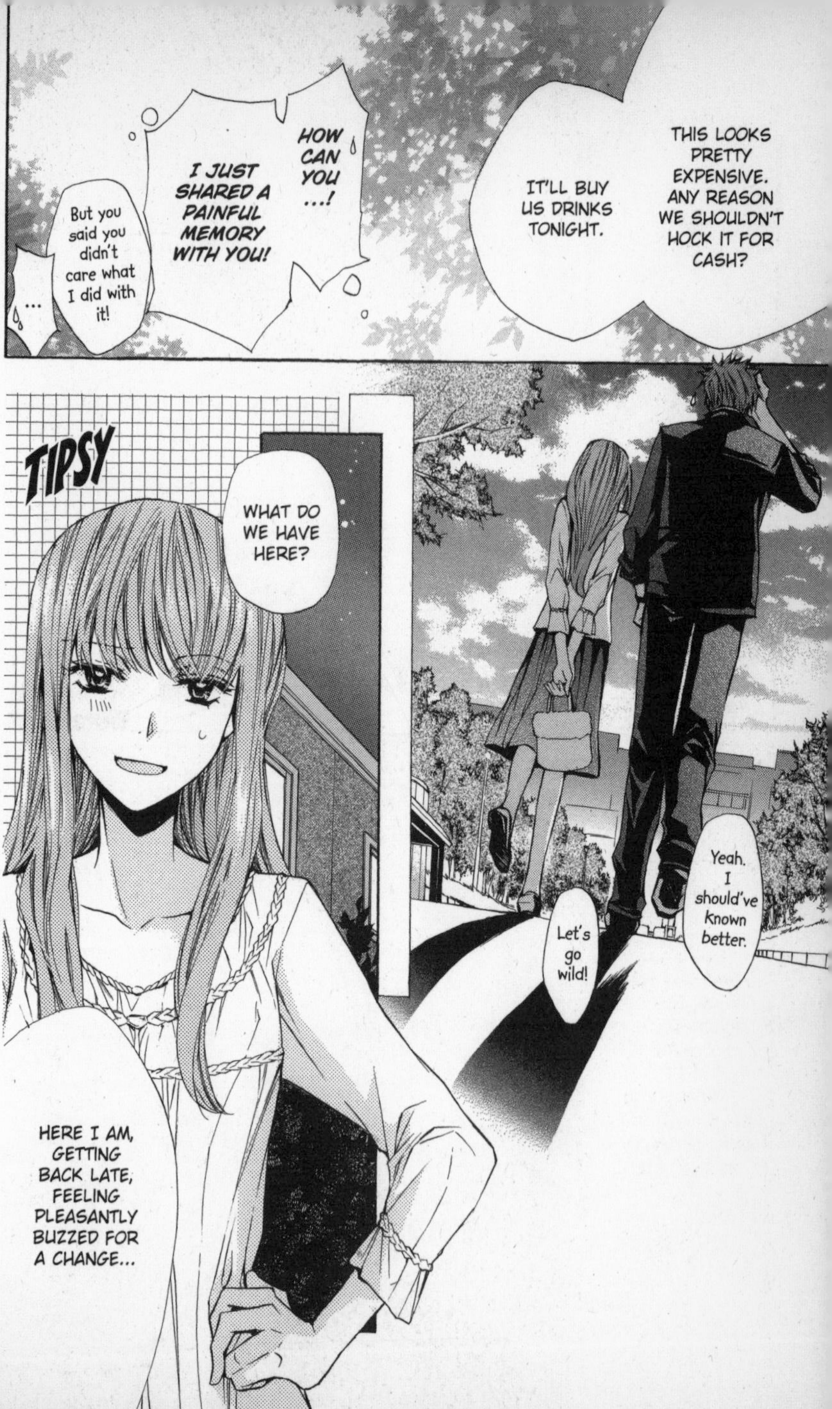
THIS LOOKS PRETTY EXPENSIVE. ANY REASON WE SHOULDN'T HOCK IT FOR CASH?
IT'LL BUY US DRINKS TONIGHT.
HOW CAN YOU ...!
I JUST SHARED A PAINFUL MEMORY WITH YOU!
But you said you didn't care what I did with it!
...
Yeah. I should've known better.
Let's go wild!
WHAT DO WE HAVE HERE?
TIPSY
HERE I AM, GETTING BACK LATE, FEELING PLEASANTLY BUZZED FOR A CHANGE...

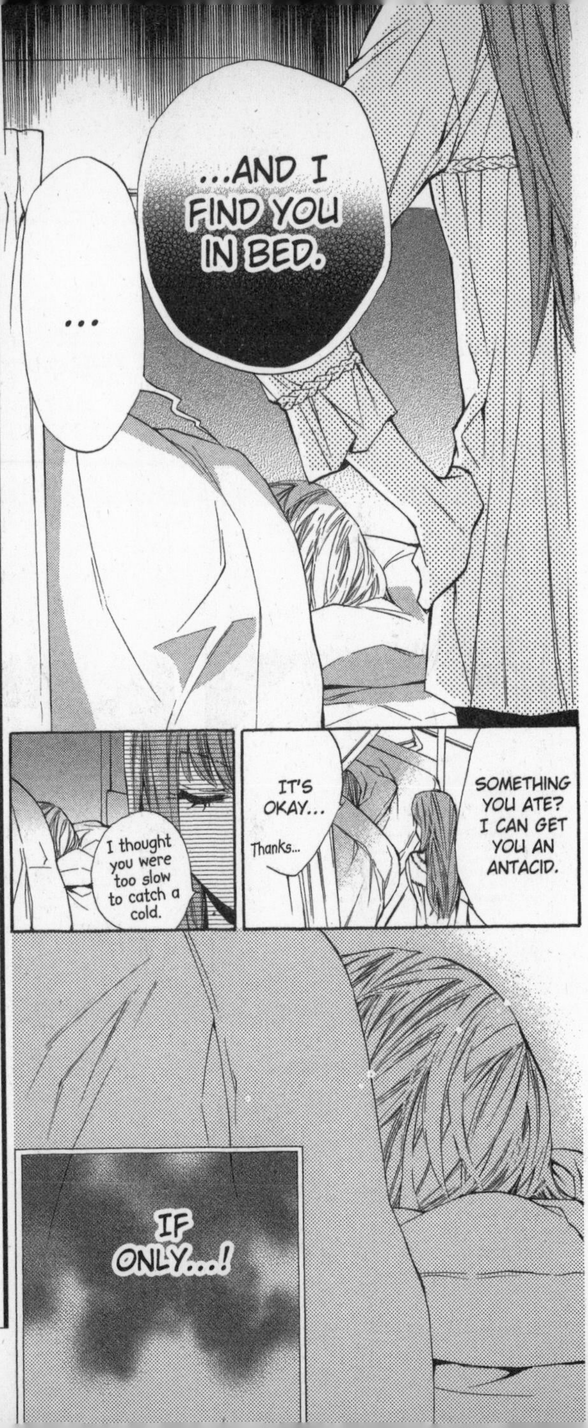
...AND I FIND YOU IN BED.
...
SOMETHING YOU ATE? I CAN GET YOU AN ANTACID.
IT'S OKAY...
Thanks...
I thought you were too slow to catch a cold.
IF ONLY...!

3

*

Remember my youngest niece that I wrote about at the end of volume 6...? She hasn't warmed up to me yet... This is kind of a shock to me...

She'd frown when I'd get close to her with a big smile on my face.

The other day, I got to feed her and spent the entire day with her. She started to open up to me toward the end of the day. Quality time spent feeding and playing together is very important...!

She's quite fond of my father, which gives him more reason to gloat.

The other two nieces are fond me, so I have reason to remain hopeful.

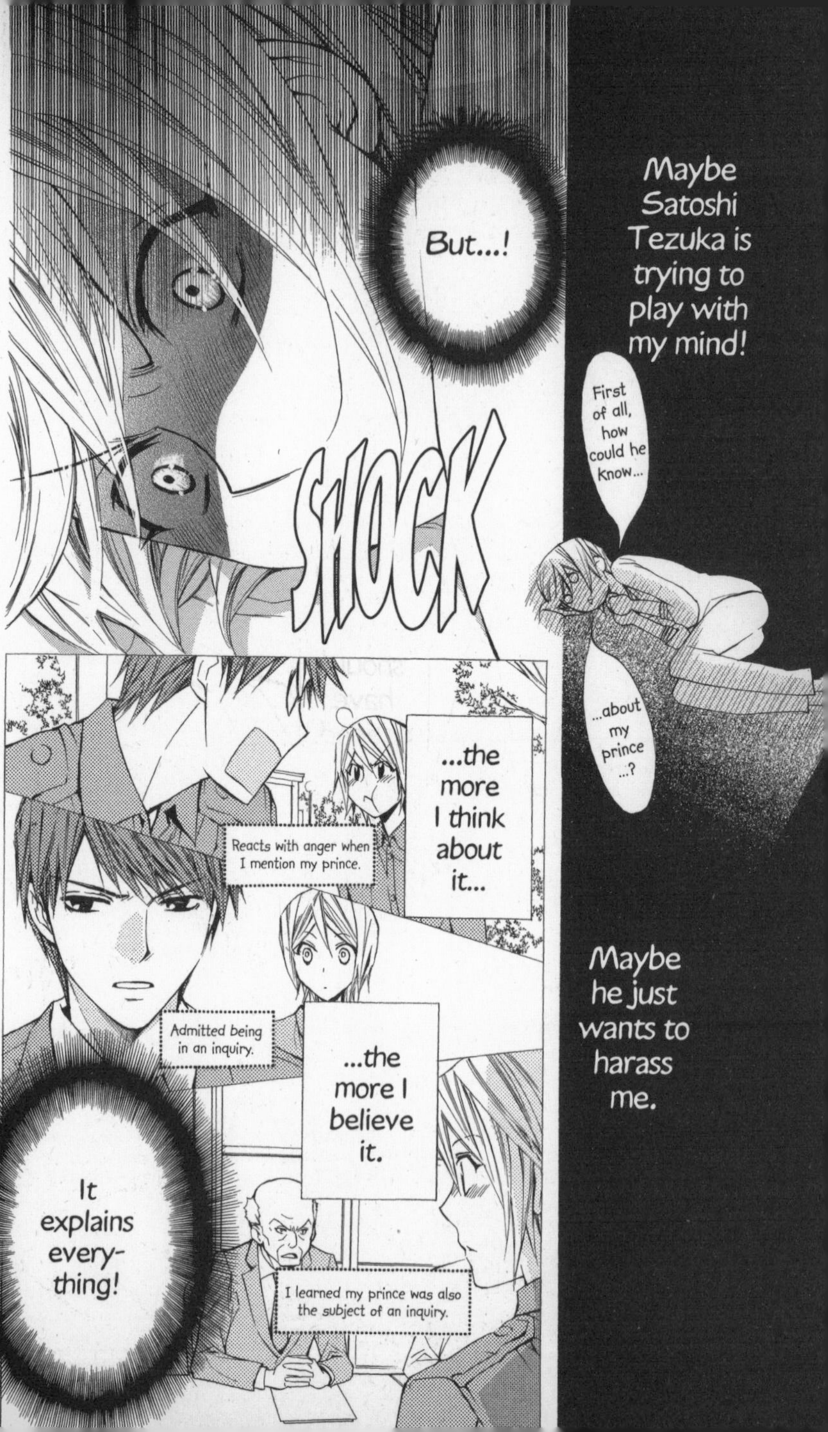
Maybe Satoshi Tezuka is trying to play with my mind!
First of all, how could he know...
...about my prince ...?
Maybe he just wants to harass me.
But...!
SHOCK
...the more I think about it...
Reacts with anger when I mention my prince.
Admitted being in an inquiry.
...the more I believe it.
I learned my prince was also the subject of an inquiry.
It explains every-thing!

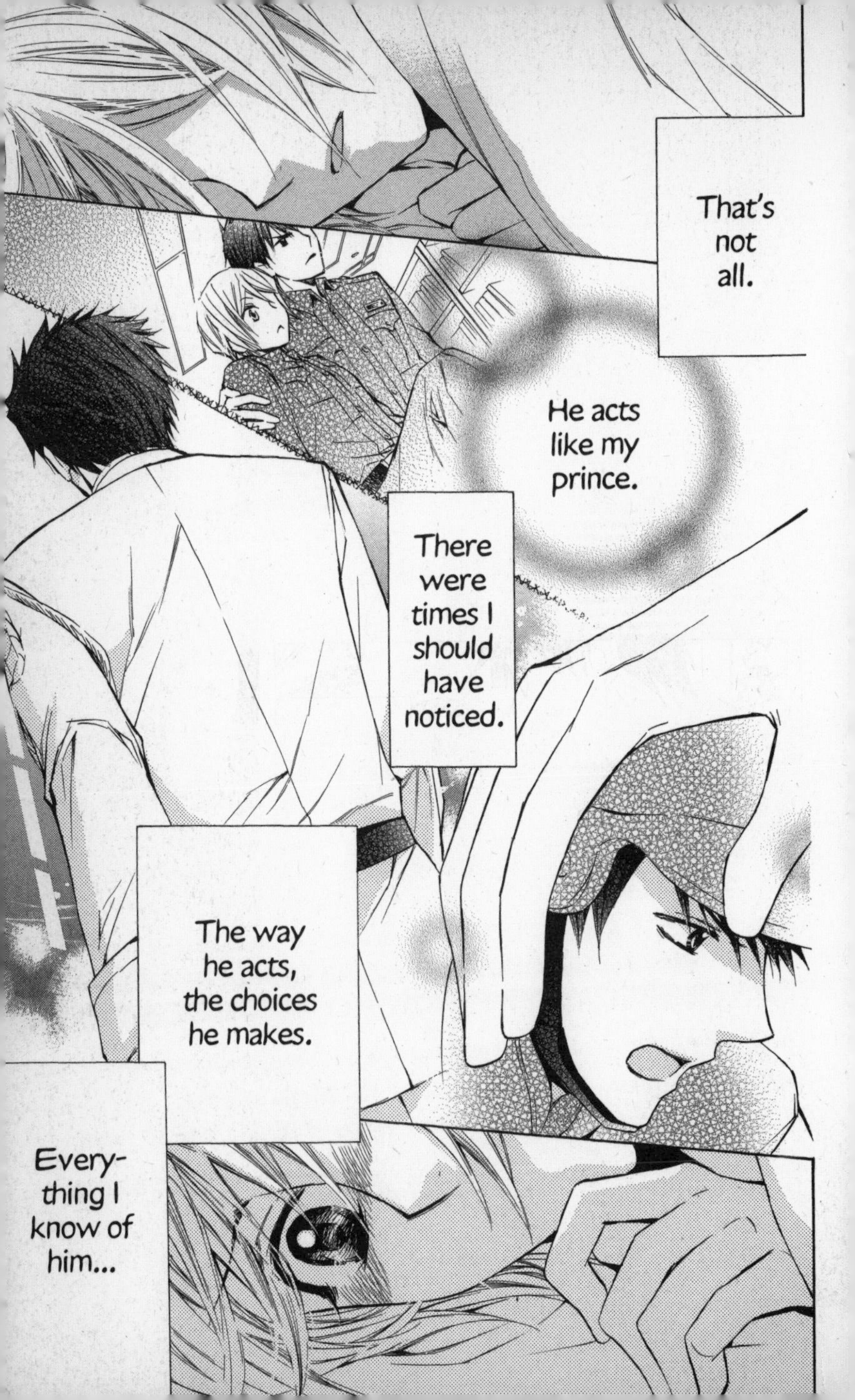
That's not all.
He acts like my prince.
There were times I should have noticed.
The way he acts, the choices he makes.
Every-thing I know of him...

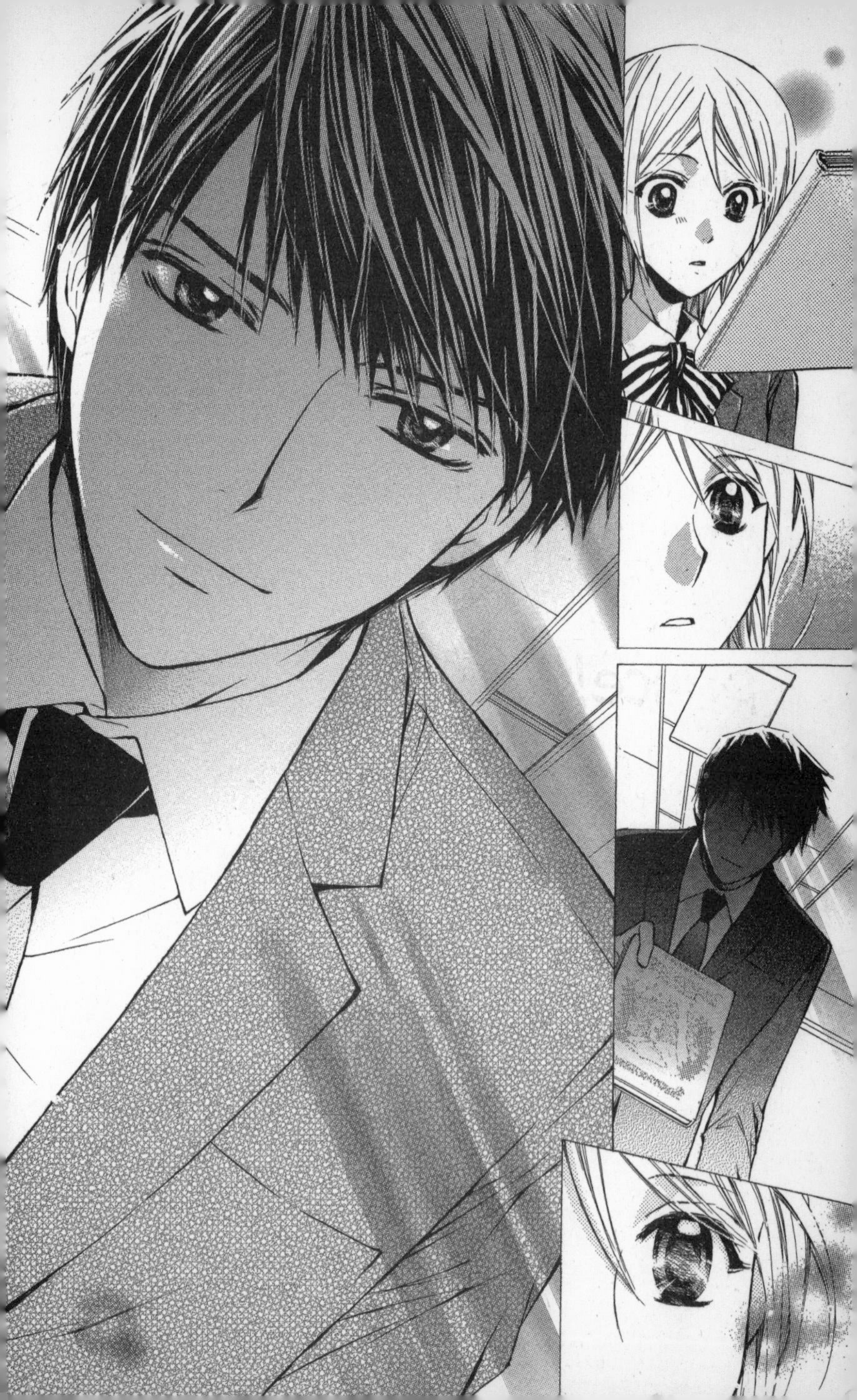

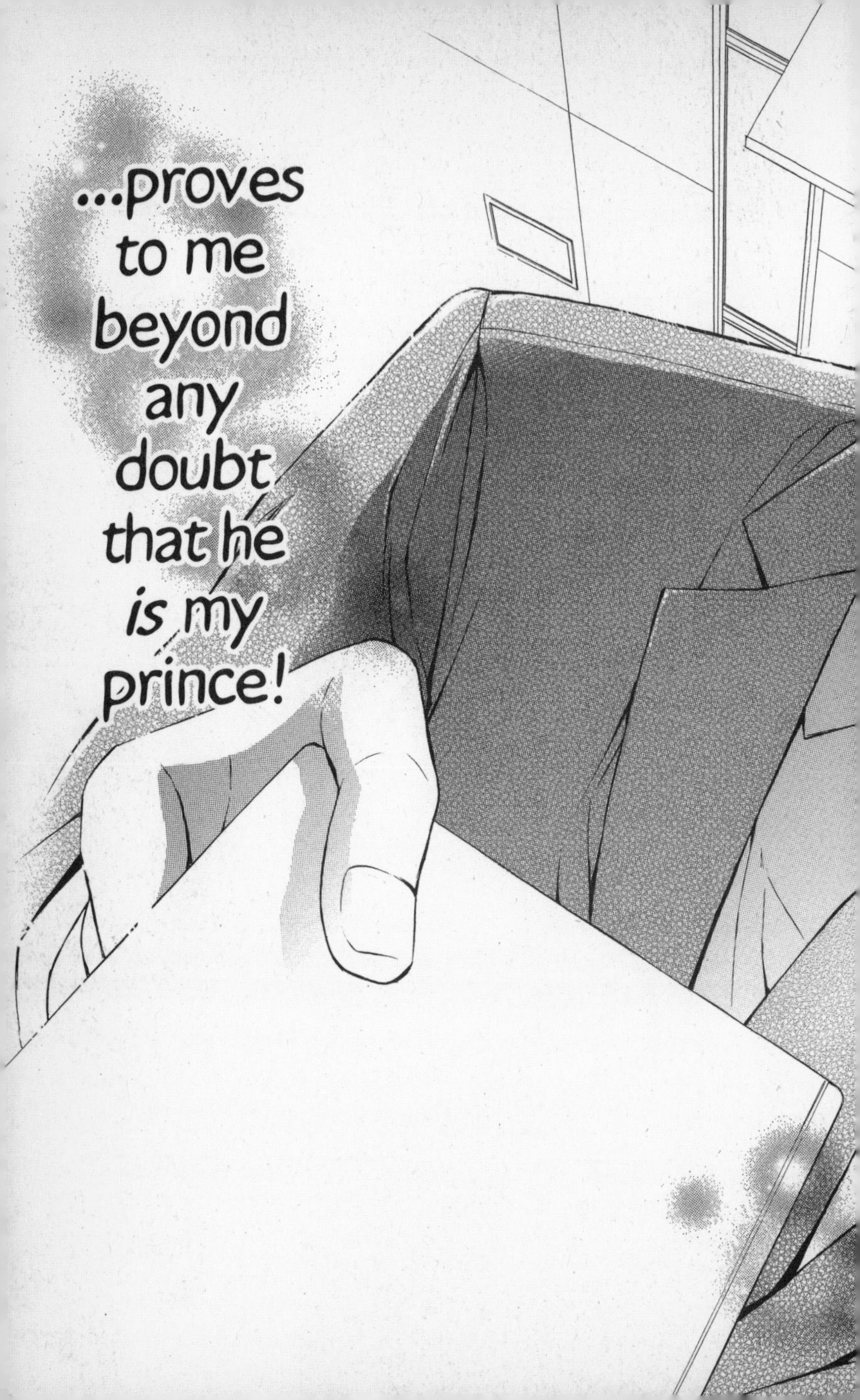
...proves to me beyond any doubt that he *is* my prince!

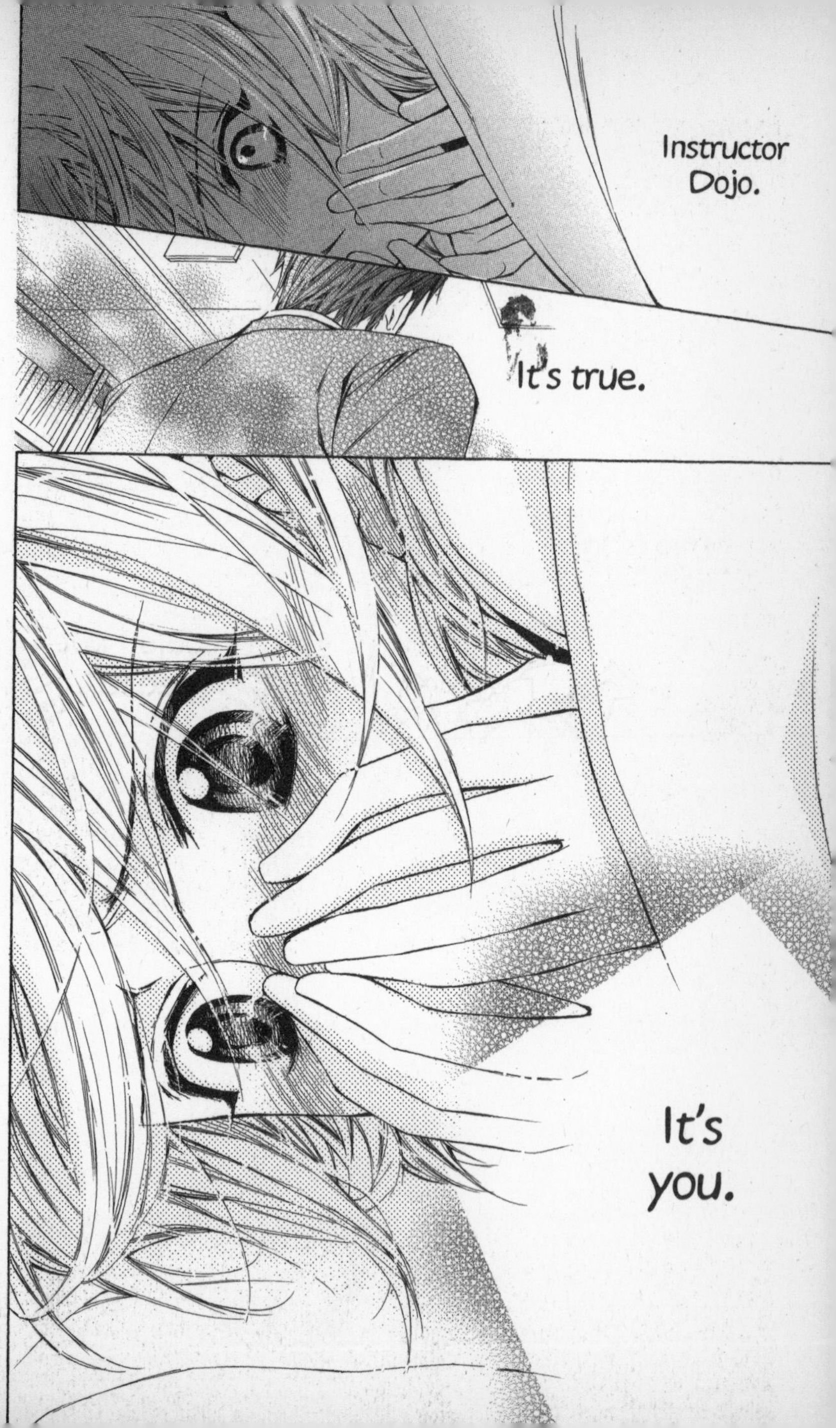
Instructor Dojo.
It's true.
It's you.

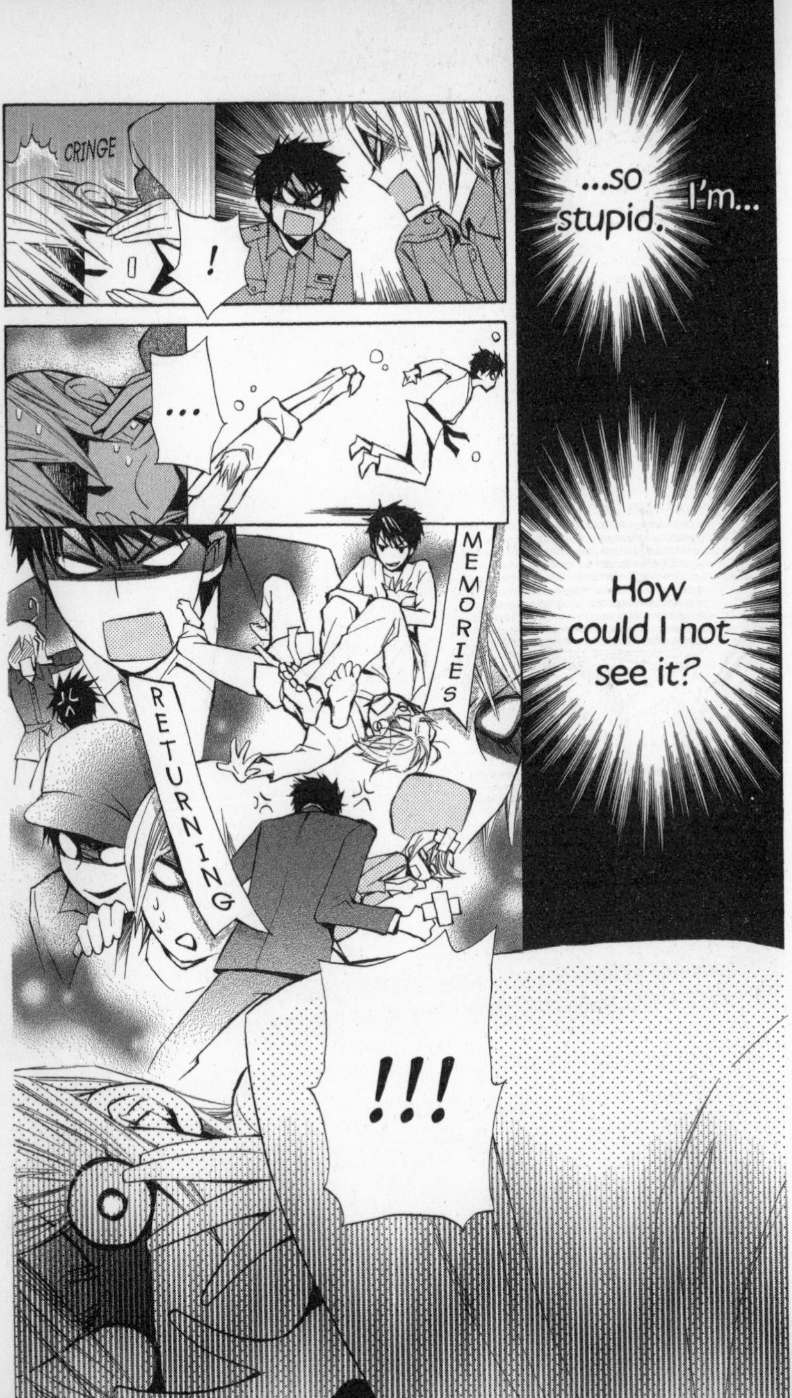
I'm...
...so stupid.
How could I not see it?
!
CRINGE
...
MEMORIES
RETURNING
!!!

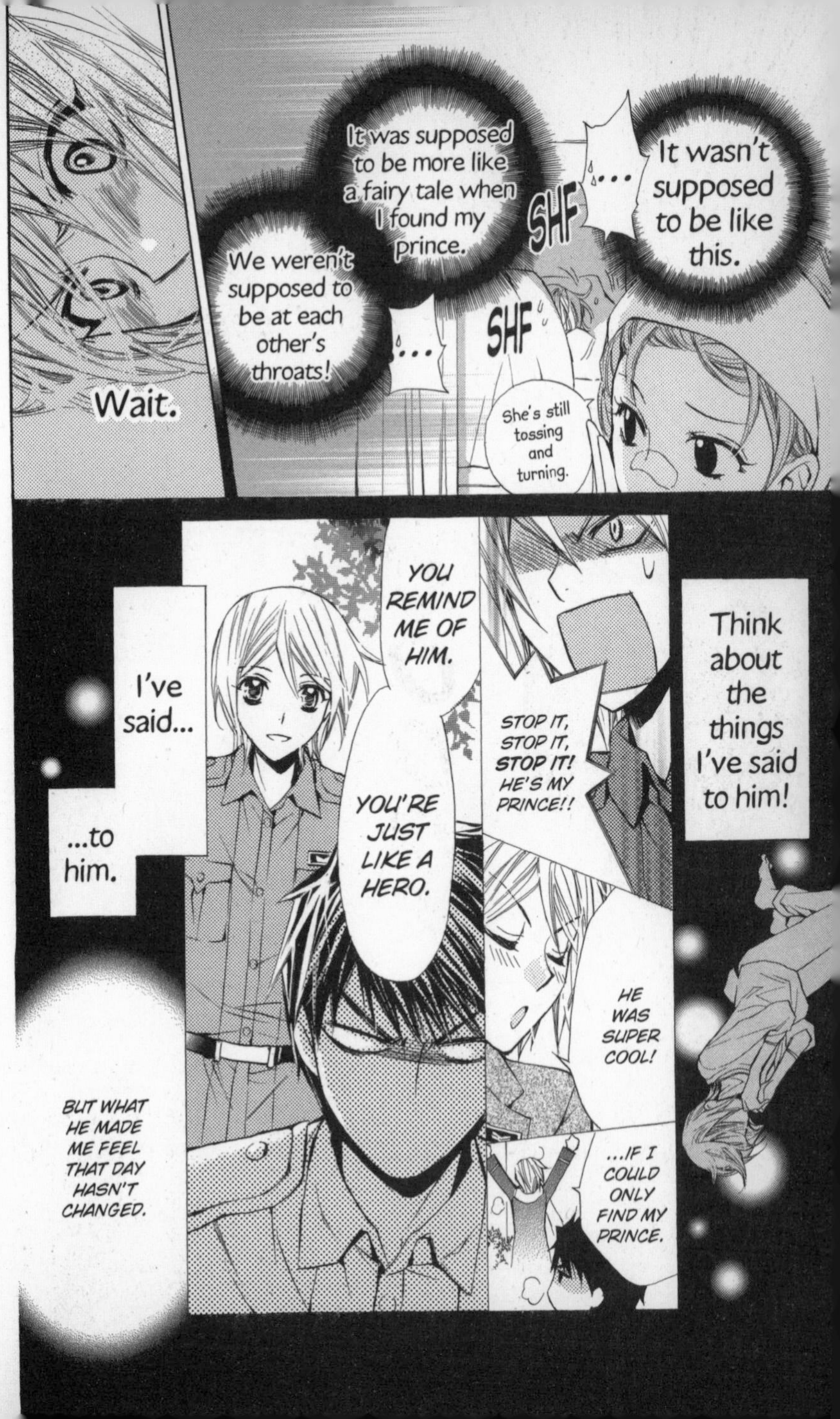
It wasn't supposed to be like this.
...
SHF
It was supposed to be more like a fairy tale when I found my prince.
We weren't supposed to be at each other's throats!
...
SHF
She's still tossing and turning.
Wait.
Think about the things I've said to him!
STOP IT, STOP IT, STOP IT! HE'S MY PRINCE!!
HE WAS SUPER COOL!
...IF I COULD ONLY FIND MY PRINCE.
YOU REMIND ME OF HIM.
YOU'RE JUST LIKE A HERO.
I've said...
...to him.
BUT WHAT HE MADE ME FEEL THAT DAY HASN'T CHANGED.

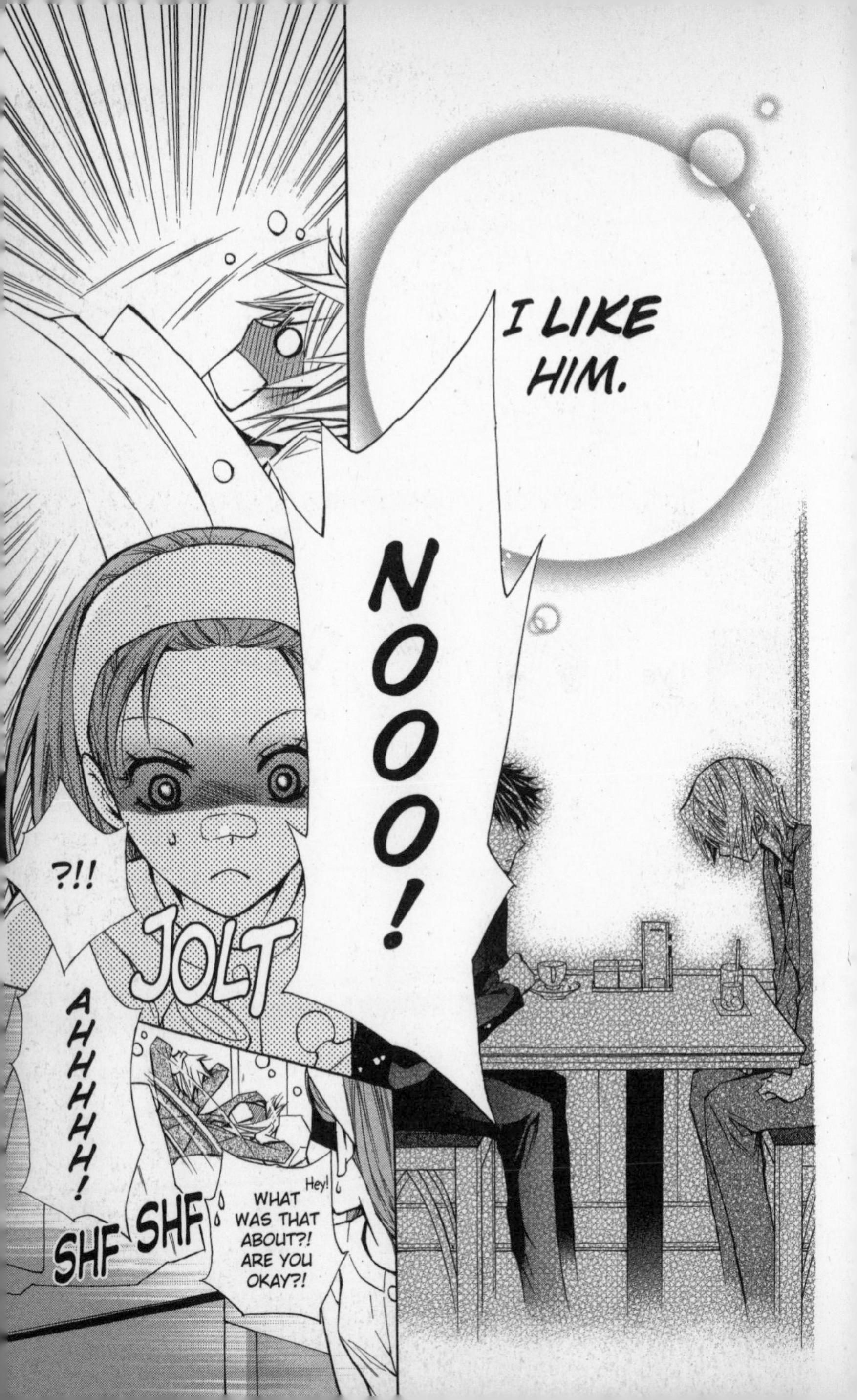
I LIKE HIM.
NOOOO!
?!!
JOLT
AHHHHHH!
Hey!
WHAT WAS THAT ABOUT?! ARE YOU OKAY?!
SHF
SHF

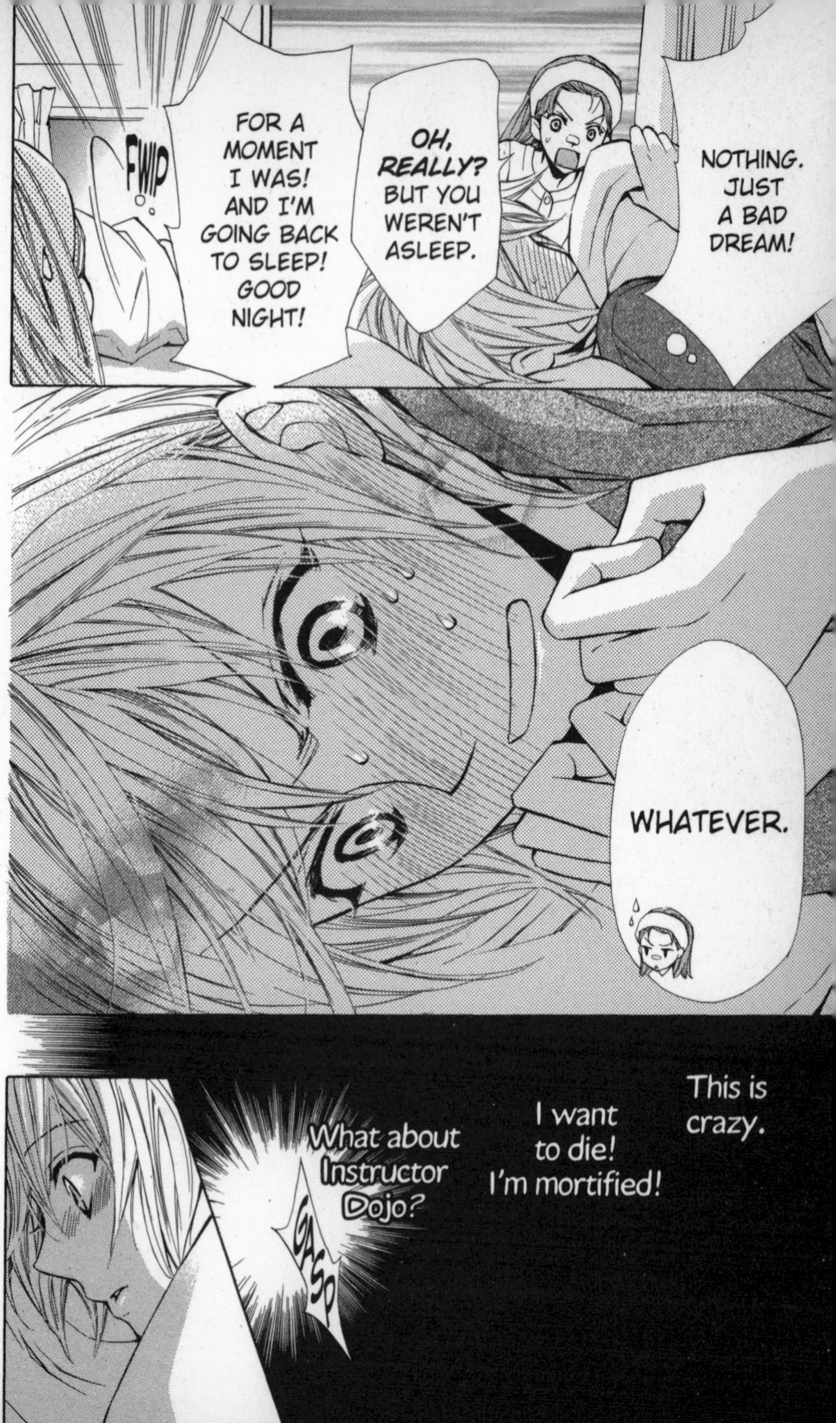
NOTHING. JUST A BAD DREAM!
OH, REALLY? BUT YOU WEREN'T ASLEEP.
FOR A MOMENT I WAS! AND I'M GOING BACK TO SLEEP! GOOD NIGHT!
FWIP
WHATEVER.
This is crazy.
I want to die! I'm mortified!
What about Instructor Dojo?
GASP

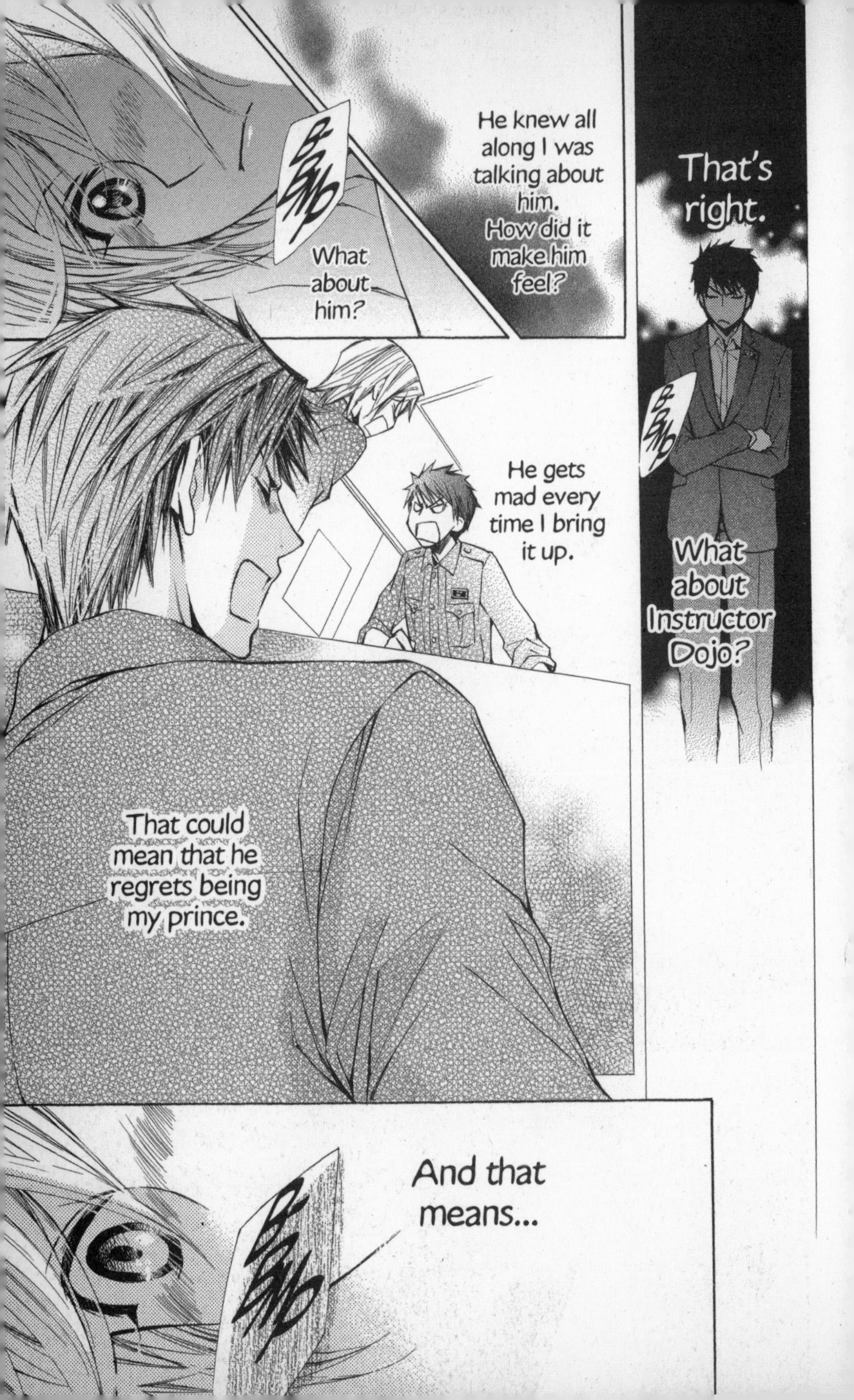
That's right.
What about Instructor Dojo?
He knew all along I was talking about him. How did it make him feel?
What about him?
He gets mad every time I bring it up.
That could mean that he regrets being my prince.
And that means...

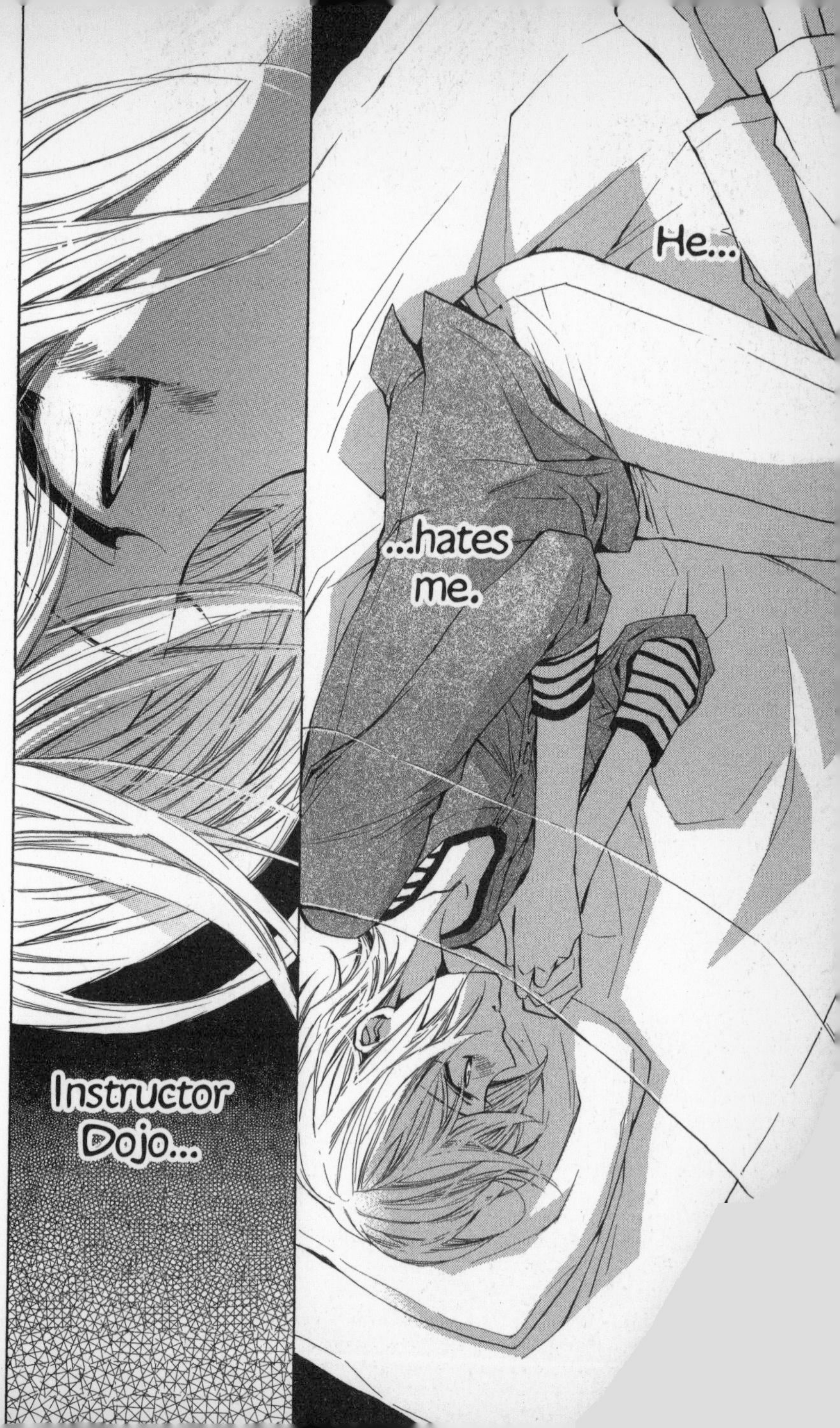
He...
...hates me.
Instructor Dojo...

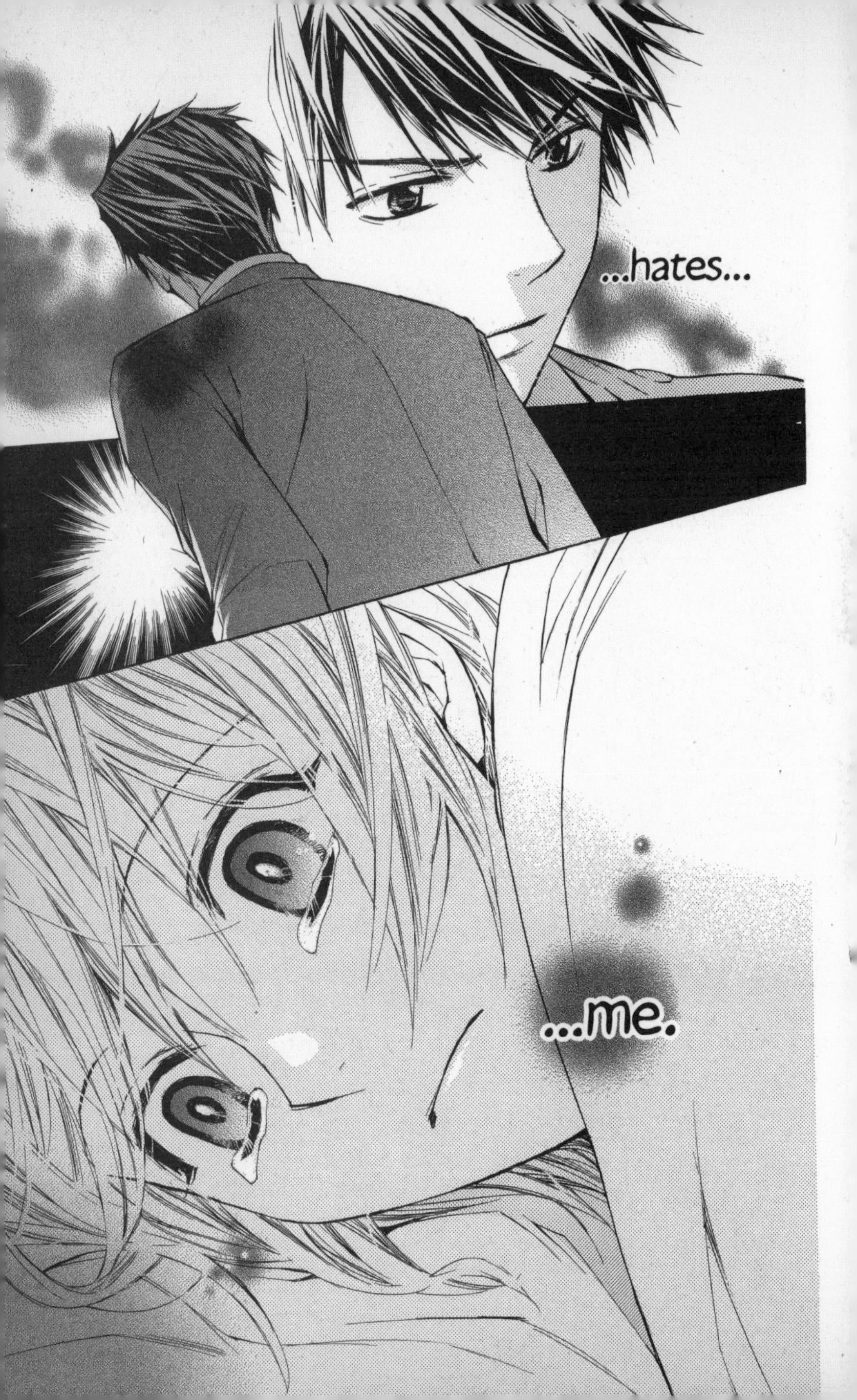
...hates...
...me.

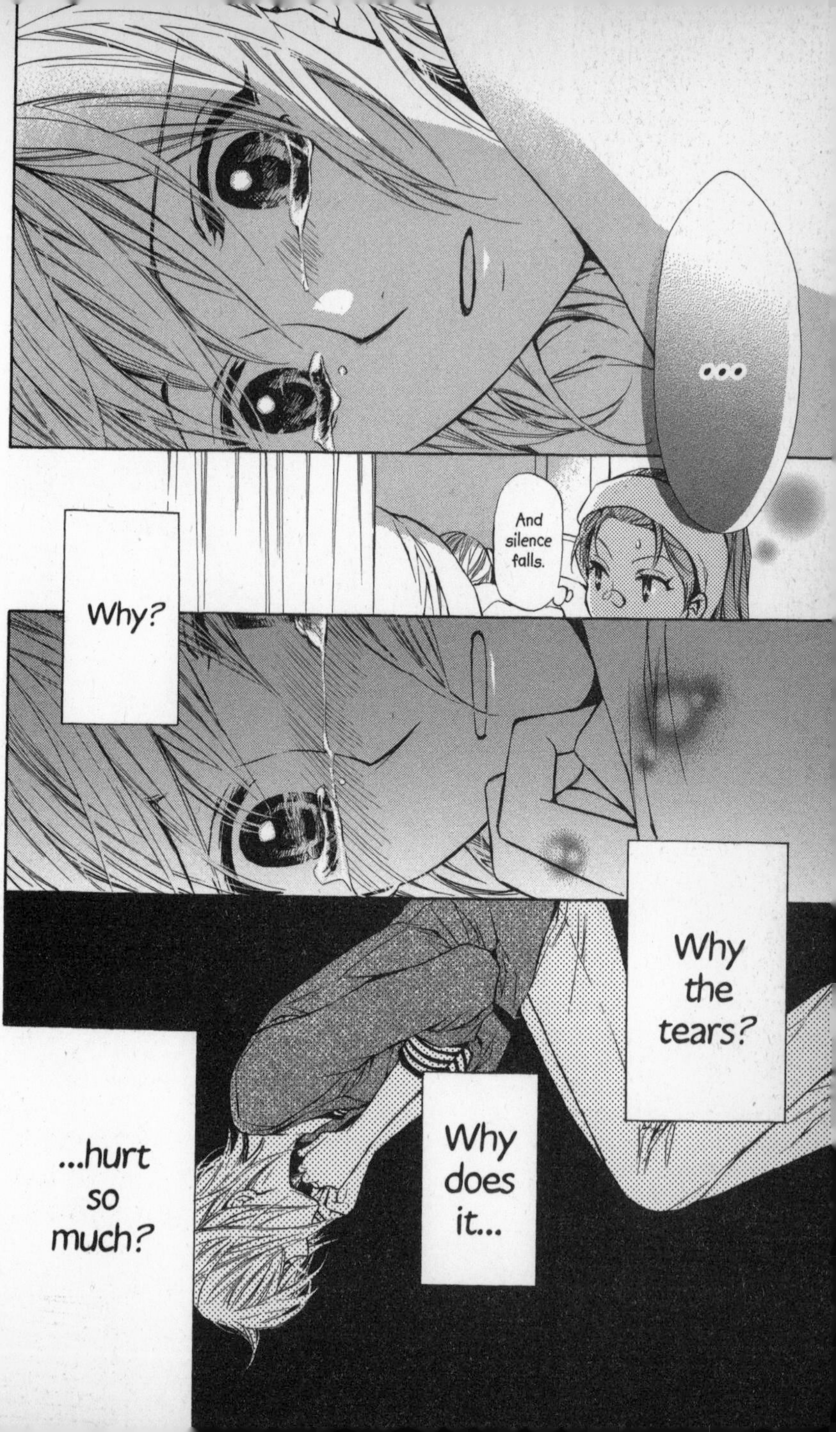
...
And silence falls.
Why?
Why the tears?
Why does it...
...hurt so much?

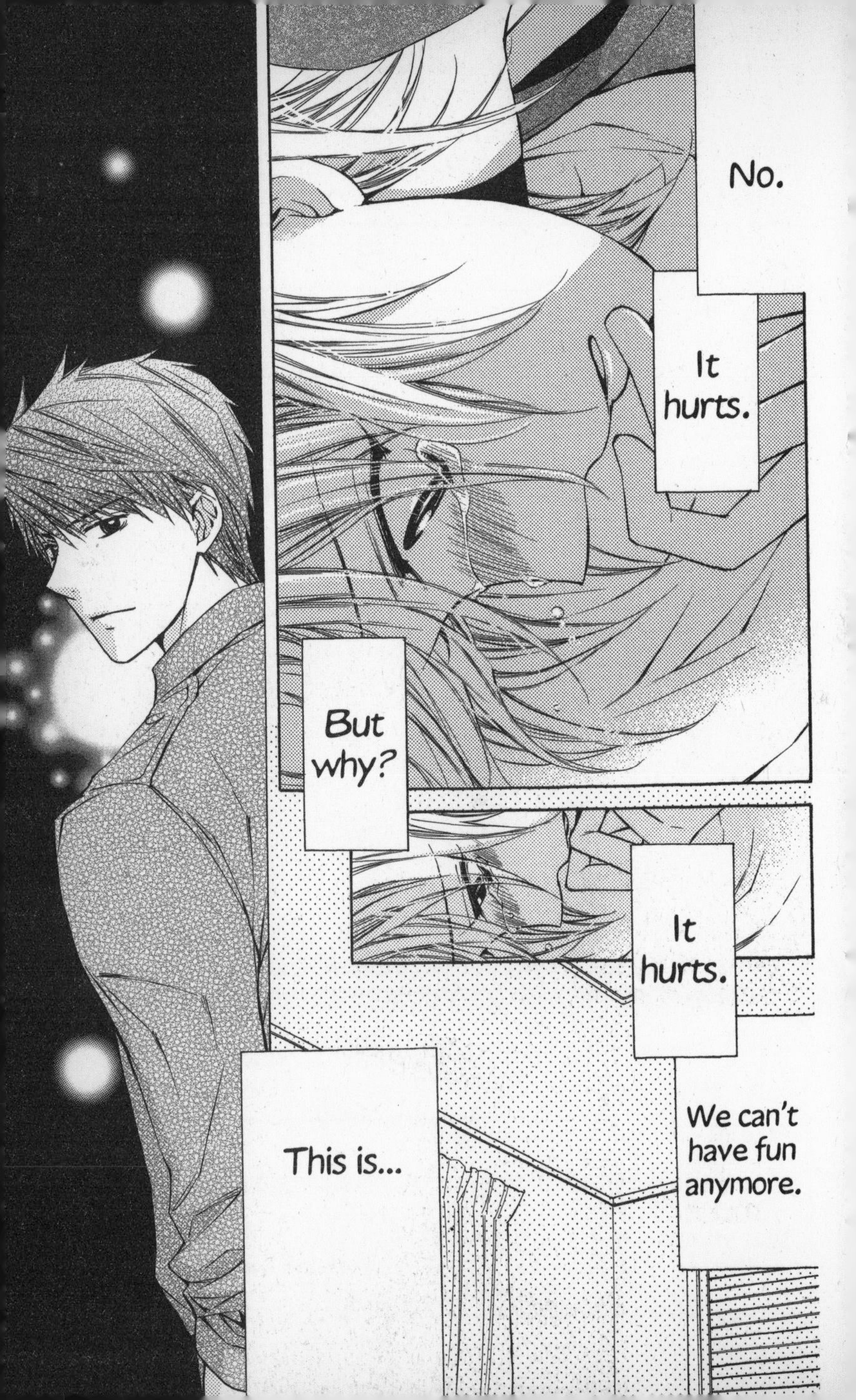
No.
It hurts.
But why?
It hurts.
We can't have fun anymore.
This is...

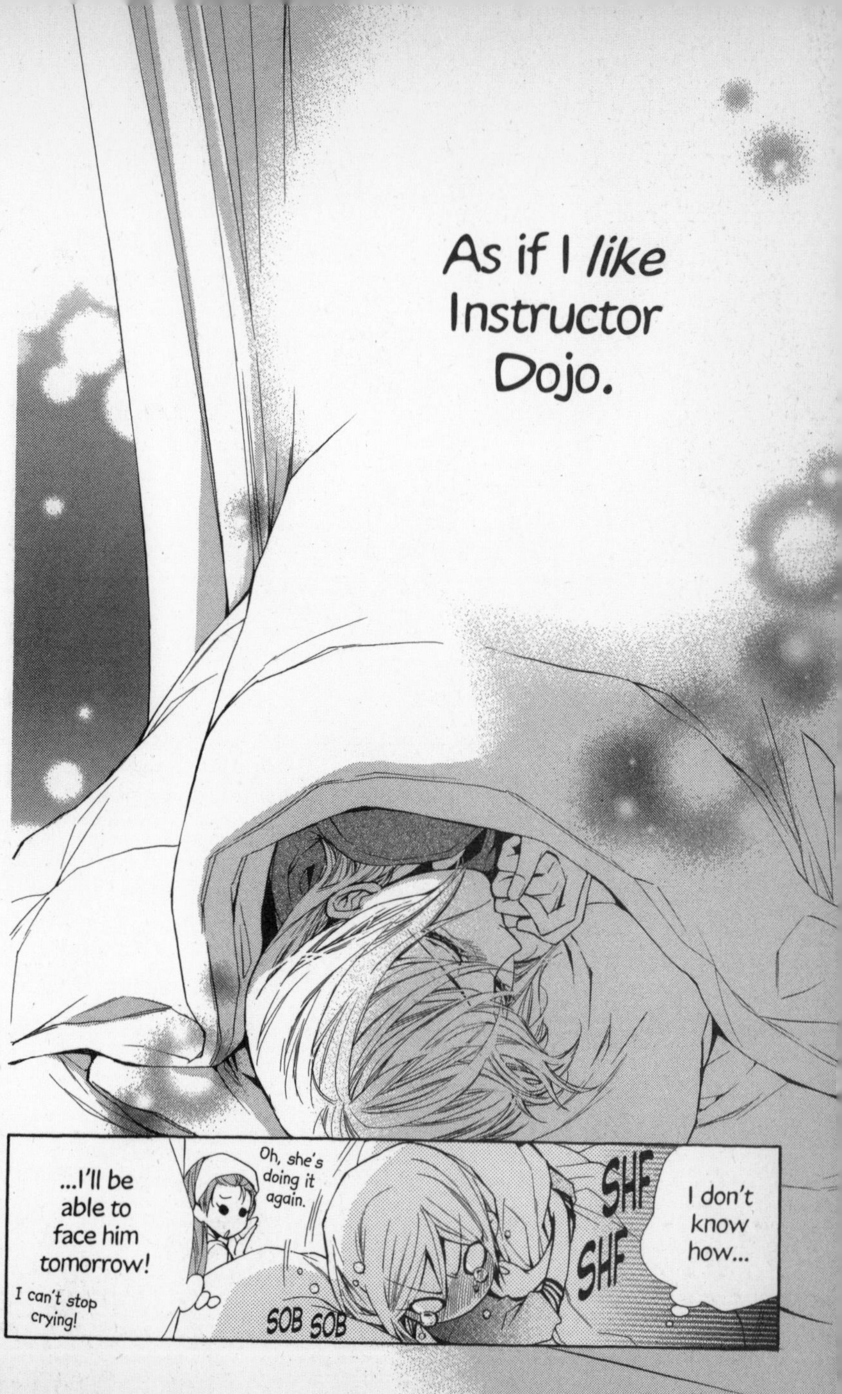
As if I *like* Instructor Dojo.
I don't know how...
SHF SHF
Oh, she's doing it again.
SOB SOB
...I'll be able to face him tomorrow!
I can't stop crying!

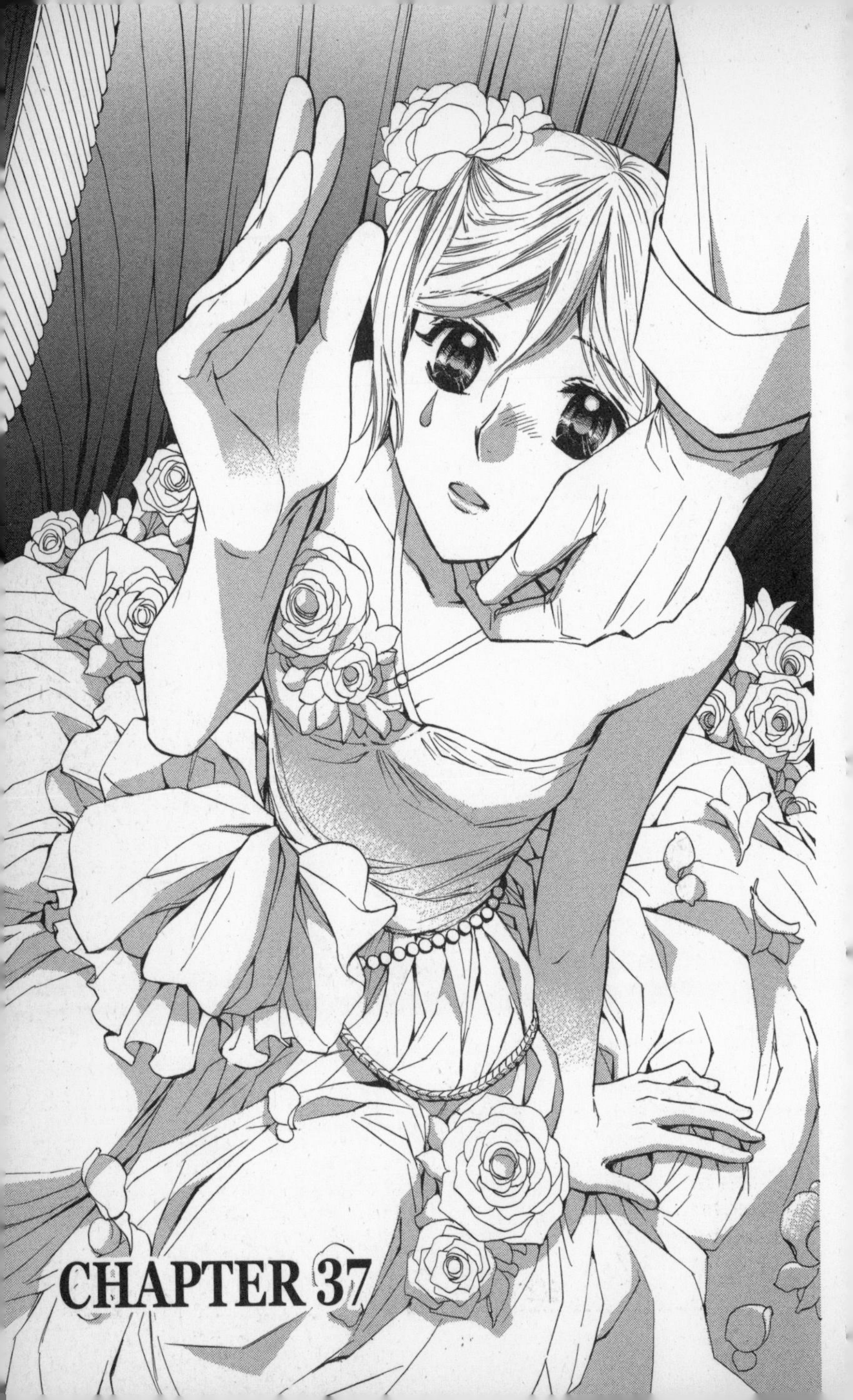
CHAPTER 37

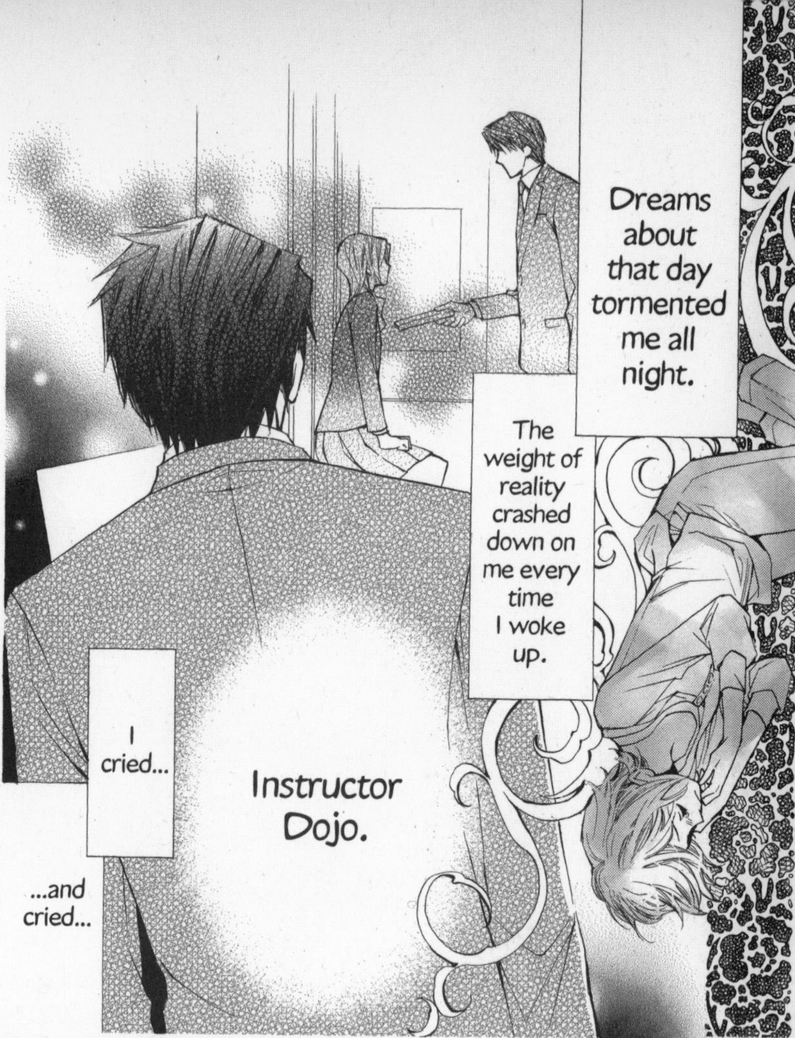
Dreams about that day tormented me all night.
The weight of reality crashed down on me every time I woke up.
I cried...
...and cried...
Instructor Dojo.

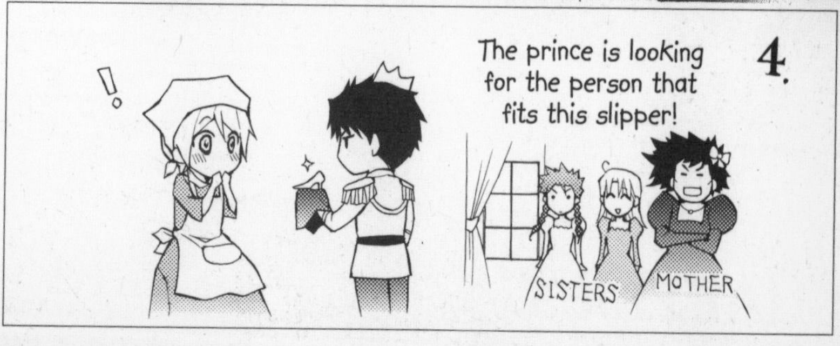
4.
The prince is looking for the person that fits this slipper!
!
SISTERS
MOTHER

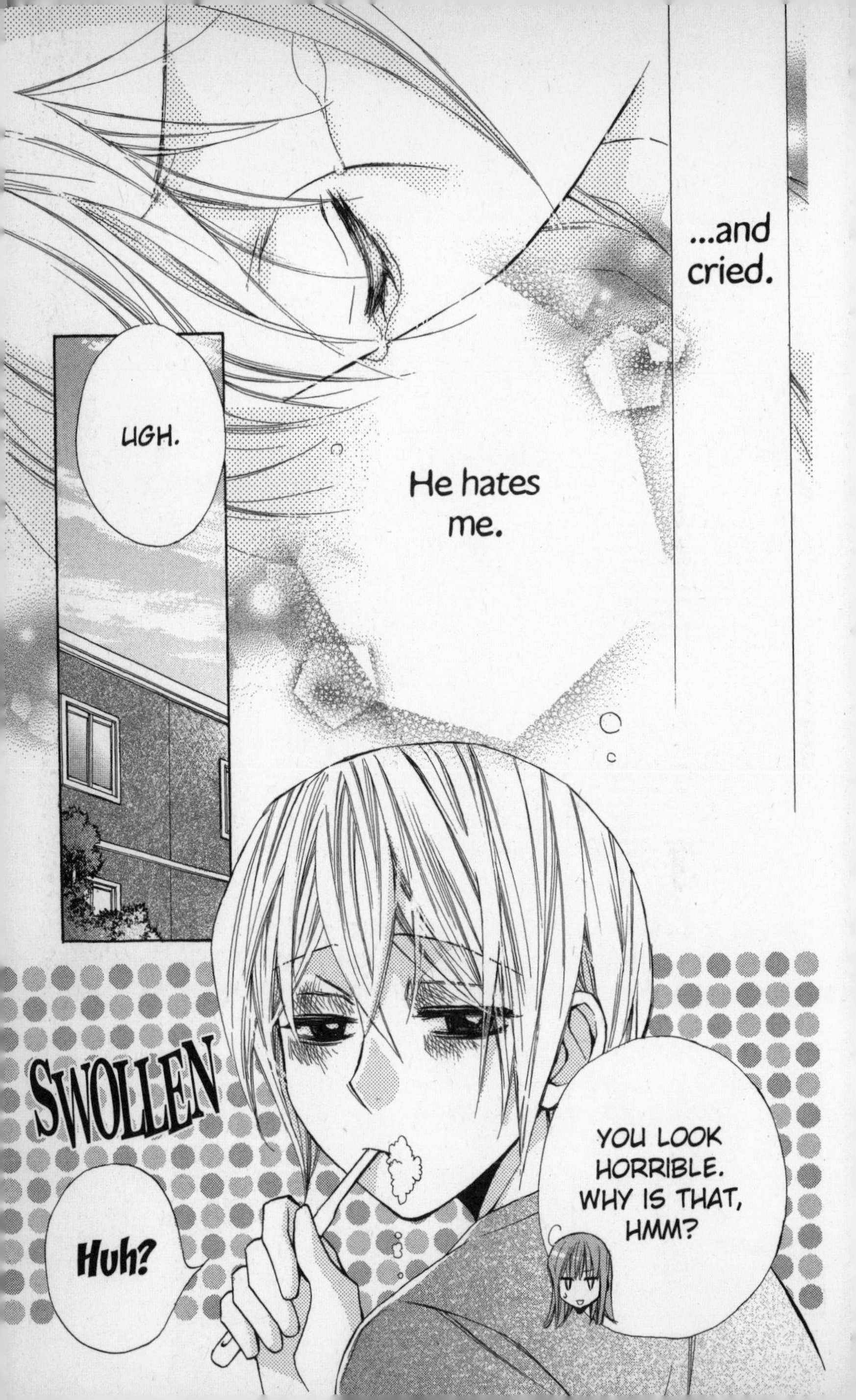
...and cried.
He hates me.
UGH.
YOU LOOK HORRIBLE. WHY IS THAT, HMM?
SWOLLEN
Huh?

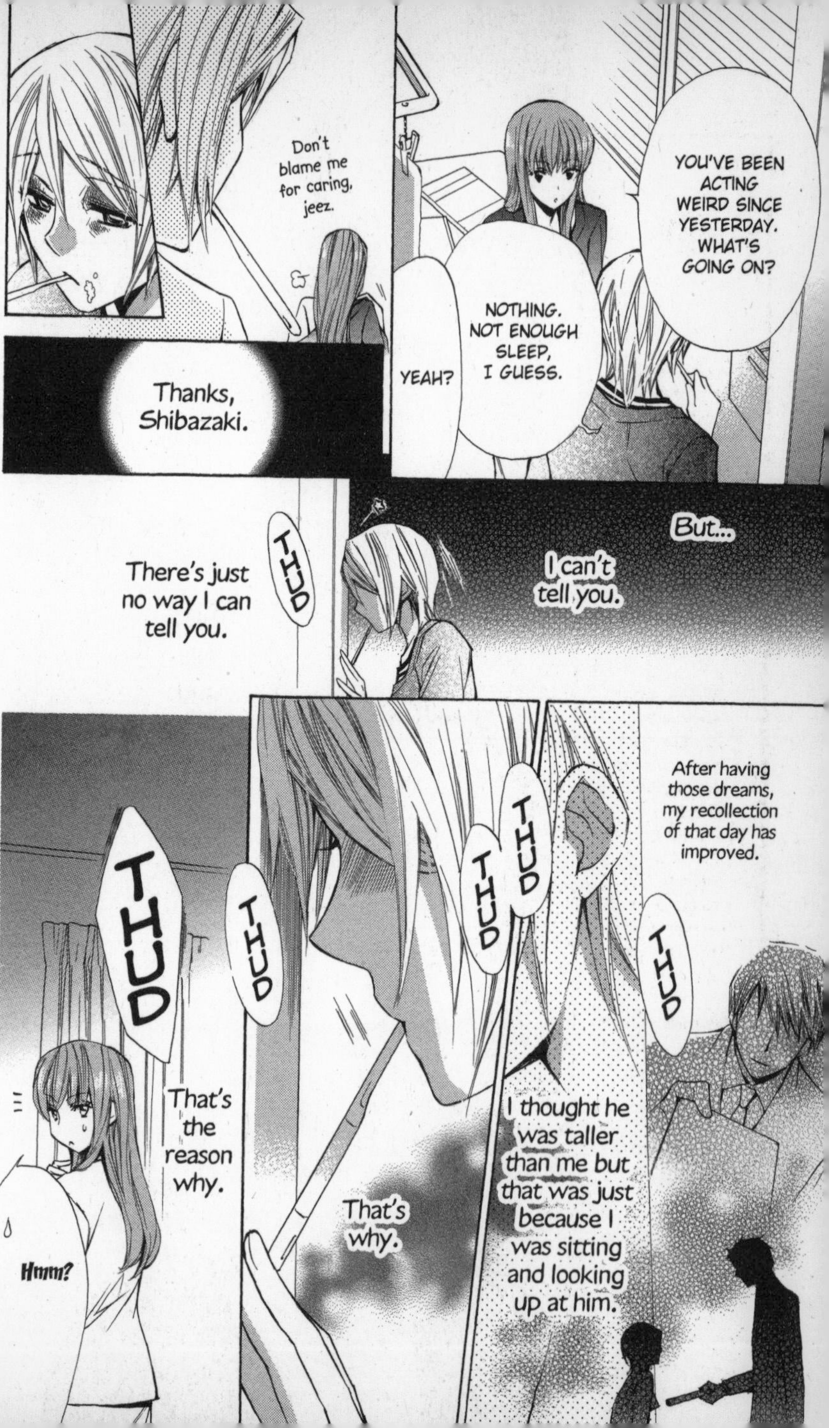
YOU'VE BEEN ACTING WEIRD SINCE YESTERDAY. WHAT'S GOING ON?
NOTHING. NOT ENOUGH SLEEP, I GUESS.
YEAH?
Don't blame me for caring, jeez.
Thanks, Shibazaki.
But...
I can't tell you.
THUD
There's just no way I can tell you.
After having those dreams, my recollection of that day has improved.
THUD
THUD
THUD
I thought he was taller than me but that was just because I was sitting and looking up at him.
THUD
That's why.
THUD
THUD
That's the reason why.
Hmm?

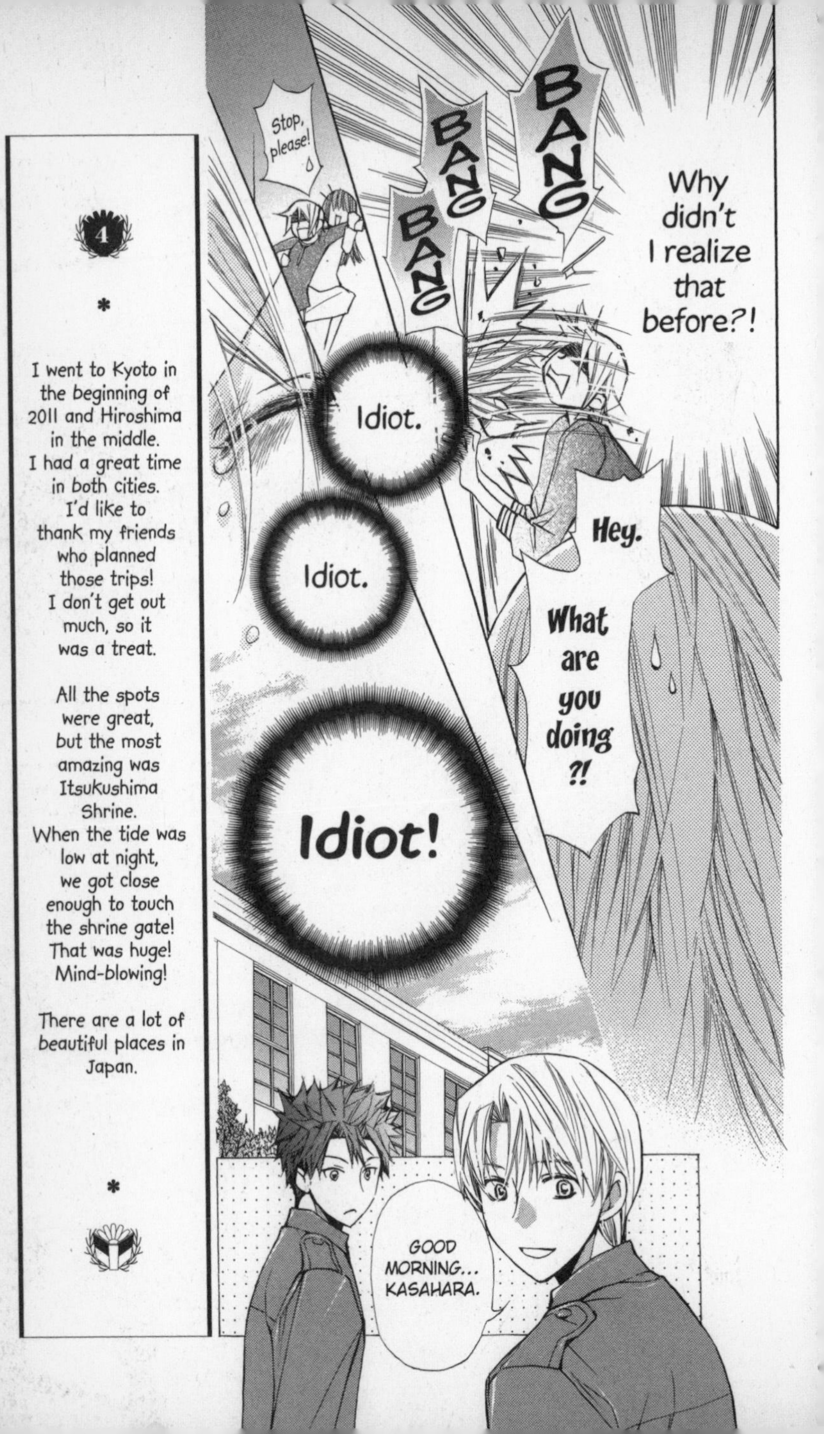
Why didn't I realize that before?!
BANG
BANG
BANG
Stop, please!
Idiot.
Idiot.
Idiot!
Hey.
What are you doing?!
GOOD MORNING... KASAHARA.

4

*

I went to Kyoto in the beginning of 2011 and Hiroshima in the middle. I had a great time in both cities. I'd like to thank my friends who planned those trips! I don't get out much, so it was a treat.

All the spots were great, but the most amazing was Itsukushima Shrine. When the tide was low at night, we got close enough to touch the shrine gate! That was huge! Mind-blowing!

There are a lot of beautiful places in Japan.

*

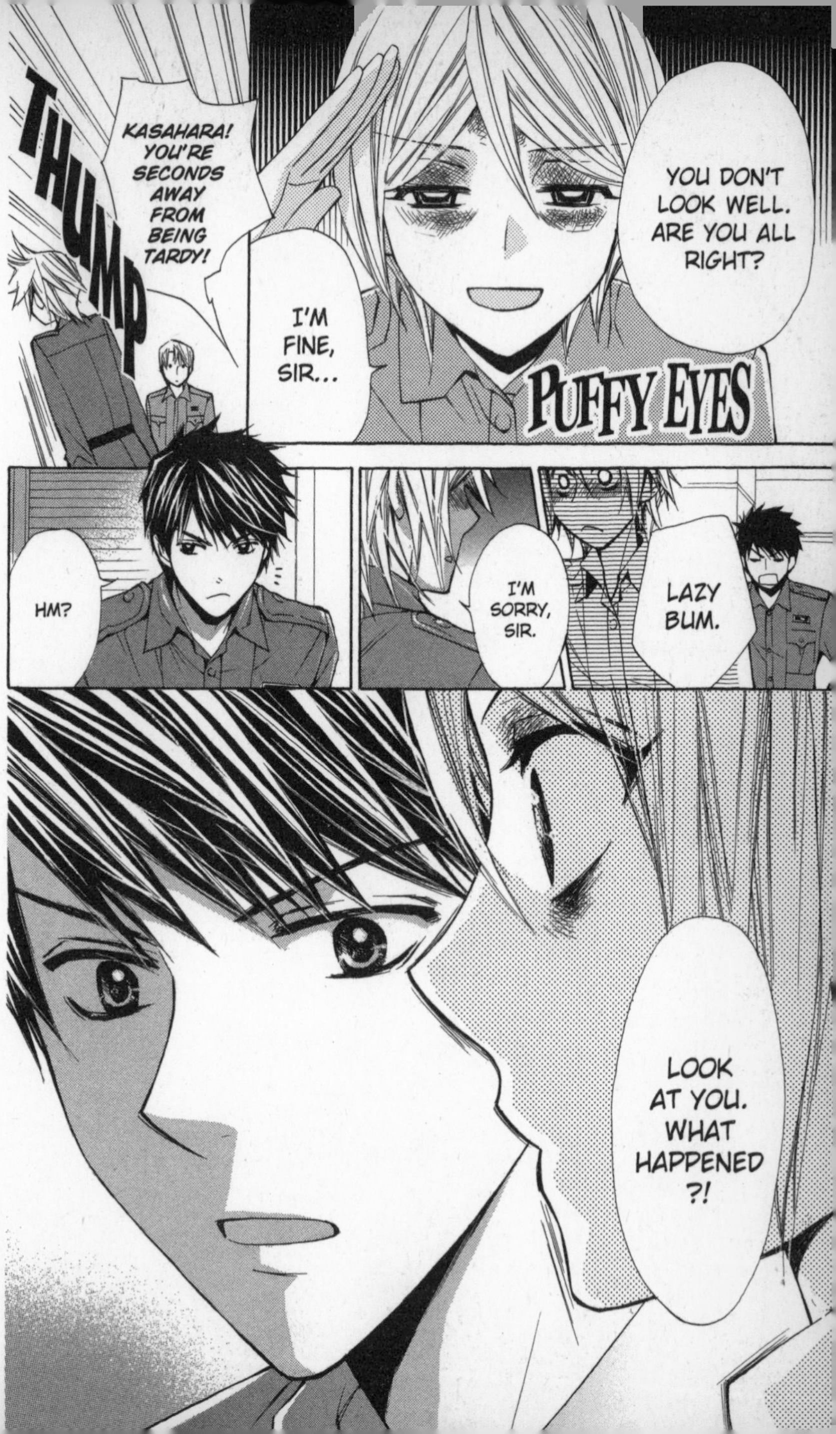
YOU DON'T LOOK WELL. ARE YOU ALL RIGHT?
I'M FINE, SIR...
PUFFY EYES
KASAHARA! YOU'RE SECONDS AWAY FROM BEING TARDY!
THUMP
LAZY BUM.
I'M SORRY, SIR.
HM?
LOOK AT YOU. WHAT HAPPENED?!

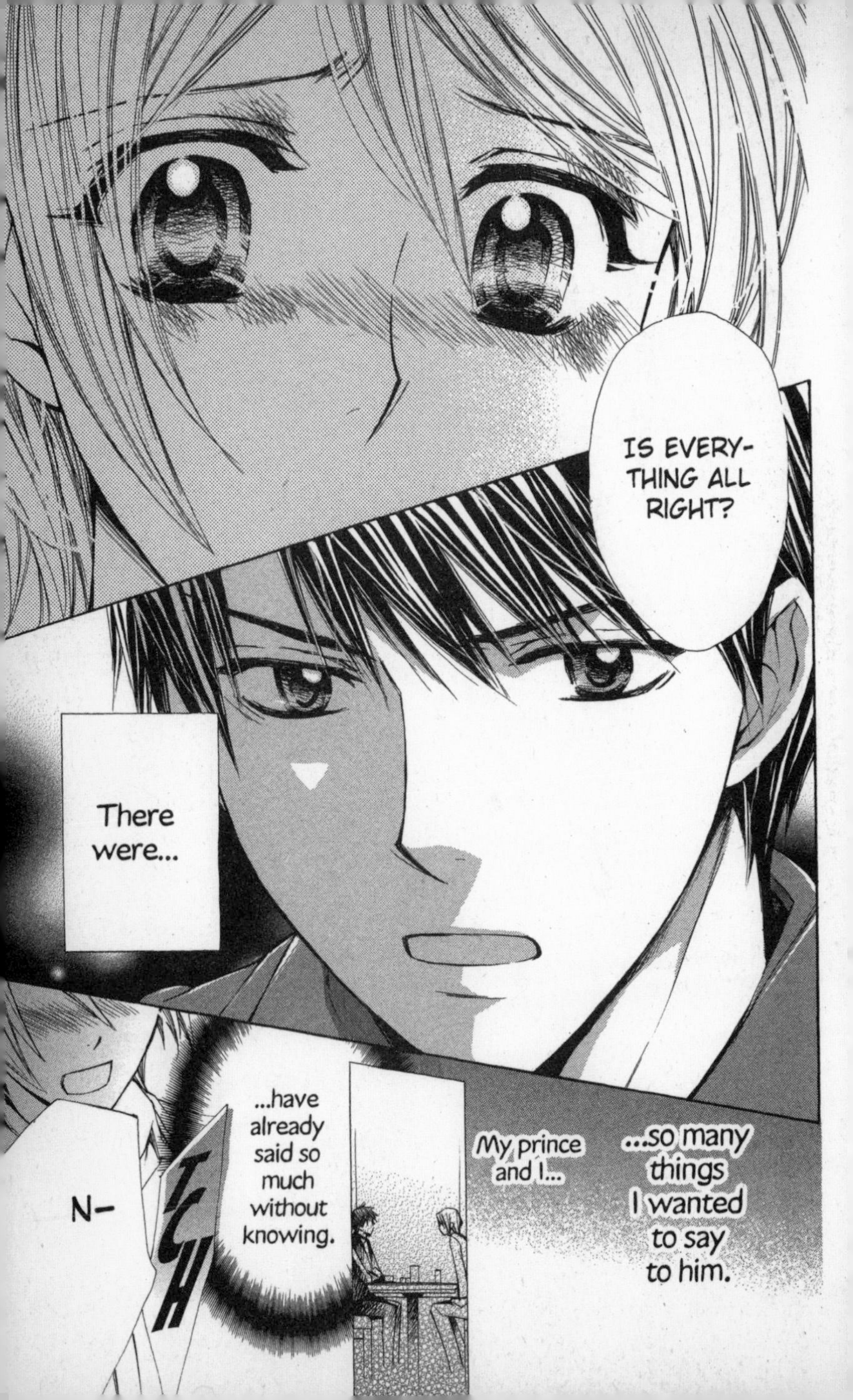
IS EVERY-THING ALL RIGHT?
There were...
...so many things I wanted to say to him.
My prince and I...
...have already said so much without knowing.
TCH
N-

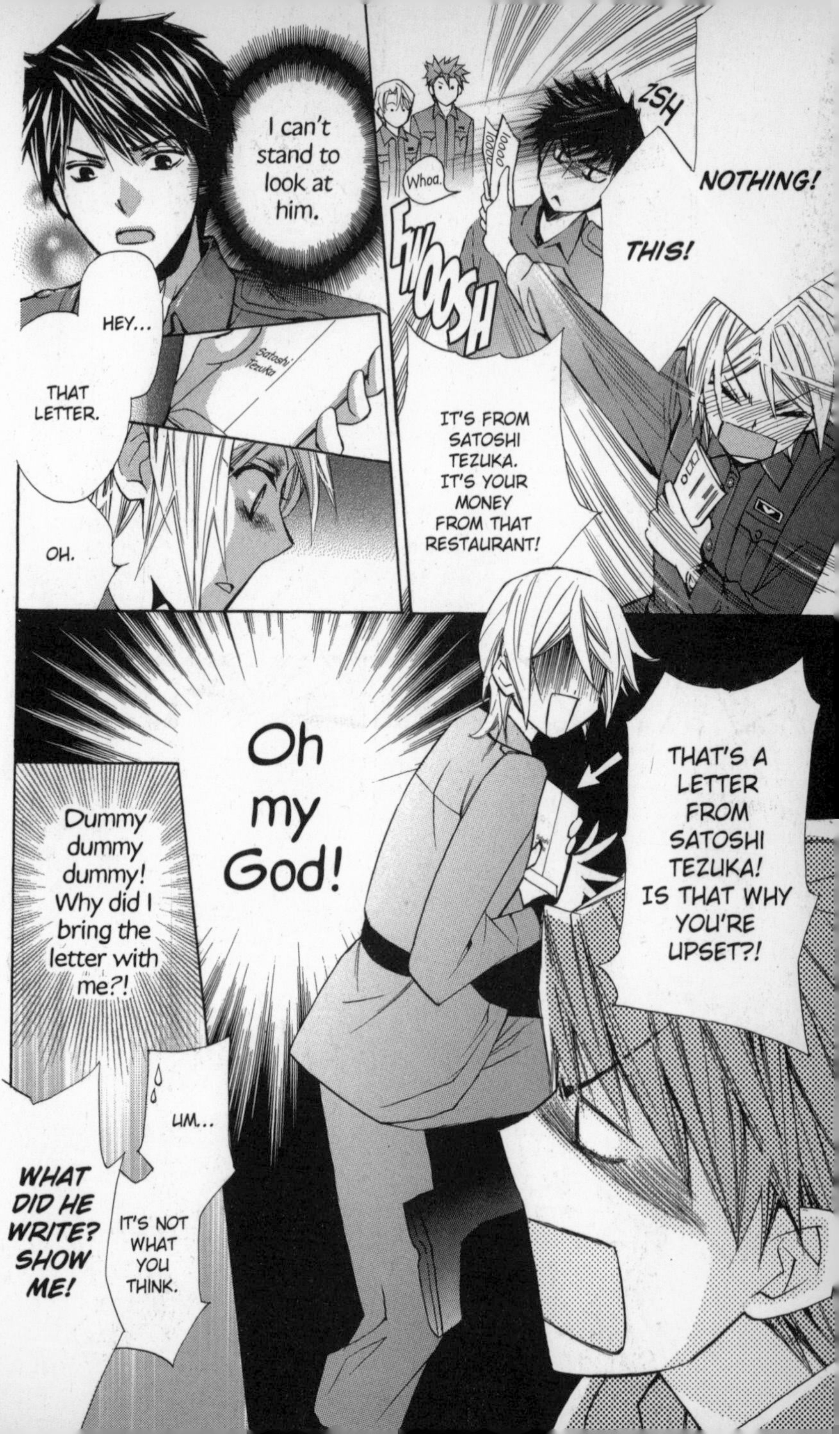
I can't stand to look at him.
HEY...
THAT LETTER.
Satoshi Tezuka
OH.
ZSH
Whoa.
FWOOSH
NOTHING!
THIS!
IT'S FROM SATOSHI TEZUKA. IT'S YOUR MONEY FROM THAT RESTAURANT!
THAT'S A LETTER FROM SATOSHI TEZUKA! IS THAT WHY YOU'RE UPSET?!
Oh my God!
Dummy dummy dummy! Why did I bring the letter with me?!
UM...
IT'S NOT WHAT YOU THINK.
WHAT DID HE WRITE? SHOW ME!

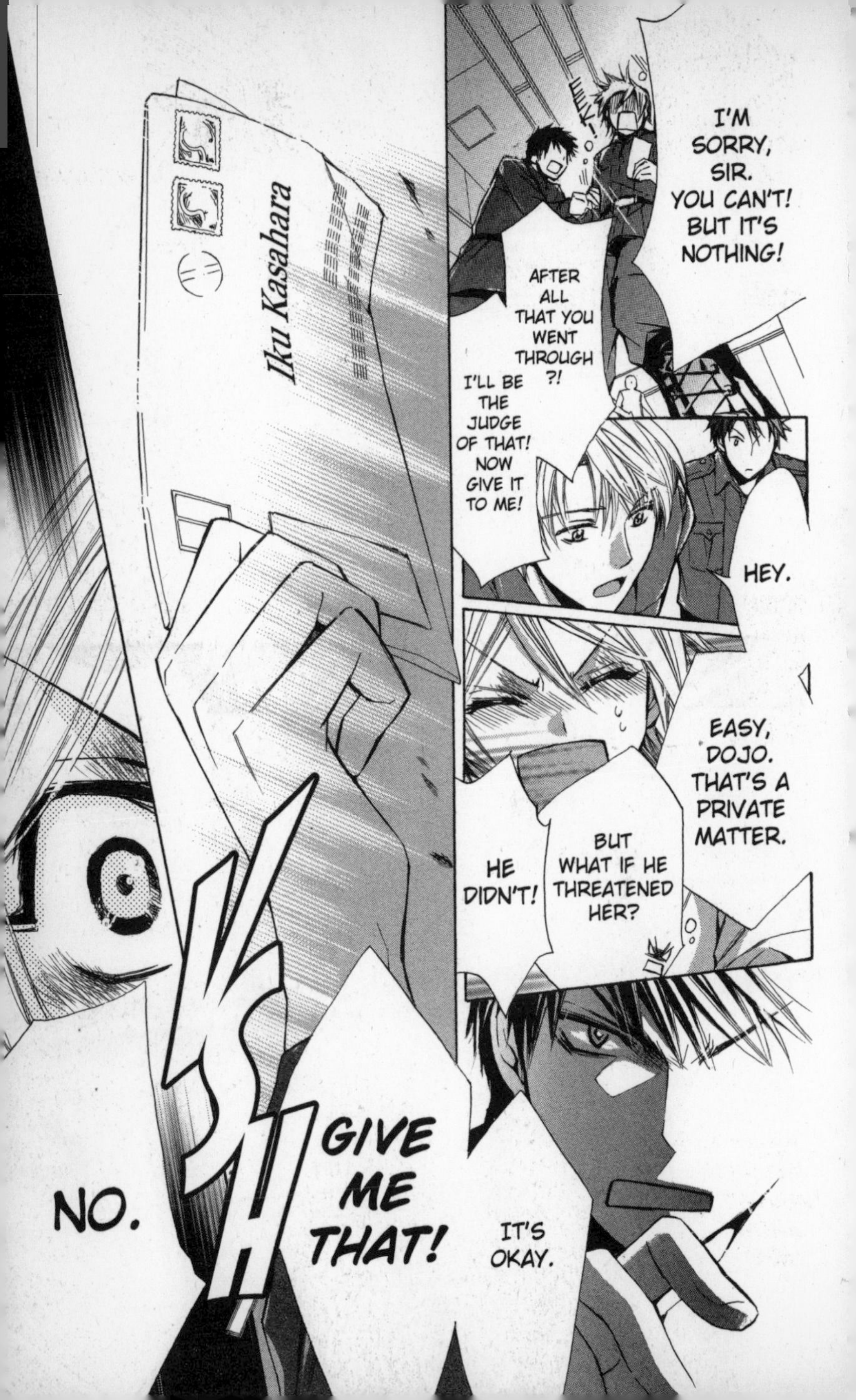
I'M SORRY, SIR. YOU CAN'T! BUT IT'S NOTHING!
AFTER ALL THAT YOU WENT THROUGH ?!
HEY.
I'LL BE THE JUDGE OF THAT! NOW GIVE IT TO ME!
EASY, DOJO. THAT'S A PRIVATE MATTER.
BUT WHAT IF HE THREATENED HER?
HE DIDN'T!
IT'S OKAY.
GIVE ME THAT!
Iku Kasahara
NO.

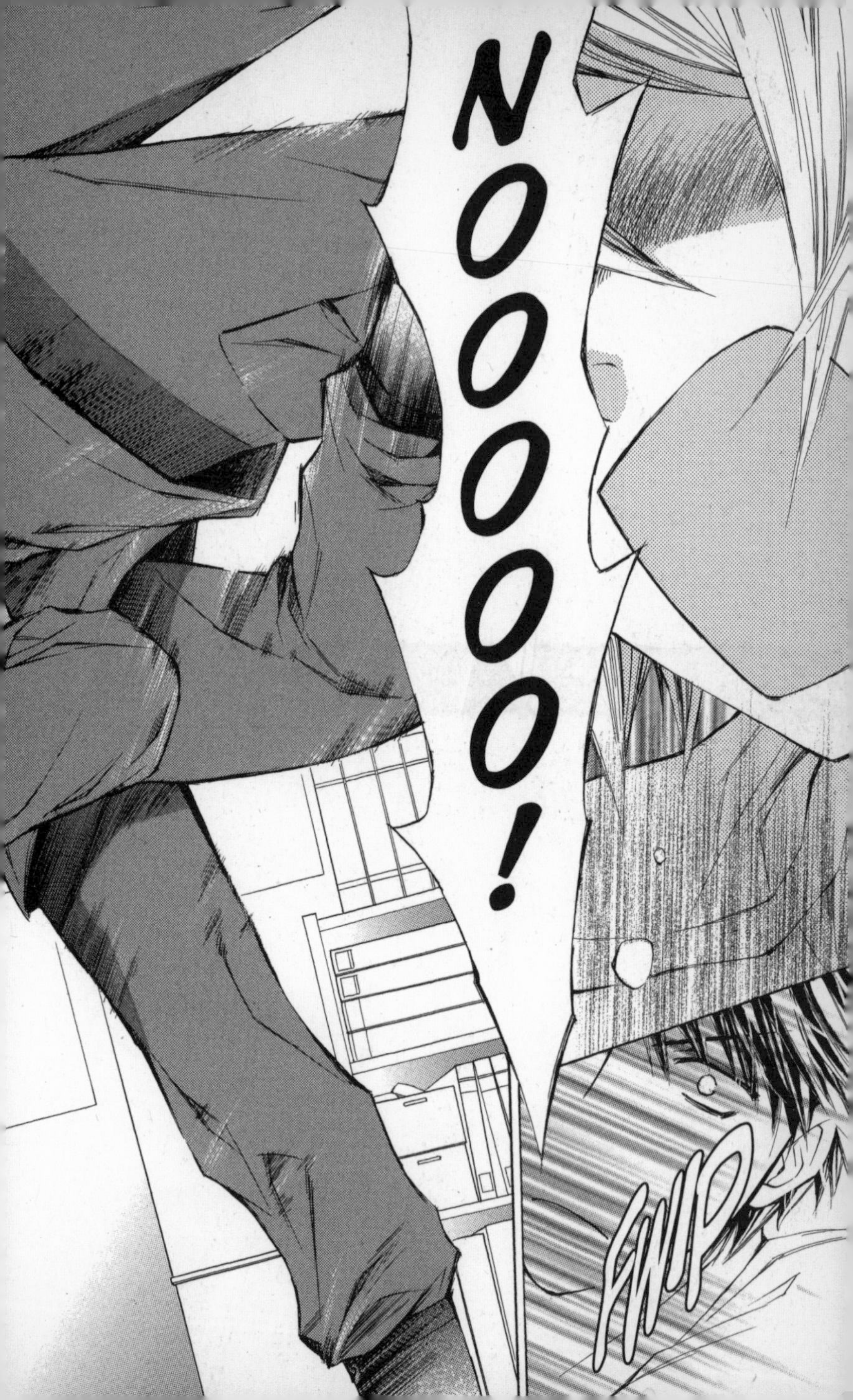
NOOOOOO!
GWIP

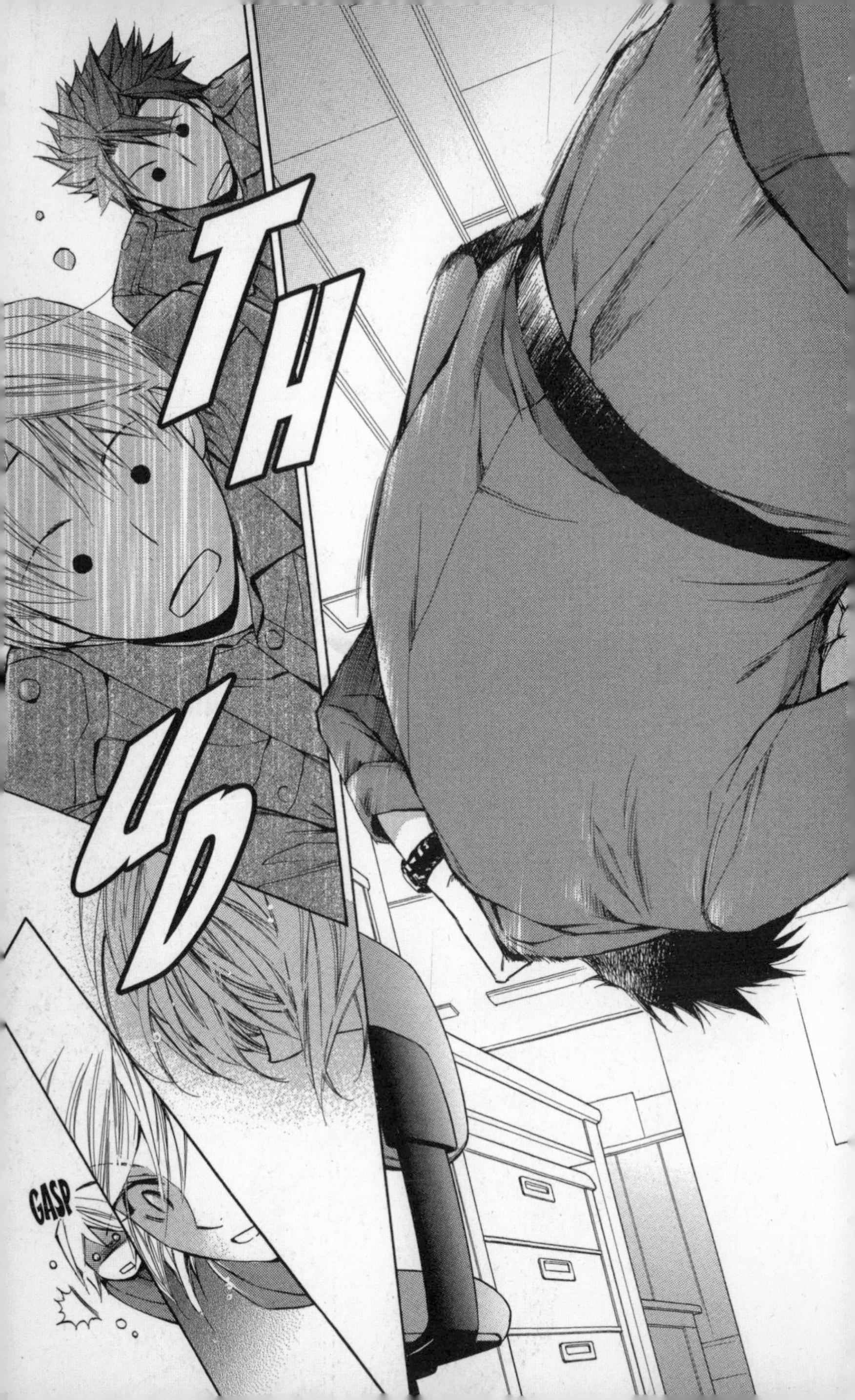
THUD
GASP

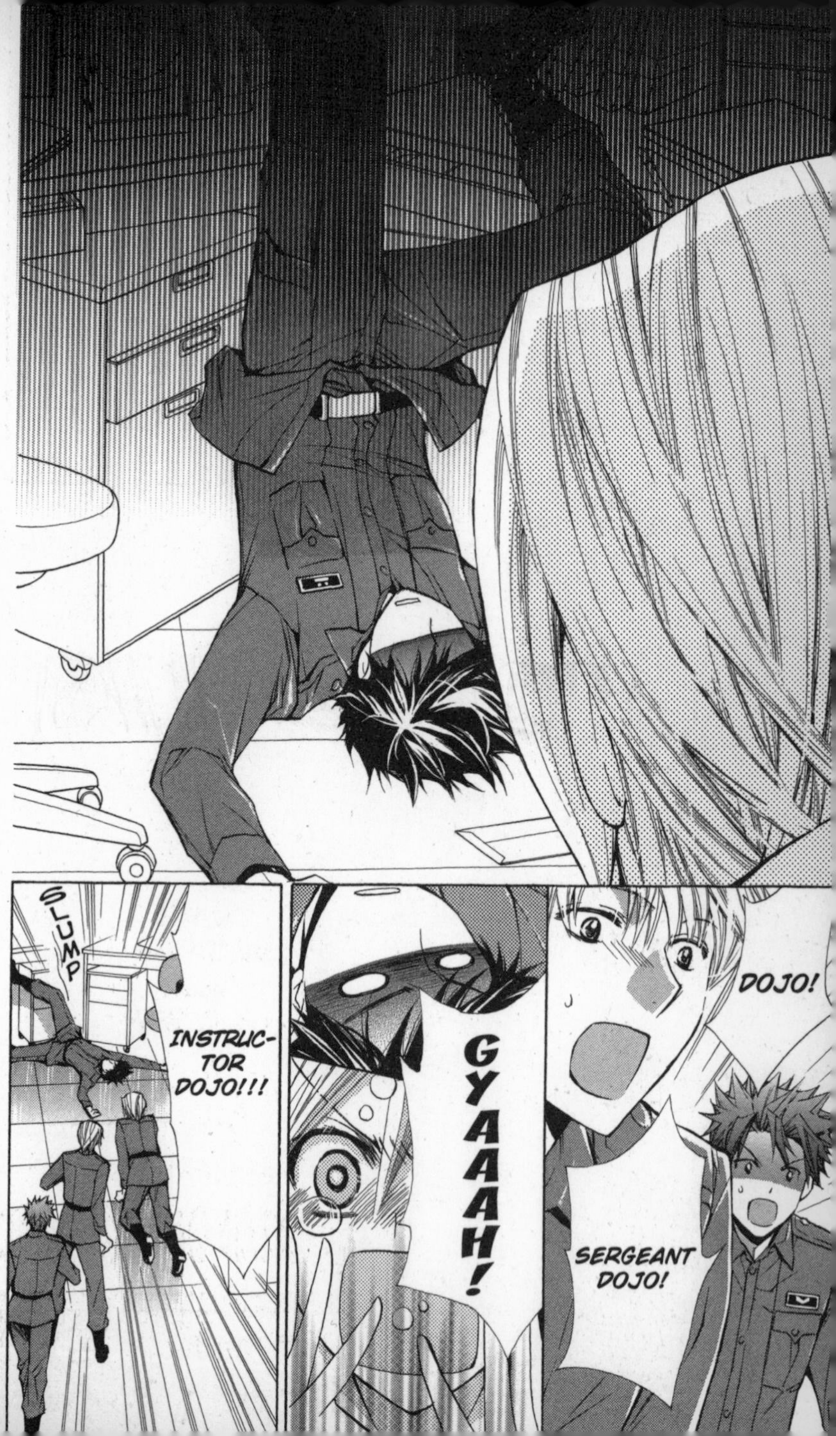
DOJO!
SERGEANT DOJO!
GYAAAAH!
SLUMP
INSTRUC-
TOR
DOJO!!!

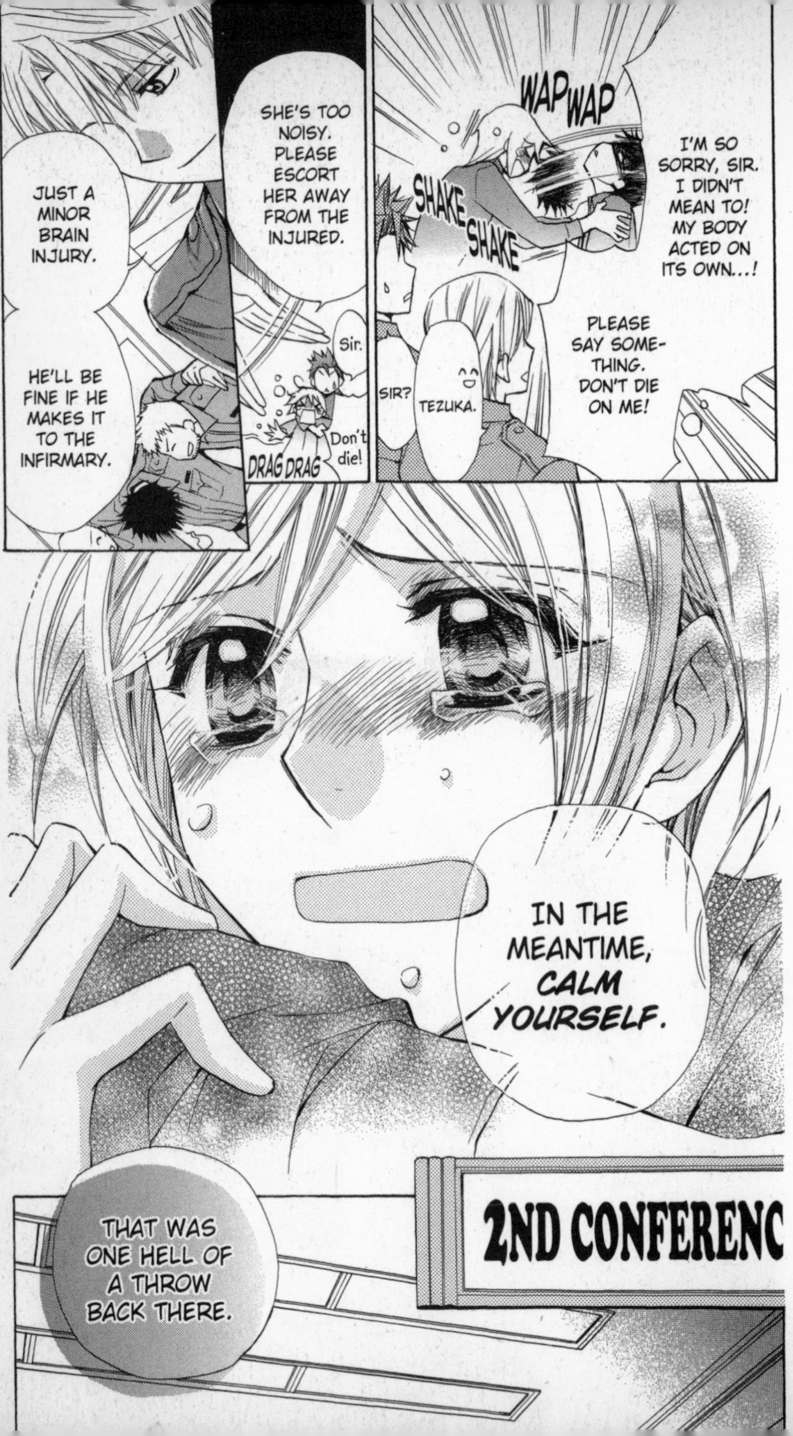
WAP WAP
I'M SO SORRY, SIR. I DIDN'T MEAN TO! MY BODY ACTED ON ITS OWN...!
SHAKE SHAKE
PLEASE SAY SOME-THING. DON'T DIE ON ME!
TEZUKA.
SIR?
SHE'S TOO NOISY. PLEASE ESCORT HER AWAY FROM THE INJURED.
Sir.
Don't die!
DRAG DRAG
JUST A MINOR BRAIN INJURY.
HE'LL BE FINE IF HE MAKES IT TO THE INFIRMARY.
IN THE MEANTIME, CALM YOURSELF.
2ND CONFERENC
THAT WAS ONE HELL OF A THROW BACK THERE.

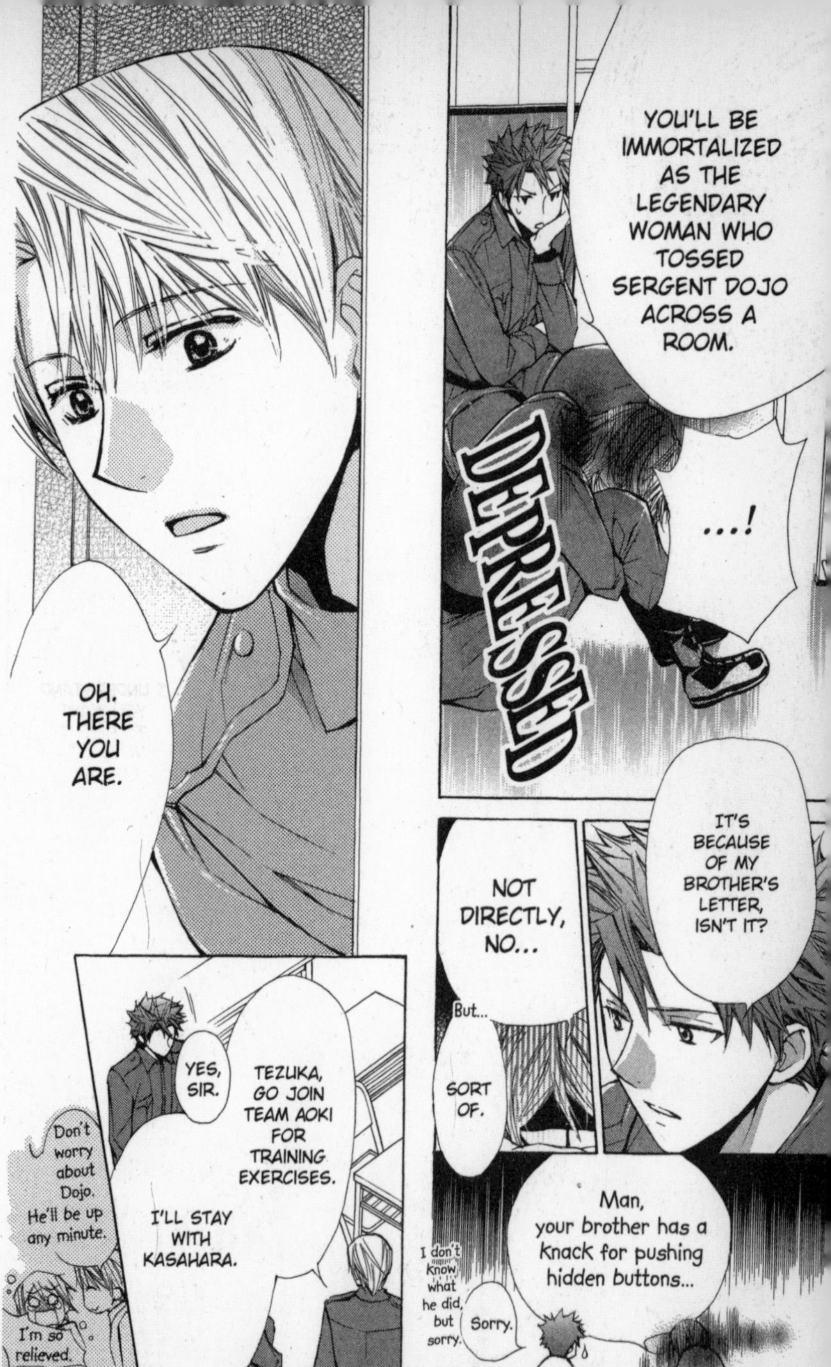
YOU'LL BE IMMORTALIZED AS THE LEGENDARY WOMAN WHO TOSSED SERGENT DOJO ACROSS A ROOM.
DEPRESSED
...!
OH. THERE YOU ARE.
IT'S BECAUSE OF MY BROTHER'S LETTER, ISN'T IT?
NOT DIRECTLY, NO...
But...
SORT OF.
Man, your brother has a knack for pushing hidden buttons...
Sorry.
I don't know what he did, but sorry.
TEZUKA, GO JOIN TEAM AOKI FOR TRAINING EXERCISES.
YES, SIR.
I'LL STAY WITH KASAHARA.
Don't worry about Dojo. He'll be up any minute.
I'm so relieved.

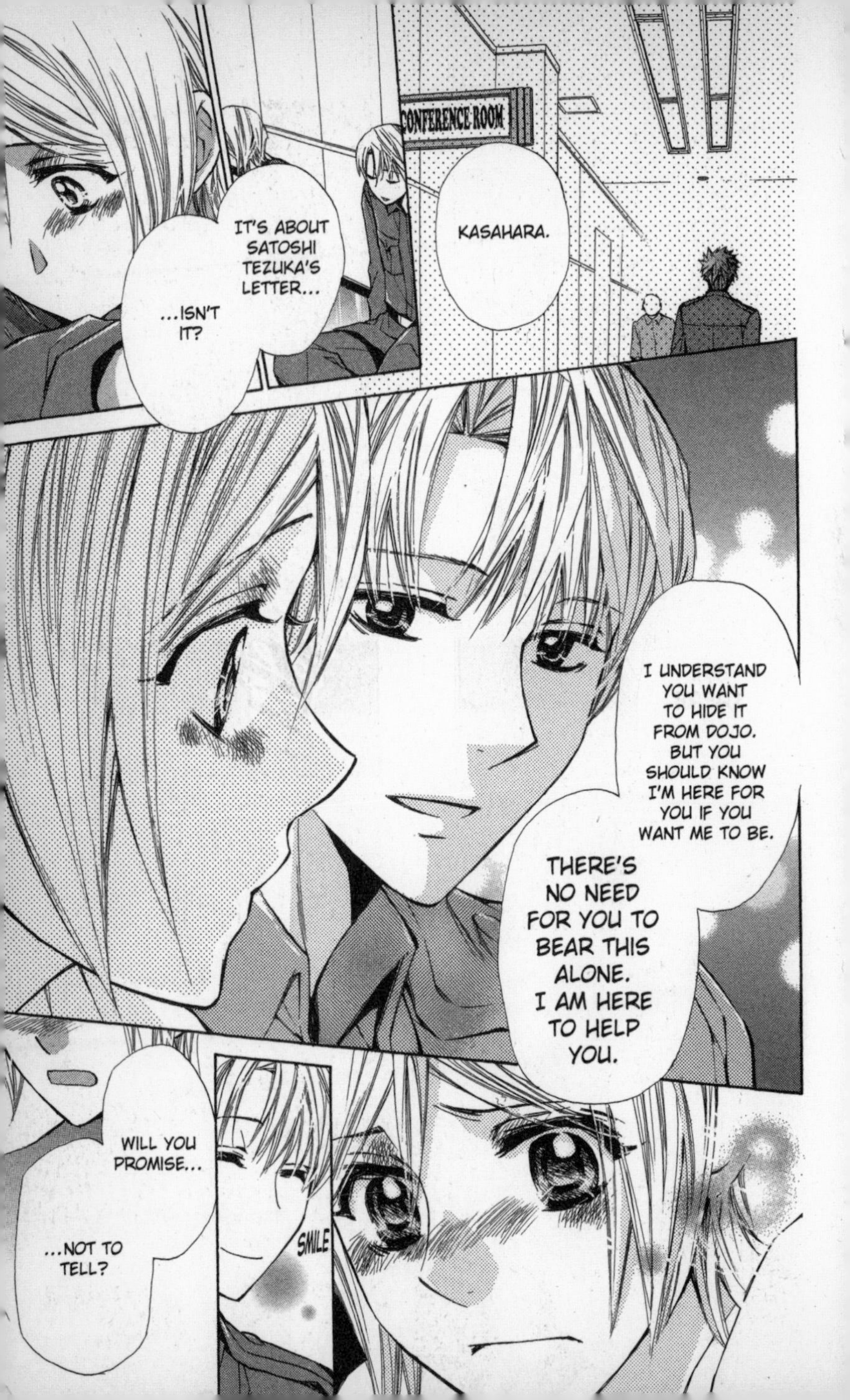
CONFERENCE ROOM
KASAHARA.
IT'S ABOUT SATOSHI TEZUKA'S LETTER...
...ISN'T IT?
I UNDERSTAND YOU WANT TO HIDE IT FROM DOJO. BUT YOU SHOULD KNOW I'M HERE FOR YOU IF YOU WANT ME TO BE.
THERE'S NO NEED FOR YOU TO BEAR THIS ALONE. I AM HERE TO HELP YOU.
SMILE
WILL YOU PROMISE...
...NOT TO TELL?

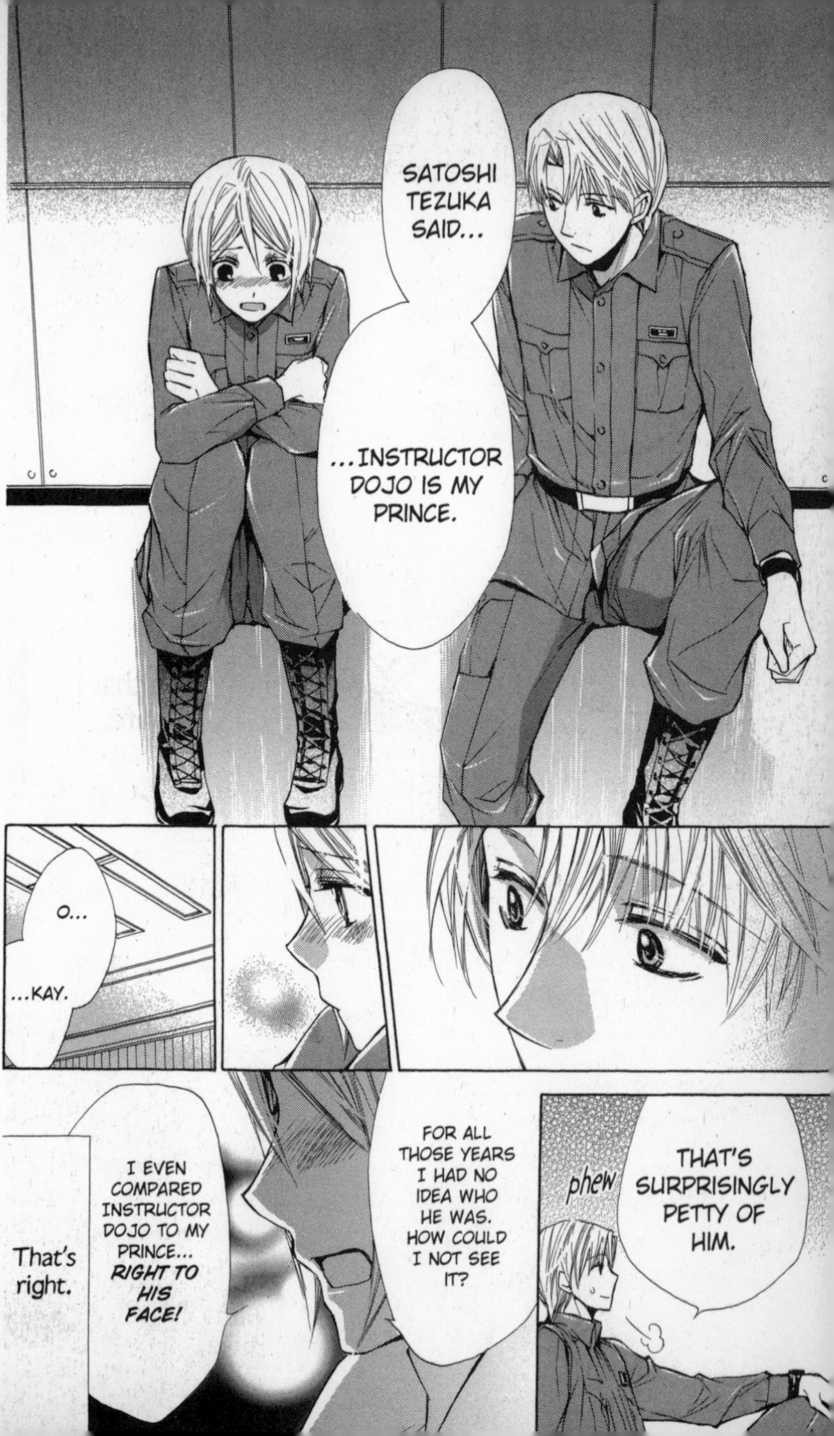
SATOSHI TEZUKA SAID...
...INSTRUCTOR DOJO IS MY PRINCE.
O...
...KAY.
THAT'S SURPRISINGLY PETTY OF HIM.
phew
FOR ALL THOSE YEARS I HAD NO IDEA WHO HE WAS. HOW COULD I NOT SEE IT?
I EVEN COMPARED INSTRUCTOR DOJO TO MY PRINCE... ***RIGHT TO HIS FACE!***
That's right.

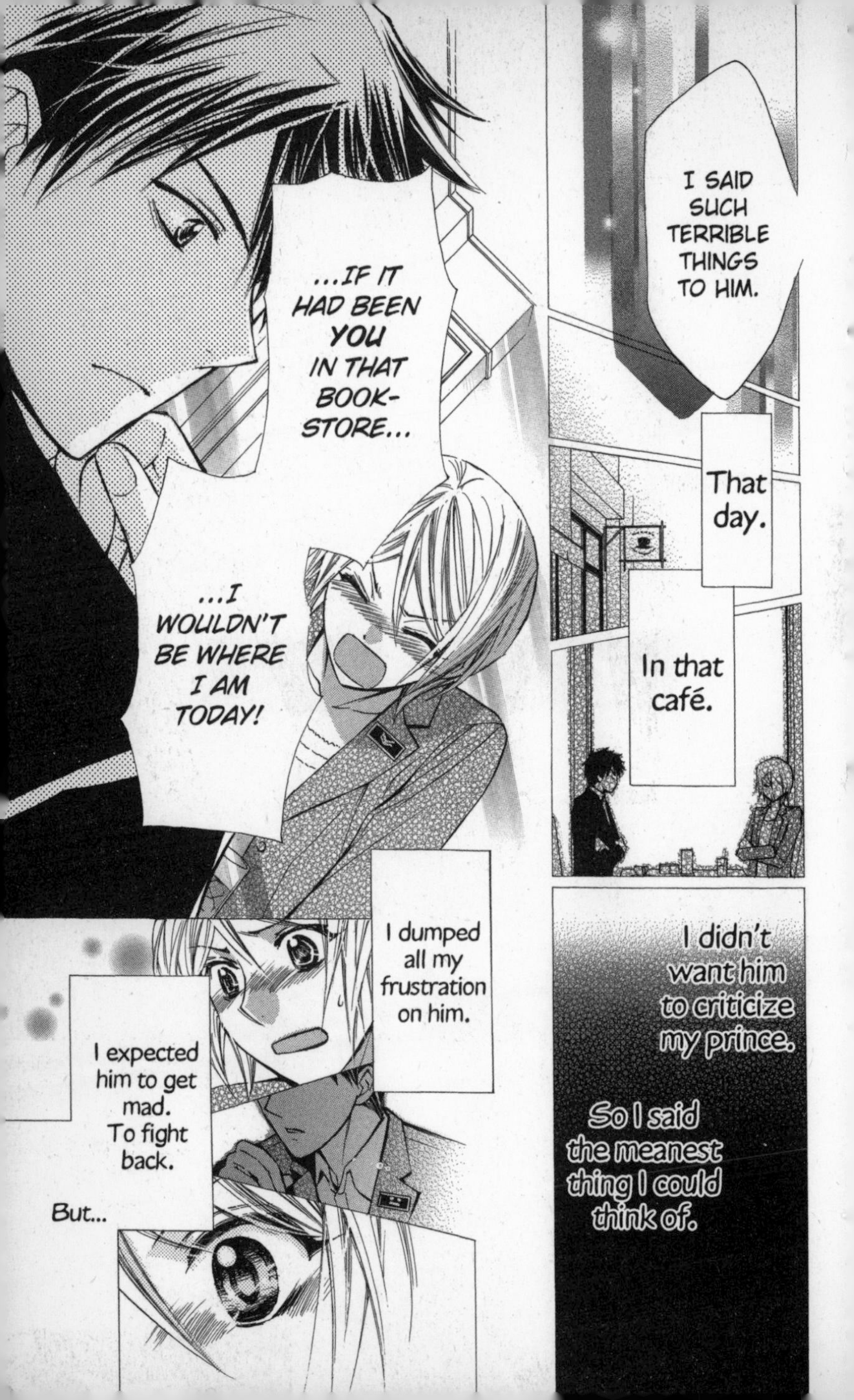

I SAID SUCH TERRIBLE THINGS TO HIM.
That day.
In that café.
...IF IT HAD BEEN YOU IN THAT BOOK-STORE...
...I WOULDN'T BE WHERE I AM TODAY!
I didn't want him to criticize my prince.
So I said the meanest thing I could think of.
I dumped all my frustration on him.
I expected him to get mad. To fight back.
But...

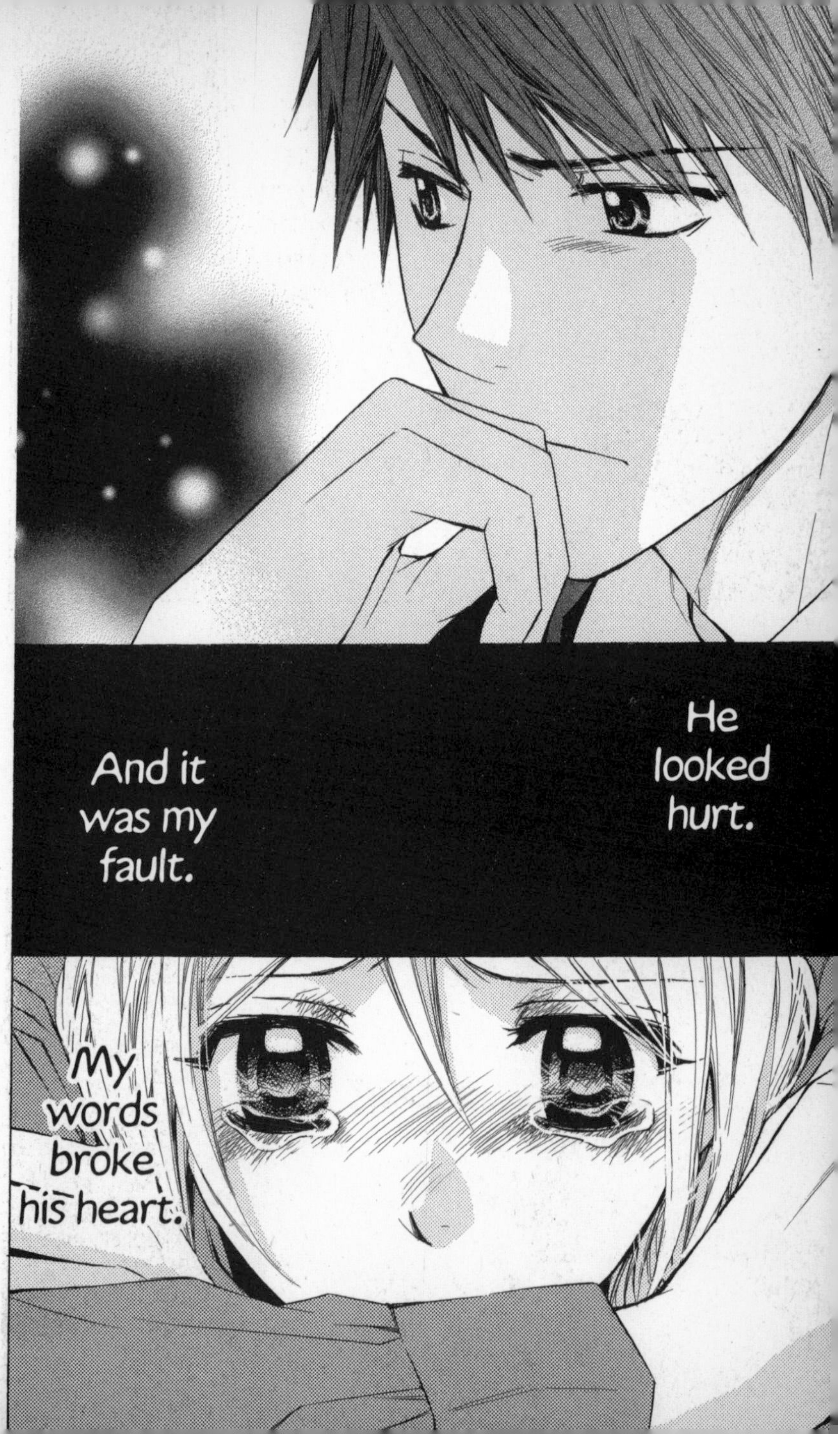
He looked hurt.
And it was my fault.
My words broke his heart.

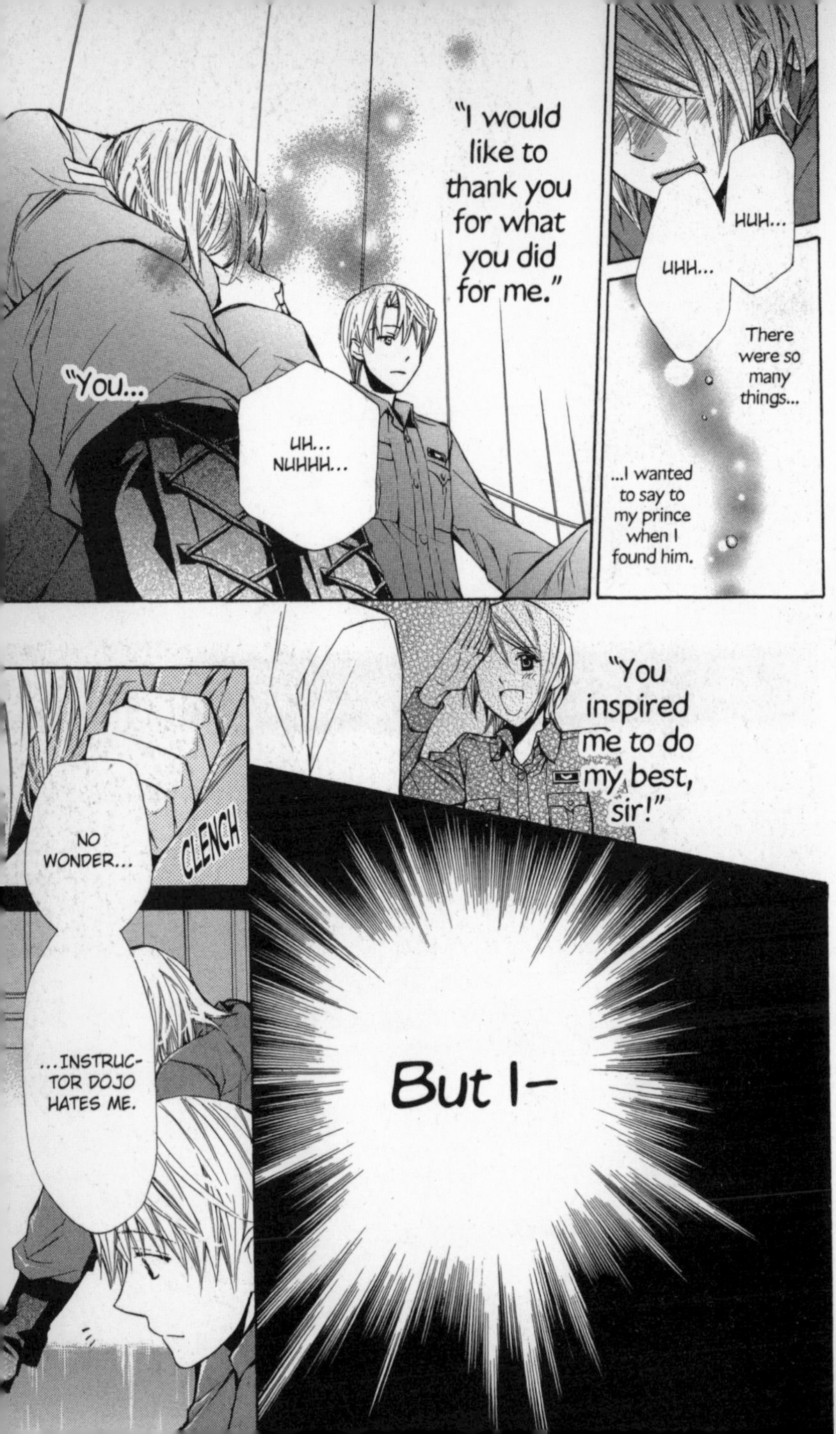
HUH...
UHH...
There were so many things...
...I wanted to say to my prince when I found him.
"I would like to thank you for what you did for me."
"You...
UH... NUHHH...
"You inspired me to do my best, sir!"
But I-
CLENCH
NO WONDER...
...INSTRUCTOR DOJO HATES ME.

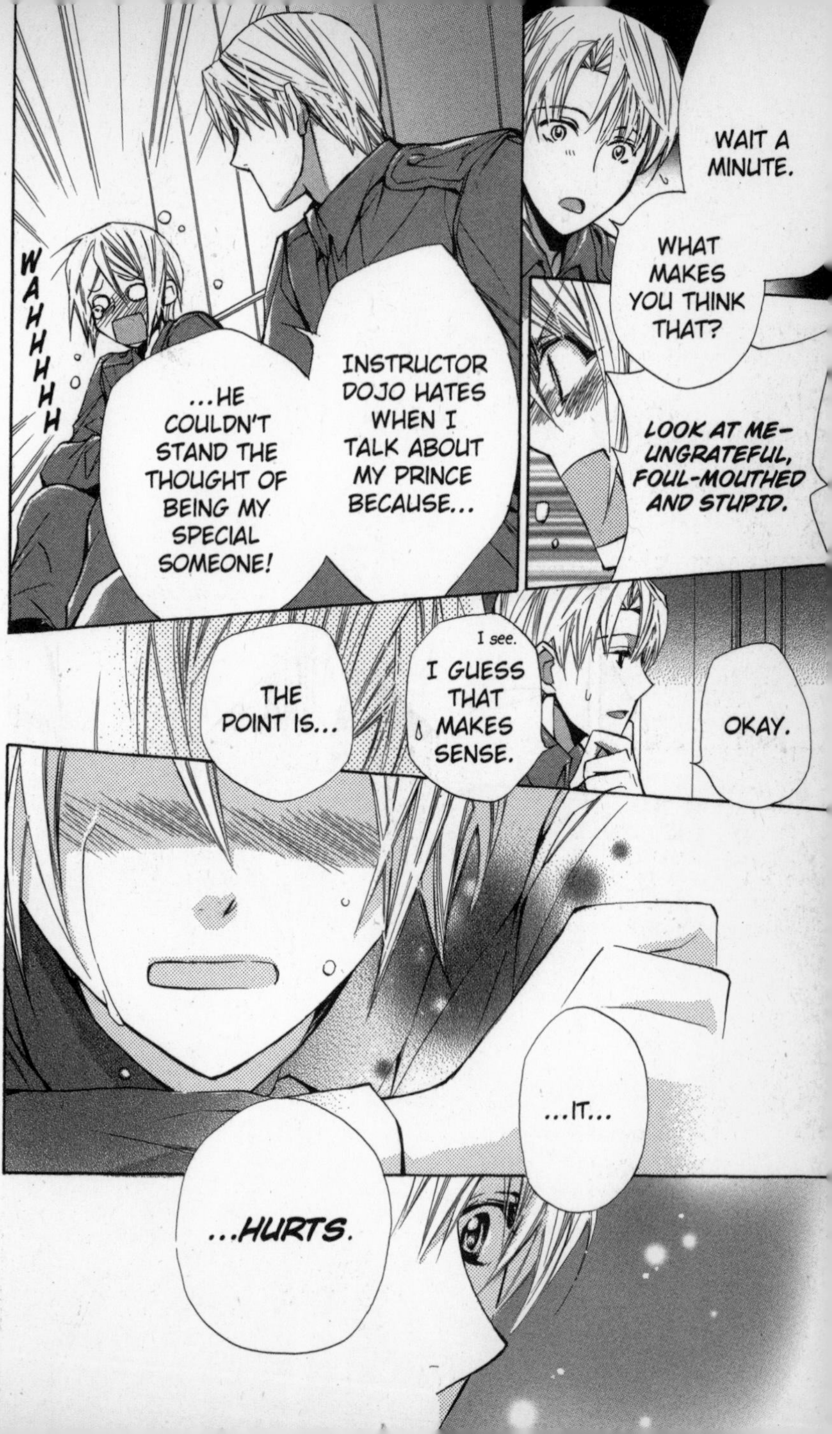
WAIT A MINUTE.
WHAT MAKES YOU THINK THAT?
LOOK AT ME—UNGRATEFUL, FOUL-MOUTHED AND STUPID.
INSTRUCTOR DOJO HATES WHEN I TALK ABOUT MY PRINCE BECAUSE...
...HE COULDN'T STAND THE THOUGHT OF BEING MY SPECIAL SOMEONE!
WAHHHHHH
OKAY.
I see.
I GUESS THAT MAKES SENSE.
THE POINT IS...
...IT...
...HURTS.

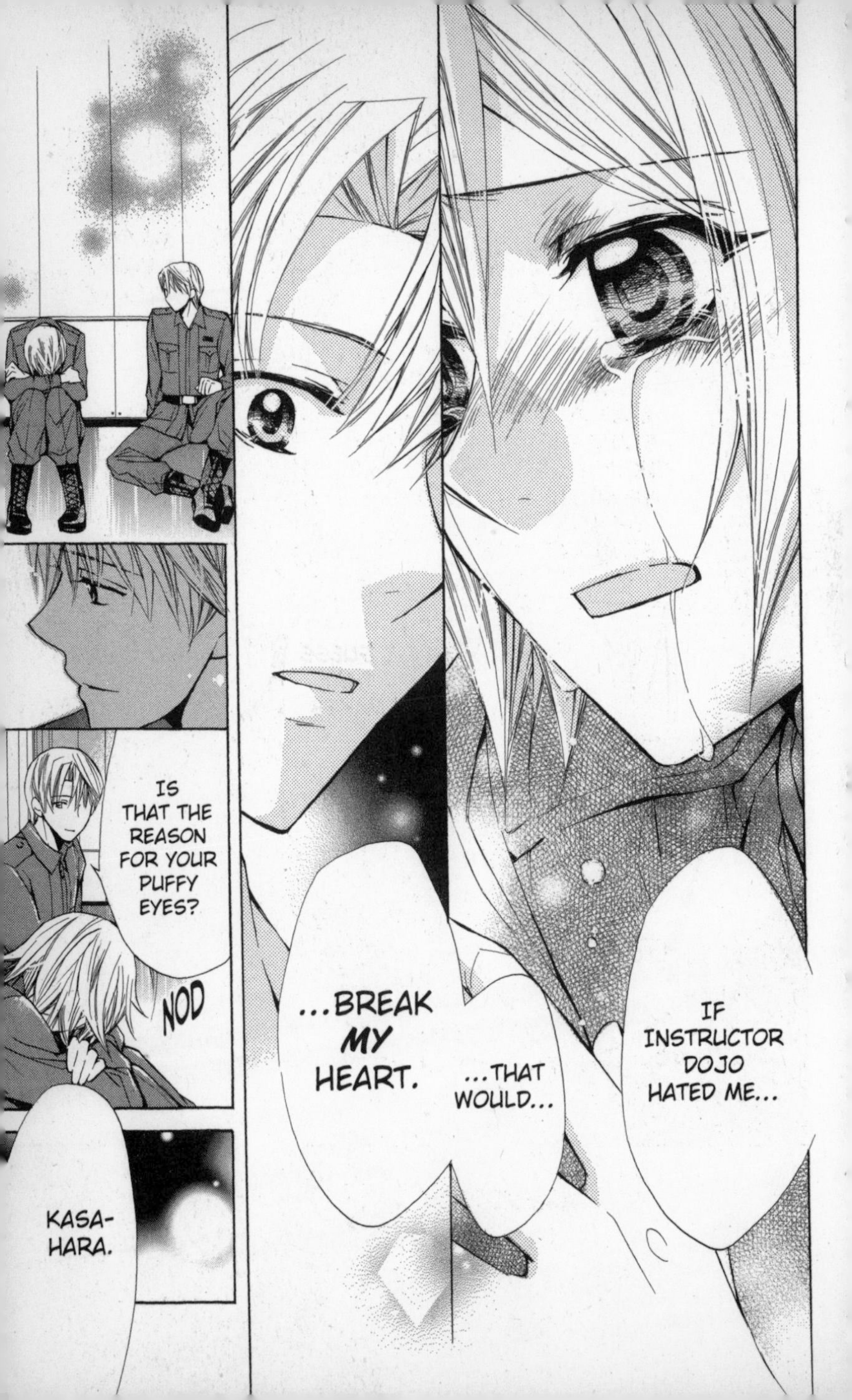
IF INSTRUCTOR DOJO HATED ME...
...THAT WOULD...
...BREAK MY HEART.
IS THAT THE REASON FOR YOUR PUFFY EYES?
NOD
KASA-HARA.

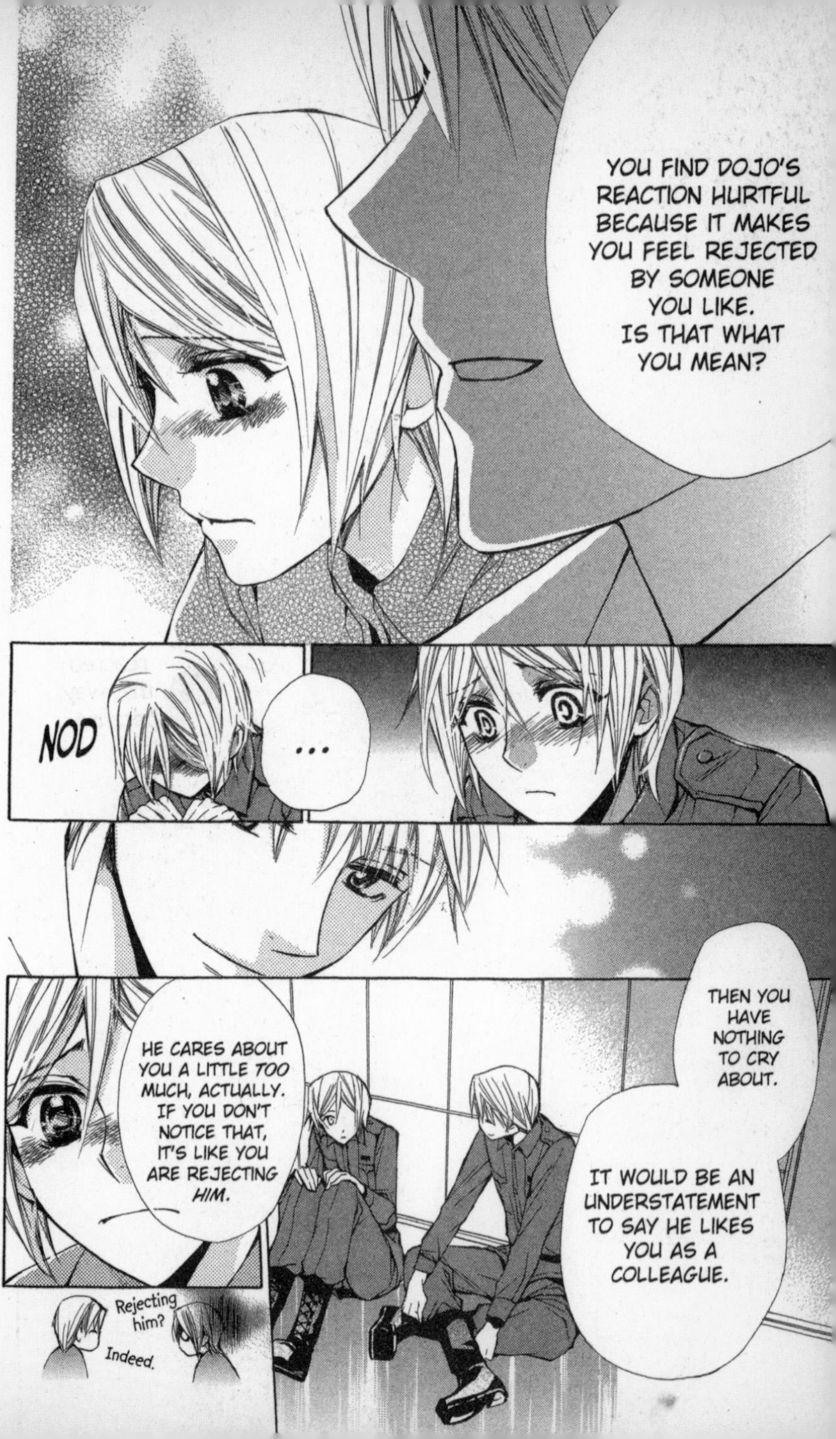
YOU FIND DOJO'S REACTION HURTFUL BECAUSE IT MAKES YOU FEEL REJECTED BY SOMEONE YOU LIKE. IS THAT WHAT YOU MEAN?
...
NOD
THEN YOU HAVE NOTHING TO CRY ABOUT.
IT WOULD BE AN UNDERSTATEMENT TO SAY HE LIKES YOU AS A COLLEAGUE.
HE CARES ABOUT YOU A LITTLE *TOO* MUCH, ACTUALLY. IF YOU DON'T NOTICE THAT, IT'S LIKE YOU ARE REJECTING *HIM*.
Rejecting him?
Indeed.

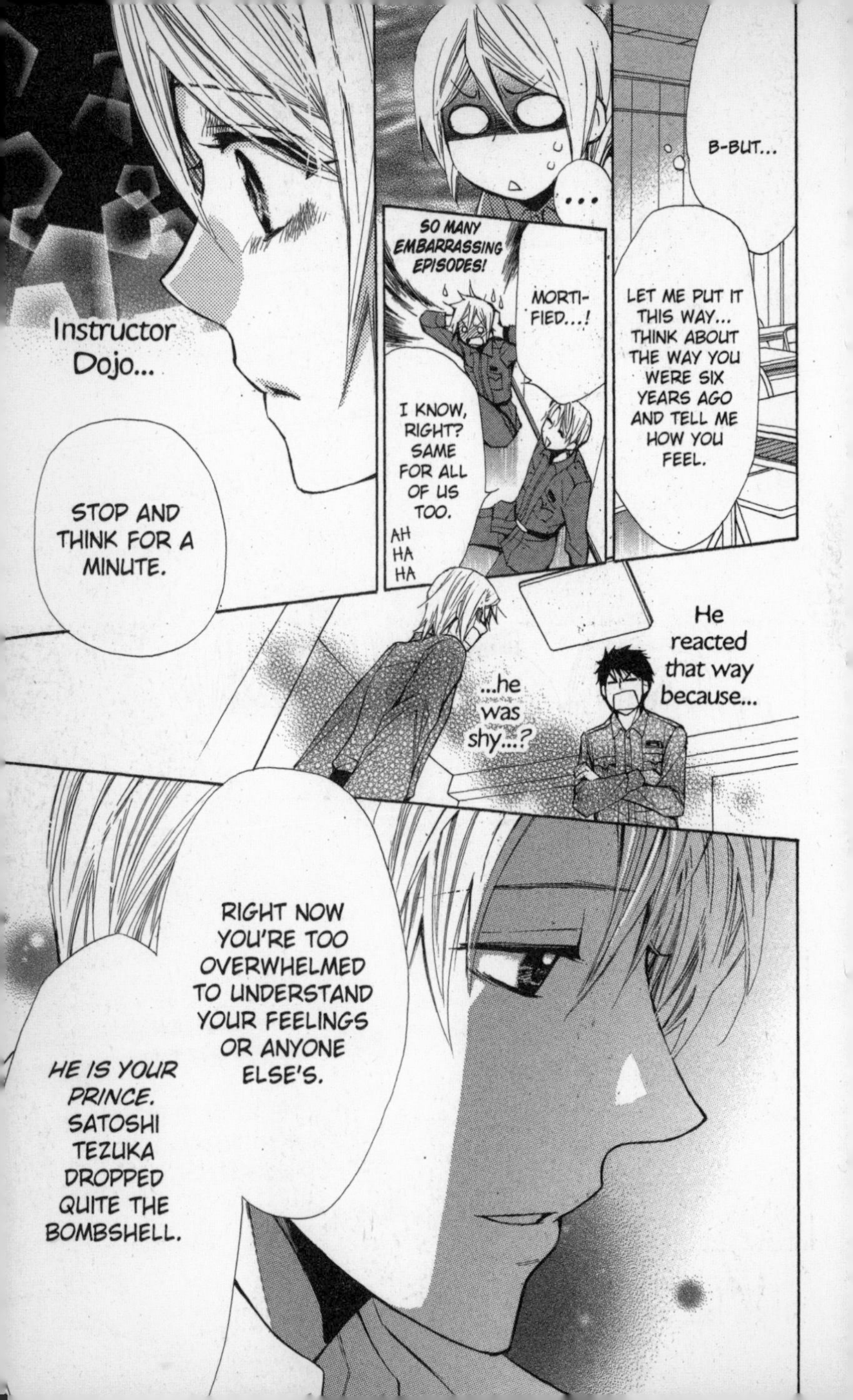
B-BUT...
LET ME PUT IT THIS WAY... THINK ABOUT THE WAY YOU WERE SIX YEARS AGO AND TELL ME HOW YOU FEEL.
...
MORTIFIED...!
SO MANY EMBARRASSING EPISODES!
I KNOW, RIGHT? SAME FOR ALL OF US TOO.
AH HA HA
Instructor Dojo...
STOP AND THINK FOR A MINUTE.
He reacted that way because...
...he was shy...?
RIGHT NOW YOU'RE TOO OVERWHELMED TO UNDERSTAND YOUR FEELINGS OR ANYONE ELSE'S.
HE IS YOUR PRINCE. SATOSHI TEZUKA DROPPED QUITE THE BOMBSHELL.

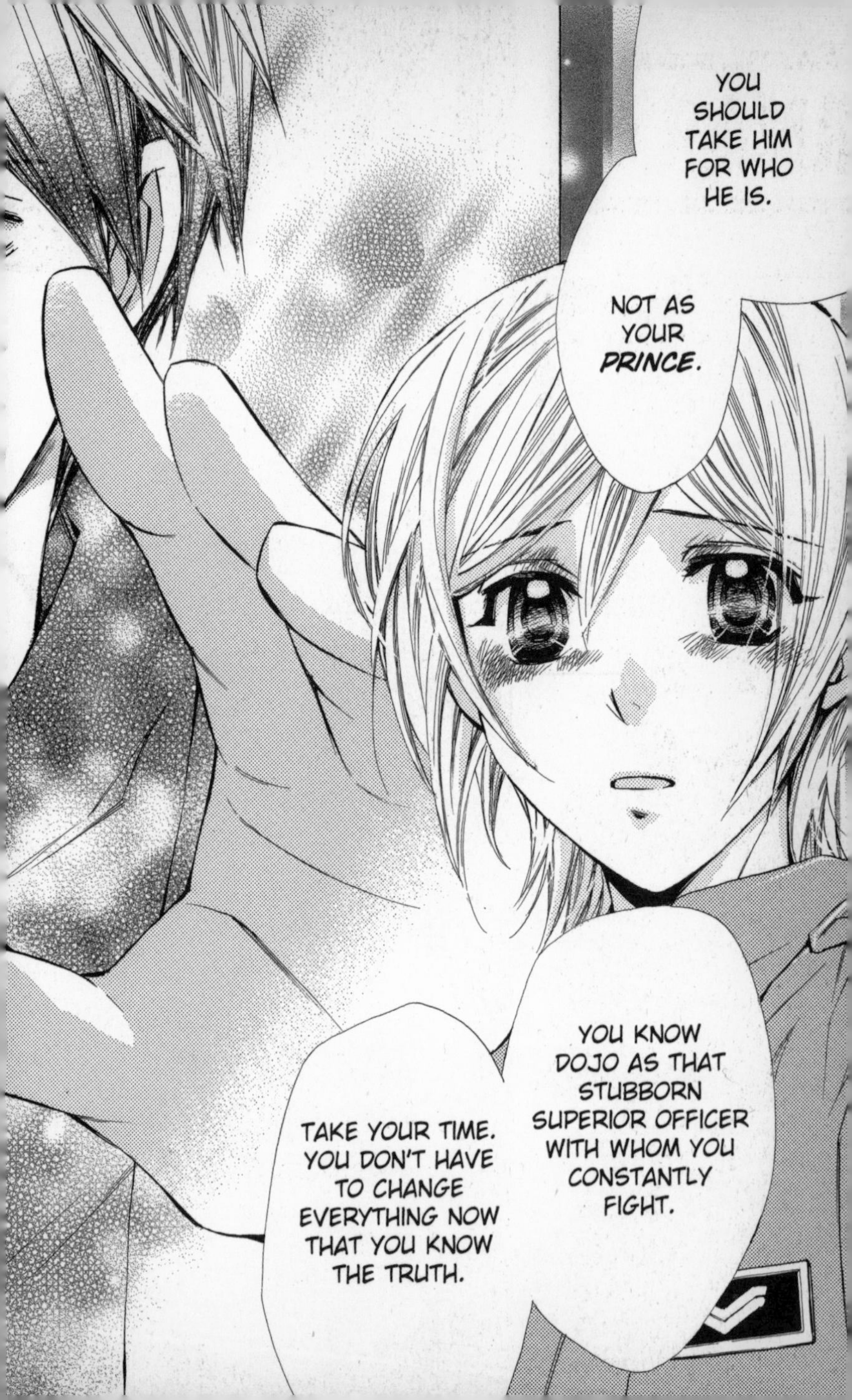
YOU SHOULD TAKE HIM FOR WHO HE IS.
NOT AS YOUR *PRINCE*.
YOU KNOW DOJO AS THAT STUBBORN SUPERIOR OFFICER WITH WHOM YOU CONSTANTLY FIGHT.
TAKE YOUR TIME. YOU DON'T HAVE TO CHANGE EVERYTHING NOW THAT YOU KNOW THE TRUTH.

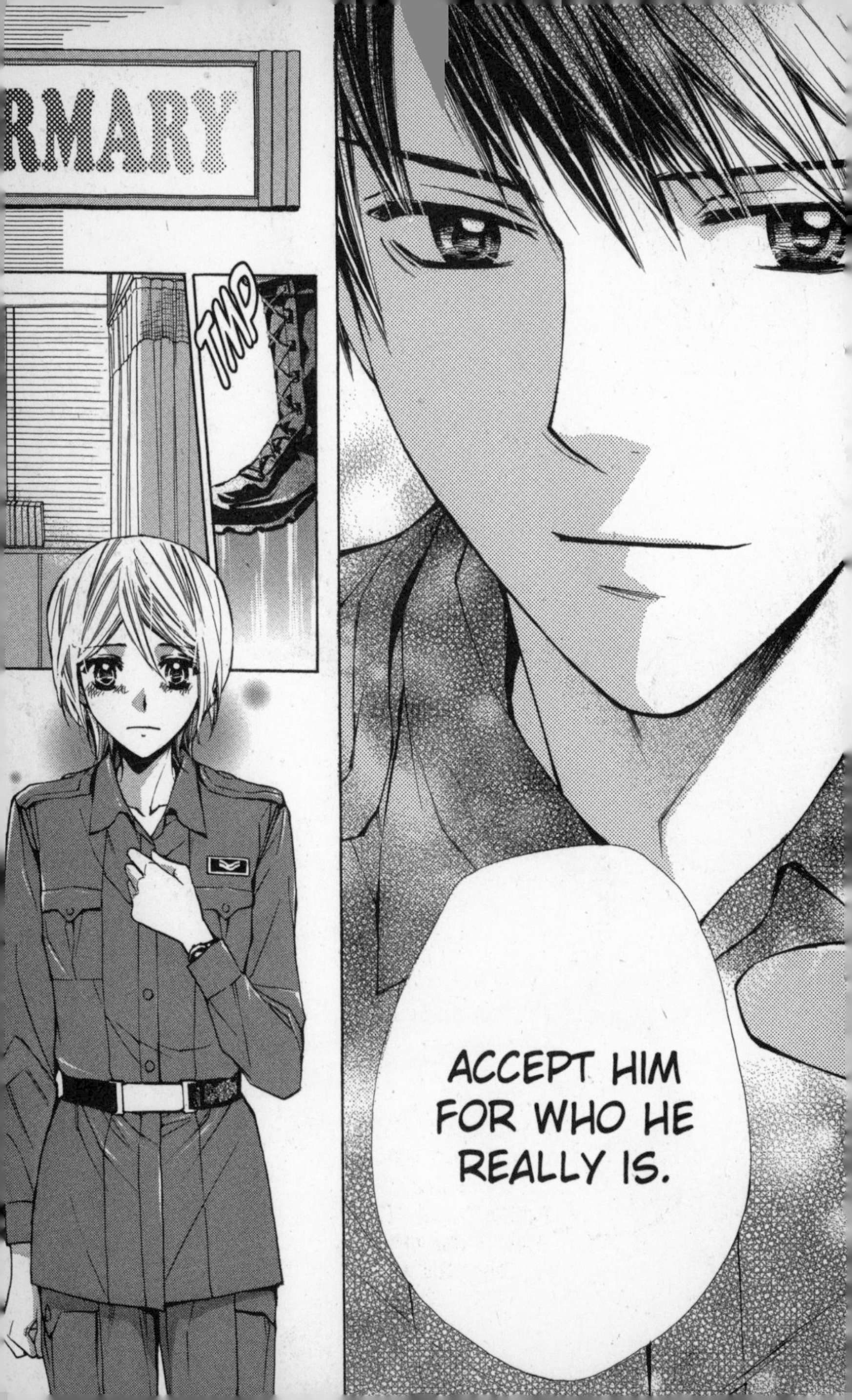
ACCEPT HIM FOR WHO HE REALLY IS.
RMARY
TMP

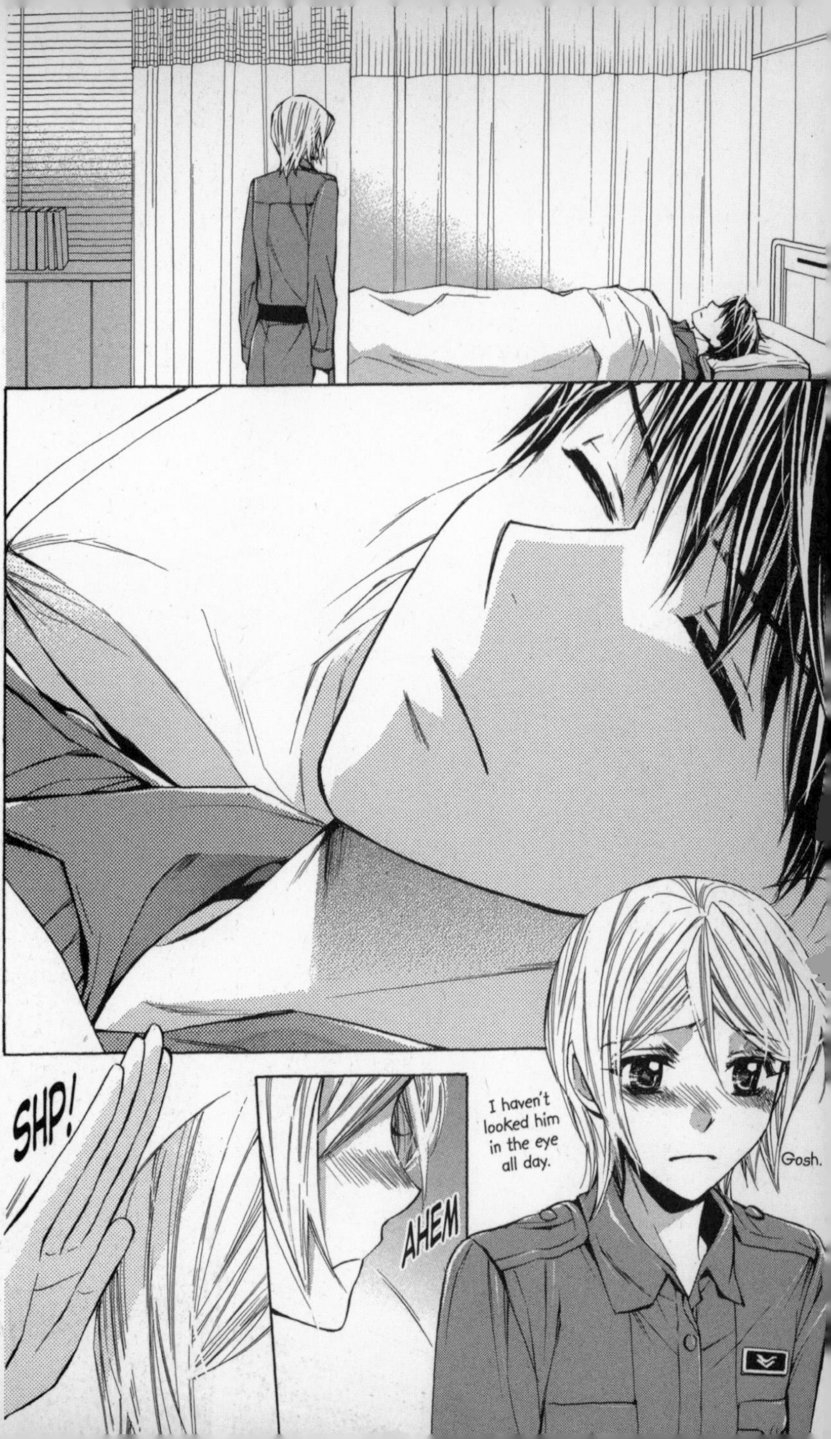
Gosh.
I haven't looked him in the eye all day.
AHEM
SHP!

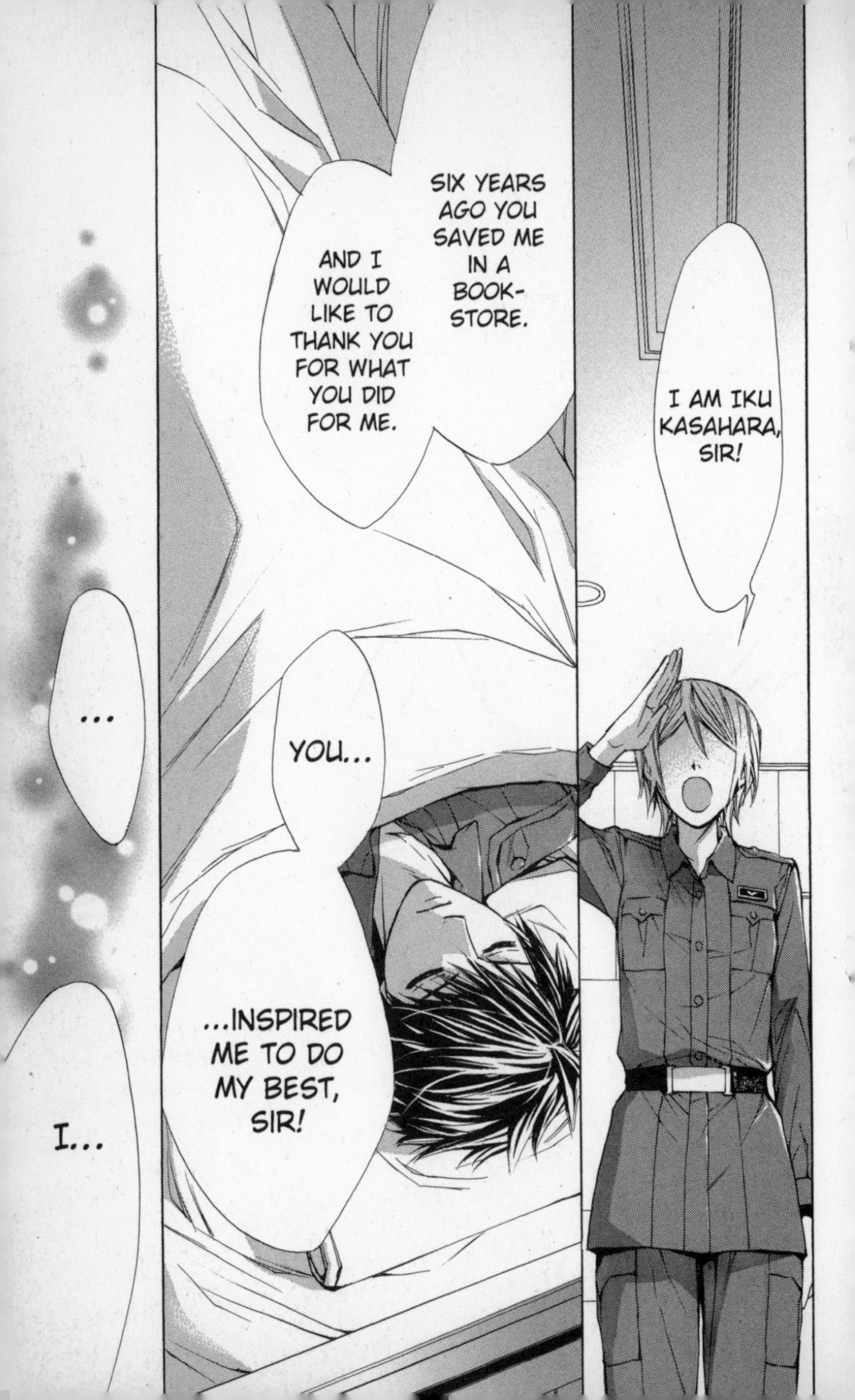
I AM IKU KASAHARA, SIR!
SIX YEARS AGO YOU SAVED ME IN A BOOK-STORE.
AND I WOULD LIKE TO THANK YOU FOR WHAT YOU DID FOR ME.
YOU...
...INSPIRED ME TO DO MY BEST, SIR!
...
I...

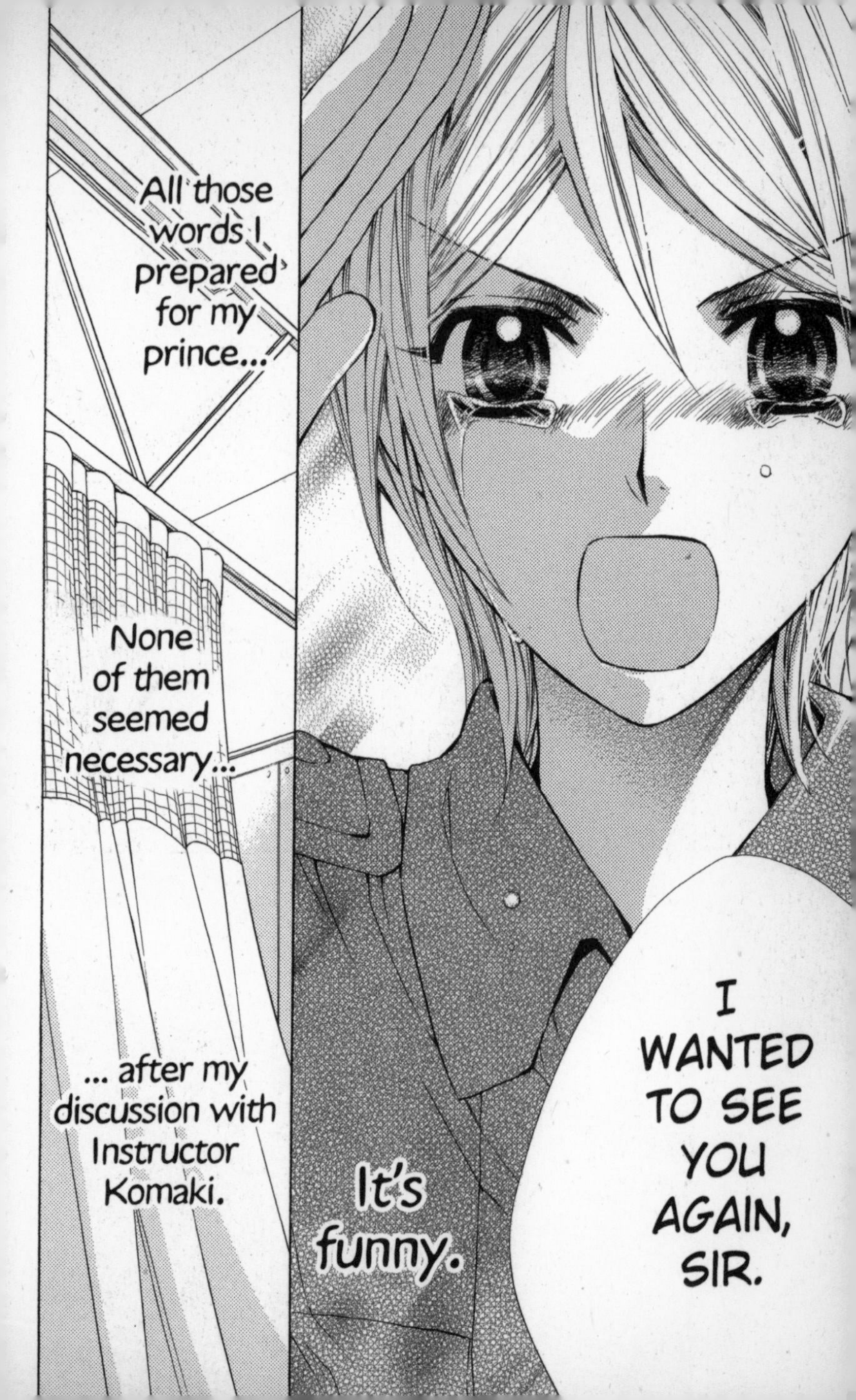
I WANTED TO SEE YOU AGAIN, SIR.
It's funny.
All those words I prepared for my prince...
None of them seemed necessary...
... after my discussion with Instructor Komaki.

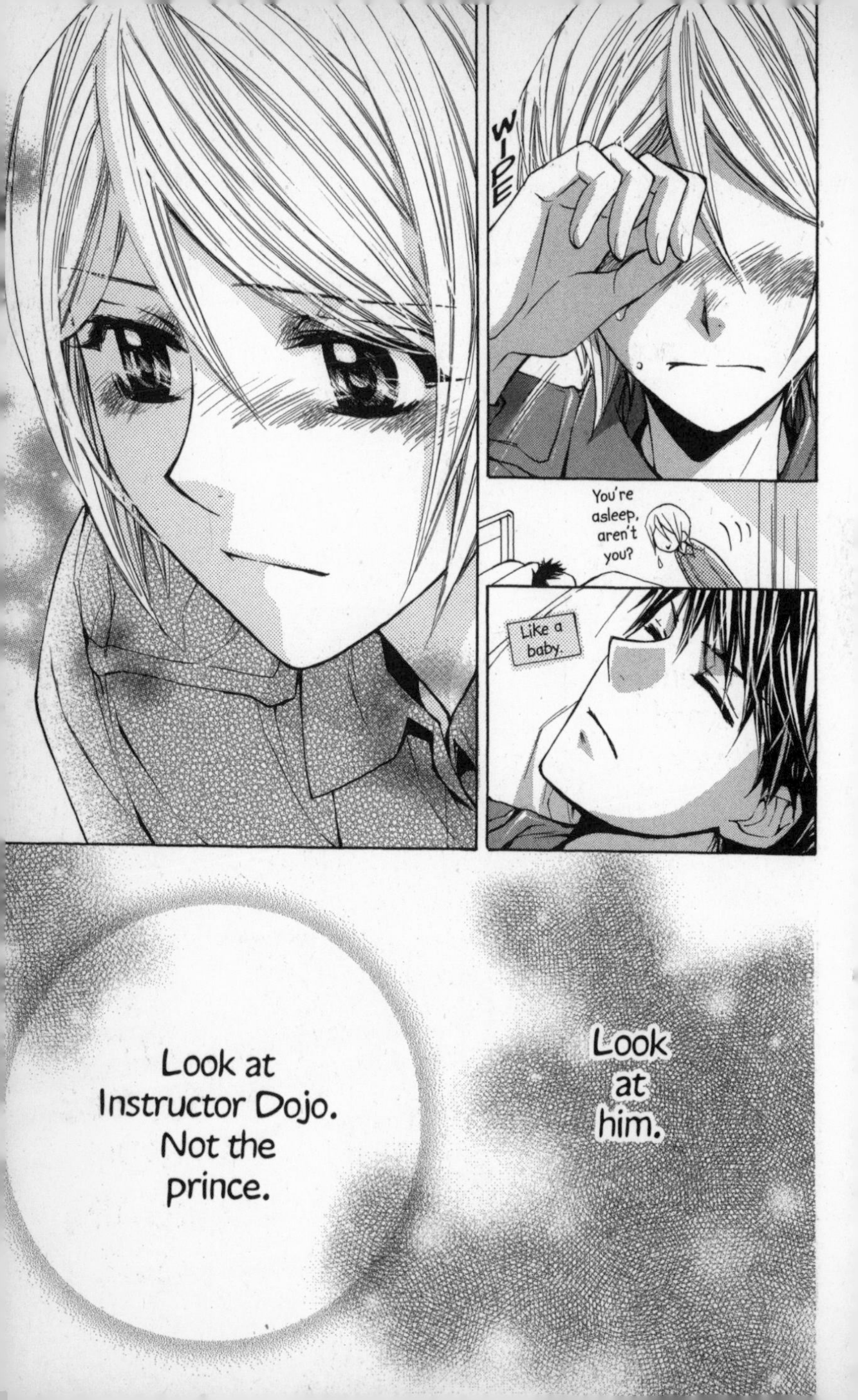
WIPE
You're asleep, aren't you?
Like a baby.
Look at him.
Look at Instructor Dojo. Not the prince.

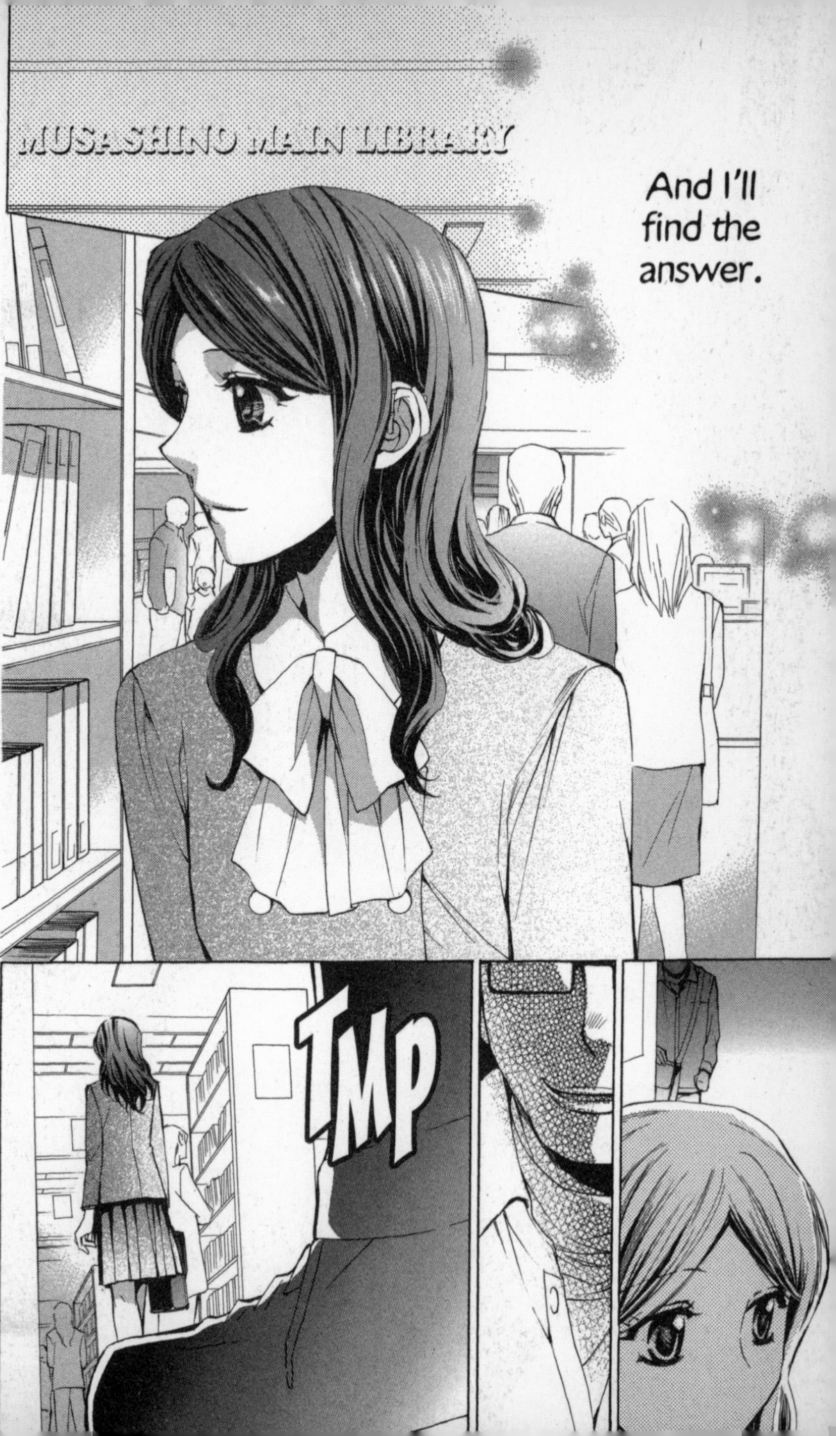
MUSASHINO MAIN LIBRARY
And I'll find the answer.
TMP

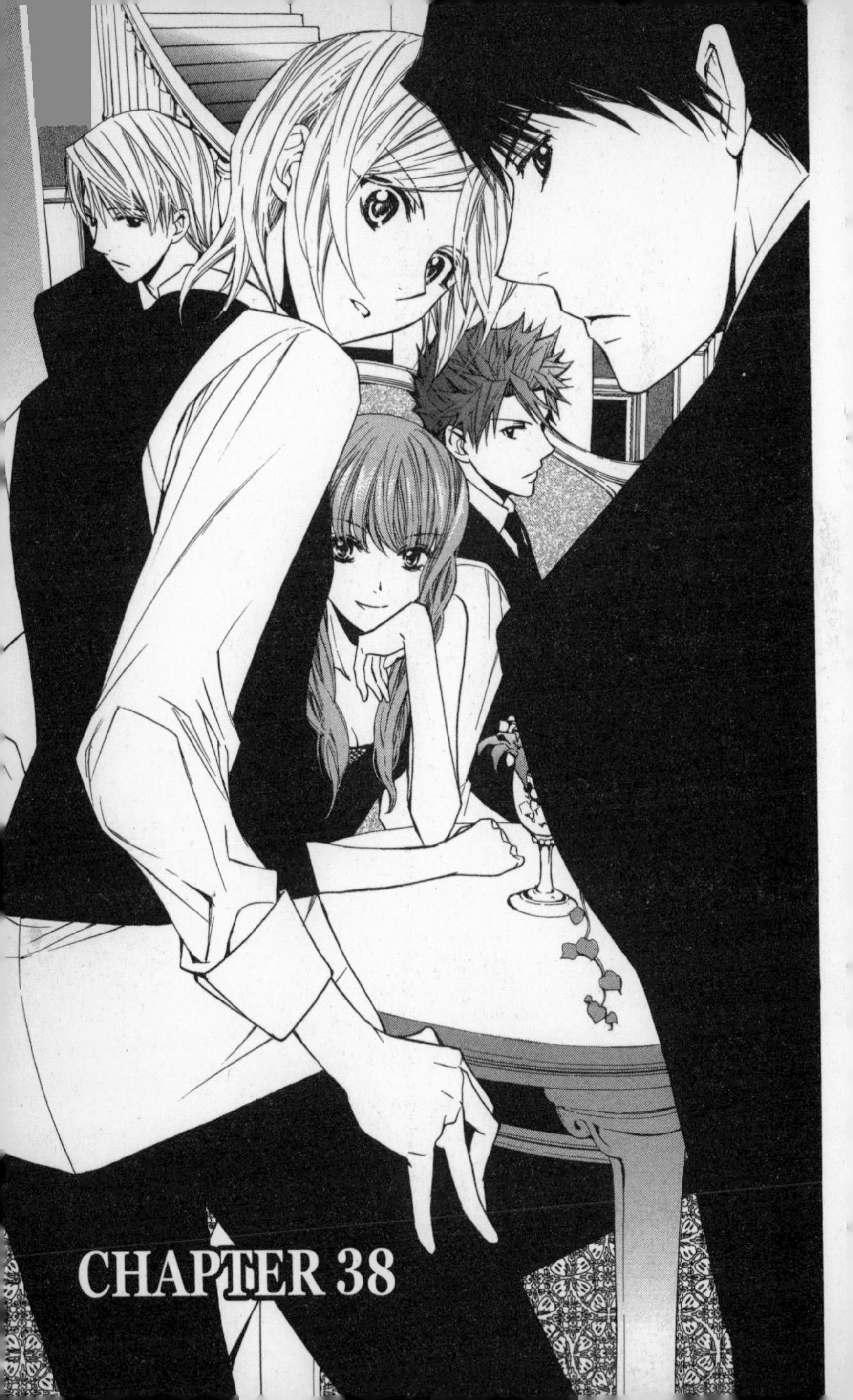
CHAPTER 38

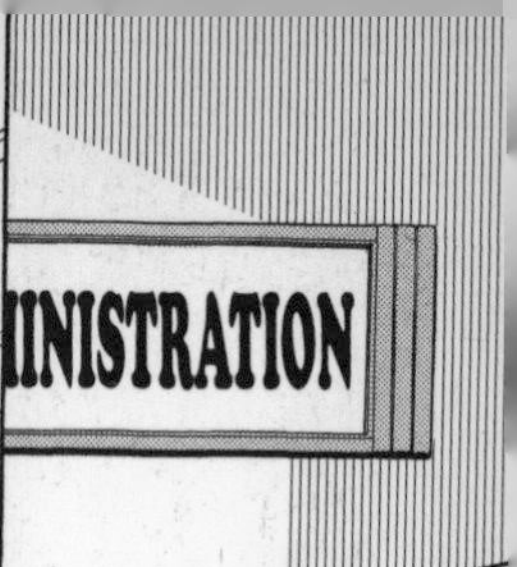
INISTRATION

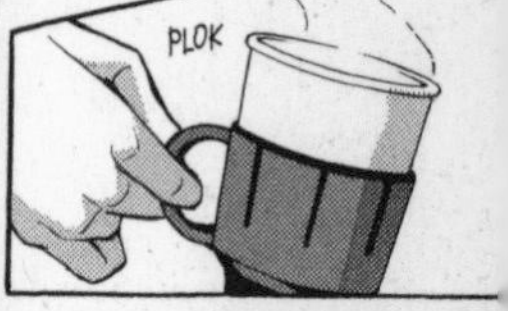
PLOK

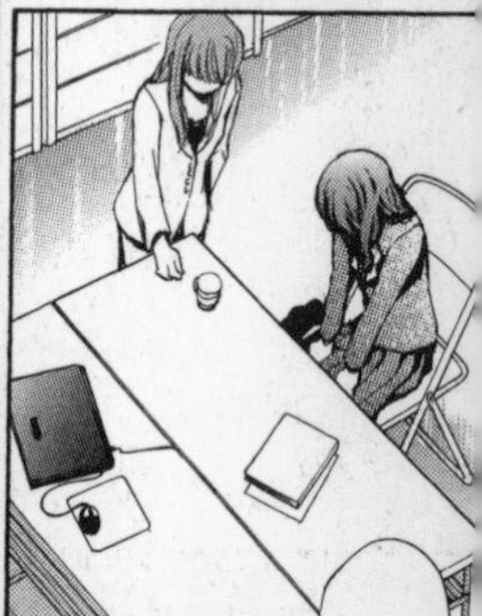

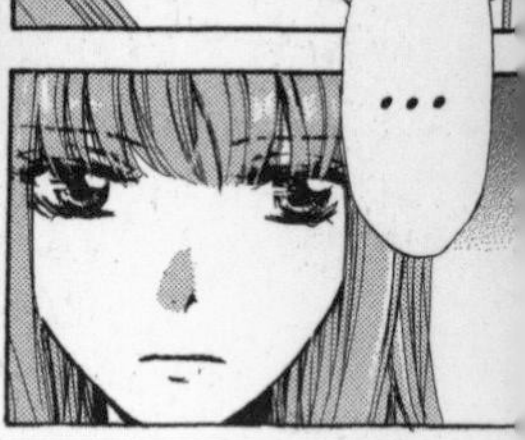
...

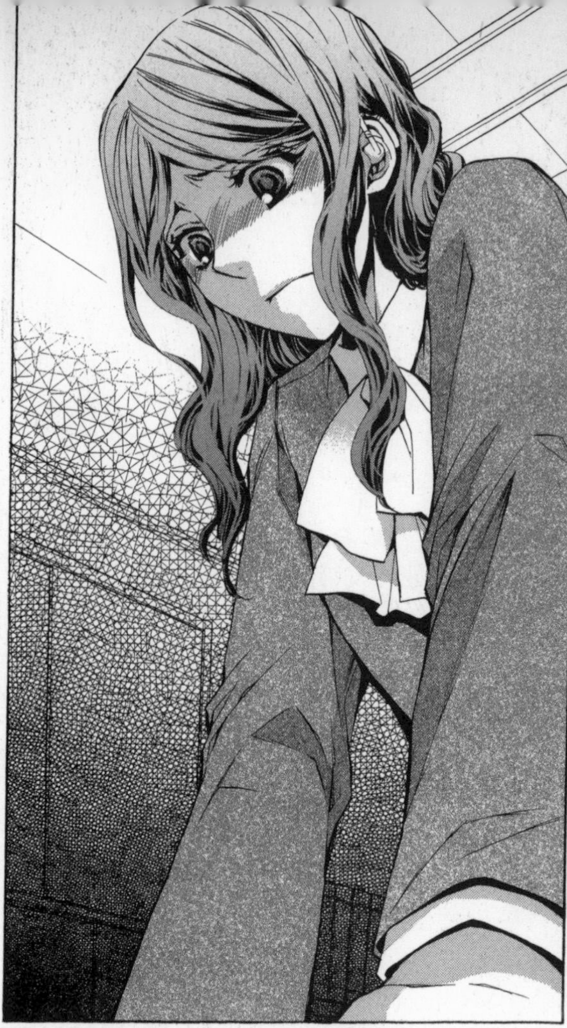

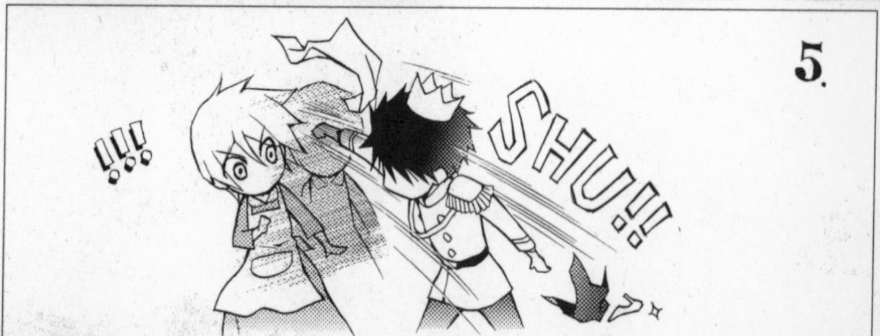
5.
SHU!!
!!!

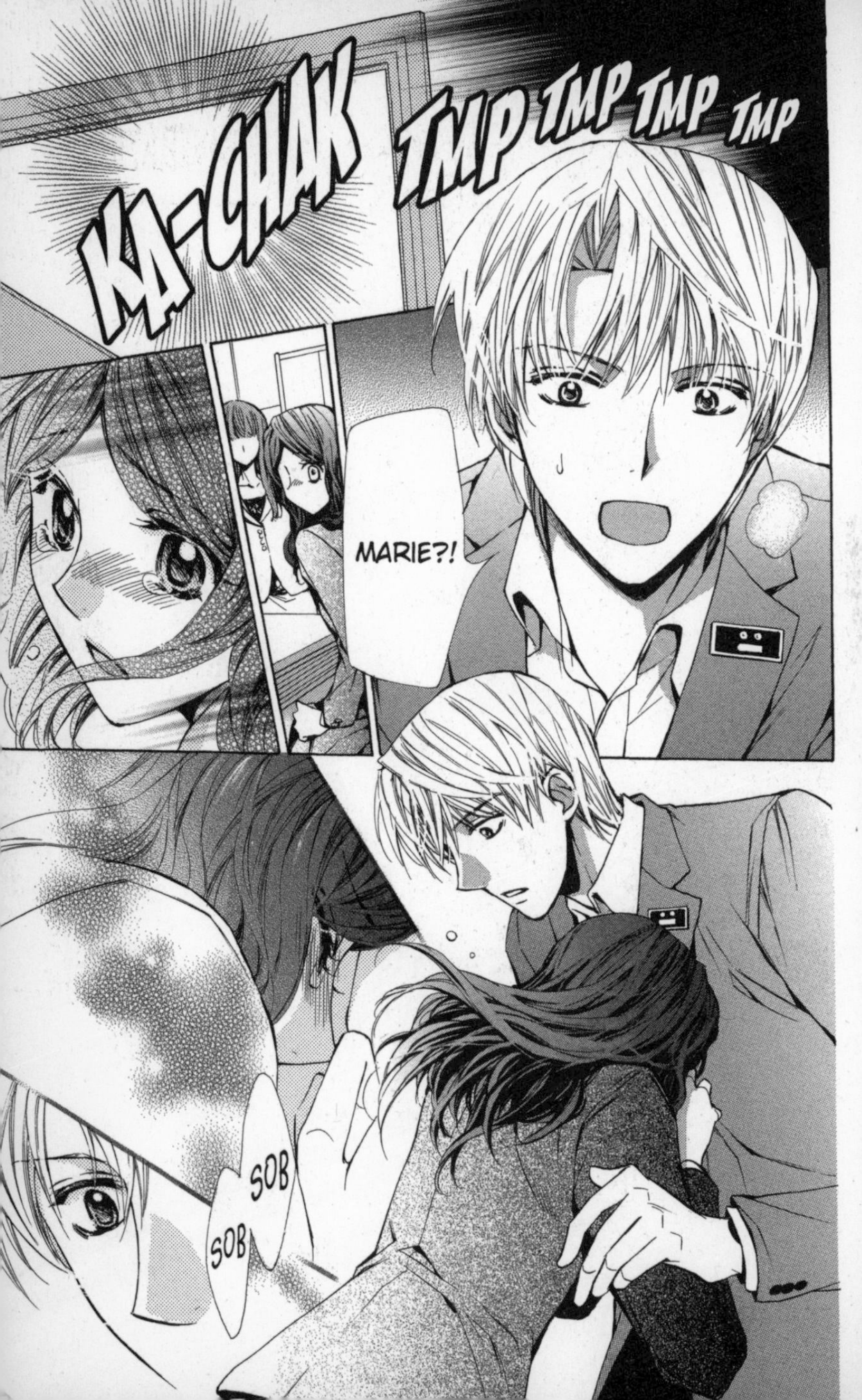
KA-CHAK
TMP TMP TMP TMP TMP
MARIE?!
SOB
SOB

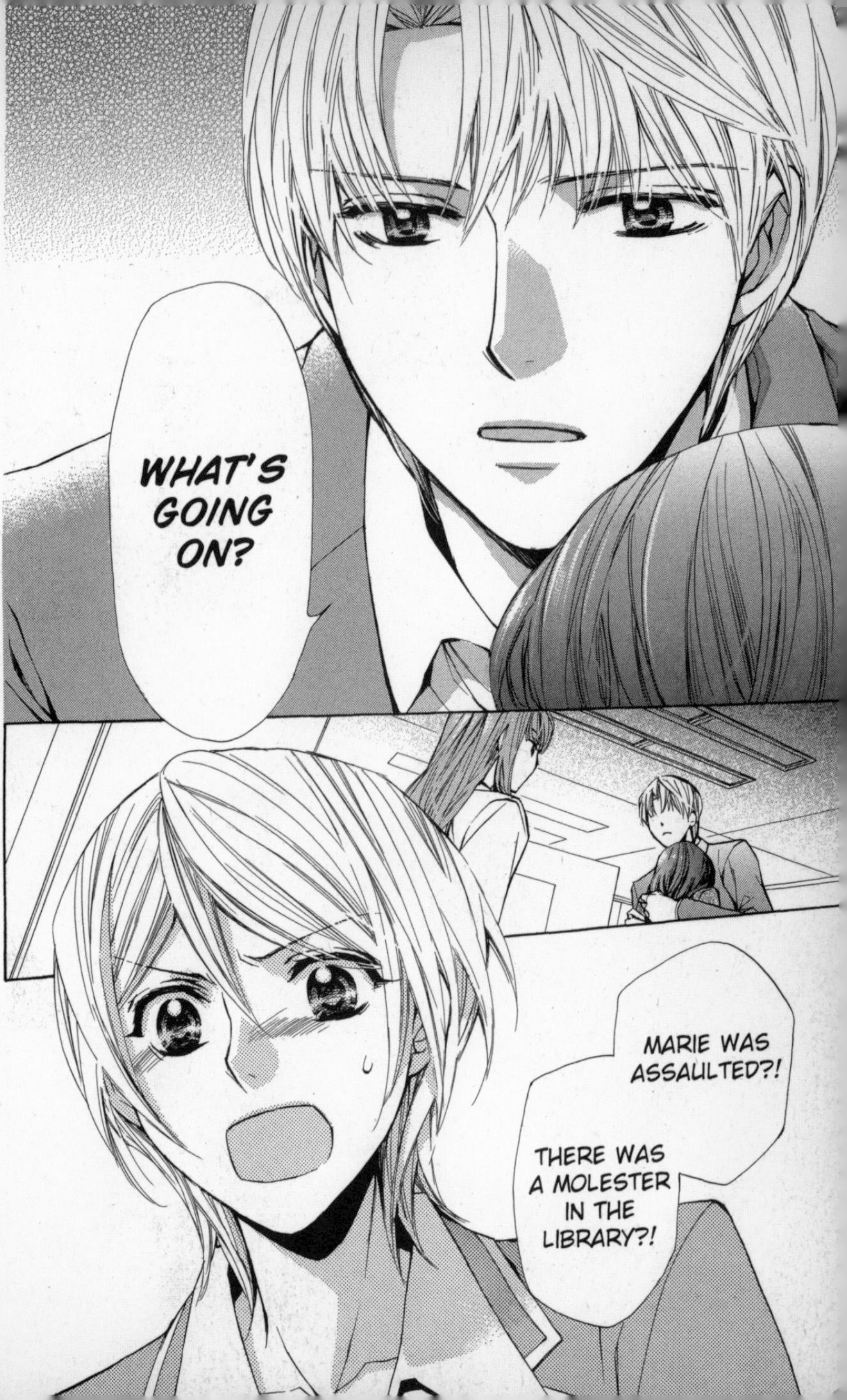
WHAT'S GOING ON?
MARIE WAS ASSAULTED?!
THERE WAS A MOLESTER IN THE LIBRARY?!

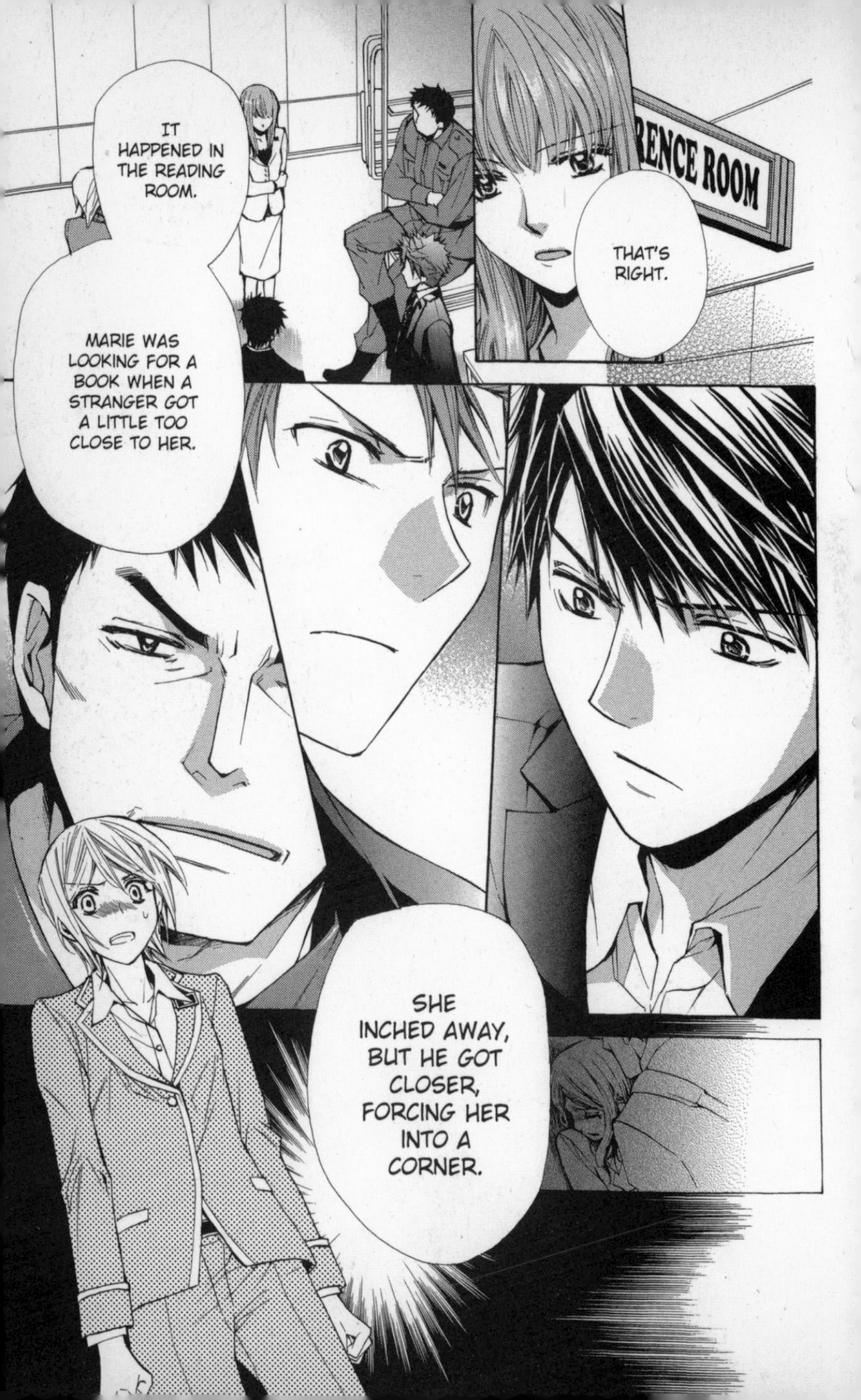
RENCE ROOM
THAT'S RIGHT.
IT HAPPENED IN THE READING ROOM.
MARIE WAS LOOKING FOR A BOOK WHEN A STRANGER GOT A LITTLE TOO CLOSE TO HER.
SHE INCHED AWAY, BUT HE GOT CLOSER, FORCING HER INTO A CORNER.

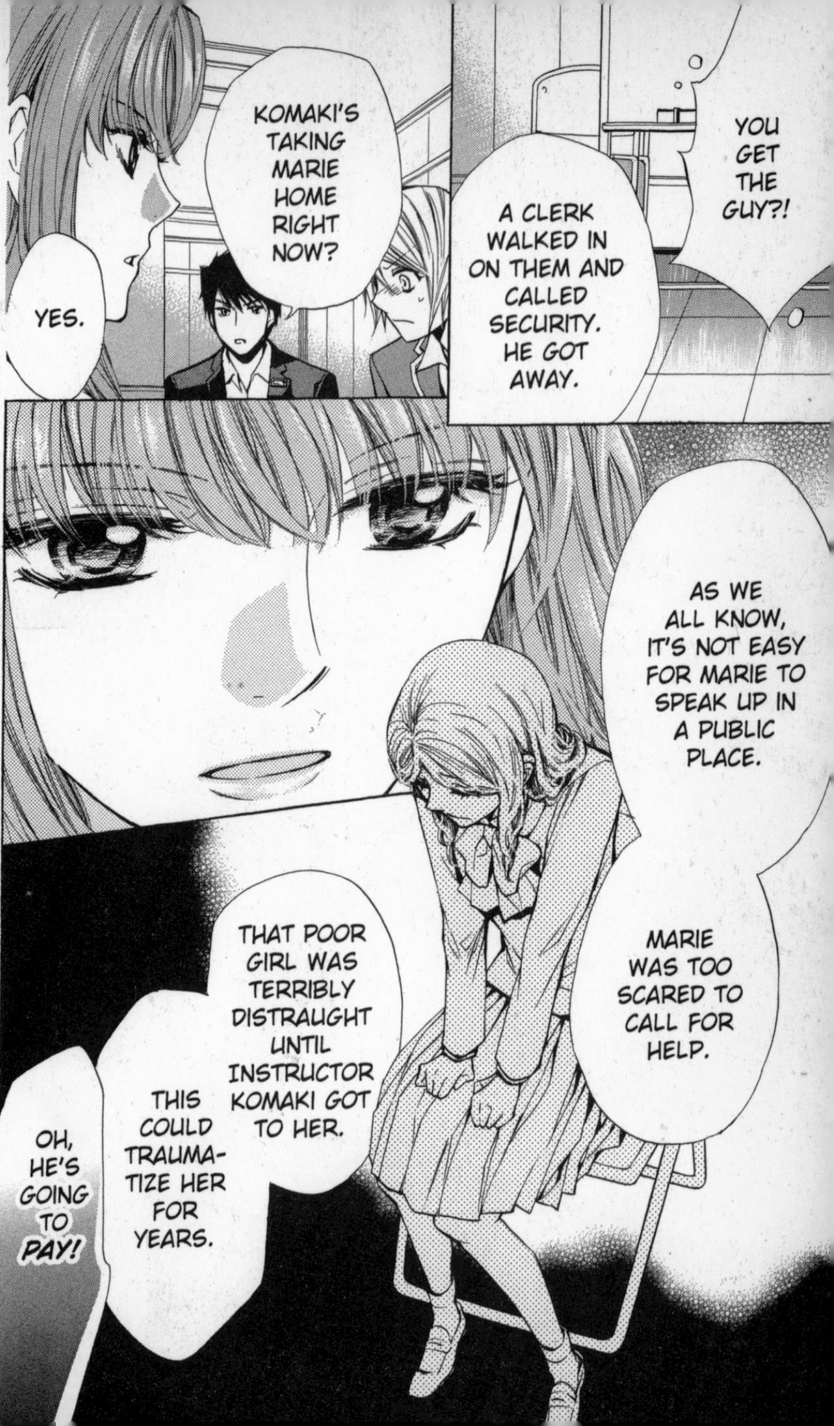
YOU GET THE GUY?!
A CLERK WALKED IN ON THEM AND CALLED SECURITY. HE GOT AWAY.
KOMAKI'S TAKING MARIE HOME RIGHT NOW?
YES.
AS WE ALL KNOW, IT'S NOT EASY FOR MARIE TO SPEAK UP IN A PUBLIC PLACE.
MARIE WAS TOO SCARED TO CALL FOR HELP.
THAT POOR GIRL WAS TERRIBLY DISTRAUGHT UNTIL INSTRUCTOR KOMAKI GOT TO HER.
THIS COULD TRAUMA-TIZE HER FOR YEARS.
OH, HE'S GOING TO *PAY!*

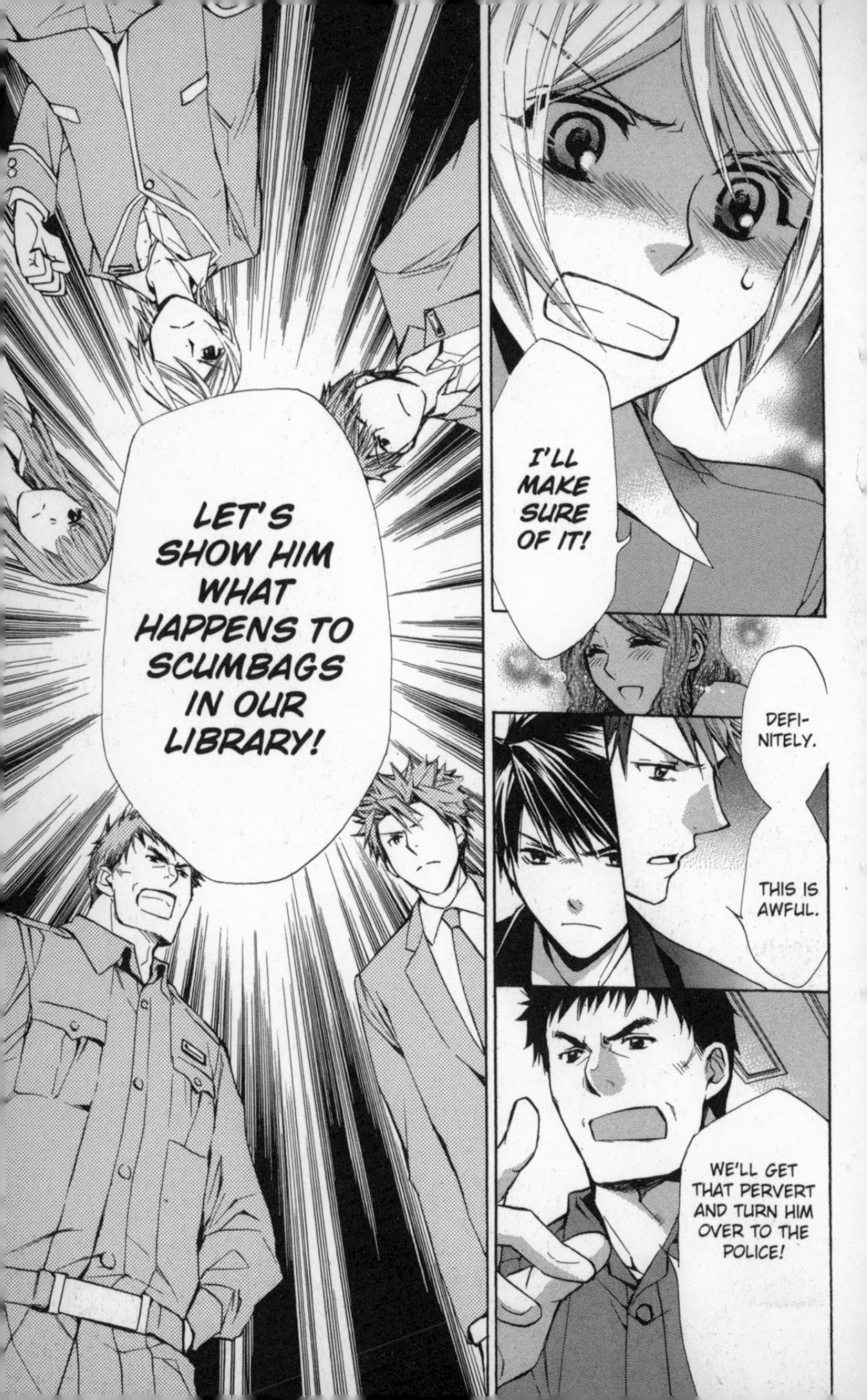
I'LL MAKE SURE OF IT!
DEFI-NITELY.
THIS IS AWFUL.
WE'LL GET THAT PERVERT AND TURN HIM OVER TO THE POLICE!
LET'S SHOW HIM WHAT HAPPENS TO SCUMBAGS IN OUR LIBRARY!

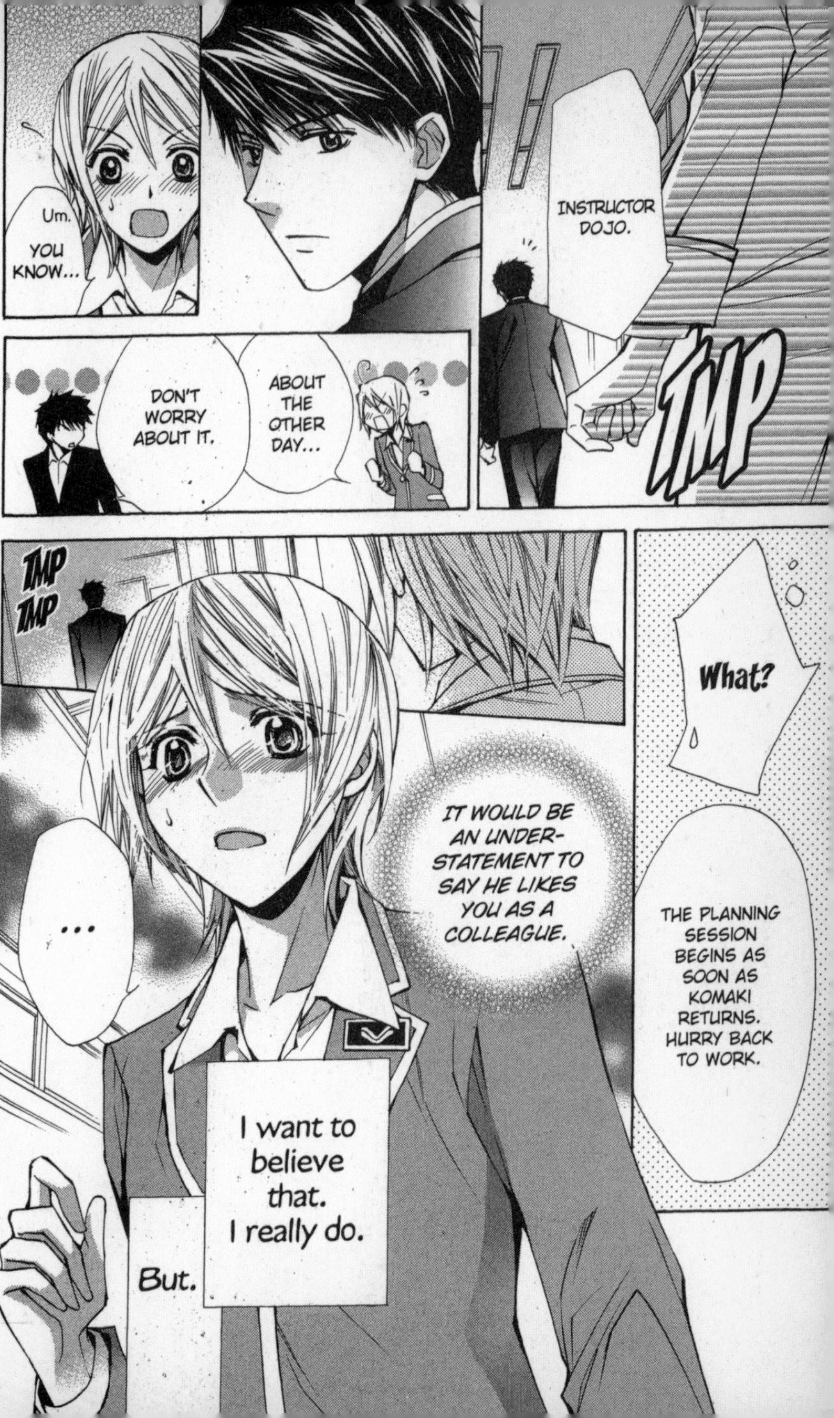
INSTRUCTOR DOJO.
TMP
Um.
YOU KNOW...
ABOUT THE OTHER DAY...
DON'T WORRY ABOUT IT.
What?
THE PLANNING SESSION BEGINS AS SOON AS KOMAKI RETURNS. HURRY BACK TO WORK.
TMP TMP
IT WOULD BE AN UNDER-STATEMENT TO SAY HE LIKES YOU AS A COLLEAGUE.
...
I want to believe that. I really do.
But.

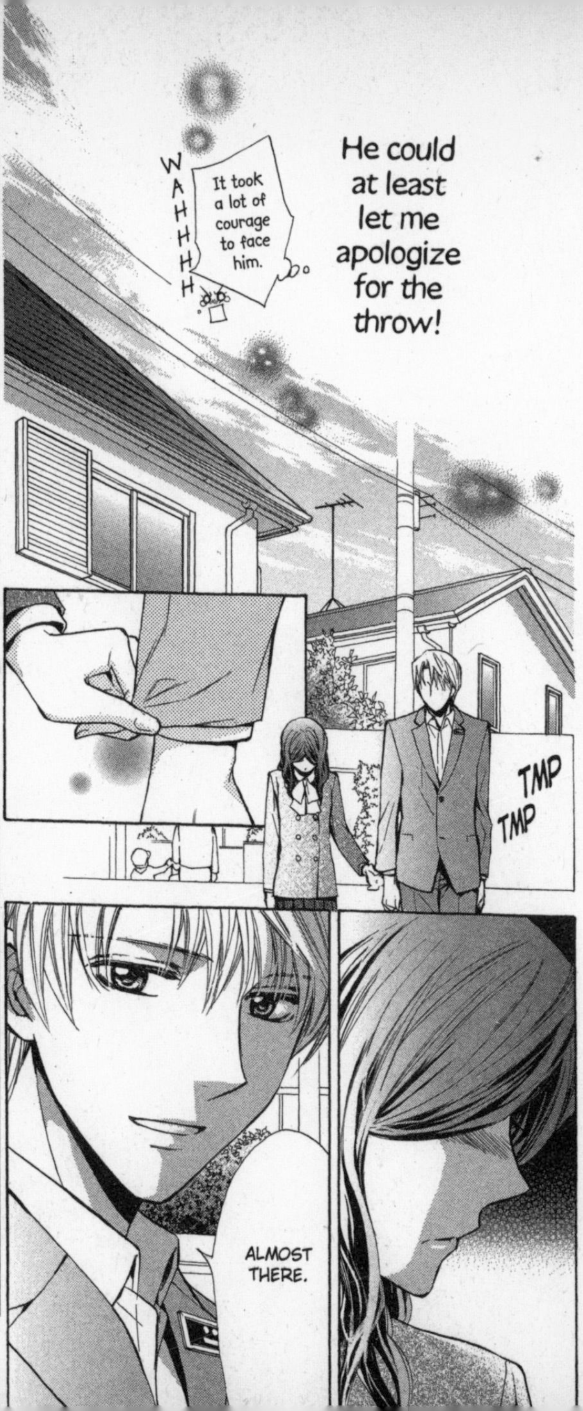
He could at least let me apologize for the throw!
It took a lot of courage to face him.
WAHHHHH
TMP TMP
ALMOST THERE.

5

*

In this volume, Iku finds out her prince's true identity. I'm glad I was able to write it. This afforded me so many more opportunities to make Iku jitter. That's fun (smile).

I wouldn't have made it this far without your support.

I'm so happy. Thank you!

A lot of you seem to enjoy the romantic atmosphere between characters.

I'm going to give you a bunch more romance.

Enjoy the jittery Iku!

*

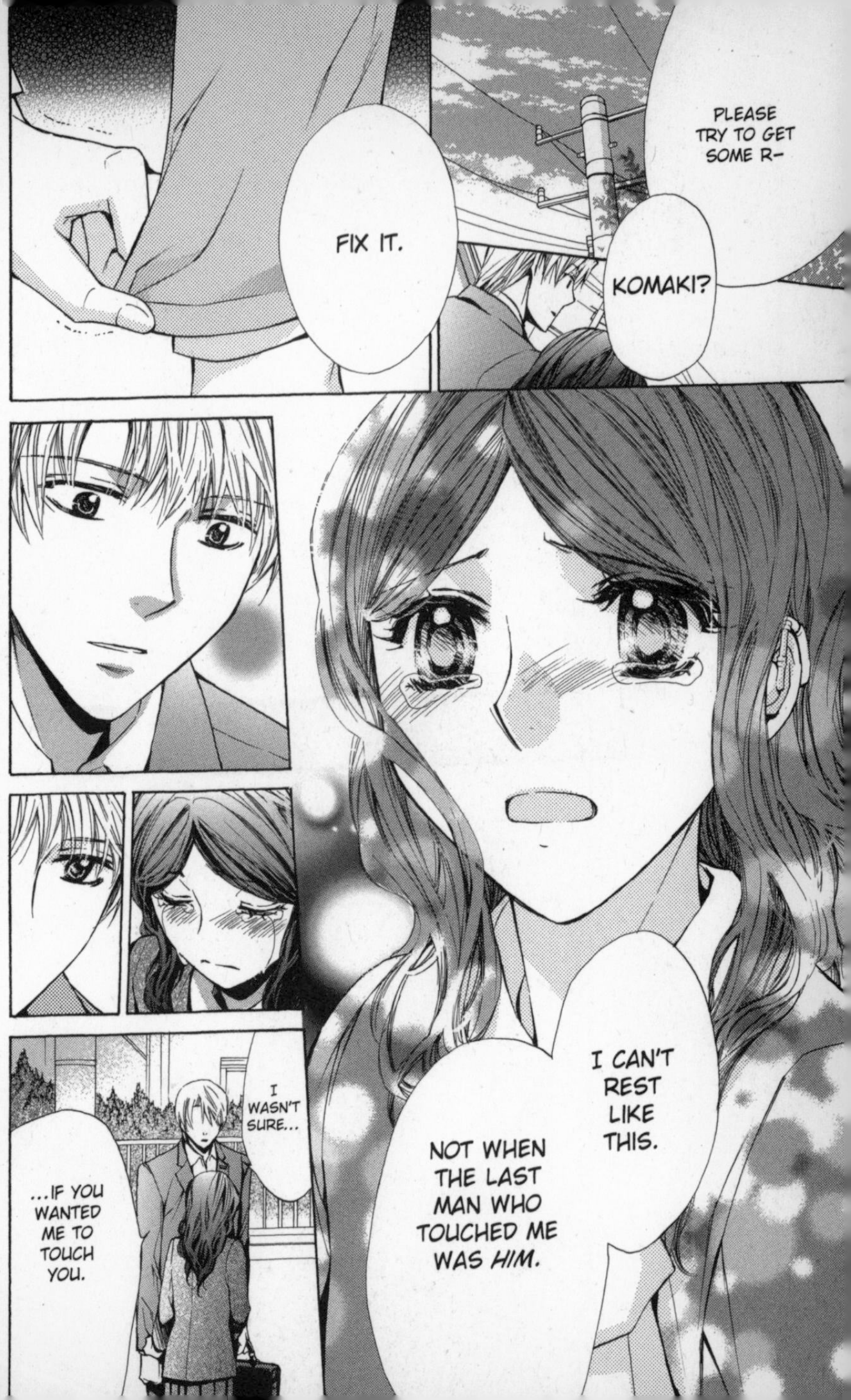
PLEASE TRY TO GET SOME R–
KOMAKI?
FIX IT.
I CAN'T REST LIKE THIS.
NOT WHEN THE LAST MAN WHO TOUCHED ME WAS *HIM*.
I WASN'T SURE...
...IF YOU WANTED ME TO TOUCH YOU.

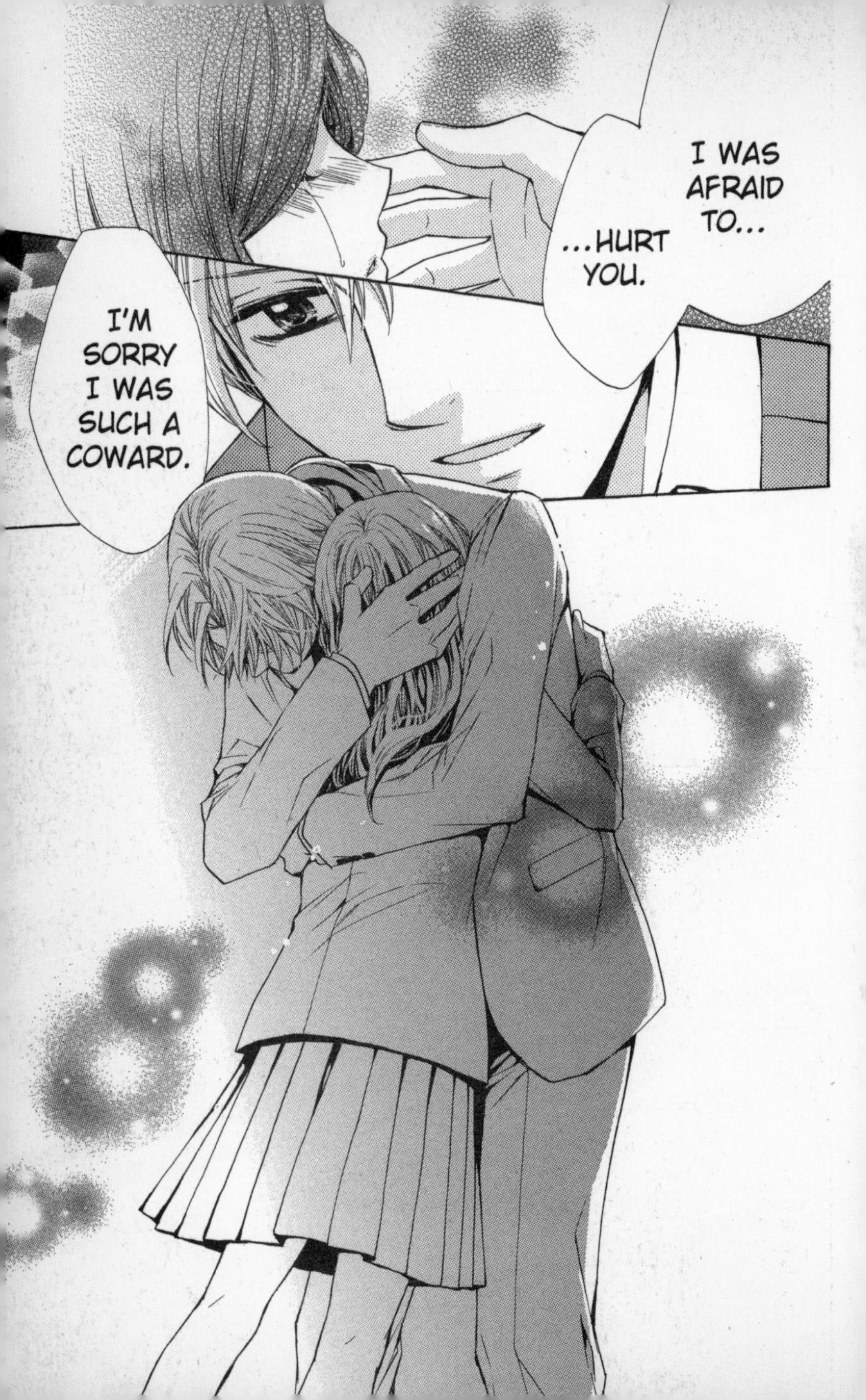
I WAS AFRAID TO...
...HURT YOU.
I'M SORRY I WAS SUCH A COWARD.

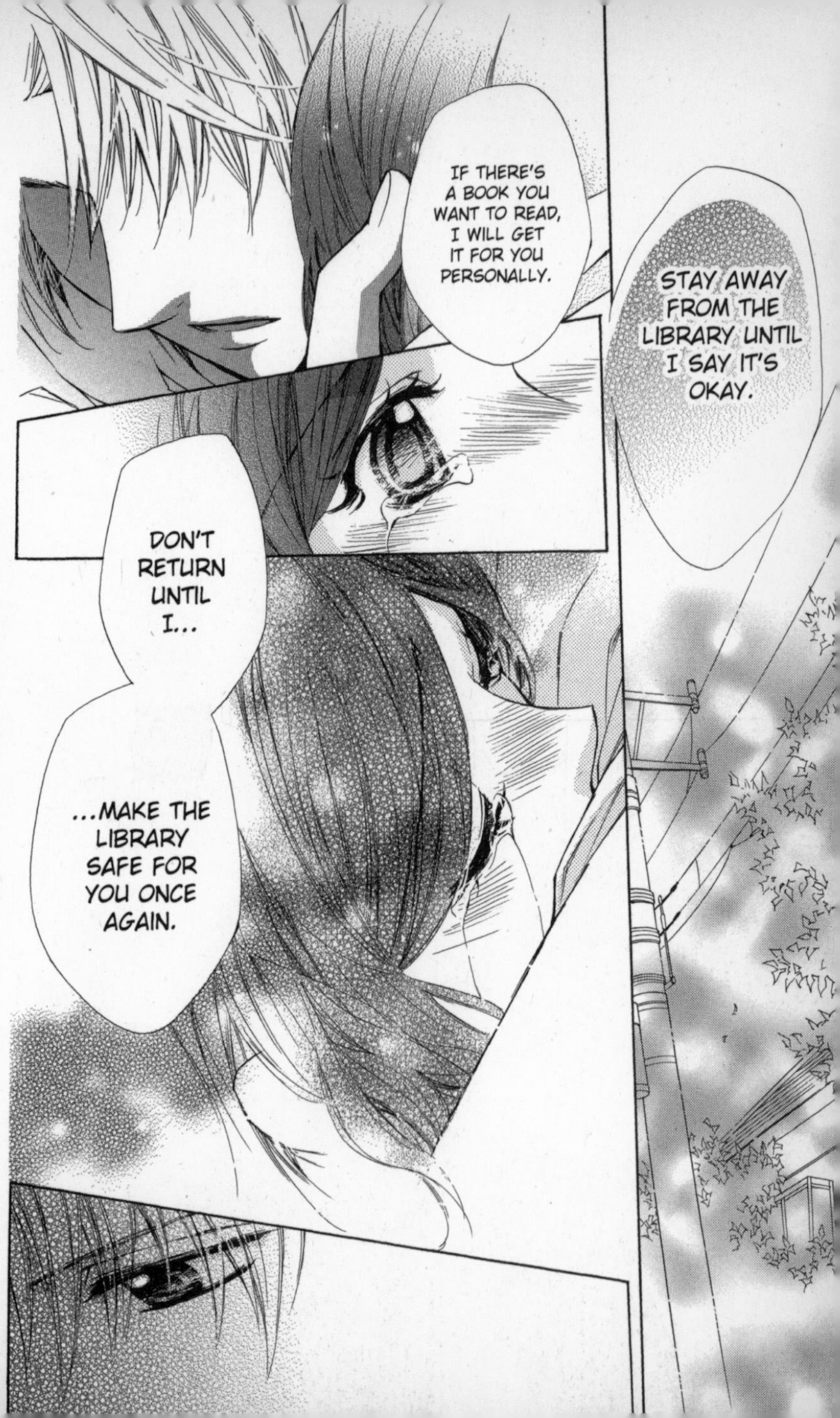

STAY AWAY FROM THE LIBRARY UNTIL I SAY IT'S OKAY.
IF THERE'S A BOOK YOU WANT TO READ, I WILL GET IT FOR YOU PERSONALLY.
DON'T RETURN UNTIL I...
...MAKE THE LIBRARY SAFE FOR YOU ONCE AGAIN.

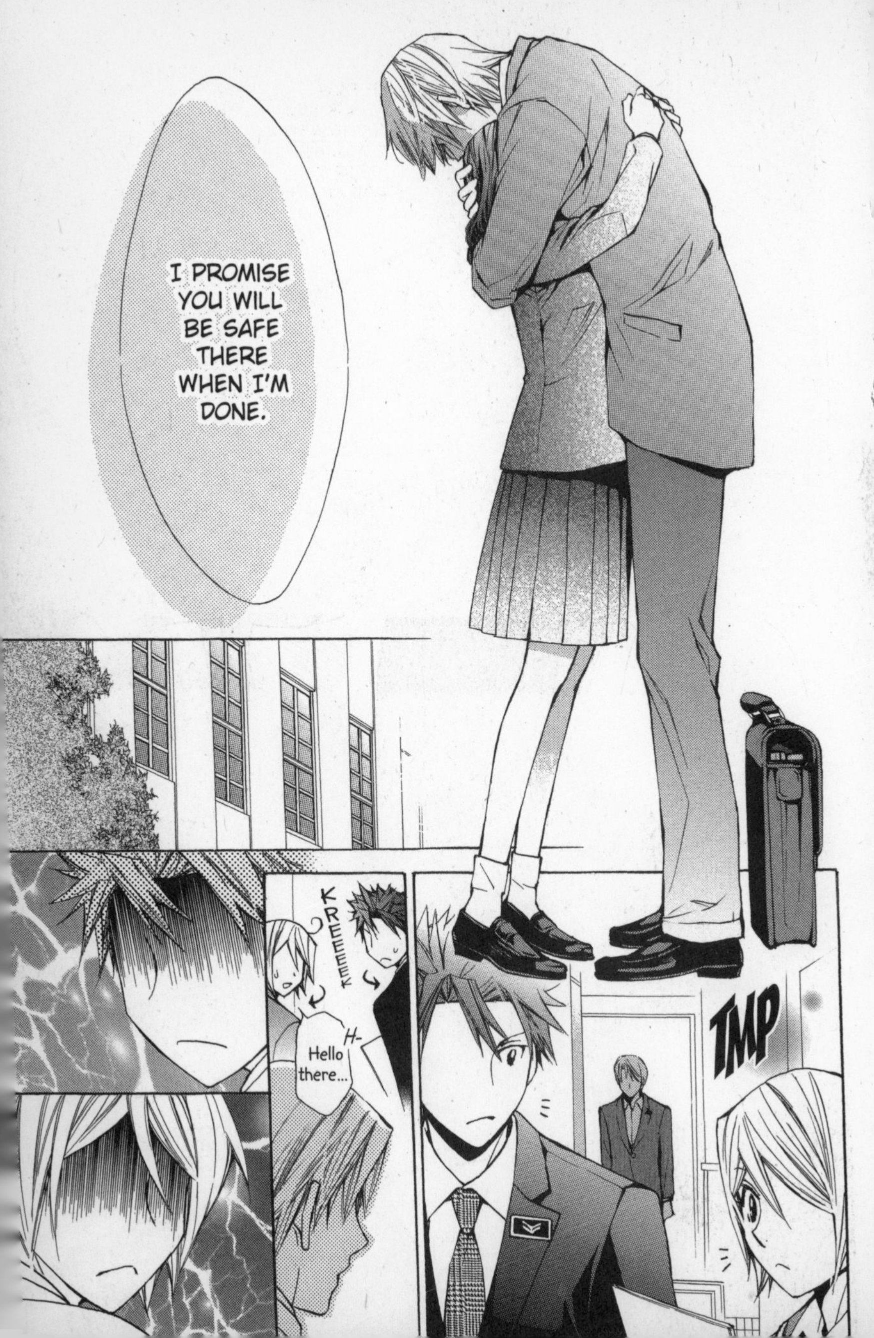
I PROMISE YOU WILL BE SAFE THERE WHEN I'M DONE.
TMP
KREEEEK
H- Hello there...

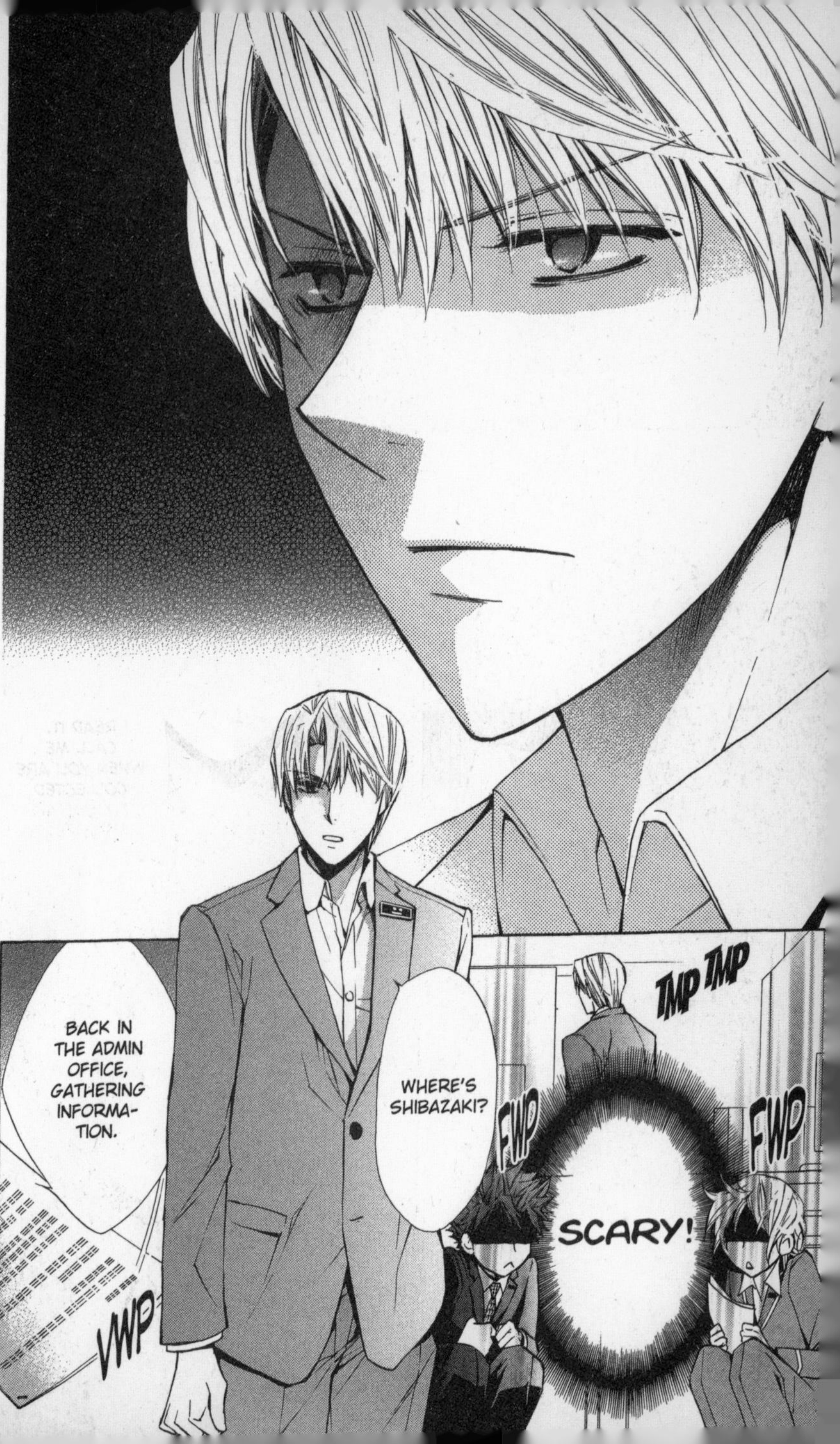
TMP TMP
FWP
FWP
SCARY!
WHERE'S SHIBAZAKI?
BACK IN THE ADMIN OFFICE, GATHERING INFORMA-TION.
VWP

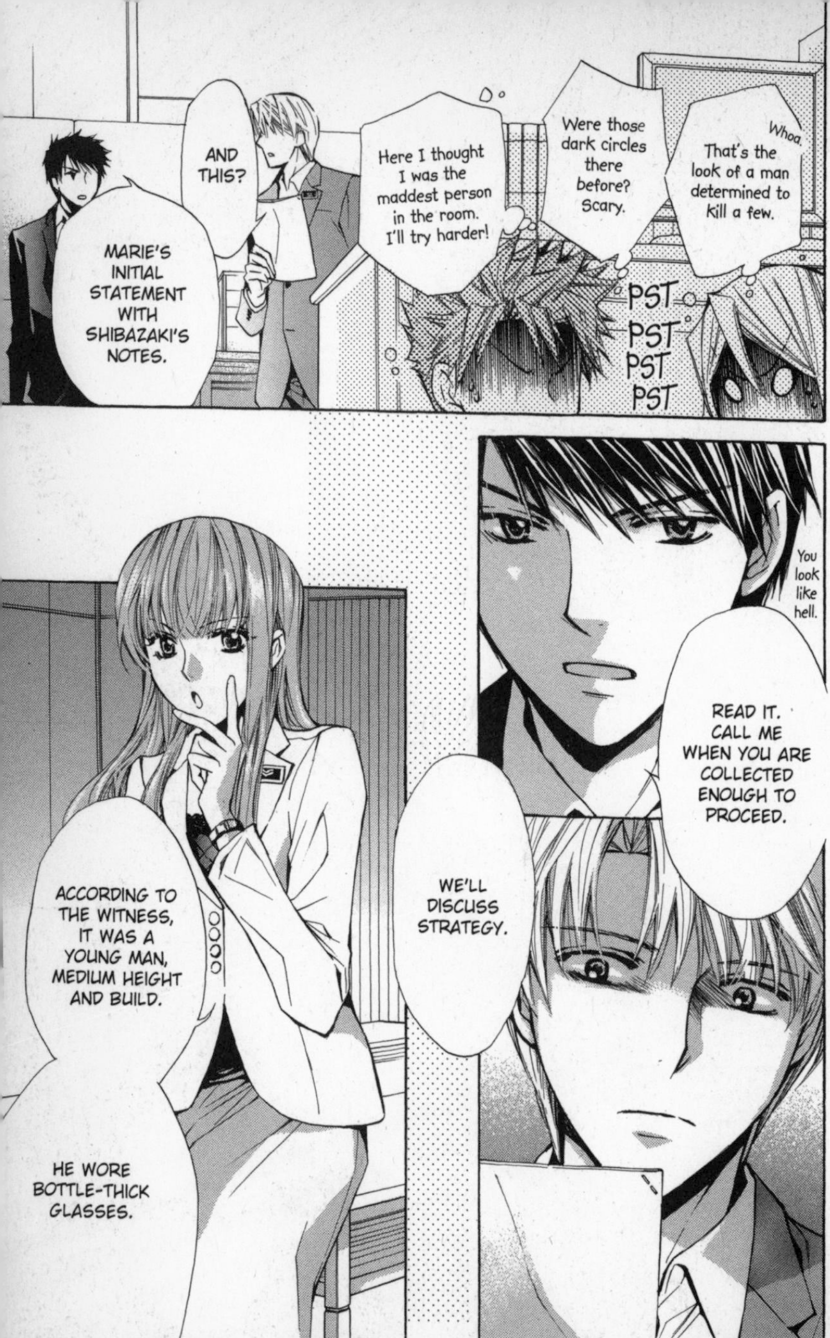
Whoa. That's the look of a man determined to kill a few.
Were those dark circles there before? Scary.
Here I thought I was the maddest person in the room. I'll try harder!
PST PST PST PST
AND THIS?
MARIE'S INITIAL STATEMENT WITH SHIBAZAKI'S NOTES.
You look like hell.
READ IT. CALL ME WHEN YOU ARE COLLECTED ENOUGH TO PROCEED.
WE'LL DISCUSS STRATEGY.
ACCORDING TO THE WITNESS, IT WAS A YOUNG MAN, MEDIUM HEIGHT AND BUILD.
HE WORE BOTTLE-THICK GLASSES.

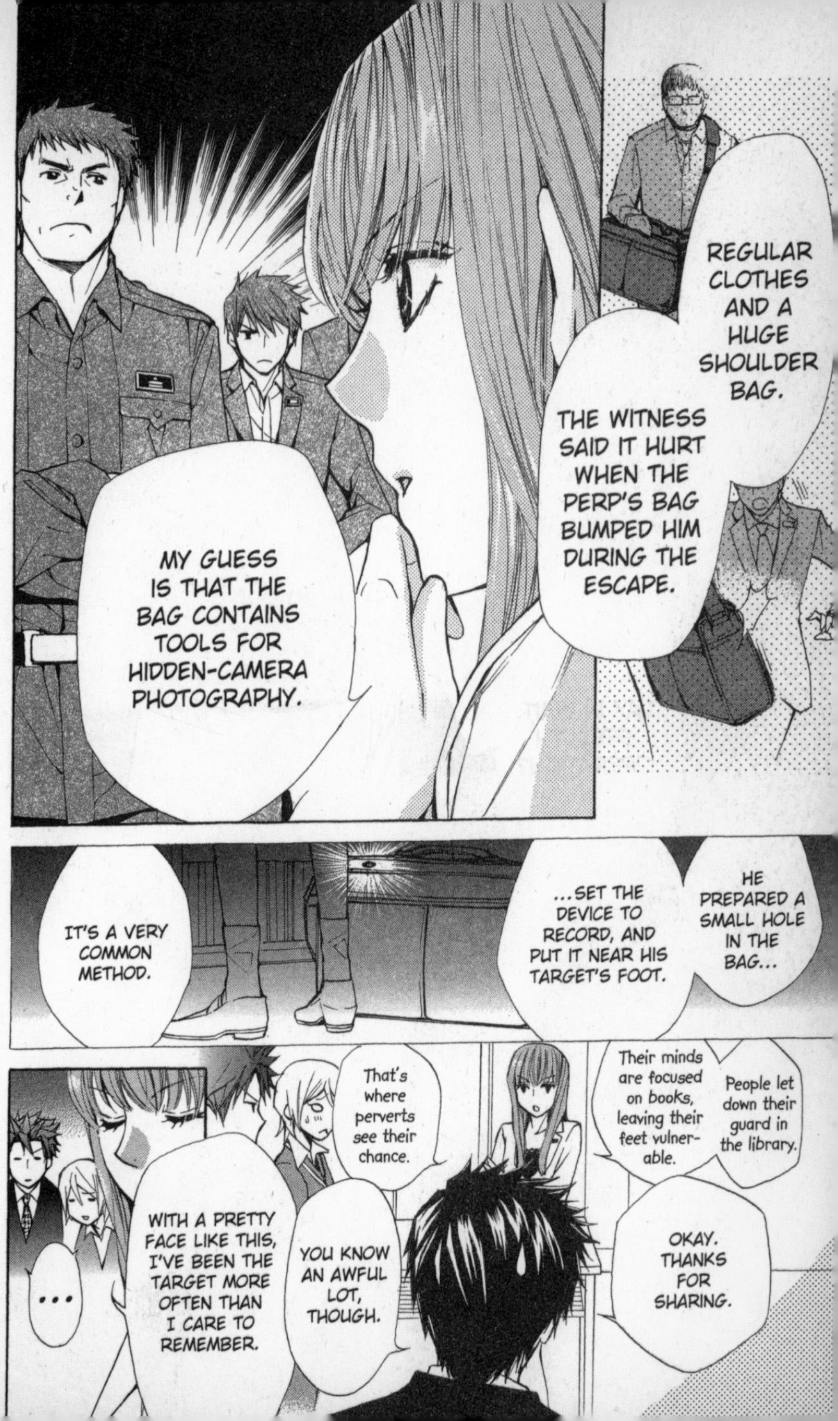
REGULAR CLOTHES AND A HUGE SHOULDER BAG.
THE WITNESS SAID IT HURT WHEN THE PERP'S BAG BUMPED HIM DURING THE ESCAPE.
MY GUESS IS THAT THE BAG CONTAINS TOOLS FOR HIDDEN-CAMERA PHOTOGRAPHY.
HE PREPARED A SMALL HOLE IN THE BAG...
...SET THE DEVICE TO RECORD, AND PUT IT NEAR HIS TARGET'S FOOT.
IT'S A VERY COMMON METHOD.
People let down their guard in the library.
Their minds are focused on books, leaving their feet vulner-able.
That's where perverts see their chance.
OKAY. THANKS FOR SHARING.
YOU KNOW AN AWFUL LOT, THOUGH.
WITH A PRETTY FACE LIKE THIS, I'VE BEEN THE TARGET MORE OFTEN THAN I CARE TO REMEMBER.
...

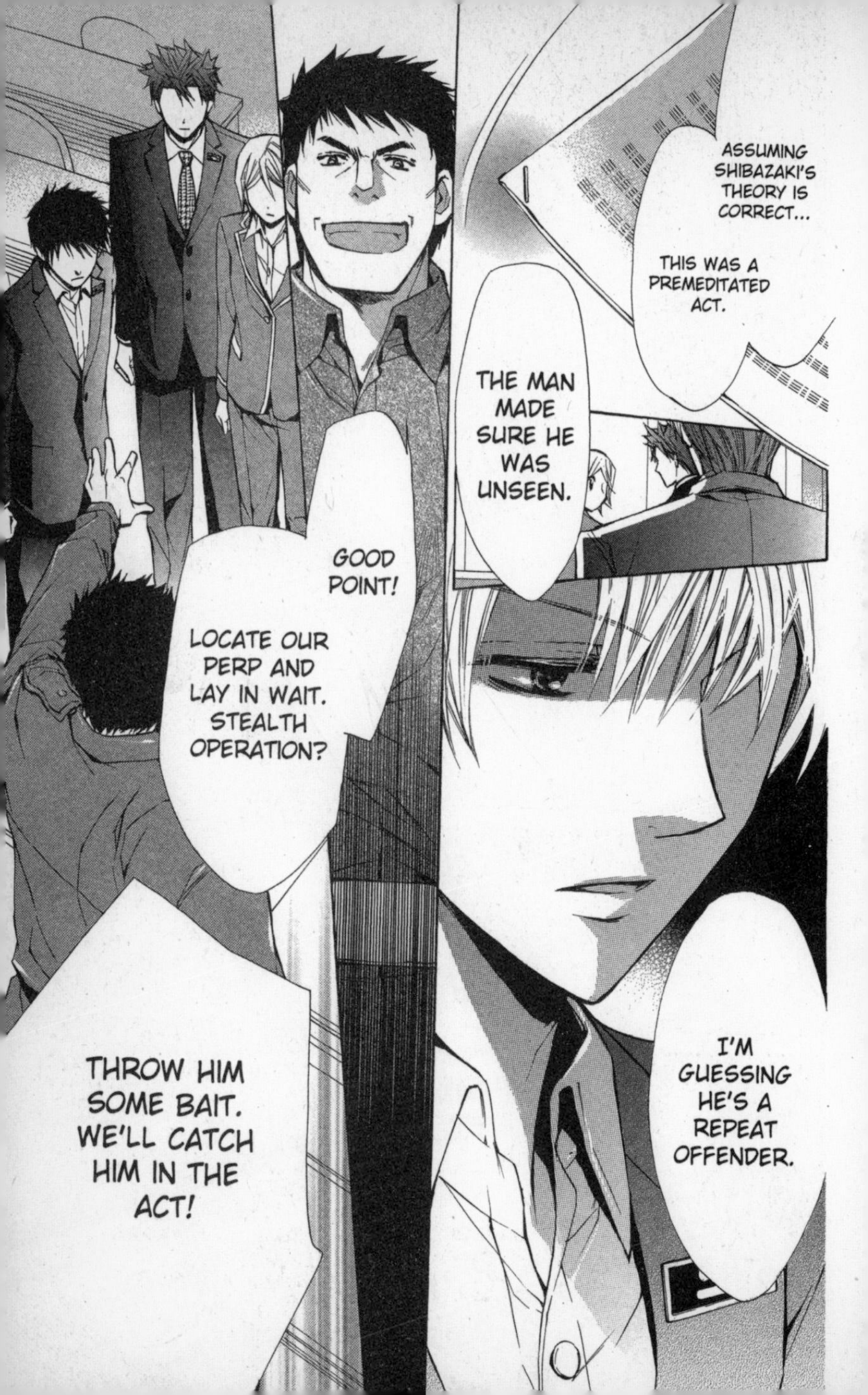
ASSUMING SHIBAZAKI'S THEORY IS CORRECT...
THIS WAS A PREMEDITATED ACT.
THE MAN MADE SURE HE WAS UNSEEN.
I'M GUESSING HE'S A REPEAT OFFENDER.
GOOD POINT!
LOCATE OUR PERP AND LAY IN WAIT. STEALTH OPERATION?
THROW HIM SOME BAIT. WE'LL CATCH HIM IN THE ACT!

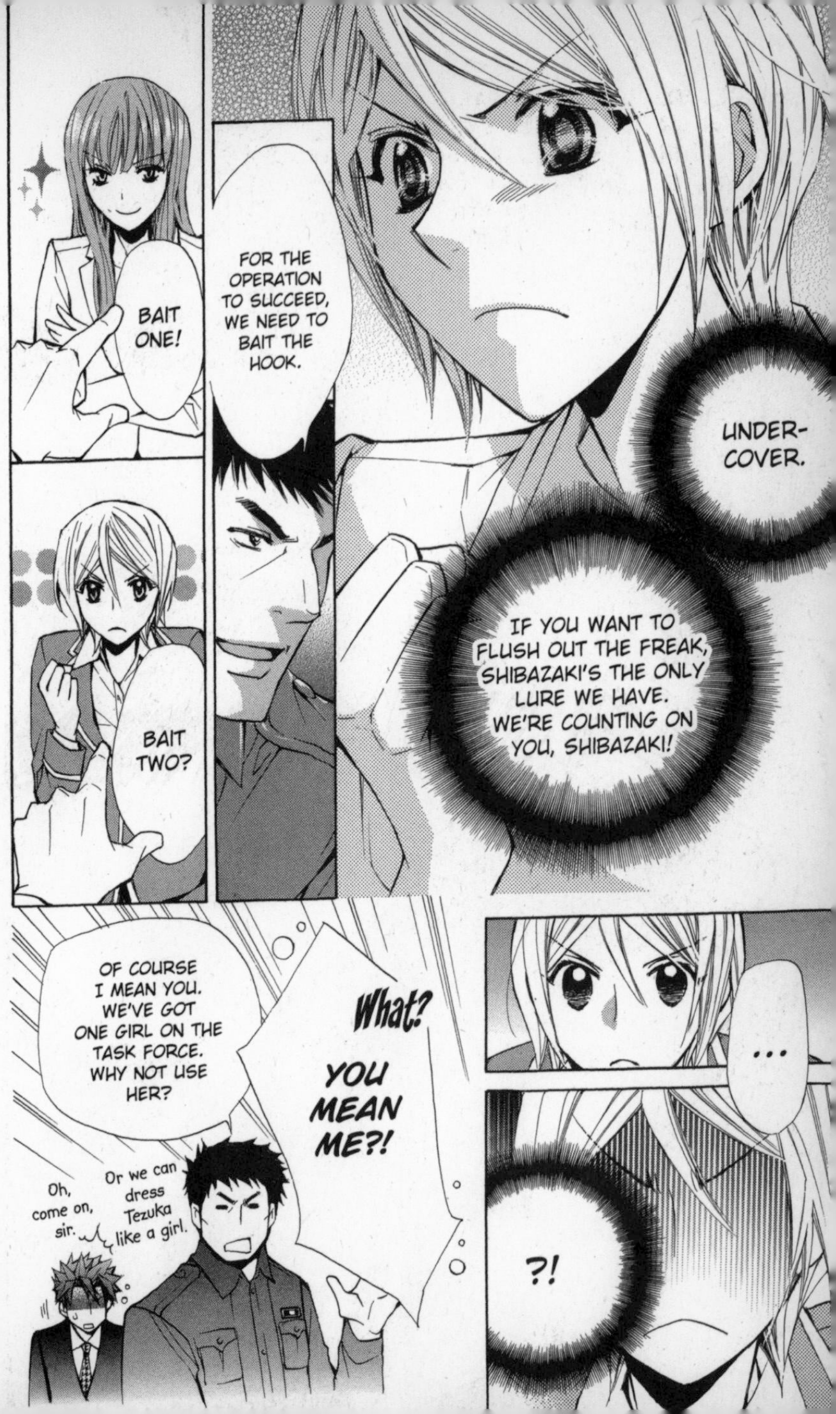

UNDER-COVER.
IF YOU WANT TO FLUSH OUT THE FREAK, SHIBAZAKI'S THE ONLY LURE WE HAVE. WE'RE COUNTING ON YOU, SHIBAZAKI!
FOR THE OPERATION TO SUCCEED, WE NEED TO BAIT THE HOOK.
BAIT ONE!
BAIT TWO?
...
?!
What?
YOU MEAN ME?!
OF COURSE I MEAN YOU. WE'VE GOT ONE GIRL ON THE TASK FORCE. WHY NOT USE HER?
Or we can dress Tezuka like a girl.
Oh, come on, sir.

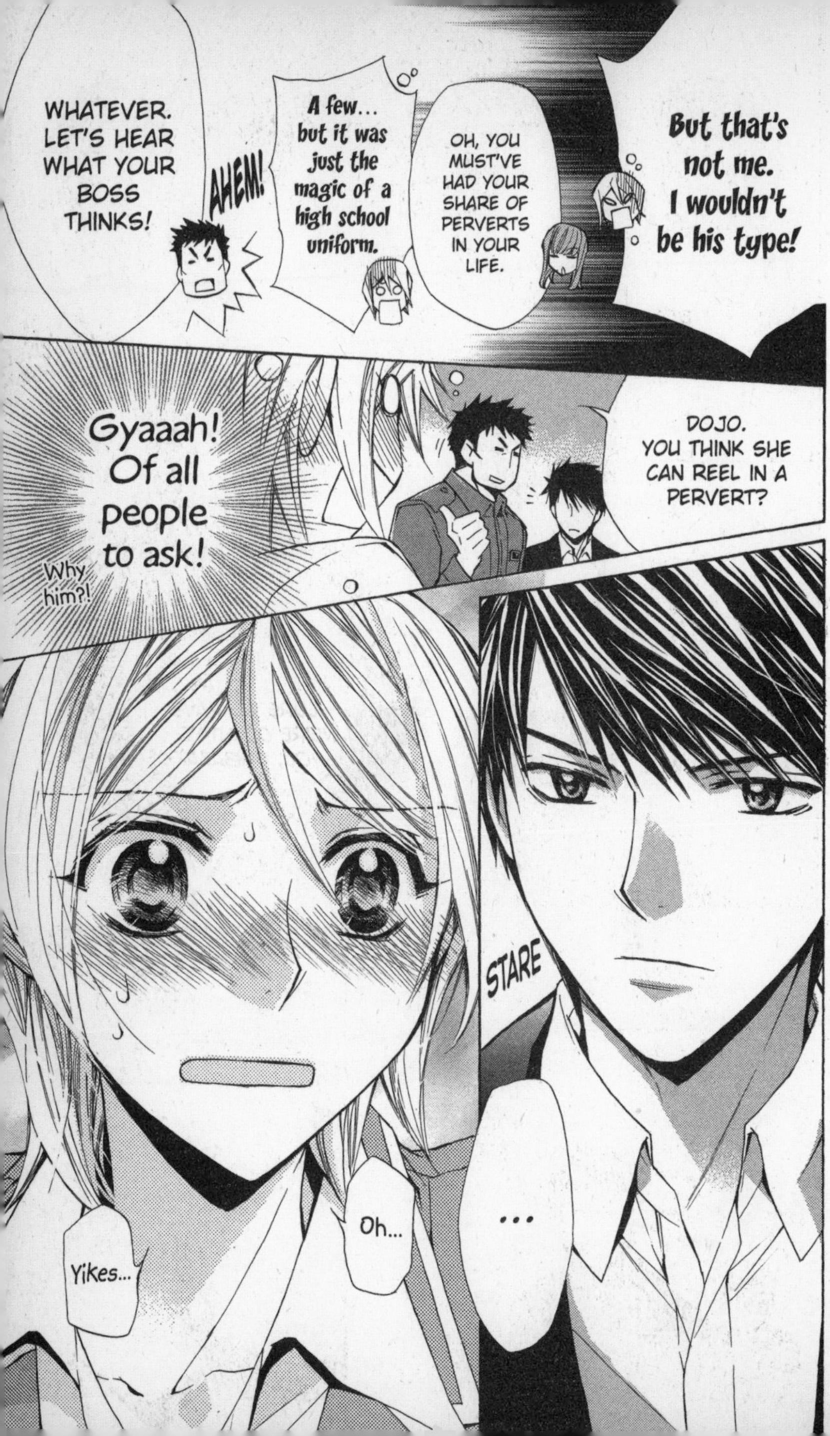
But that's not me. I wouldn't be his type!
OH, YOU MUST'VE HAD YOUR SHARE OF PERVERTS IN YOUR LIFE.
A few... but it was just the magic of a high school uniform.
AHEM!
WHATEVER. LET'S HEAR WHAT YOUR BOSS THINKS!
DOJO. YOU THINK SHE CAN REEL IN A PERVERT?
Gyaaah! Of all people to ask!
Why him?!
STARE
...
Oh...
Yikes...

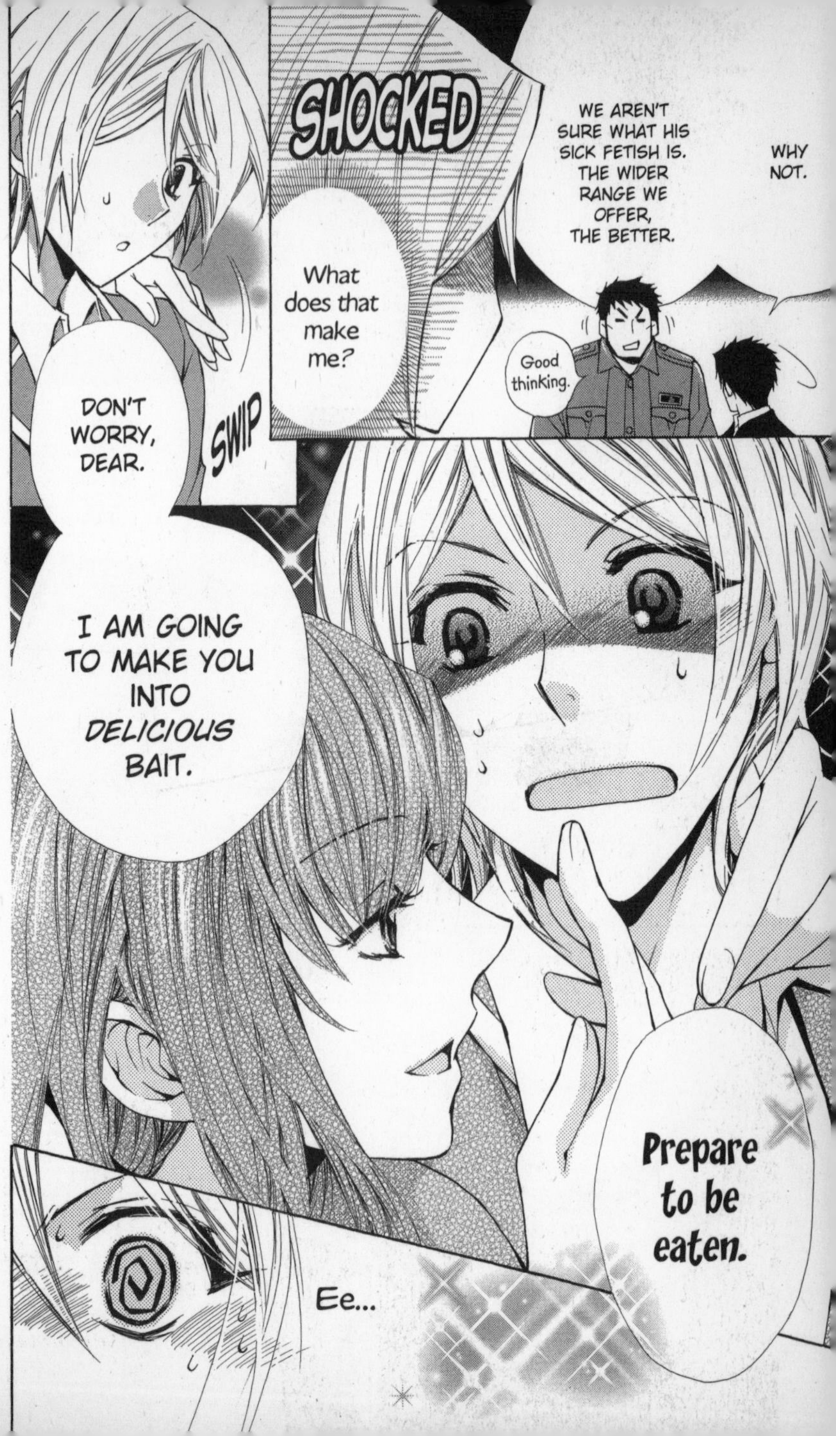

WHY NOT.
WE AREN'T SURE WHAT HIS SICK FETISH IS. THE WIDER RANGE WE OFFER, THE BETTER.
Good thinking.
SHOCKED
What does that make me?
SWIP
DON'T WORRY, DEAR.
I AM GOING TO MAKE YOU INTO DELICIOUS BAIT.
Prepare to be eaten.
Ee...

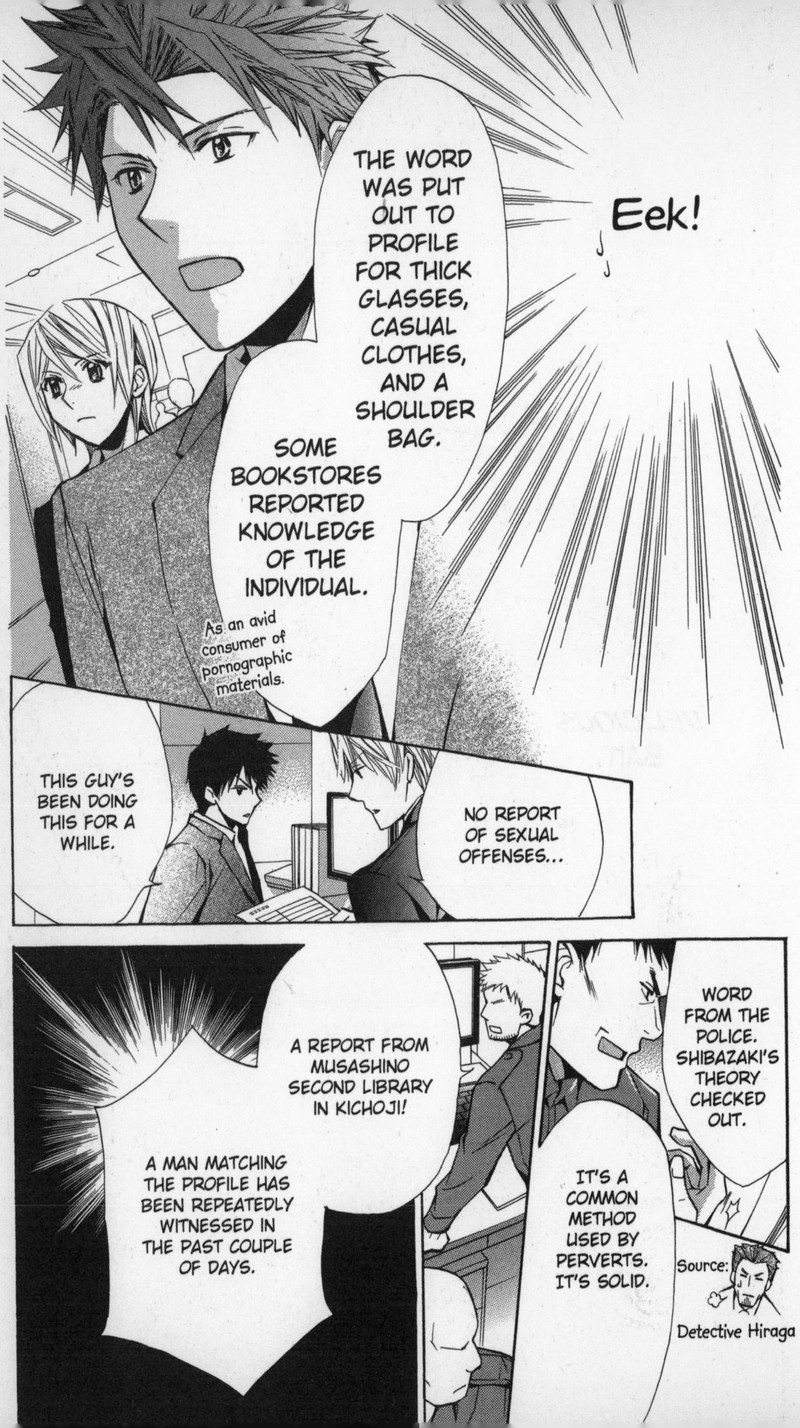
Eek!
THE WORD WAS PUT OUT TO PROFILE FOR THICK GLASSES, CASUAL CLOTHES, AND A SHOULDER BAG.
SOME BOOKSTORES REPORTED KNOWLEDGE OF THE INDIVIDUAL.
As an avid consumer of pornographic materials.
NO REPORT OF SEXUAL OFFENSES...
THIS GUY'S BEEN DOING THIS FOR A WHILE.
WORD FROM THE POLICE. SHIBAZAKI'S THEORY CHECKED OUT.
IT'S A COMMON METHOD USED BY PERVERTS. IT'S SOLID.
Source:
Detective Hiraga
A REPORT FROM MUSASHINO SECOND LIBRARY IN KICHOJI!
A MAN MATCHING THE PROFILE HAS BEEN REPEATEDLY WITNESSED IN THE PAST COUPLE OF DAYS.

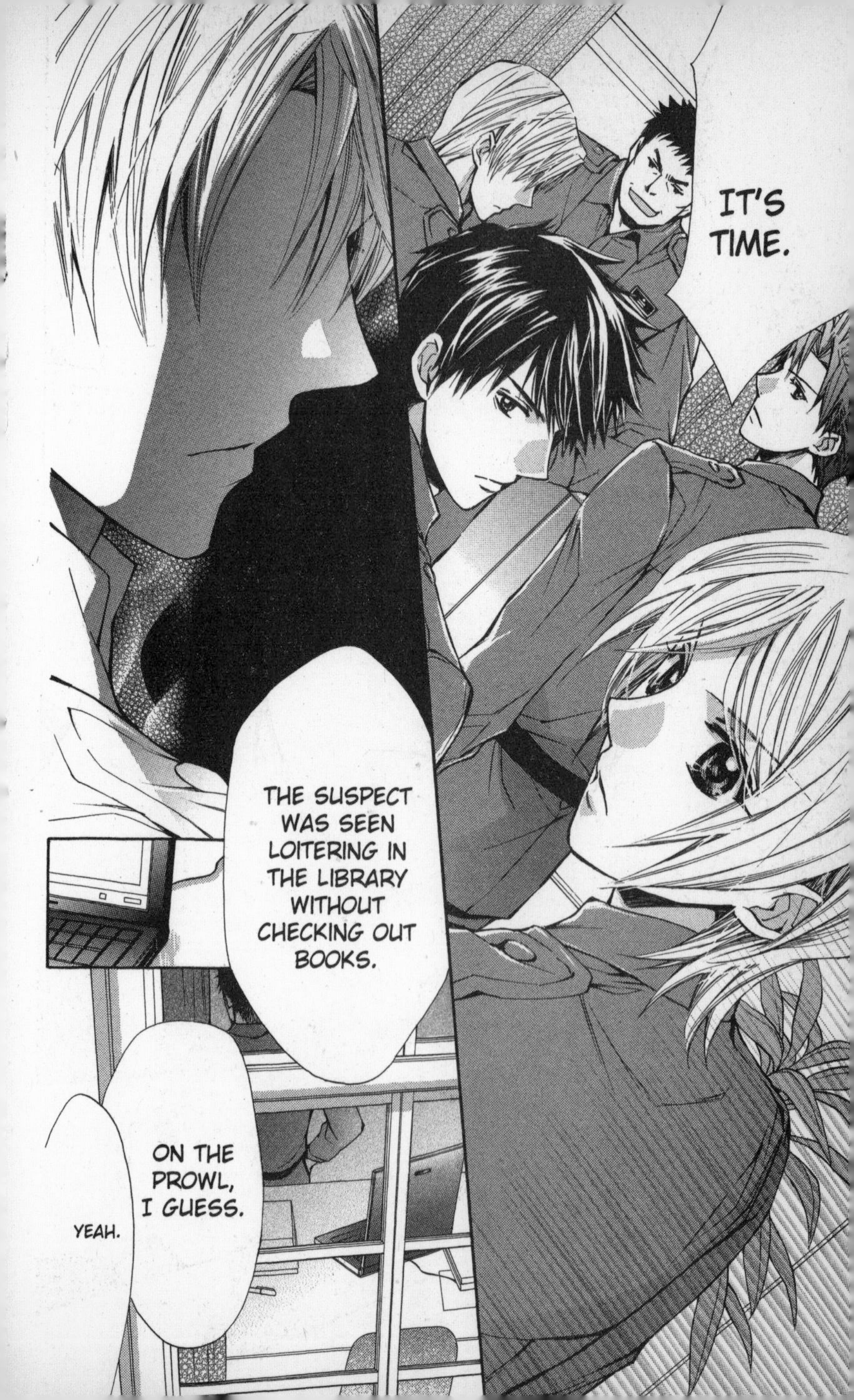
IT'S TIME.
THE SUSPECT WAS SEEN LOITERING IN THE LIBRARY WITHOUT CHECKING OUT BOOKS.
ON THE PROWL, I GUESS.
YEAH.

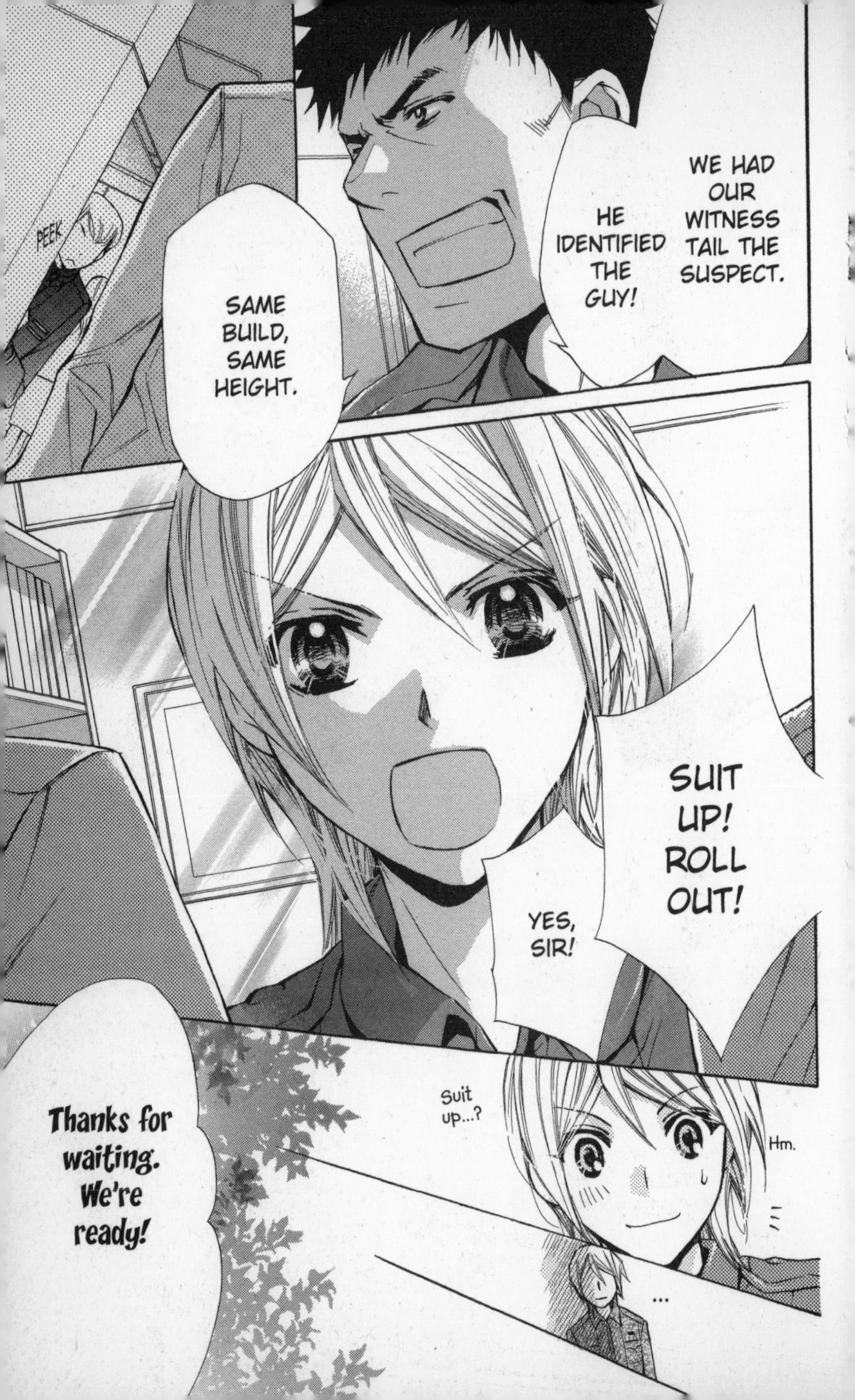

WE HAD OUR WITNESS TAIL THE SUSPECT.
HE IDENTIFIED THE GUY!
SAME BUILD, SAME HEIGHT.
PEEK
SUIT UP! ROLL OUT!
YES, SIR!
Hm.
Suit up...?
...
Thanks for waiting. We're ready!

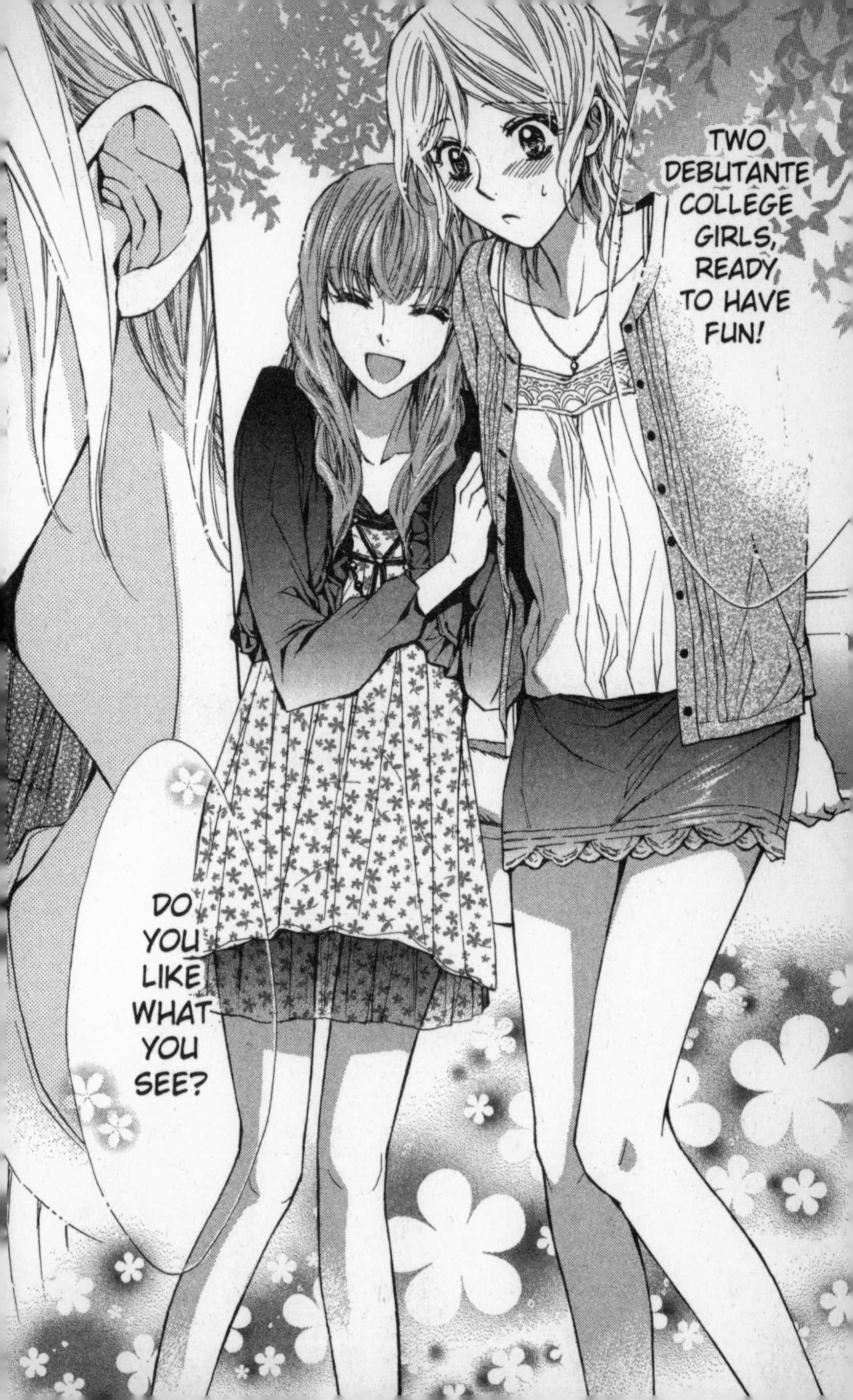
TWO DEBUTANTE COLLEGE GIRLS, READY TO HAVE FUN!
DO YOU LIKE WHAT YOU SEE?

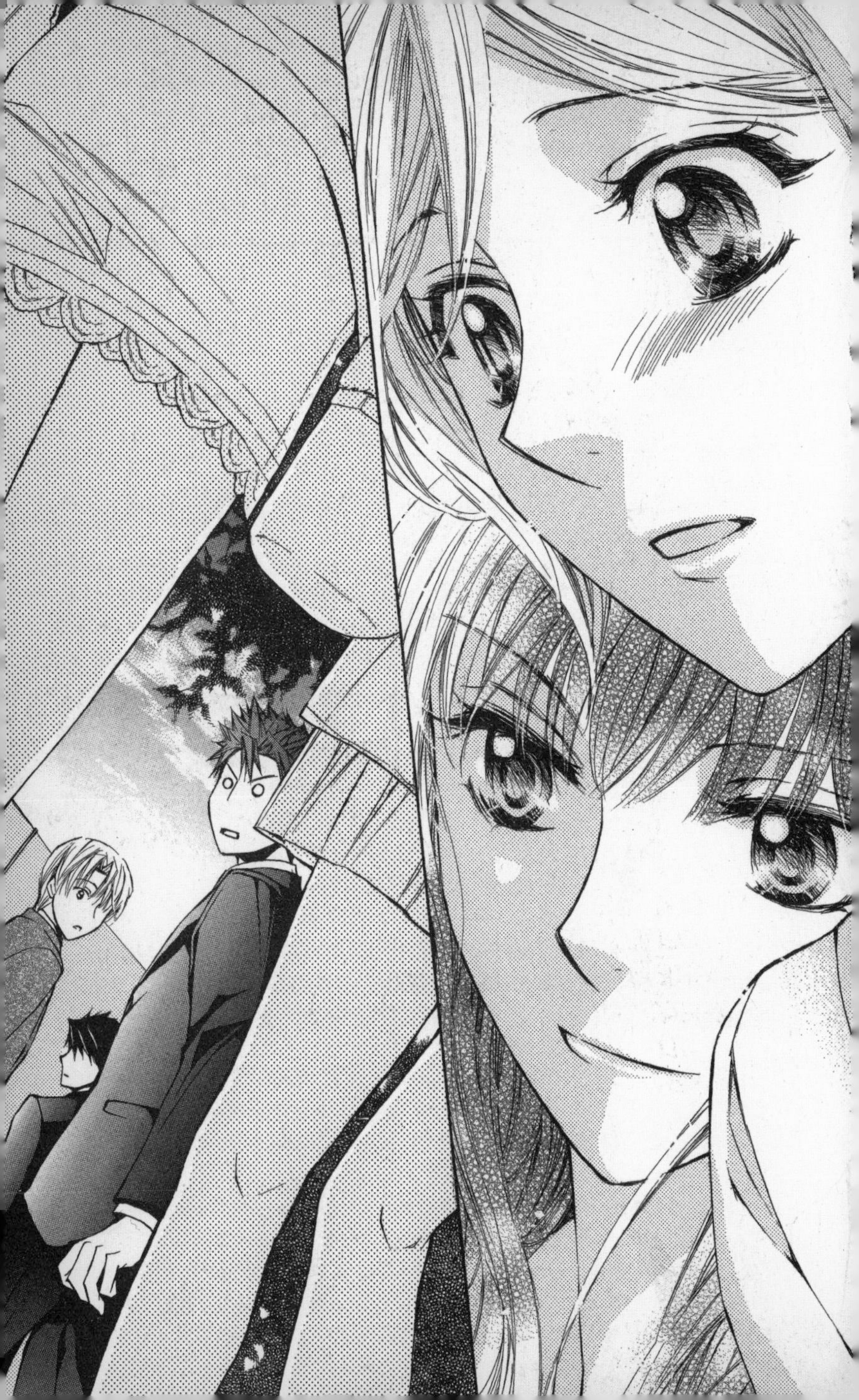

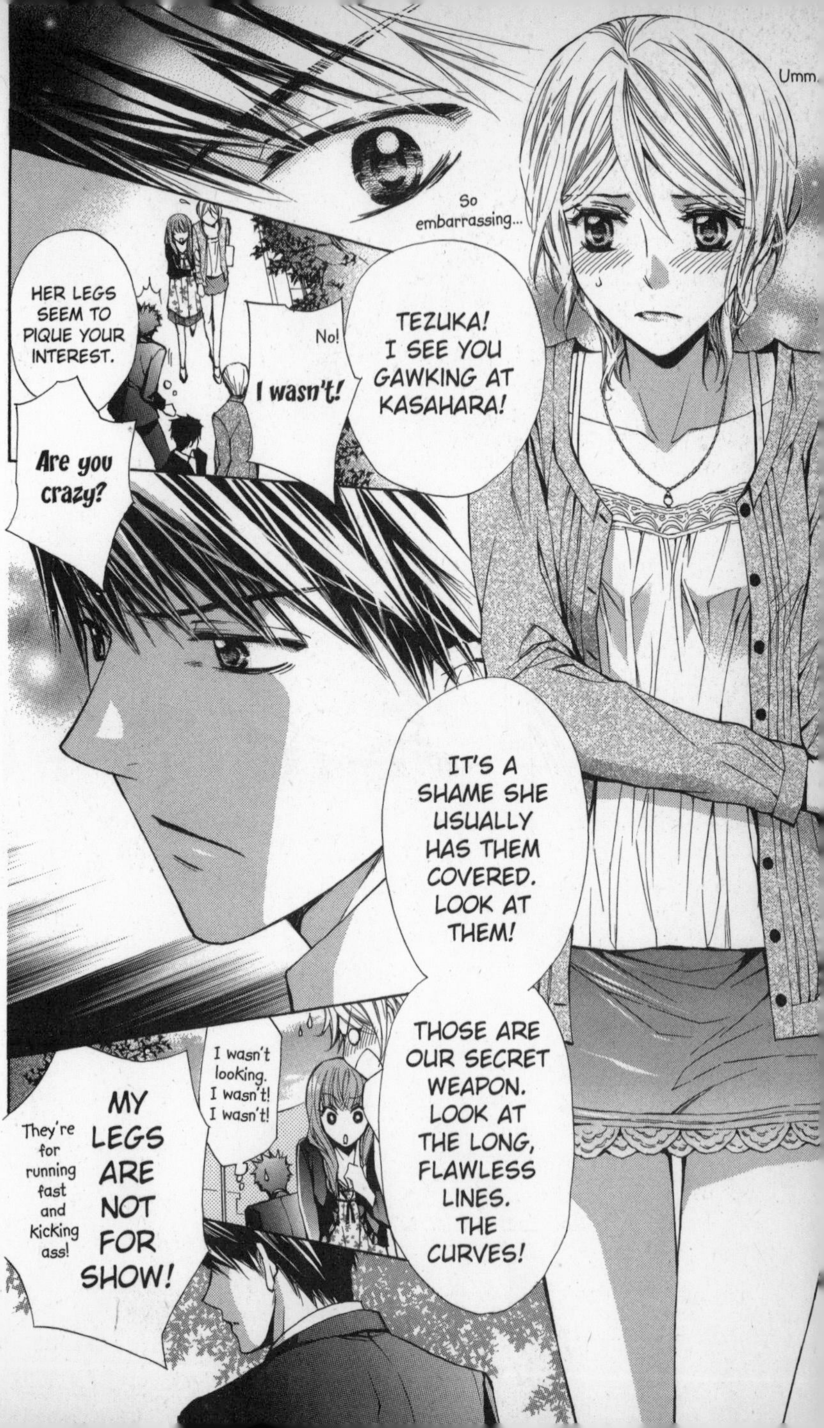
Umm.
So embarrassing...
TEZUKA! I SEE YOU GAWKING AT KASAHARA!
No! I wasn't!
HER LEGS SEEM TO PIQUE YOUR INTEREST.
Are you crazy?
IT'S A SHAME SHE USUALLY HAS THEM COVERED. LOOK AT THEM!
THOSE ARE OUR SECRET WEAPON. LOOK AT THE LONG, FLAWLESS LINES. THE CURVES!
I wasn't looking. I wasn't! I wasn't!
MY LEGS ARE NOT FOR SHOW!
They're for running fast and kicking ass!

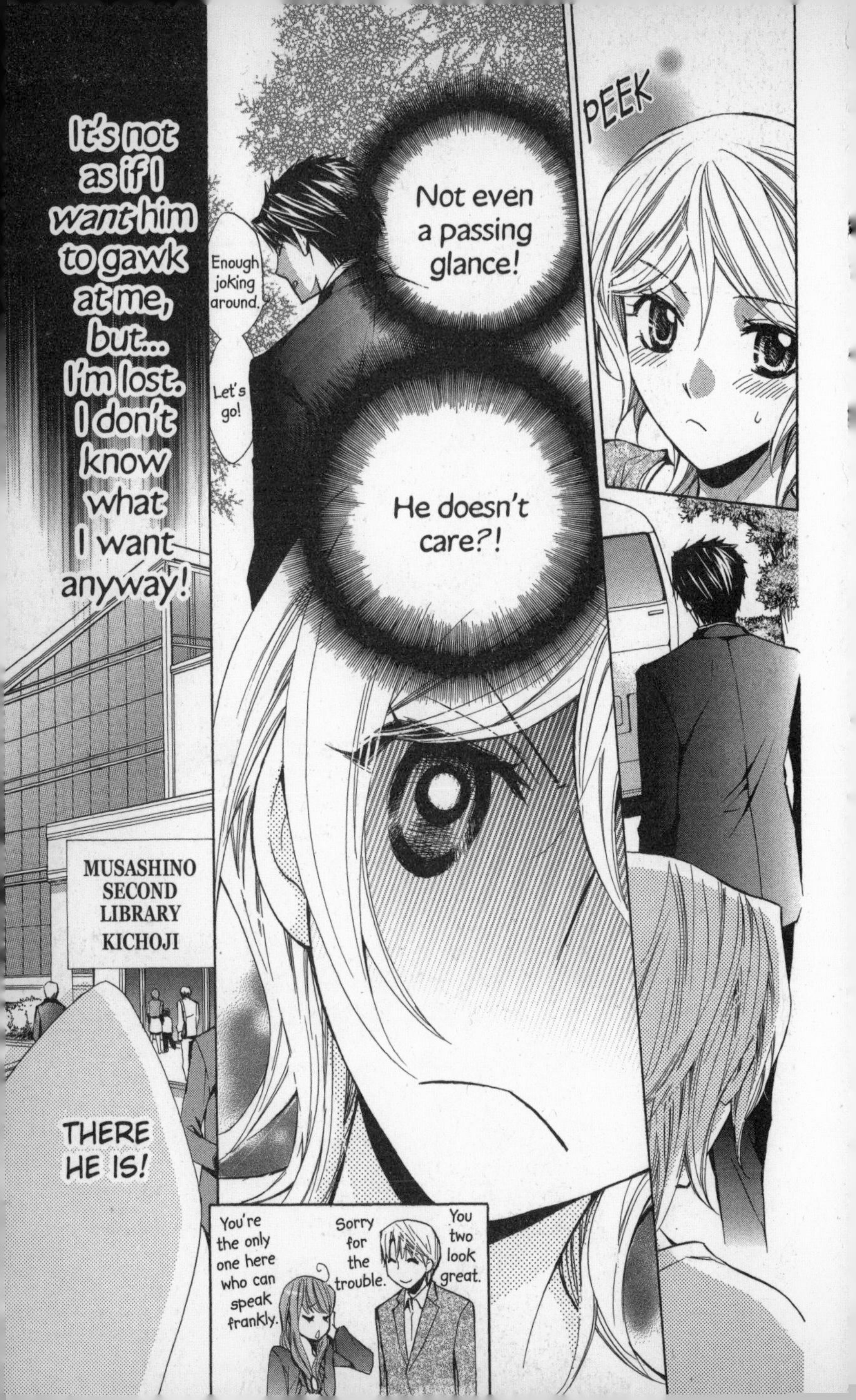
PEEK
Not even a passing glance!
He doesn't care?!
Enough joking around.
Let's go!
You two look great.
Sorry for the trouble.
You're the only one here who can speak frankly.
It's not as if I want him to gawk at me, but... I'm lost. I don't know what I want anyway!
MUSASHINO SECOND LIBRARY KICHOJI
THERE HE IS!

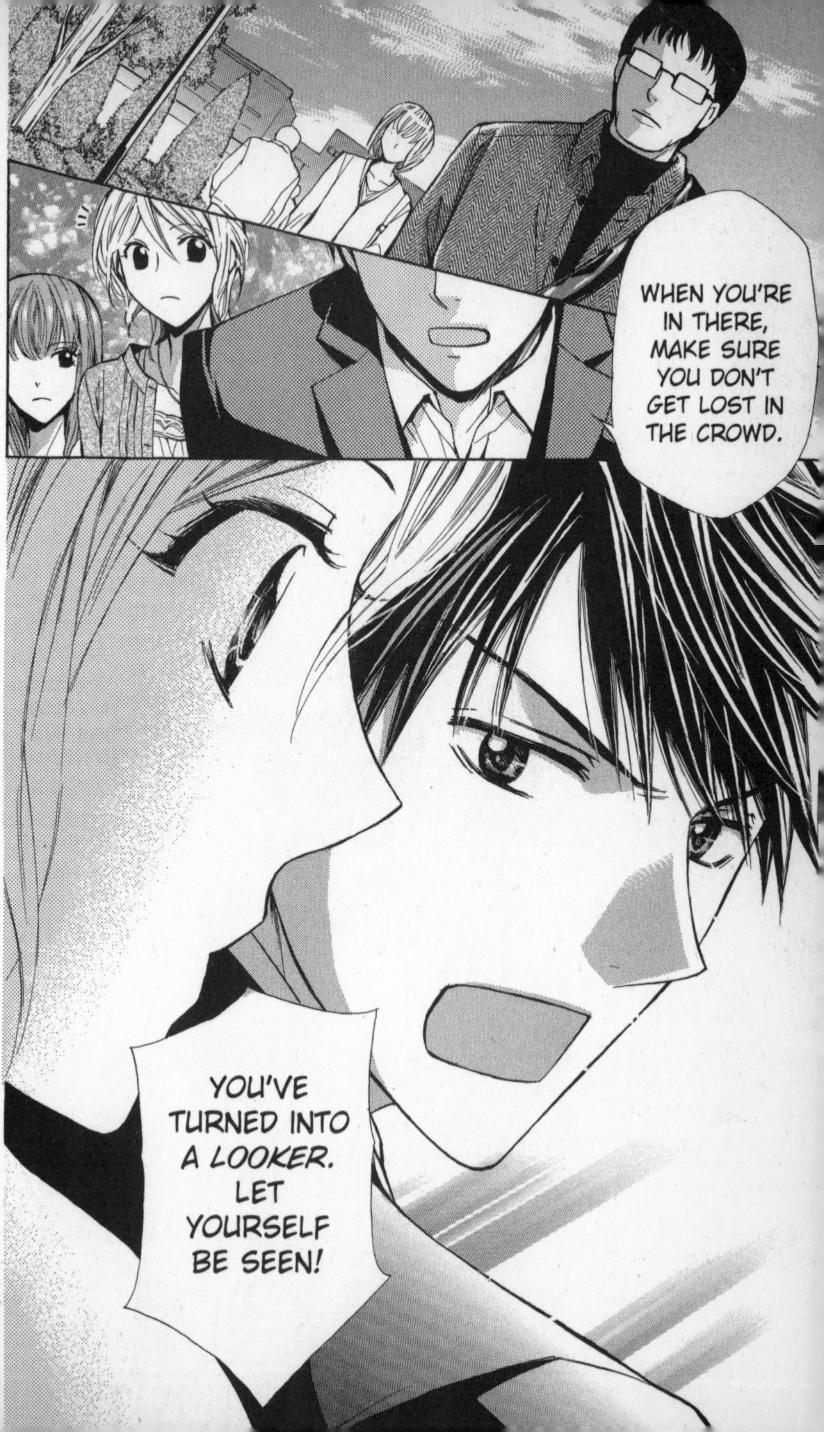
WHEN YOU'RE IN THERE, MAKE SURE YOU DON'T GET LOST IN THE CROWD.
YOU'VE TURNED INTO A *LOOKER*. LET YOURSELF BE SEEN!

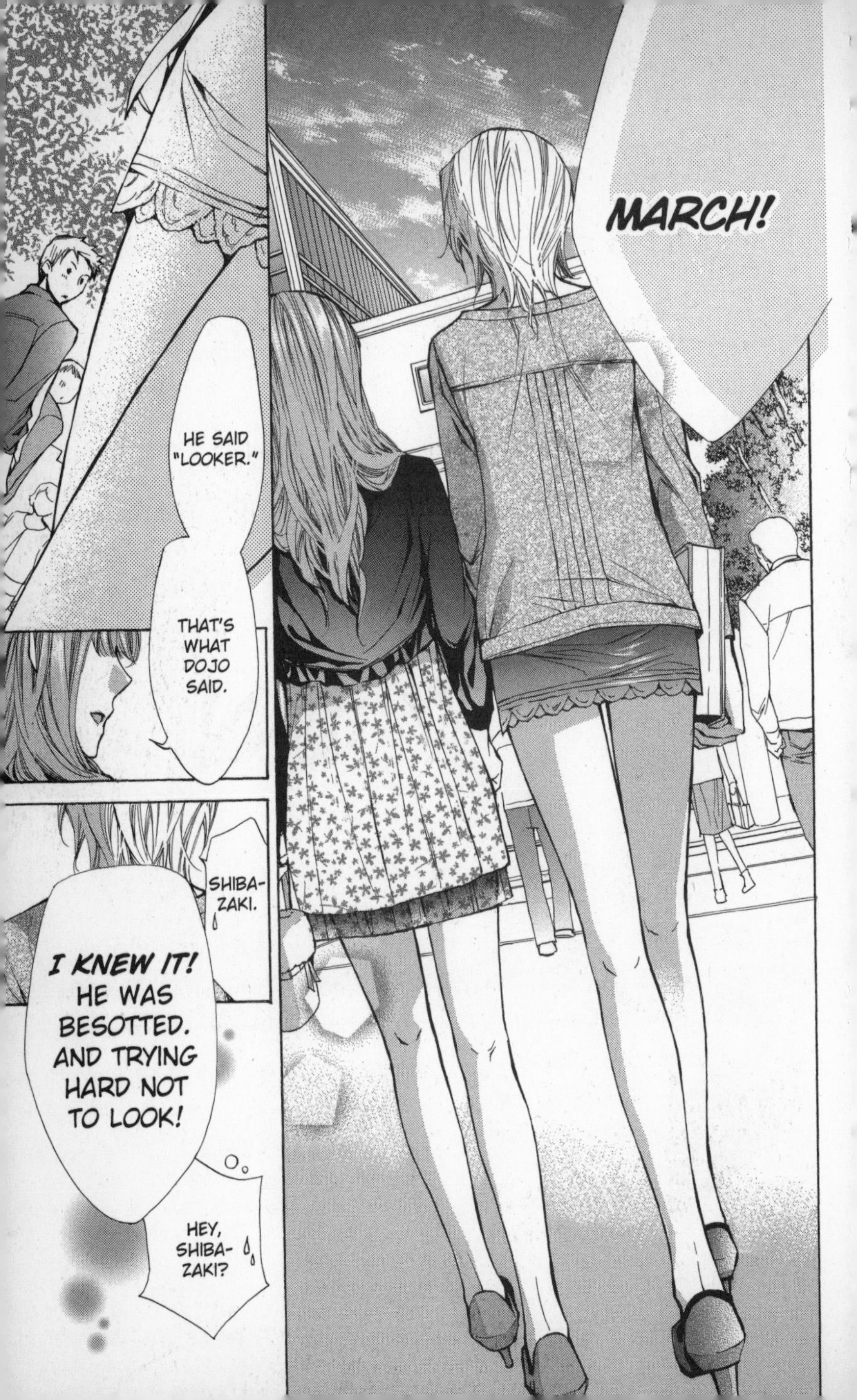
MARCH!
HE SAID "LOOKER."
THAT'S WHAT DOJO SAID.
SHIBA-ZAKI.
I KNEW IT! HE WAS BESOTTED. AND TRYING HARD NOT TO LOOK!
HEY, SHIBA-ZAKI?

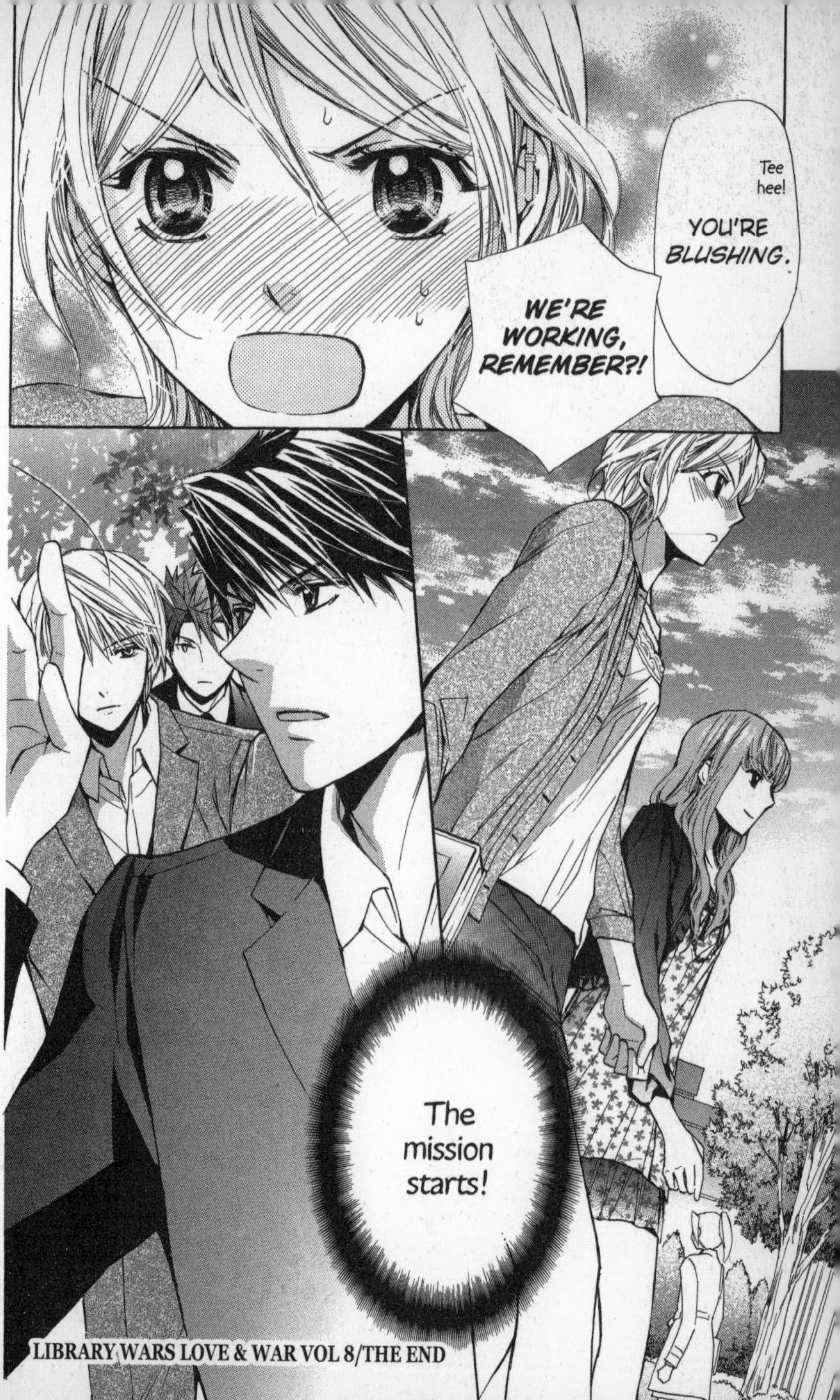
Tee hee! YOU'RE BLUSHING.
WE'RE WORKING, REMEMBER?!
The mission starts!
LIBRARY WARS LOVE & WAR VOL 8/THE END

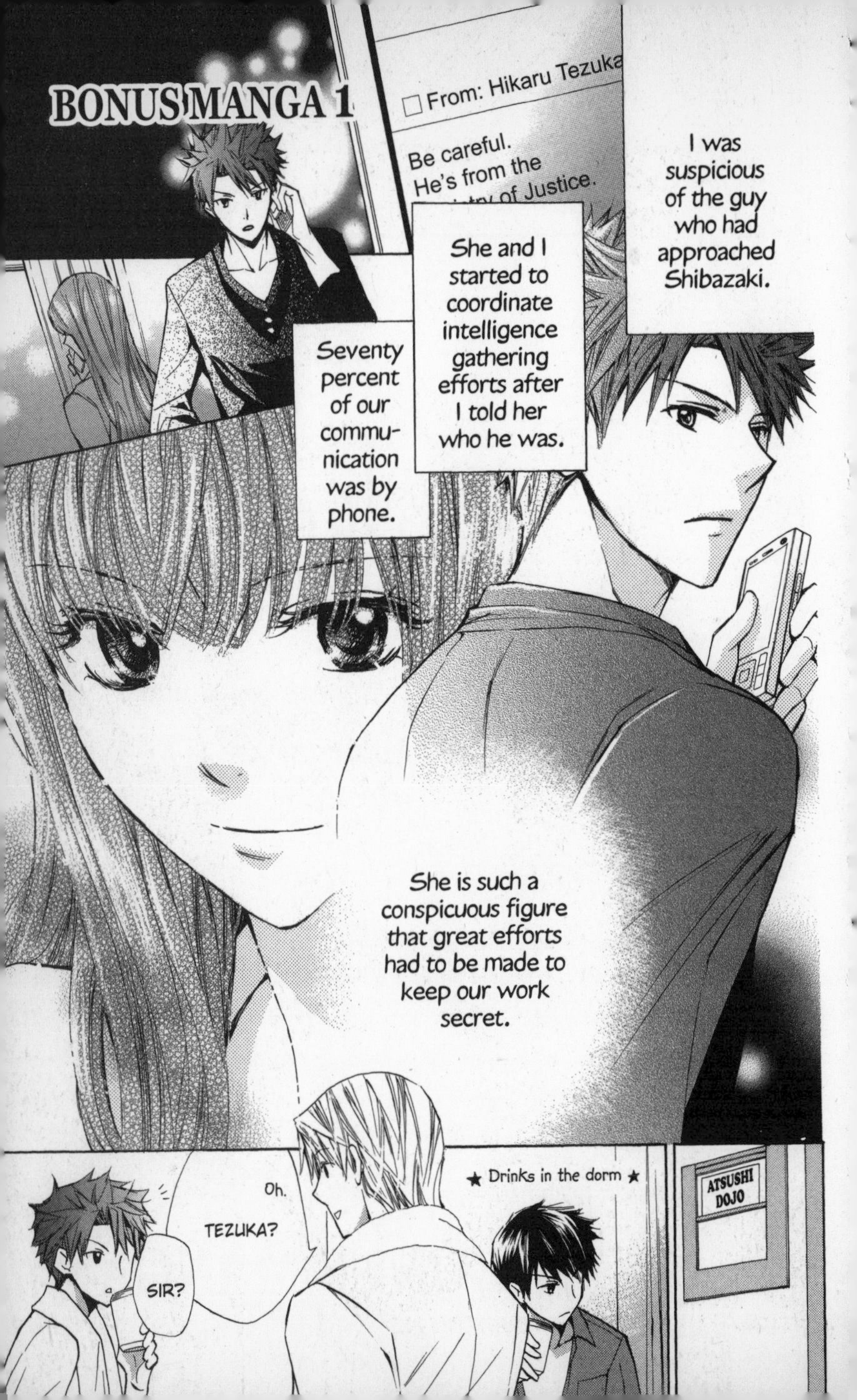
BONUS MANGA 1
I was suspicious of the guy who had approached Shibazaki.
From: Hikaru Tezuka
Be careful.
He's from the
of Justice.
She and I started to coordinate intelligence gathering efforts after I told her who he was.
Seventy percent of our communication was by phone.
She is such a conspicuous figure that great efforts had to be made to keep our work secret.
ATSUSHI DOJO
★ Drinks in the dorm ★
Oh.
TEZUKA?
SIR?

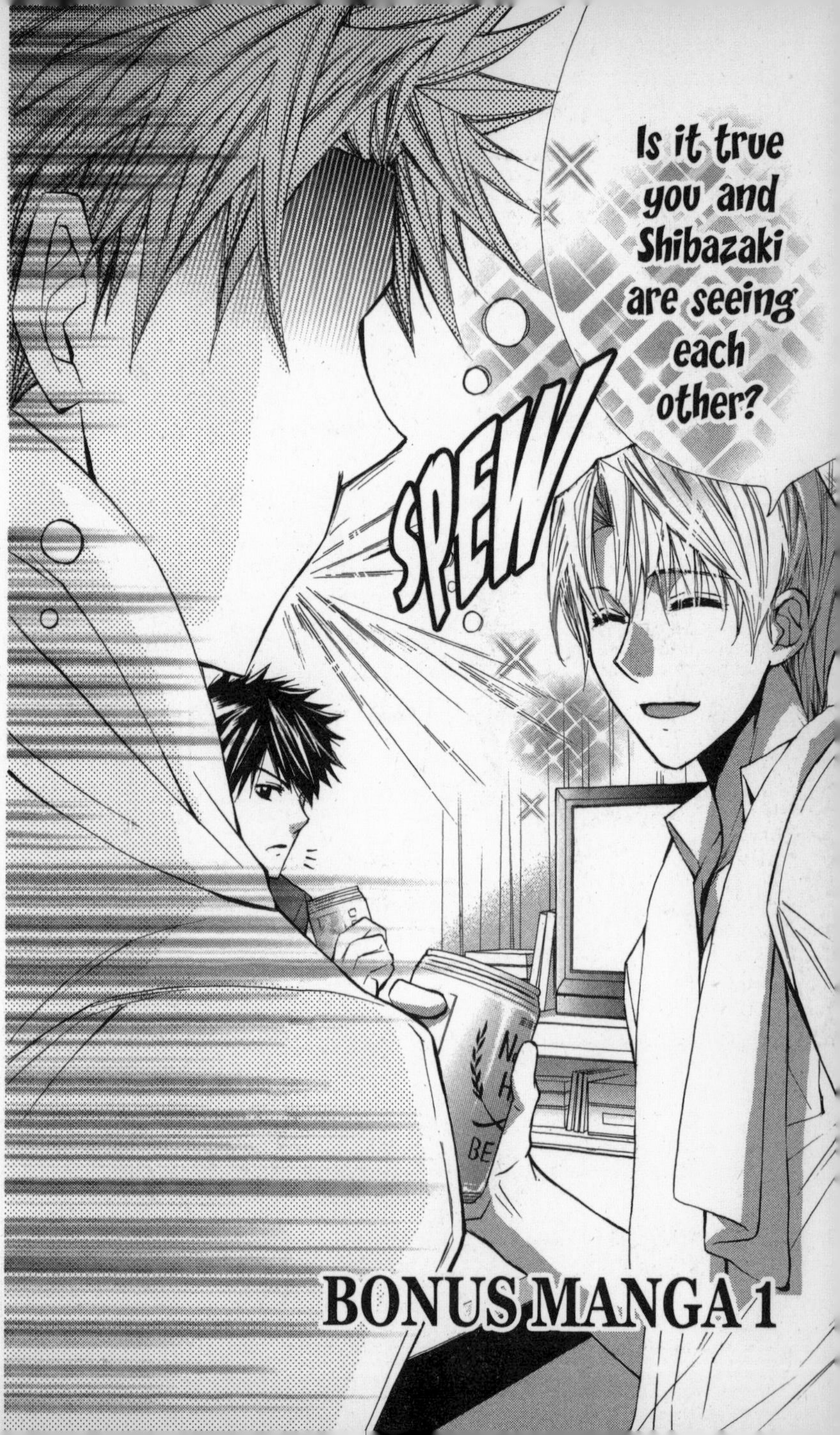
Is it true you and Shibazaki are seeing each other?
SPEW
BONUS MANGA 1

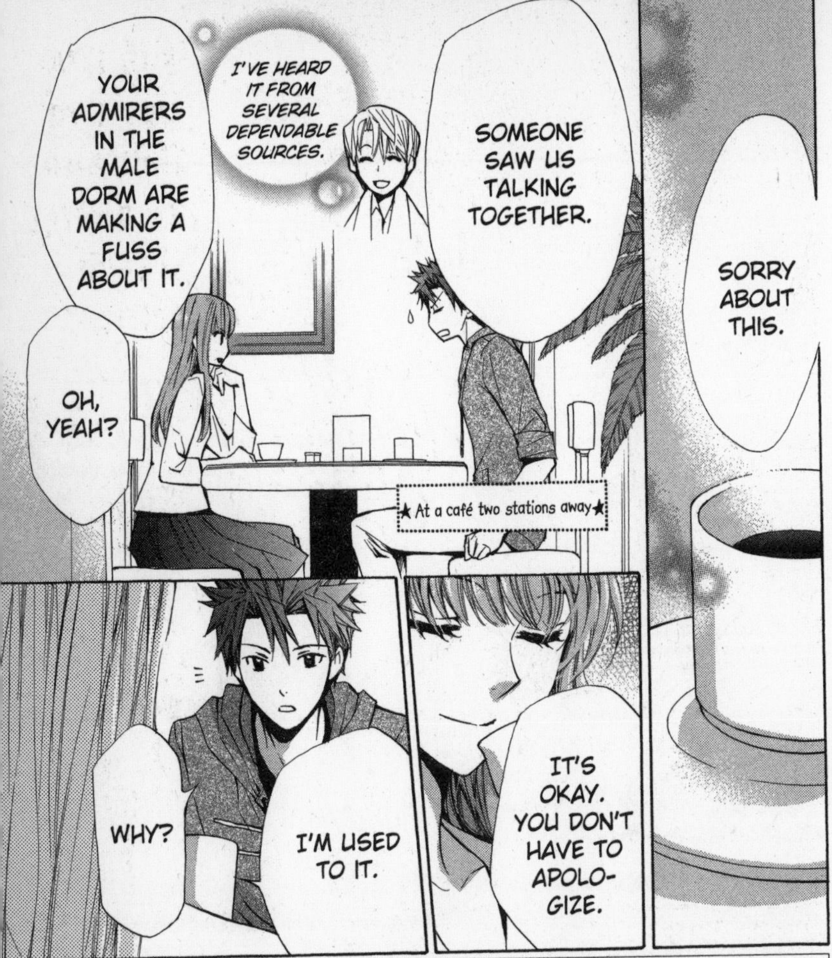
SORRY ABOUT THIS.
★At a café two stations away★
SOMEONE SAW US TALKING TOGETHER.
I'VE HEARD IT FROM SEVERAL DEPENDABLE SOURCES.
YOUR ADMIRERS IN THE MALE DORM ARE MAKING A FUSS ABOUT IT.
OH, YEAH?
IT'S OKAY. YOU DON'T HAVE TO APOLO-GIZE.
I'M USED TO IT.
WHY?

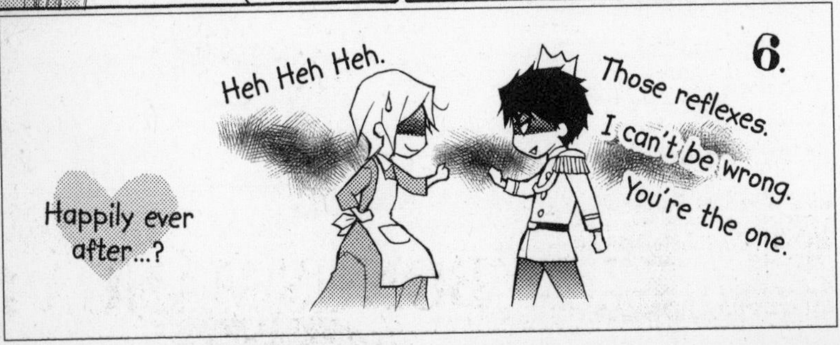
6.
Those reflexes. I can't be wrong. You're the one.
Heh Heh Heh.
Happily ever after...?

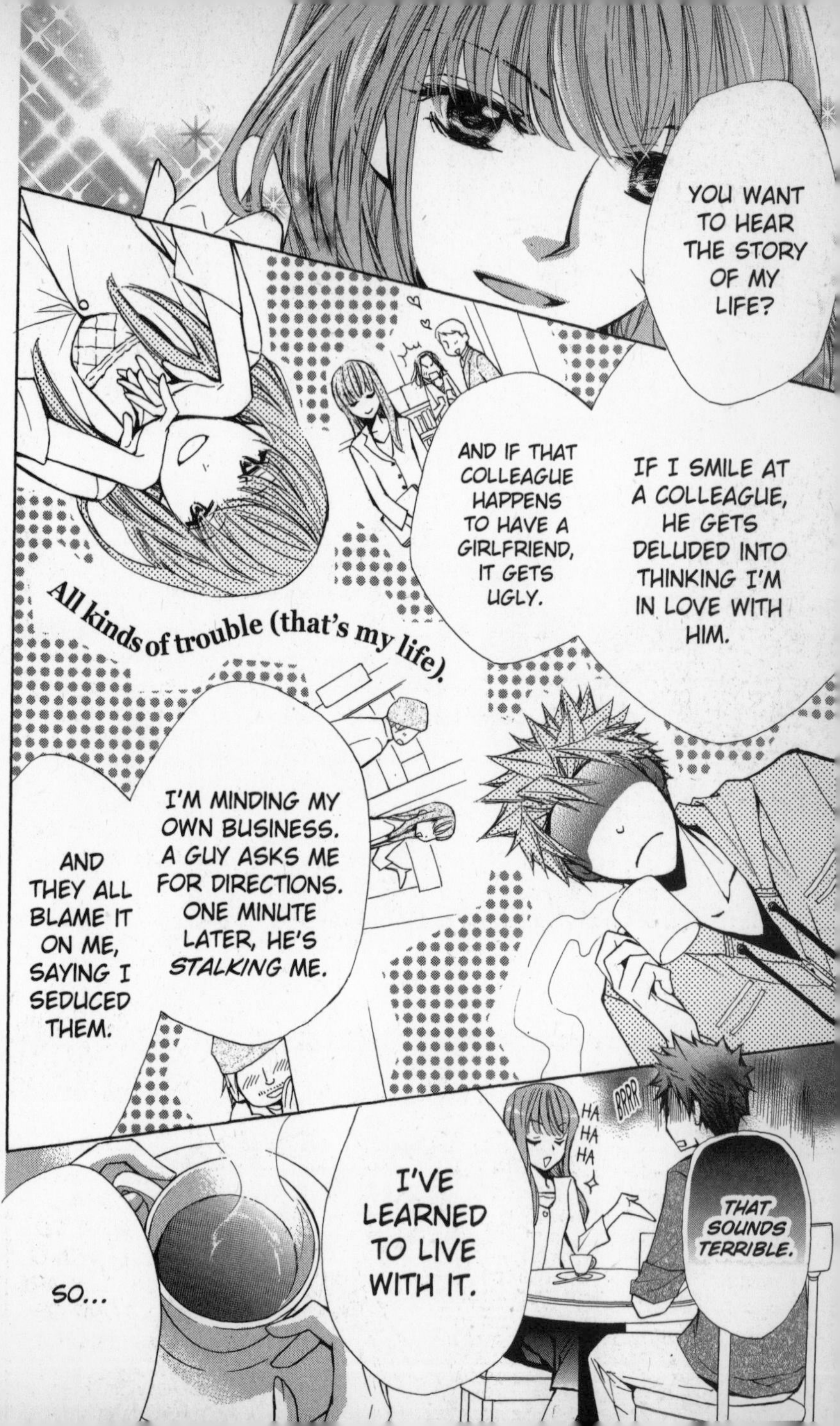
YOU WANT TO HEAR THE STORY OF MY LIFE?
IF I SMILE AT A COLLEAGUE, HE GETS DELUDED INTO THINKING I'M IN LOVE WITH HIM.
AND IF THAT COLLEAGUE HAPPENS TO HAVE A GIRLFRIEND, IT GETS UGLY.
All kinds of trouble (that's my life).
I'M MINDING MY OWN BUSINESS. A GUY ASKS ME FOR DIRECTIONS. ONE MINUTE LATER, HE'S STALKING ME.
AND THEY ALL BLAME IT ON ME, SAYING I SEDUCED THEM.
THAT SOUNDS TERRIBLE.
BRRR
HA HA HA HA
I'VE LEARNED TO LIVE WITH IT.
SO...

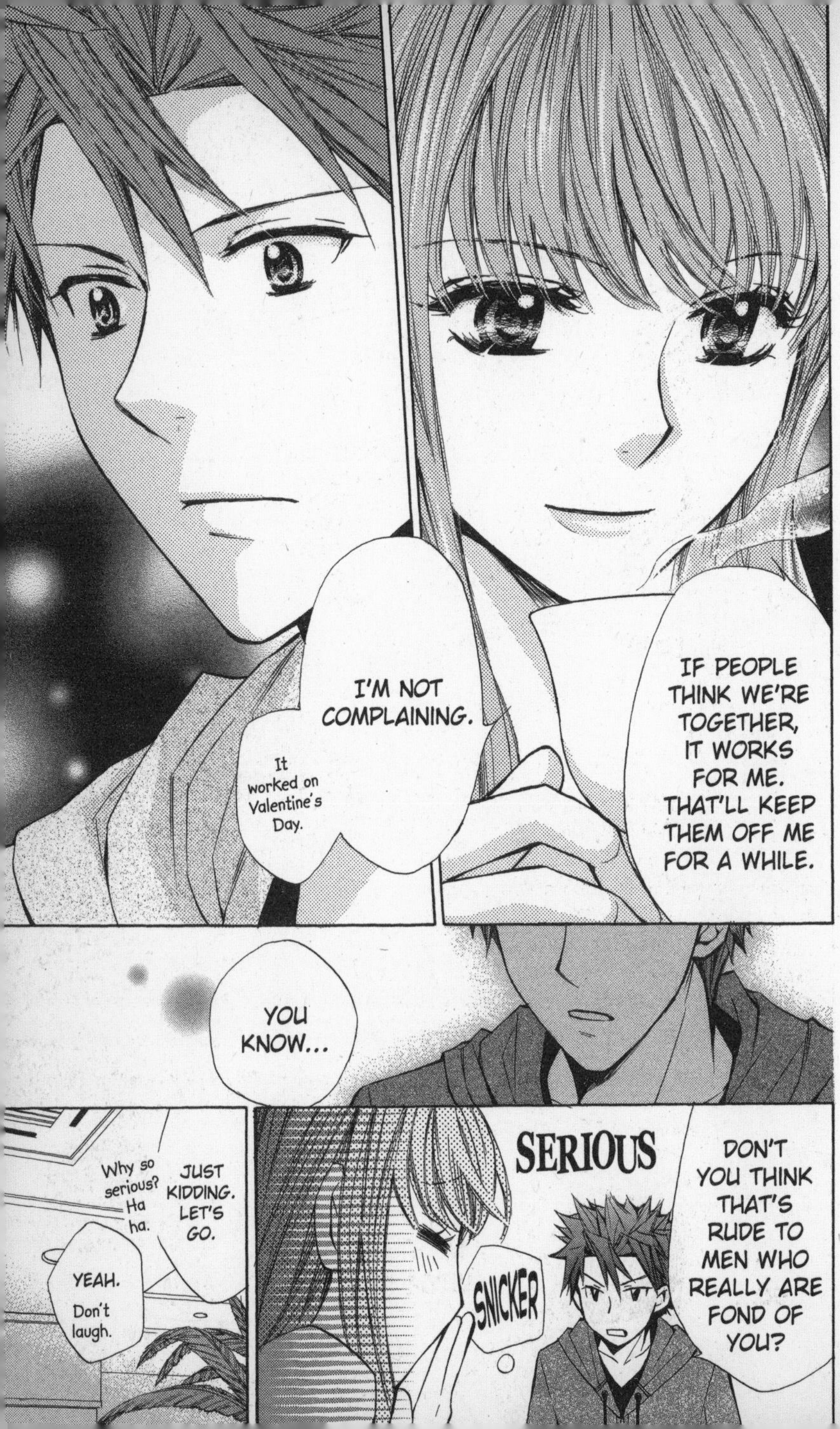
IF PEOPLE THINK WE'RE TOGETHER, IT WORKS FOR ME. THAT'LL KEEP THEM OFF ME FOR A WHILE.
I'M NOT COMPLAINING.
It worked on Valentine's Day.
YOU KNOW...
DON'T YOU THINK THAT'S RUDE TO MEN WHO REALLY ARE FOND OF YOU?
SERIOUS
SNICKER
JUST KIDDING. LET'S GO.
Why so serious? Ha ha.
YEAH.
Don't laugh.

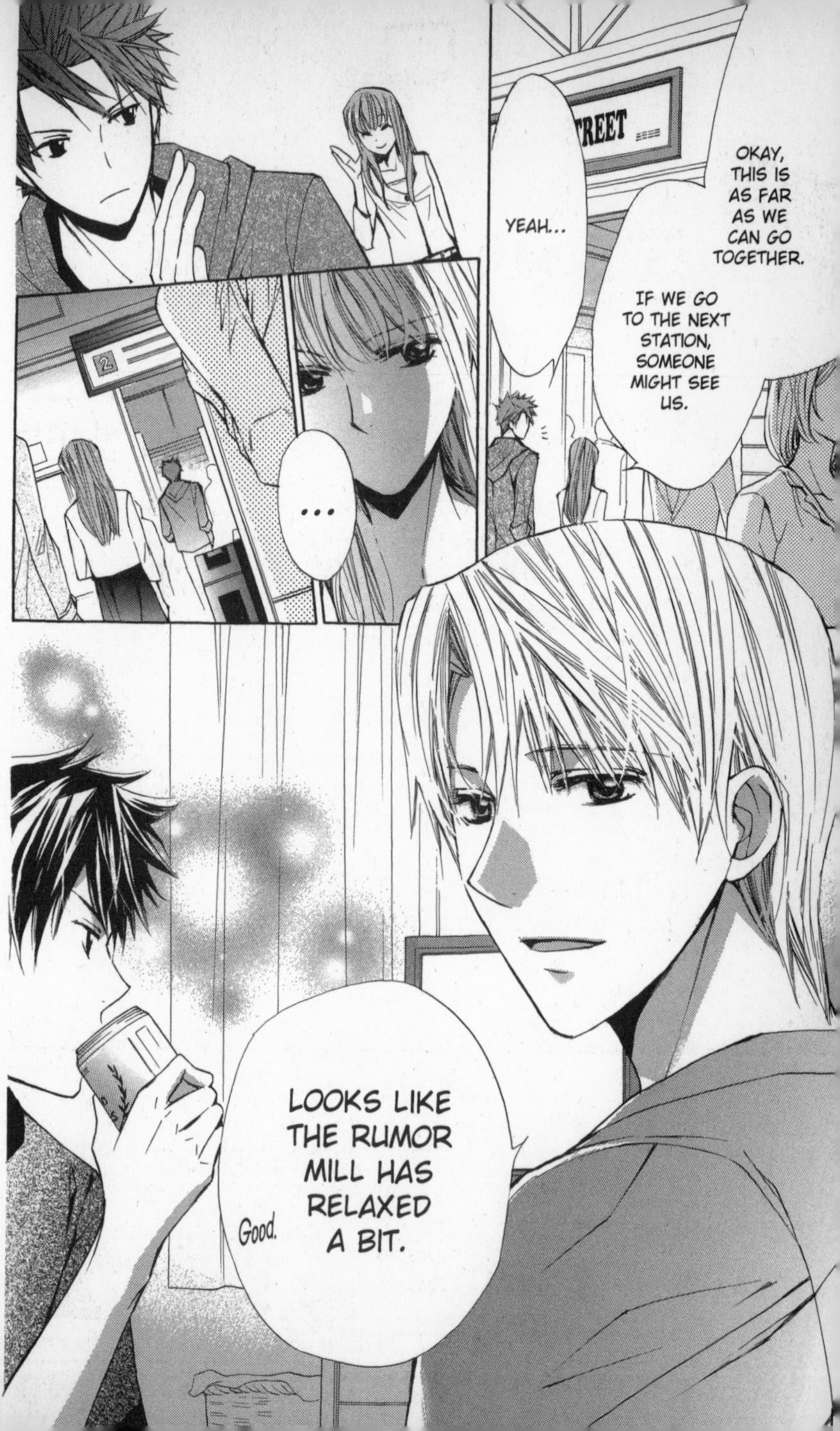
OKAY, THIS IS AS FAR AS WE CAN GO TOGETHER.
IF WE GO TO THE NEXT STATION, SOMEONE MIGHT SEE US.
YEAH...
...
LOOKS LIKE THE RUMOR MILL HAS RELAXED A BIT.
Good.

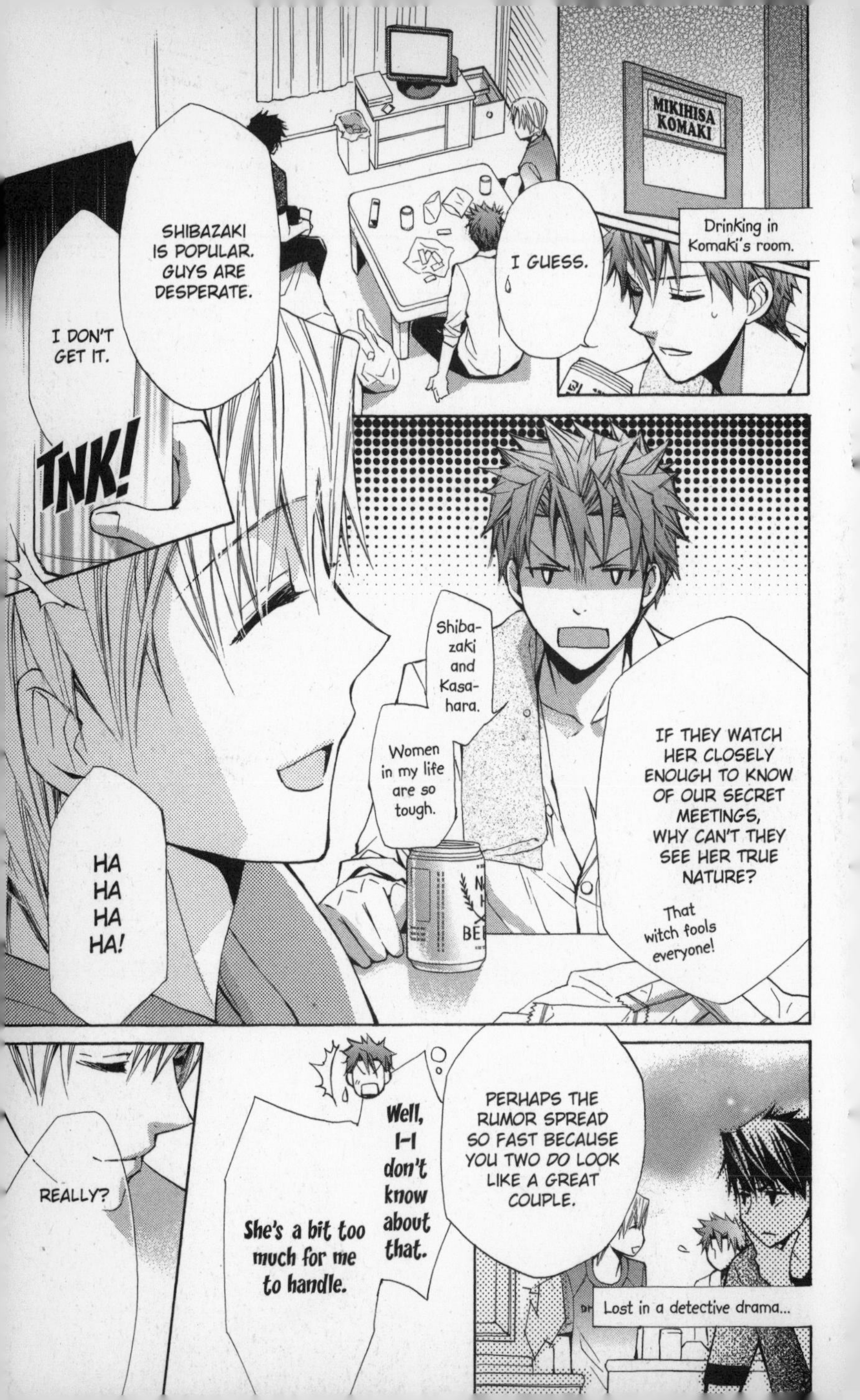
MIKIHISA KOMAKI
Drinking in Komaki's room.
I GUESS.
SHIBAZAKI IS POPULAR. GUYS ARE DESPERATE.
IF THEY WATCH HER CLOSELY ENOUGH TO KNOW OF OUR SECRET MEETINGS, WHY CAN'T THEY SEE HER TRUE NATURE?
That witch fools everyone!
Shibazaki and Kasahara.
Women in my life are so tough.
I DON'T GET IT.
TNK!
HA HA HA HA!
Lost in a detective drama...
PERHAPS THE RUMOR SPREAD SO FAST BECAUSE YOU TWO *DO* LOOK LIKE A GREAT COUPLE.
Well, I-I don't know about that.
She's a bit too much for me to handle.
REALLY?

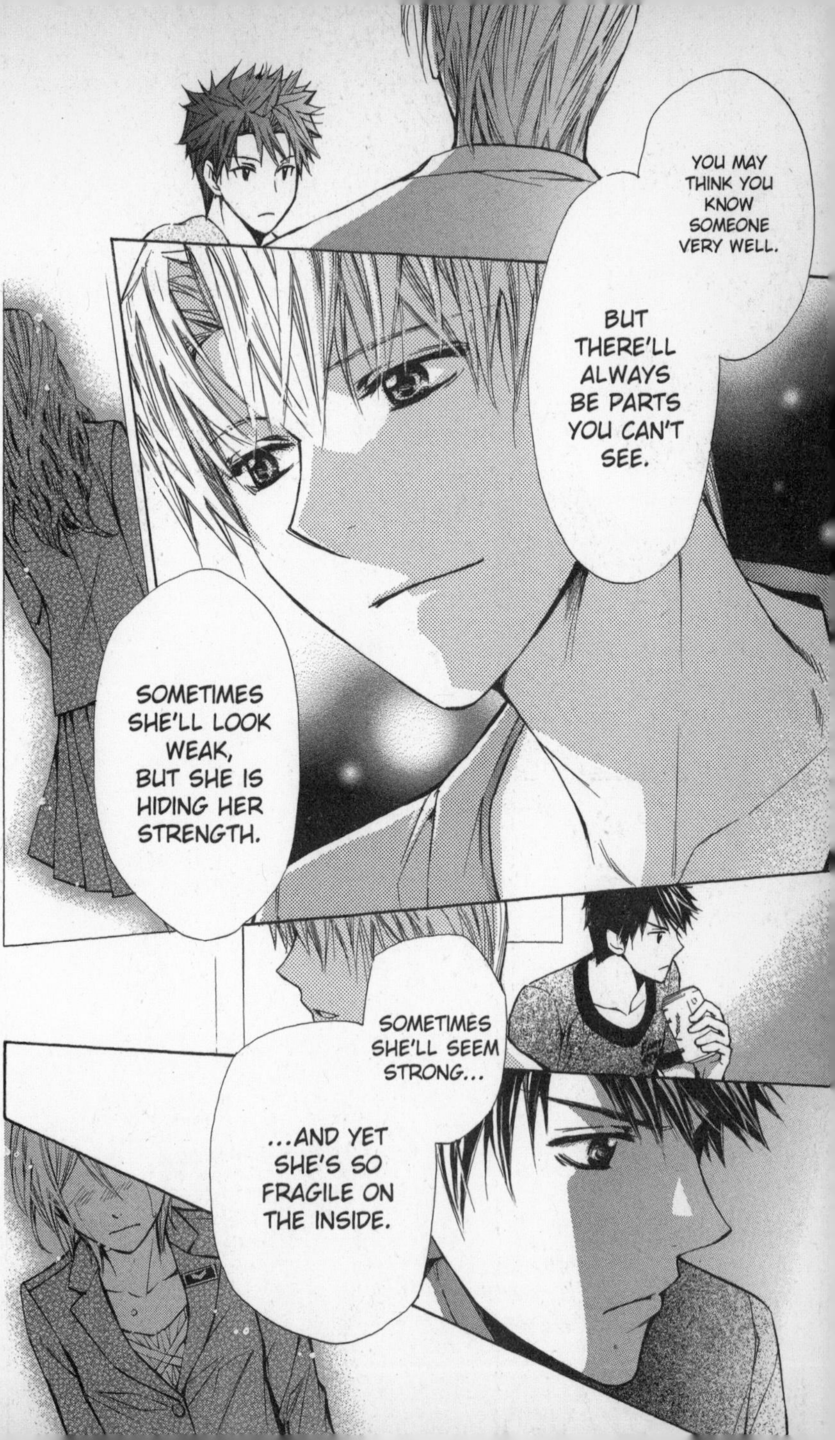
YOU MAY THINK YOU KNOW SOMEONE VERY WELL.
BUT THERE'LL ALWAYS BE PARTS YOU CAN'T SEE.
SOMETIMES SHE'LL LOOK WEAK, BUT SHE IS HIDING HER STRENGTH.
SOMETIMES SHE'LL SEEM STRONG...
...AND YET SHE'S SO FRAGILE ON THE INSIDE.

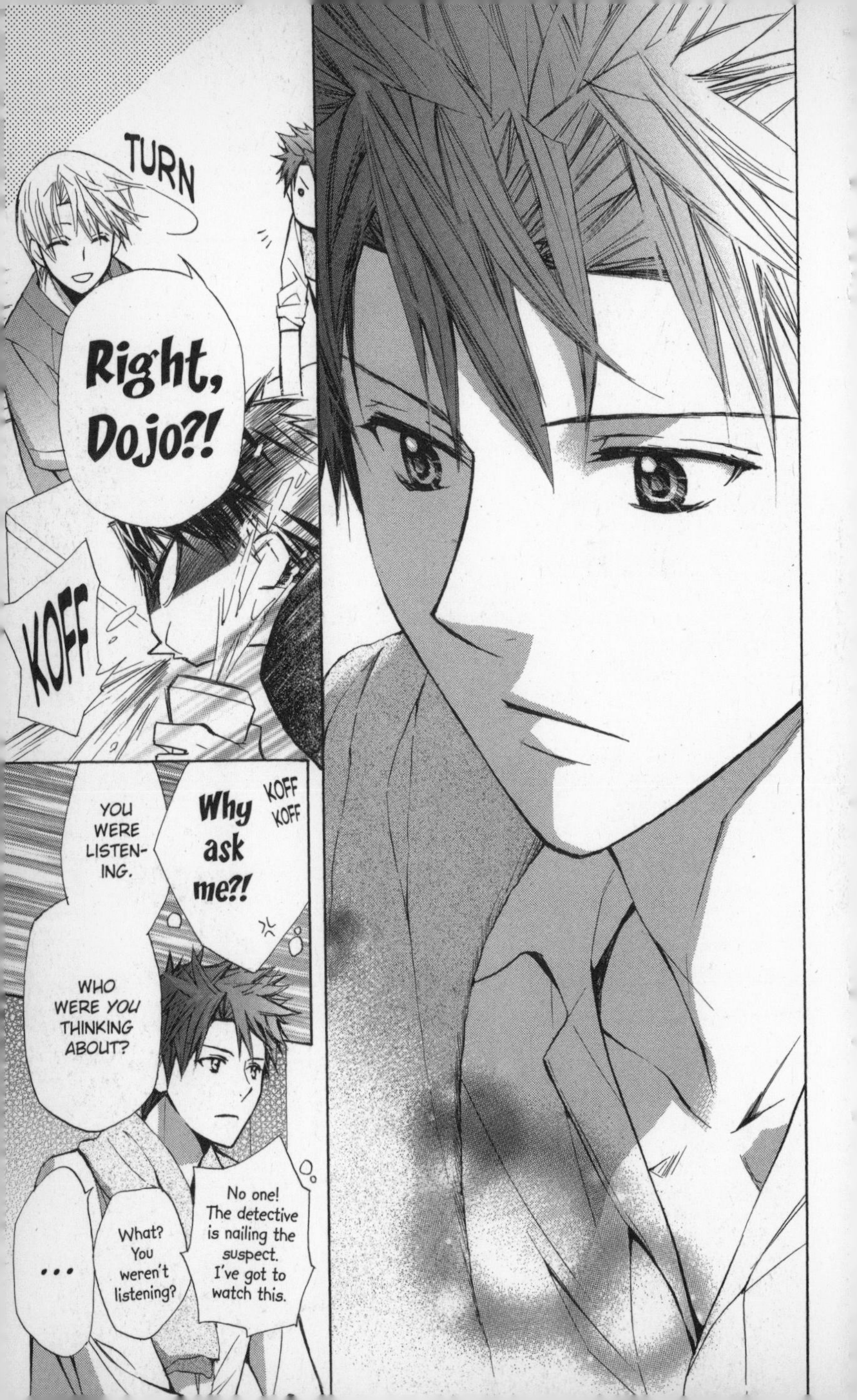
TURN
Right, Dojo?!
KOFF
KOFF KOFF
Why ask me?!
YOU WERE LISTENING.
WHO WERE YOU THINKING ABOUT?
No one! The detective is nailing the suspect. I've got to watch this.
What? You weren't listening?
...

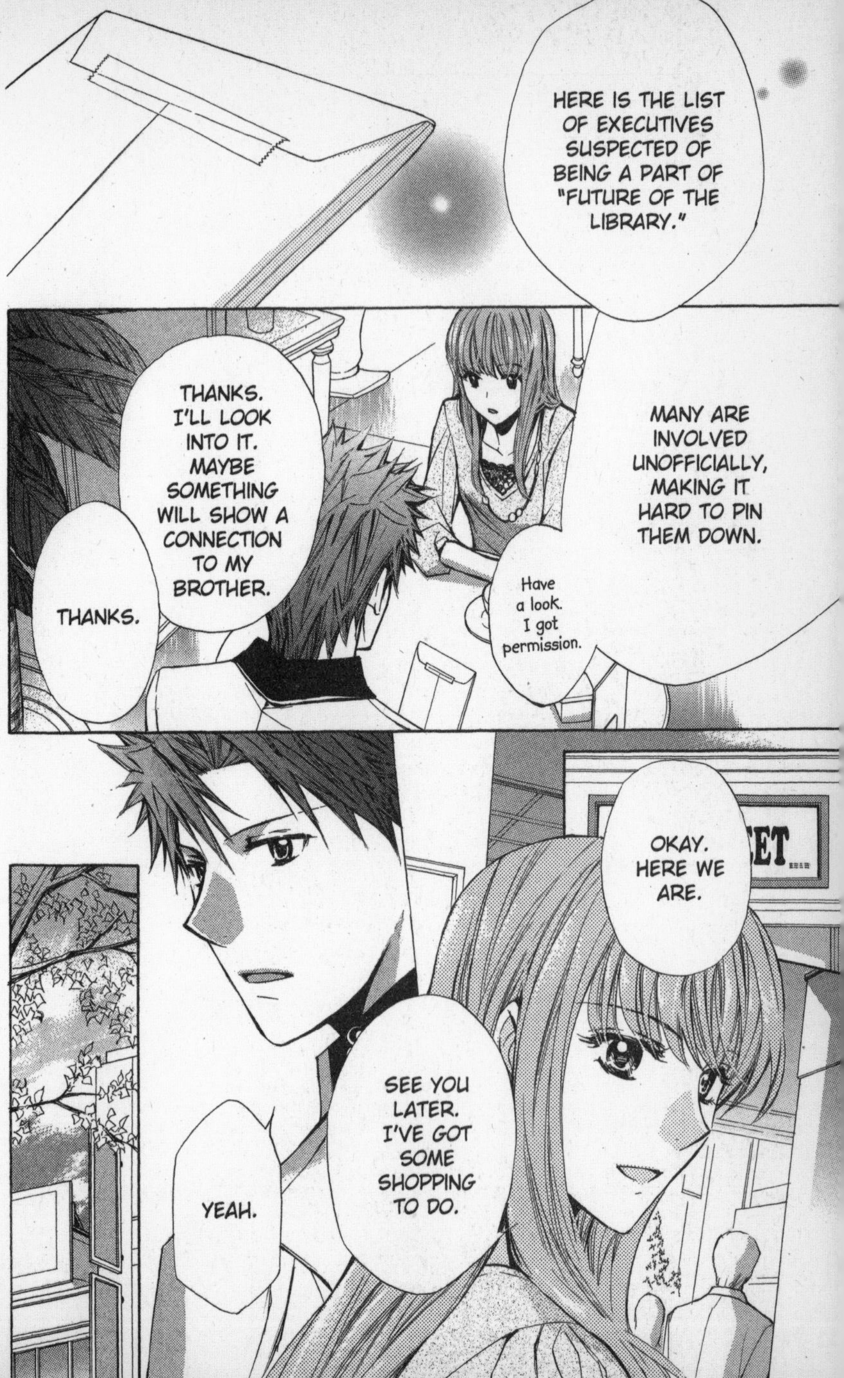
HERE IS THE LIST OF EXECUTIVES SUSPECTED OF BEING A PART OF "FUTURE OF THE LIBRARY."
MANY ARE INVOLVED UNOFFICIALLY, MAKING IT HARD TO PIN THEM DOWN.
Have a look. I got permission.
THANKS. I'LL LOOK INTO IT. MAYBE SOMETHING WILL SHOW A CONNECTION TO MY BROTHER.
THANKS.
OKAY. HERE WE ARE.
SEE YOU LATER. I'VE GOT SOME SHOPPING TO DO.
YEAH.

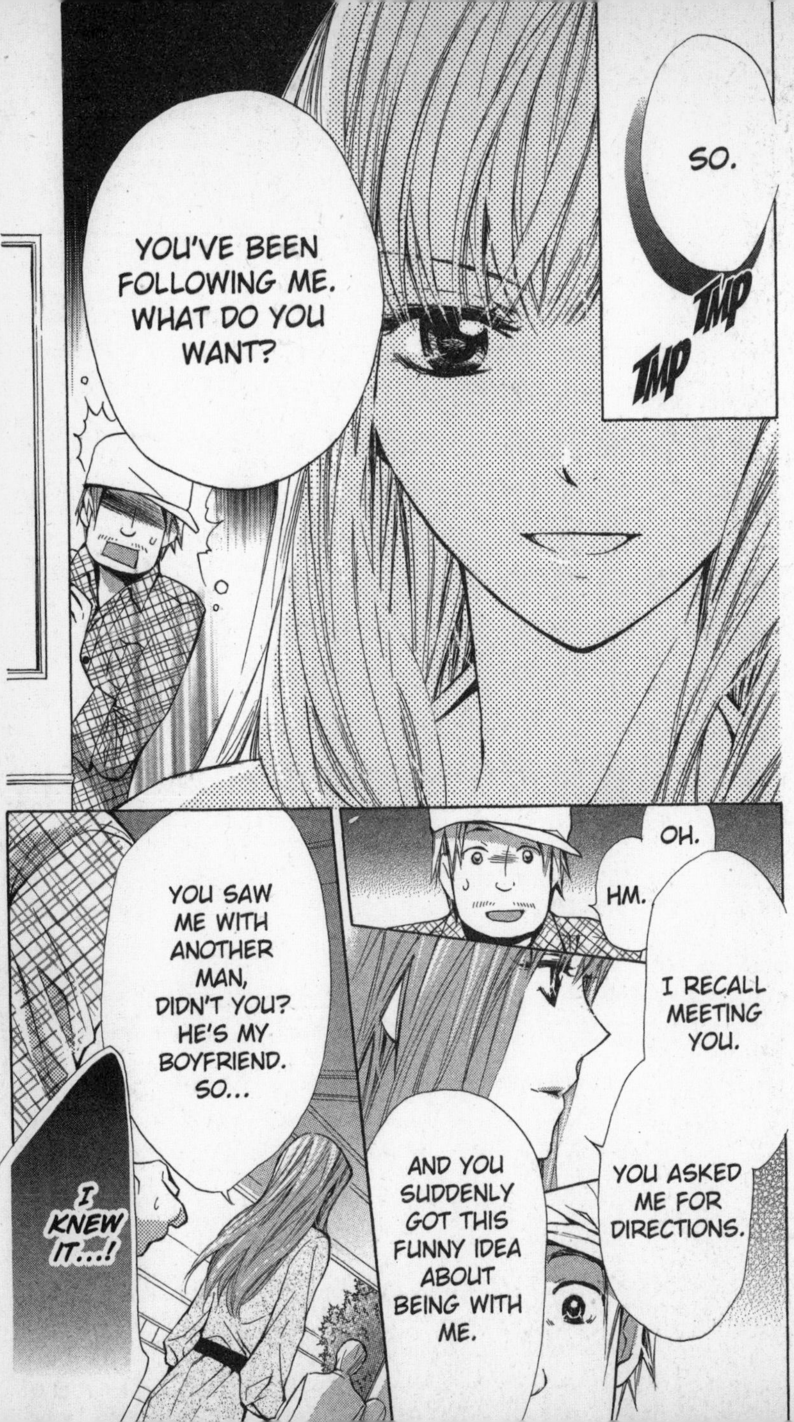
SO.
TMP TMP
YOU'VE BEEN FOLLOWING ME. WHAT DO YOU WANT?
OH.
HM.
I RECALL MEETING YOU.
YOU ASKED ME FOR DIRECTIONS.
AND YOU SUDDENLY GOT THIS FUNNY IDEA ABOUT BEING WITH ME.
YOU SAW ME WITH ANOTHER MAN, DIDN'T YOU? HE'S MY BOYFRIEND. SO...
I KNEW IT...!

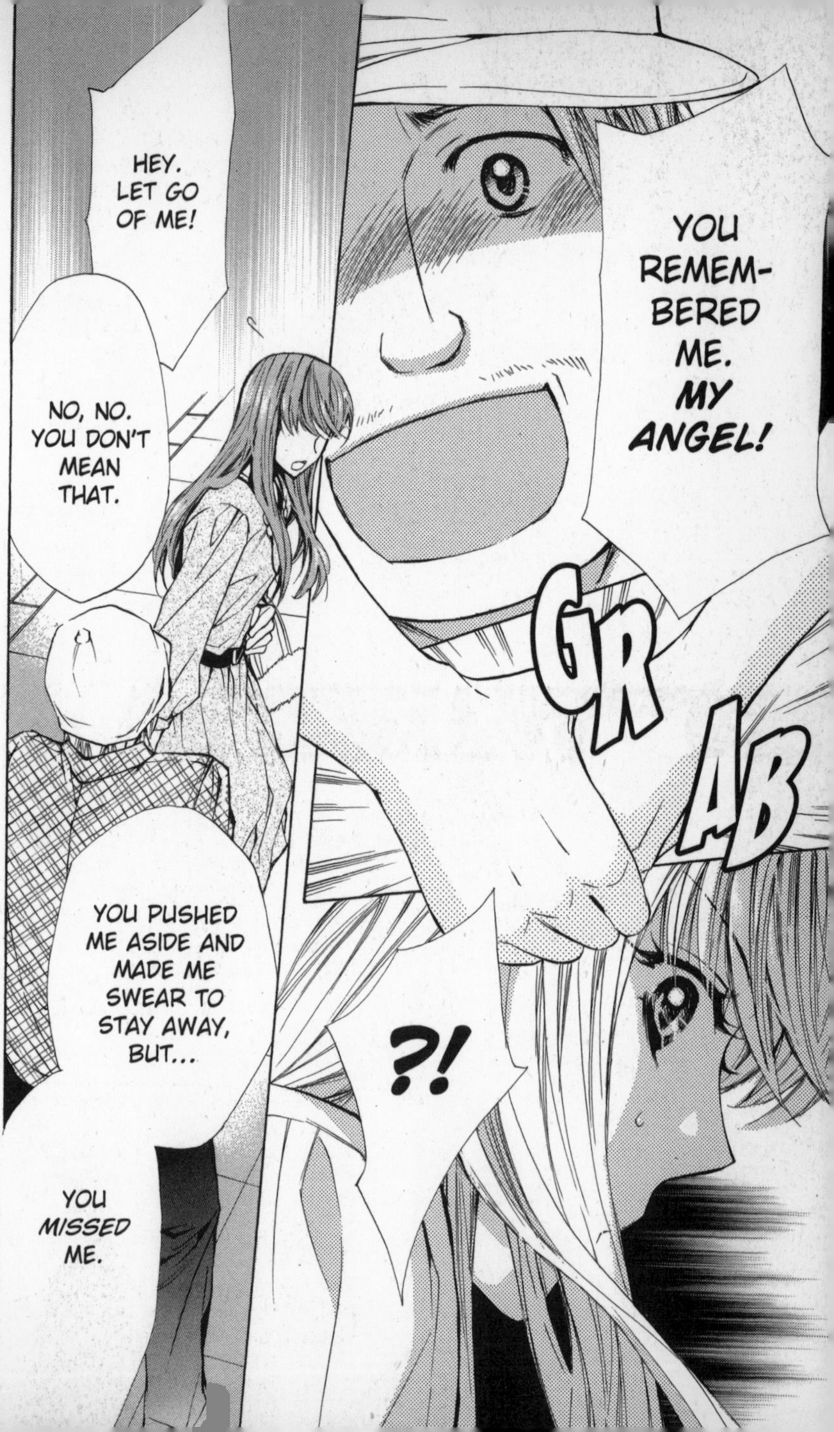
YOU REMEM-BERED ME. MY ANGEL!
GRAB
?!
HEY. LET GO OF ME!
NO, NO. YOU DON'T MEAN THAT.
YOU PUSHED ME ASIDE AND MADE ME SWEAR TO STAY AWAY, BUT...
YOU MISSED ME.

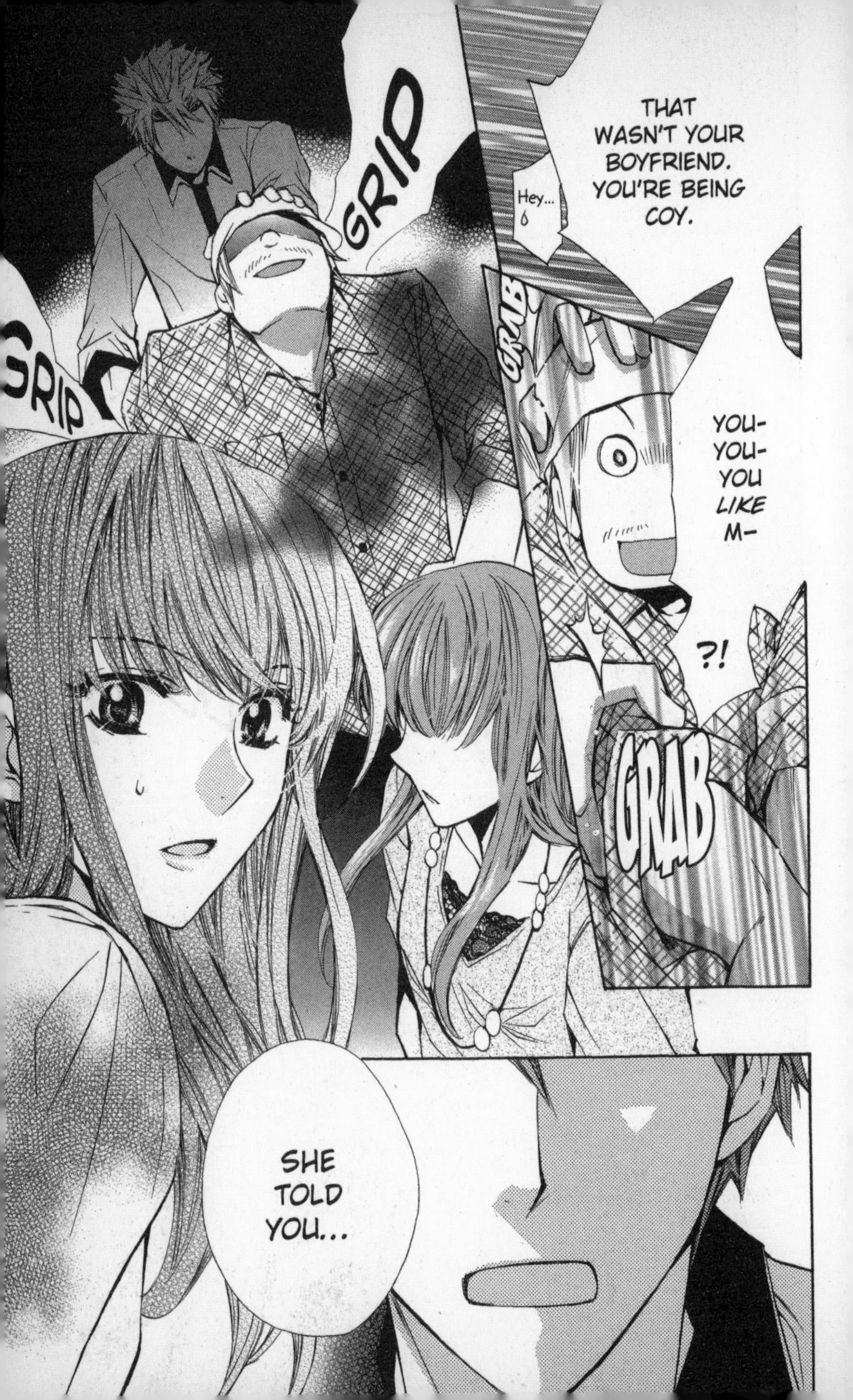
THAT WASN'T YOUR BOYFRIEND. YOU'RE BEING COY.
Hey...
GRAB
YOU-YOU-YOU LIKE M-
?!
GRAB
GRIP
GRIP
SHE TOLD YOU...

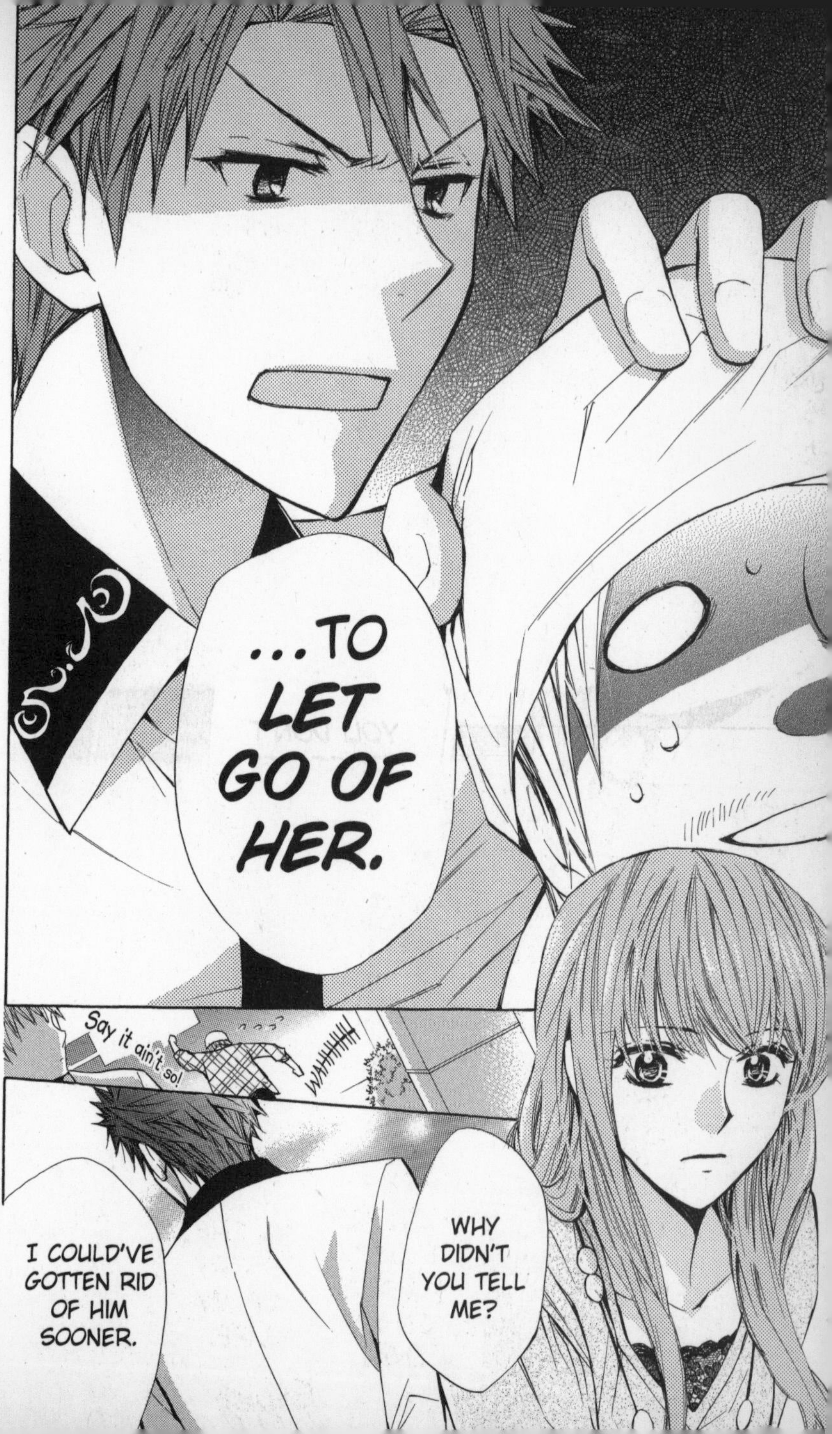
...TO LET GO OF HER.
WHY DIDN'T YOU TELL ME?
Say it ain't so!
WAHHHH
I COULD'VE GOTTEN RID OF HIM SOONER.

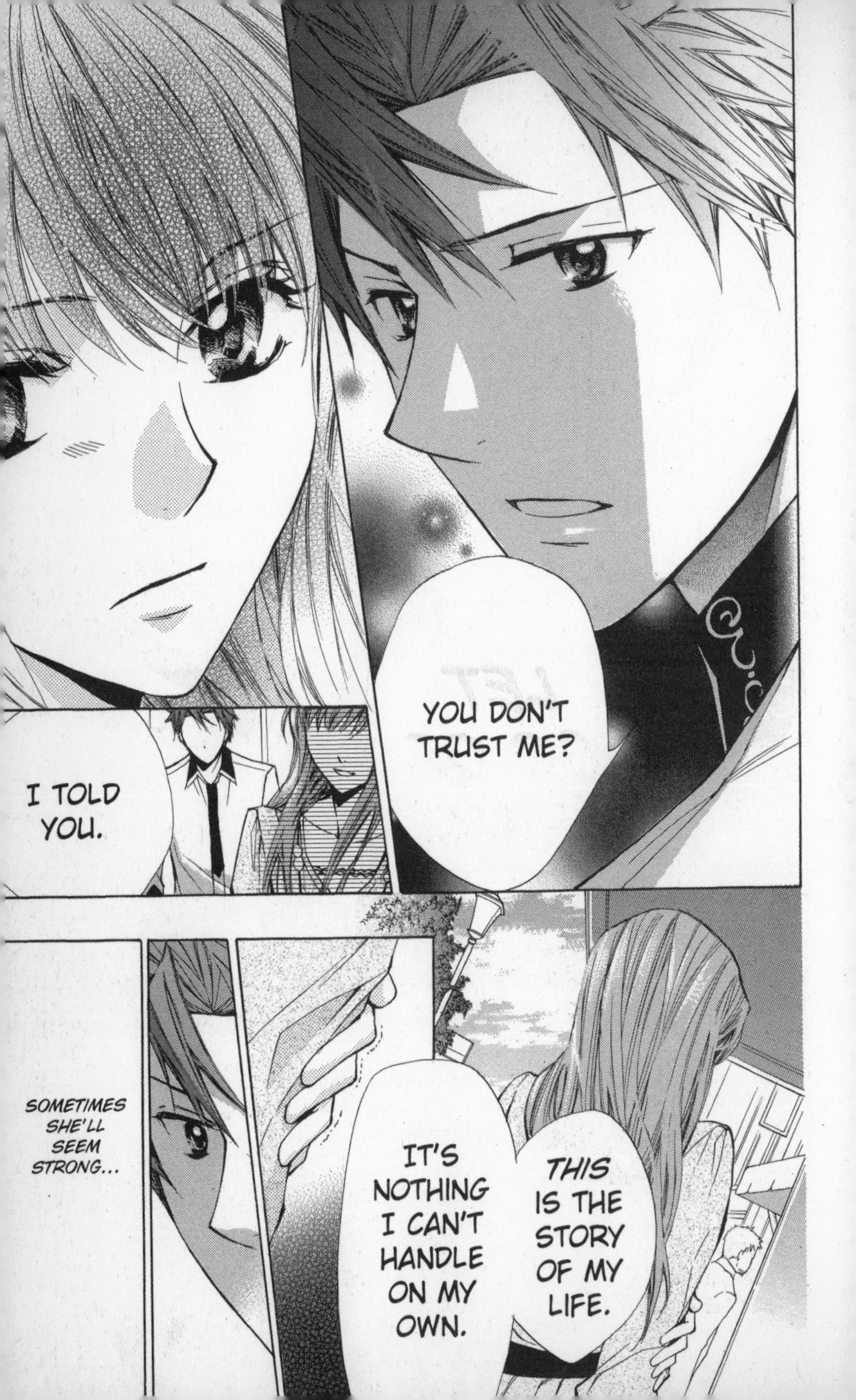
YOU DON'T TRUST ME?
I TOLD YOU.
THIS IS THE STORY OF MY LIFE.
IT'S NOTHING I CAN'T HANDLE ON MY OWN.
SOMETIMES SHE'LL SEEM STRONG...

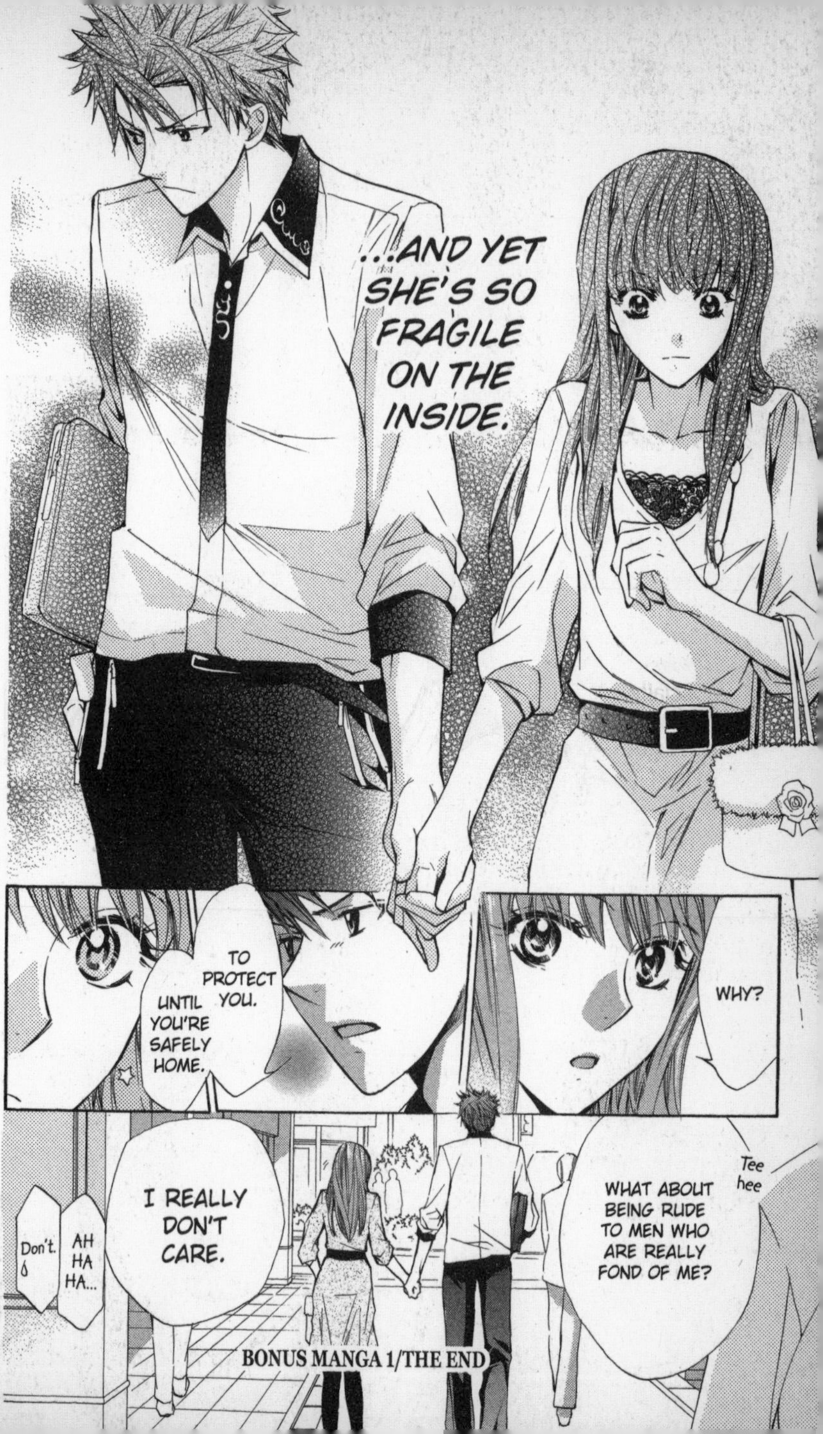
...AND YET SHE'S SO FRAGILE ON THE INSIDE.
WHY?
TO PROTECT YOU.
UNTIL YOU'RE SAFELY HOME.
Tee hee
WHAT ABOUT BEING RUDE TO MEN WHO ARE REALLY FOND OF ME?
I REALLY DON'T CARE.
AH HA HA...
Don't.
BONUS MANGA 1/THE END

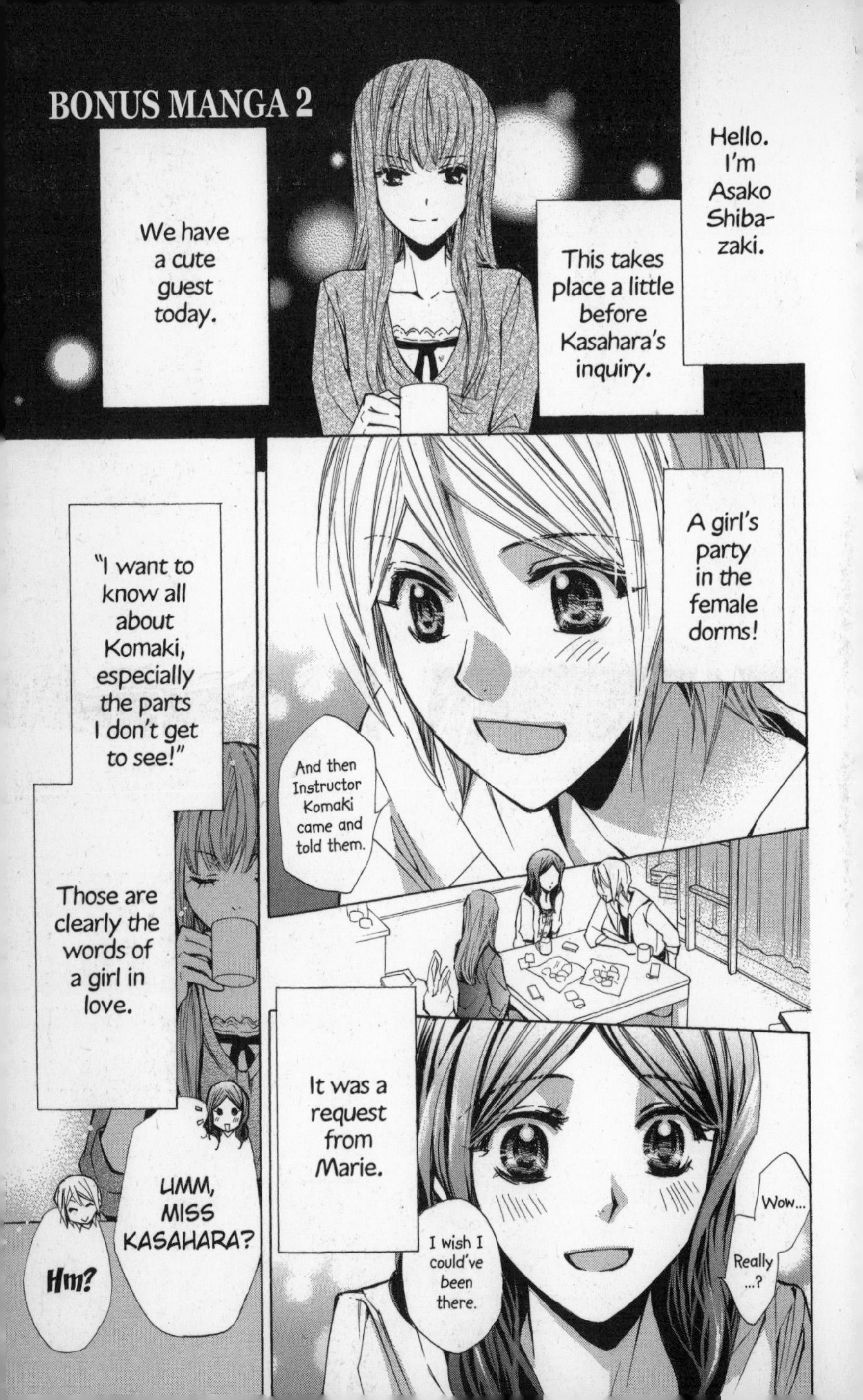
BONUS MANGA 2
Hello. I'm Asako Shiba-zaki.
This takes place a little before Kasahara's inquiry.
We have a cute guest today.
A girl's party in the female dorms!
And then Instructor Komaki came and told them.
It was a request from Marie.
Wow...
Really ...?
I wish I could've been there.
"I want to know all about Komaki, especially the parts I don't get to see!"
Those are clearly the words of a girl in love.
UMM, MISS KASAHARA?
Hm?

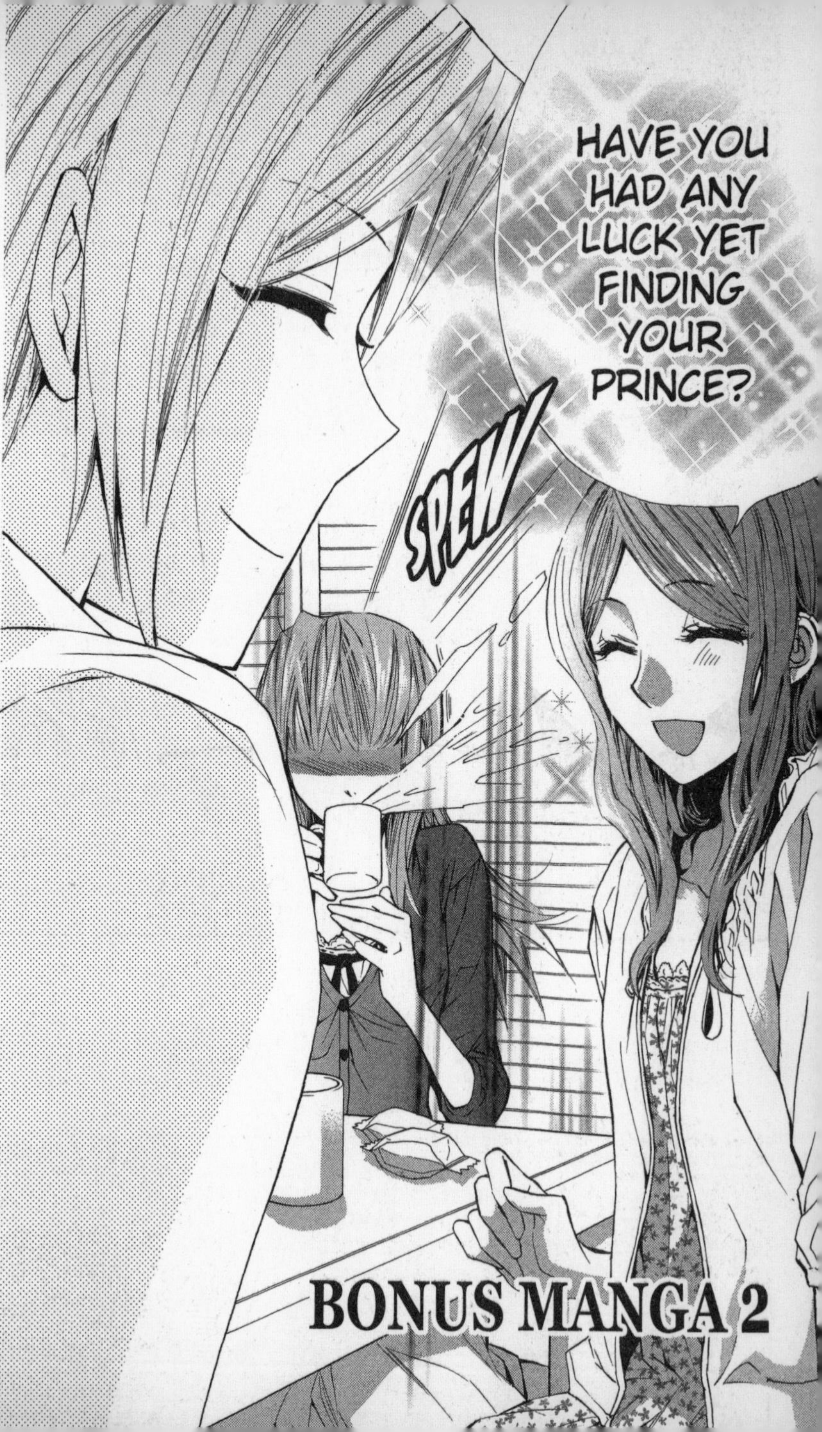
HAVE YOU HAD ANY LUCK YET FINDING YOUR PRINCE?
SPEW
BONUS MANGA 2

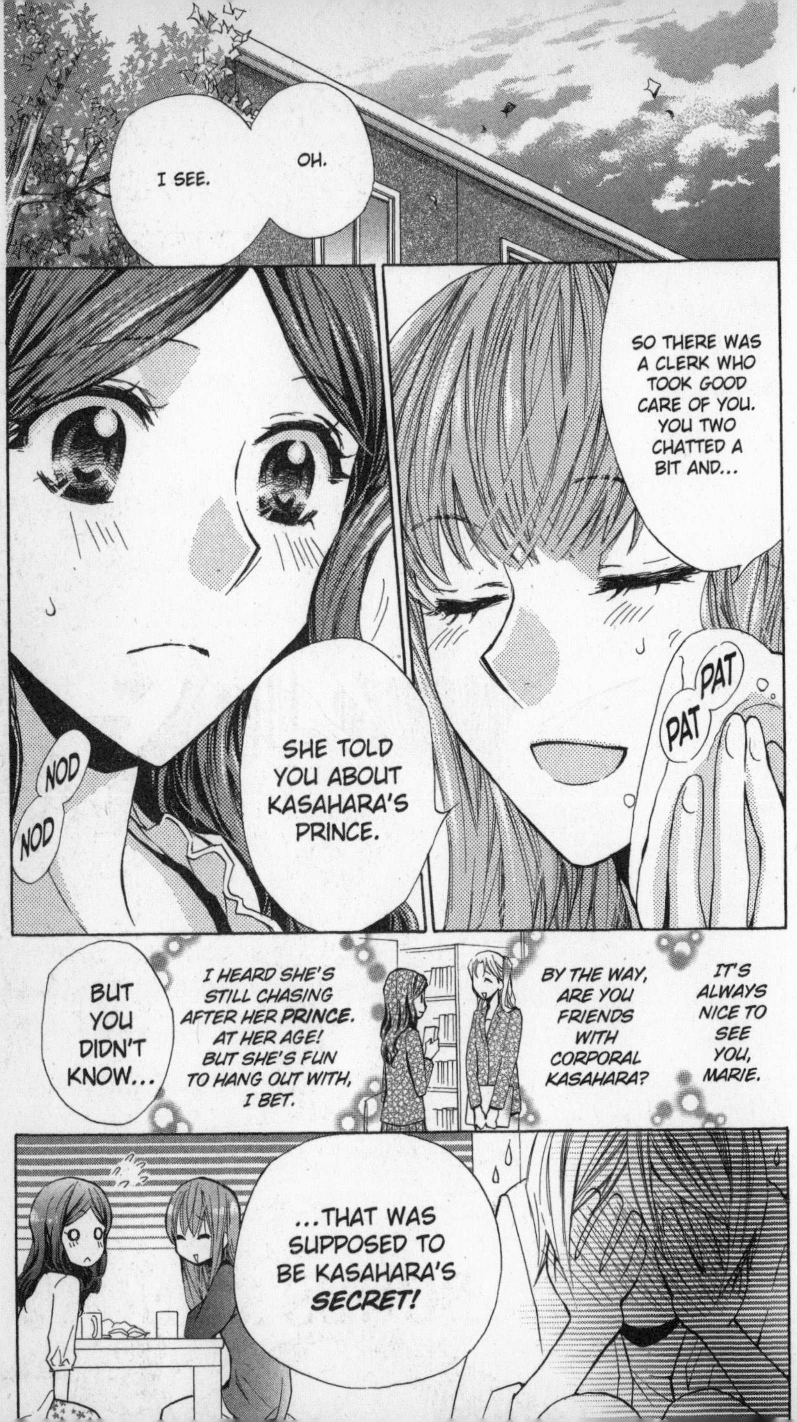
OH.
I SEE.
SO THERE WAS A CLERK WHO TOOK GOOD CARE OF YOU. YOU TWO CHATTED A BIT AND...
PAT PAT
SHE TOLD YOU ABOUT KASAHARA'S PRINCE.
NOD NOD
IT'S ALWAYS NICE TO SEE YOU, MARIE.
BY THE WAY, ARE YOU FRIENDS WITH CORPORAL KASAHARA?
I HEARD SHE'S STILL CHASING AFTER HER PRINCE. AT HER AGE! BUT SHE'S FUN TO HANG OUT WITH, I BET.
BUT YOU DIDN'T KNOW...
...THAT WAS SUPPOSED TO BE KASAHARA'S SECRET!

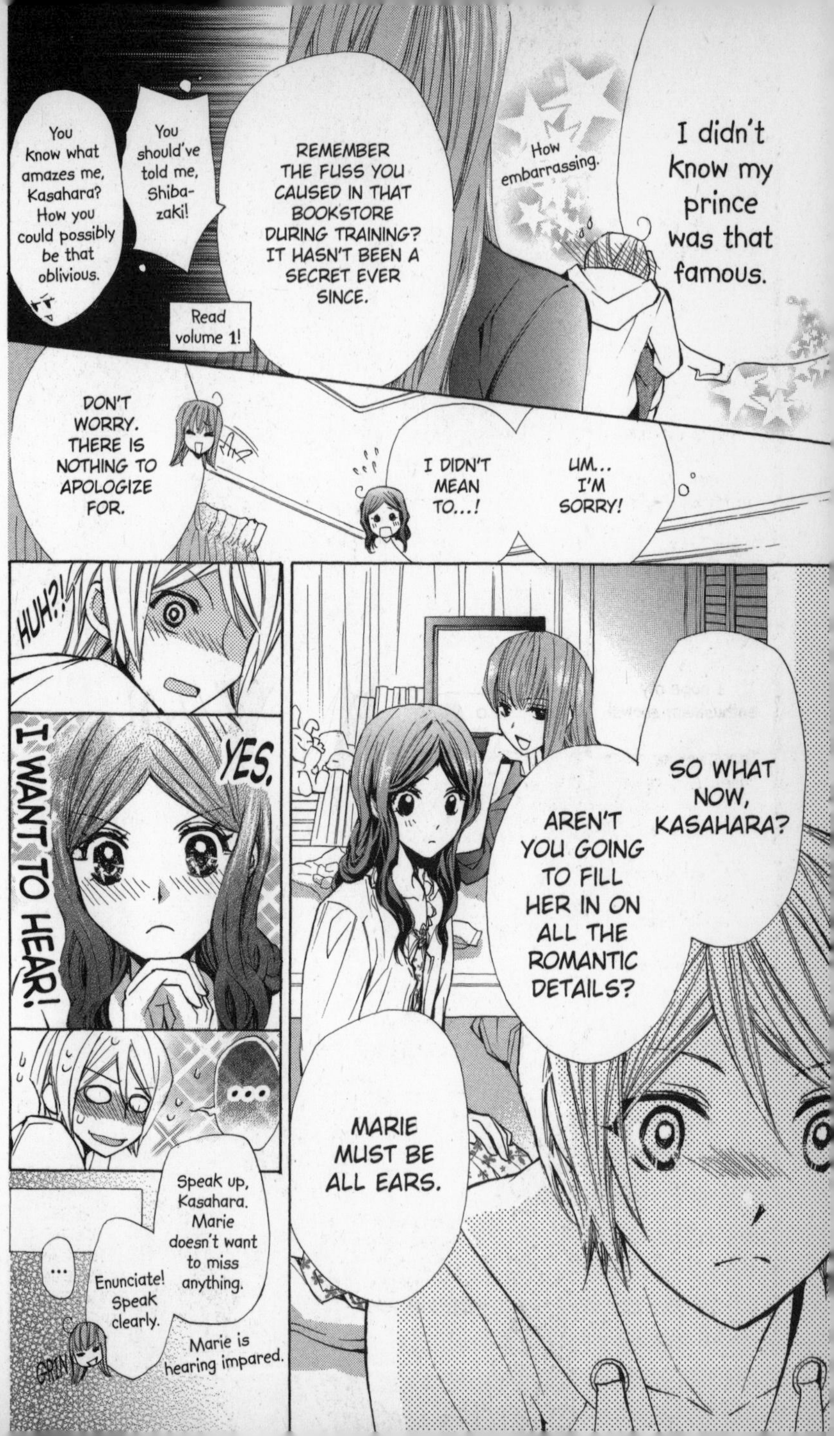
I didn't know my prince was that famous.
How embarrassing.
REMEMBER THE FUSS YOU CAUSED IN THAT BOOKSTORE DURING TRAINING? IT HASN'T BEEN A SECRET EVER SINCE.
Read volume 1!
You should've told me, Shiba-zaki!
You know what amazes me, Kasahara? How you could possibly be that oblivious.
UM... I'M SORRY!
I DIDN'T MEAN TO...!
DON'T WORRY. THERE IS NOTHING TO APOLOGIZE FOR.
SO WHAT NOW, KASAHARA?
AREN'T YOU GOING TO FILL HER IN ON ALL THE ROMANTIC DETAILS?
MARIE MUST BE ALL EARS.
HUH?!
YES.
I WANT TO HEAR!
...
Speak up, Kasahara. Marie doesn't want to miss anything.
Enunciate! Speak clearly.
...
Marie is hearing impared.
GRIN

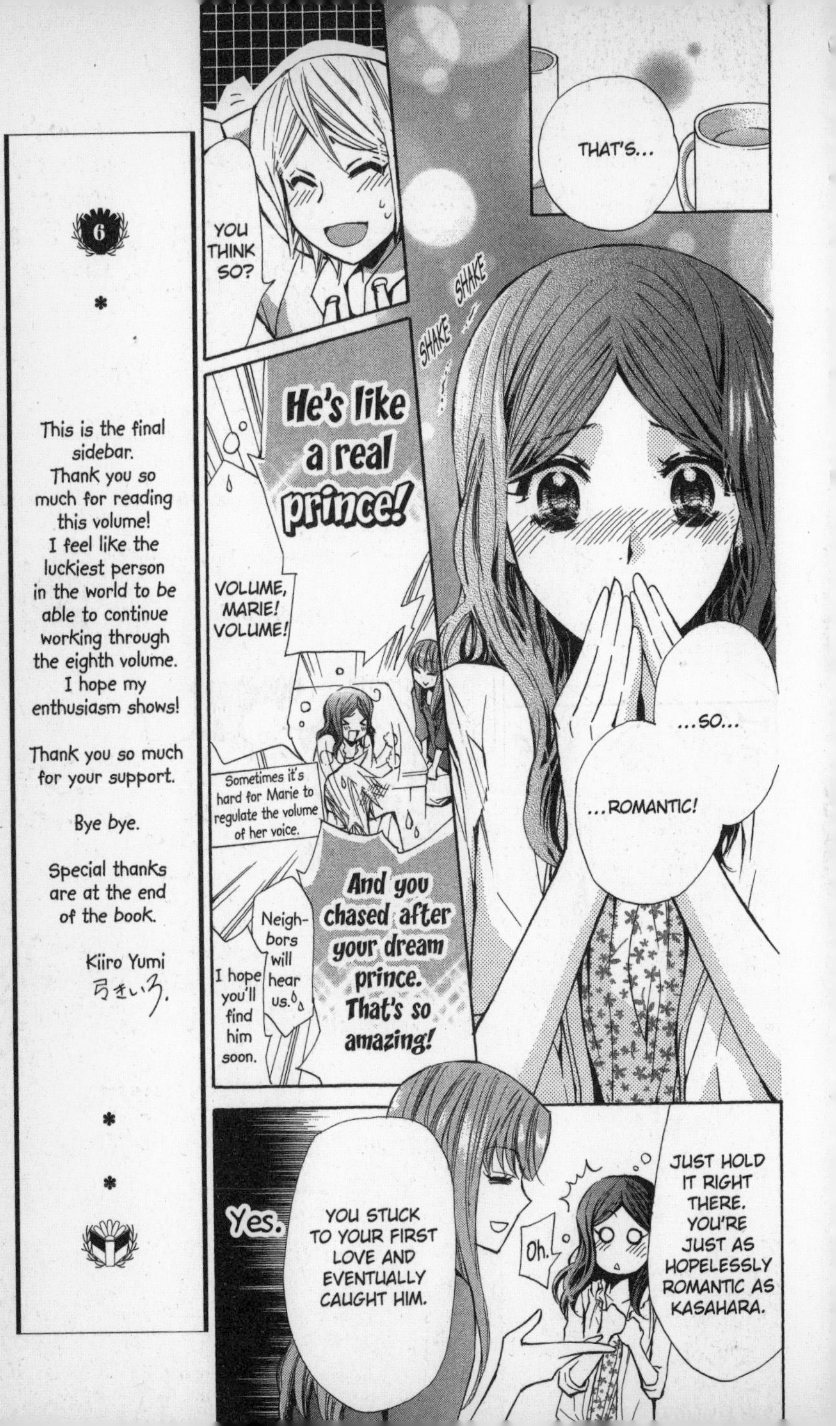
THAT'S...
SHAKE SHAKE
...SO...
...ROMANTIC!
YOU THINK SO?
He's like a real prince!
VOLUME, MARIE! VOLUME!
Sometimes it's hard for Marie to regulate the volume of her voice.
And you chased after your dream prince. That's so amazing!
Neighbors will hear us.
I hope you'll find him soon.
JUST HOLD IT RIGHT THERE. YOU'RE JUST AS HOPELESSLY ROMANTIC AS KASAHARA.
Oh.
YOU STUCK TO YOUR FIRST LOVE AND EVENTUALLY CAUGHT HIM.
Yes.

6

*

This is the final sidebar. Thank you so much for reading this volume! I feel like the luckiest person in the world to be able to continue working through the eighth volume. I hope my enthusiasm shows!

Thank you so much for your support.

Bye bye.

Special thanks are at the end of the book.

Kiiro Yumi
弓きいろ

*

*

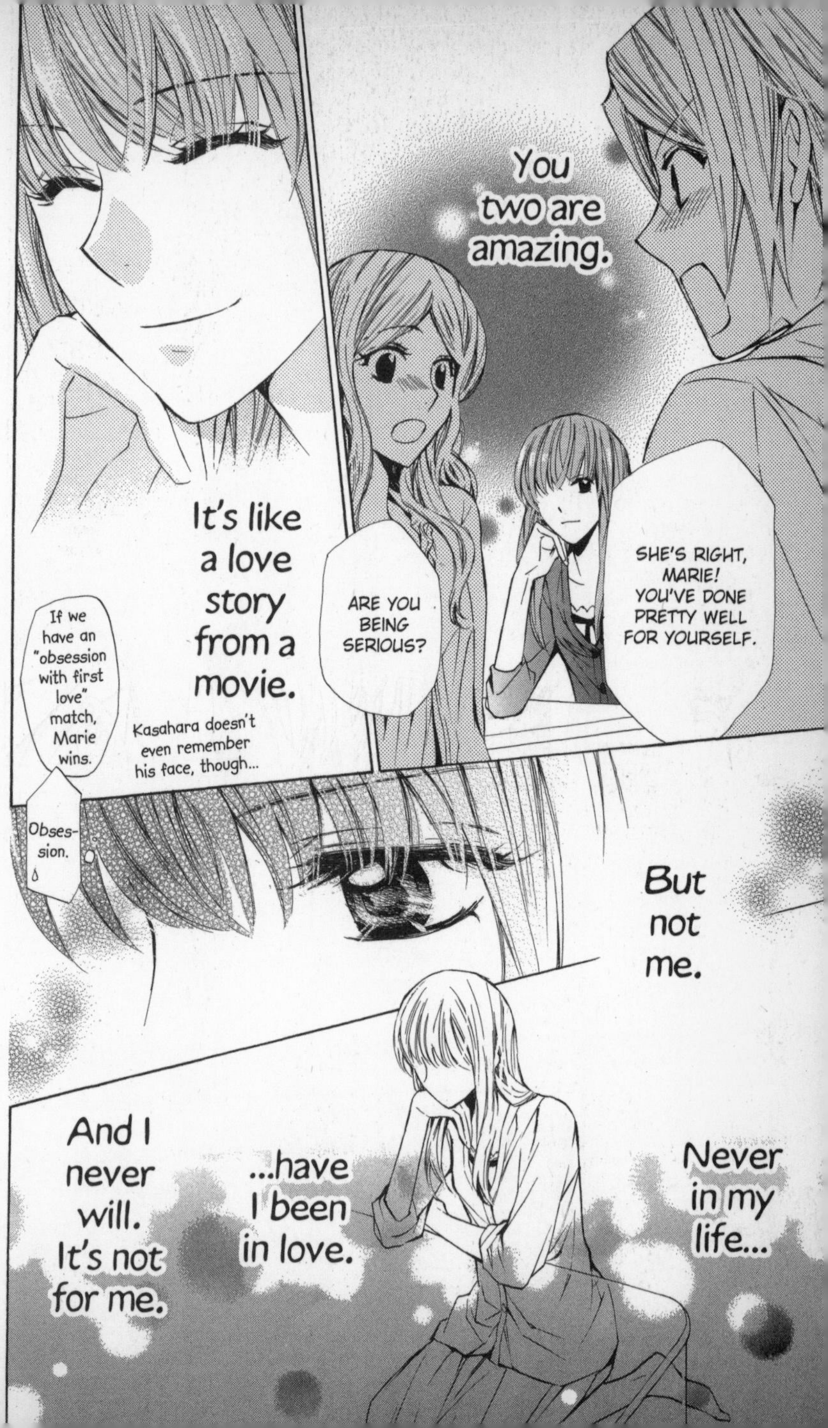
You two are amazing.
SHE'S RIGHT, MARIE! YOU'VE DONE PRETTY WELL FOR YOURSELF.
ARE YOU BEING SERIOUS?
It's like a love story from a movie.
Kasahara doesn't even remember his face, though...
If we have an "obsession with first love" match, Marie wins.
Obses-sion.
But not me.
Never in my life...
...have I been in love.
And I never will. It's not for me.

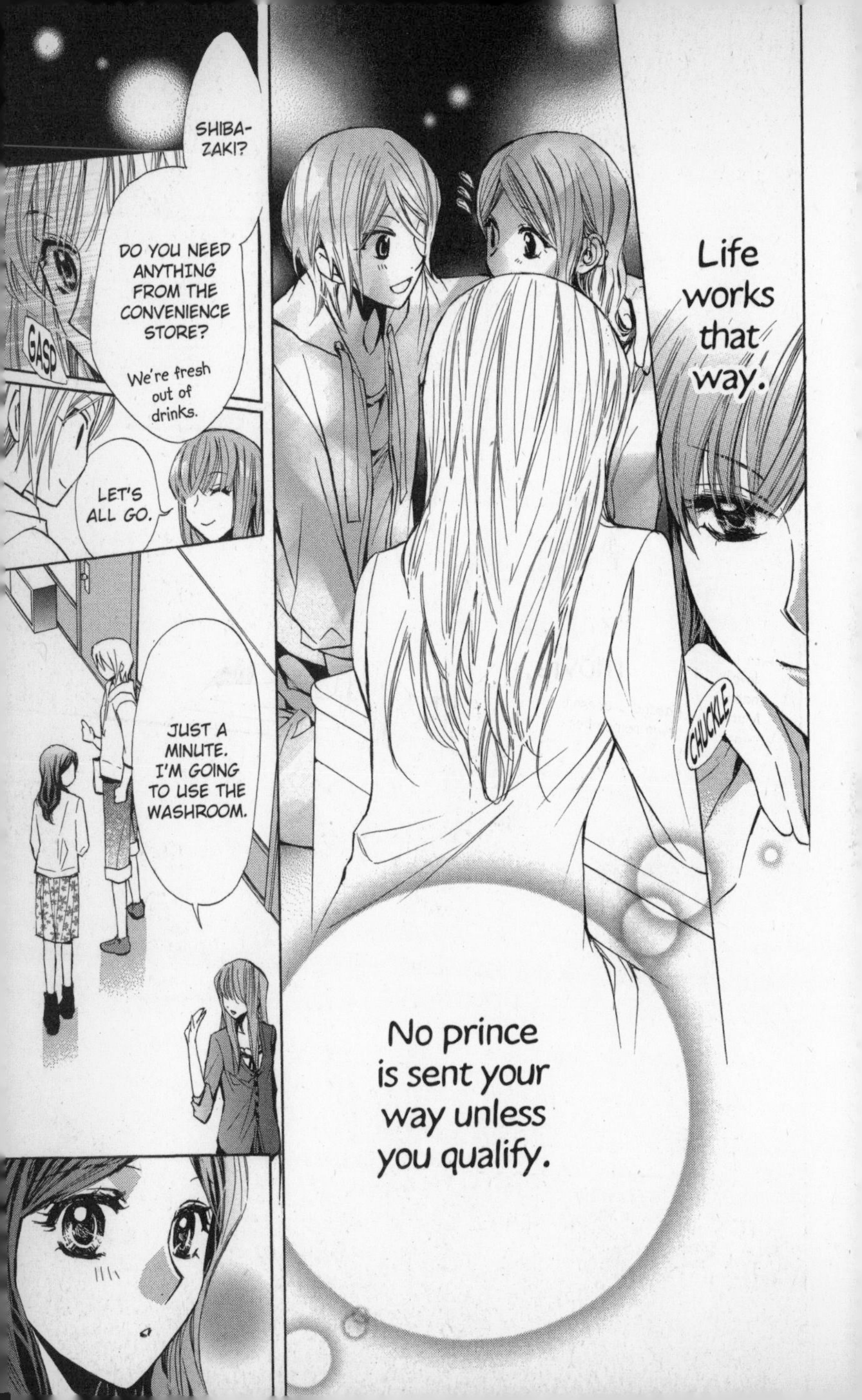

Life works that way.
CHUCKLE
No prince is sent your way unless you qualify.
SHIBA-ZAKI?
DO YOU NEED ANYTHING FROM THE CONVENIENCE STORE?
We're fresh out of drinks.
GASP
LET'S ALL GO.
JUST A MINUTE. I'M GOING TO USE THE WASHROOM.

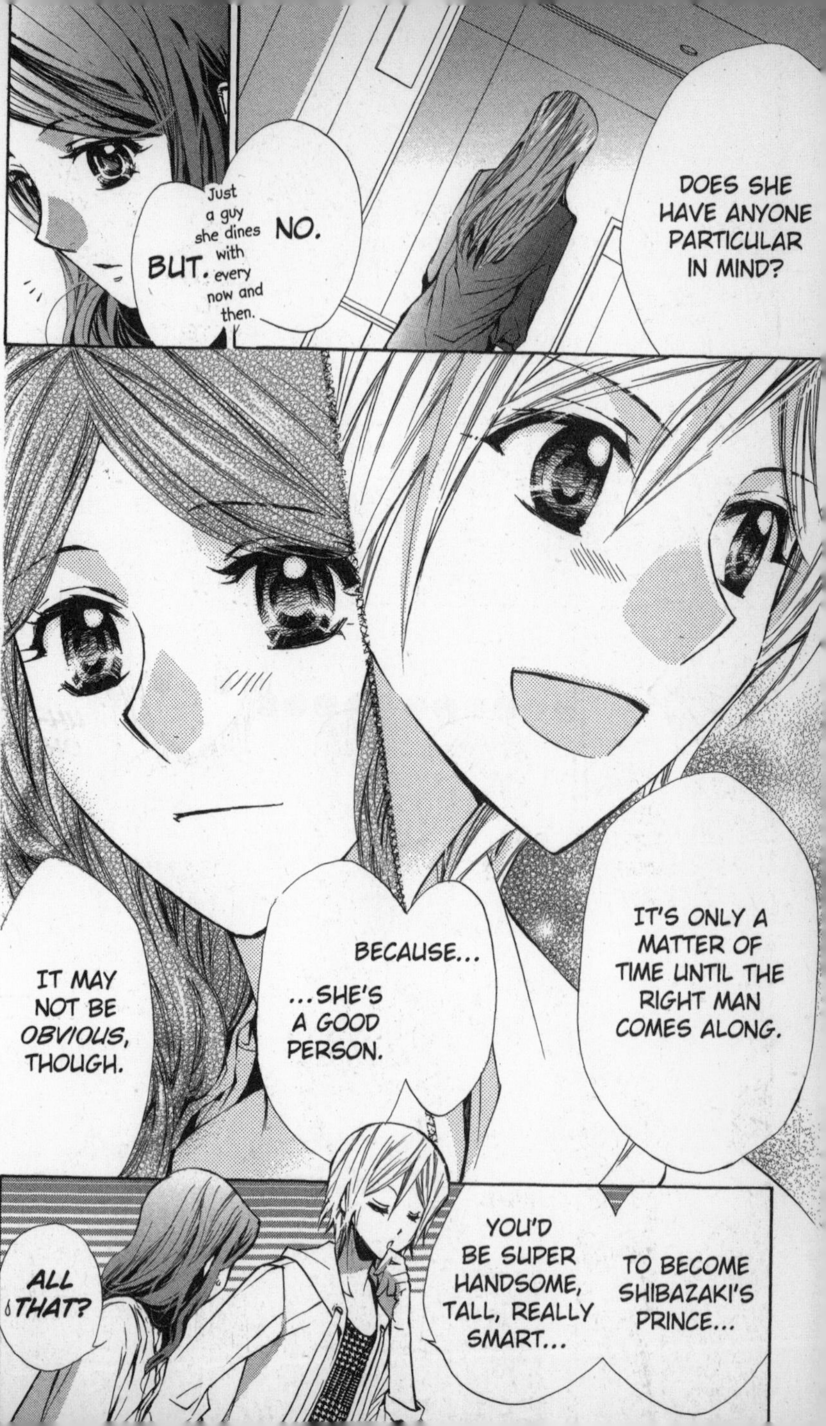
DOES SHE HAVE ANYONE PARTICULAR IN MIND?
NO.
BUT.
Just a guy she dines with every now and then.
IT'S ONLY A MATTER OF TIME UNTIL THE RIGHT MAN COMES ALONG.
BECAUSE...
...SHE'S A GOOD PERSON.
IT MAY NOT BE OBVIOUS, THOUGH.
TO BECOME SHIBAZAKI'S PRINCE...
YOU'D BE SUPER HANDSOME, TALL, REALLY SMART...
ALL THAT?

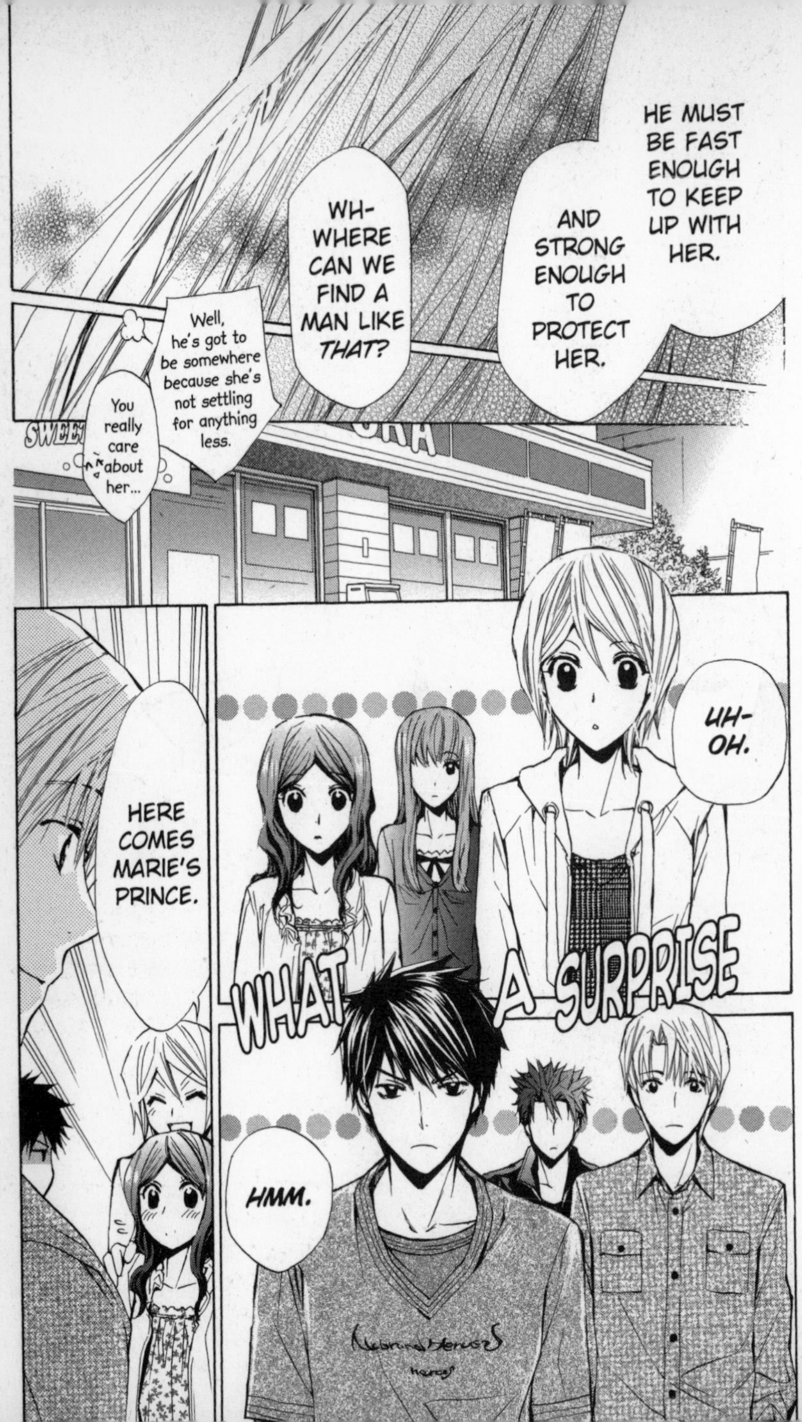
HE MUST BE FAST ENOUGH TO KEEP UP WITH HER.
AND STRONG ENOUGH TO PROTECT HER.
WH-WHERE CAN WE FIND A MAN LIKE *THAT?*
Well, he's got to be somewhere because she's not settling for anything less.
You really care about her...
UH-OH.
WHAT A SURPRISE
HMM.
HERE COMES MARIE'S PRINCE.

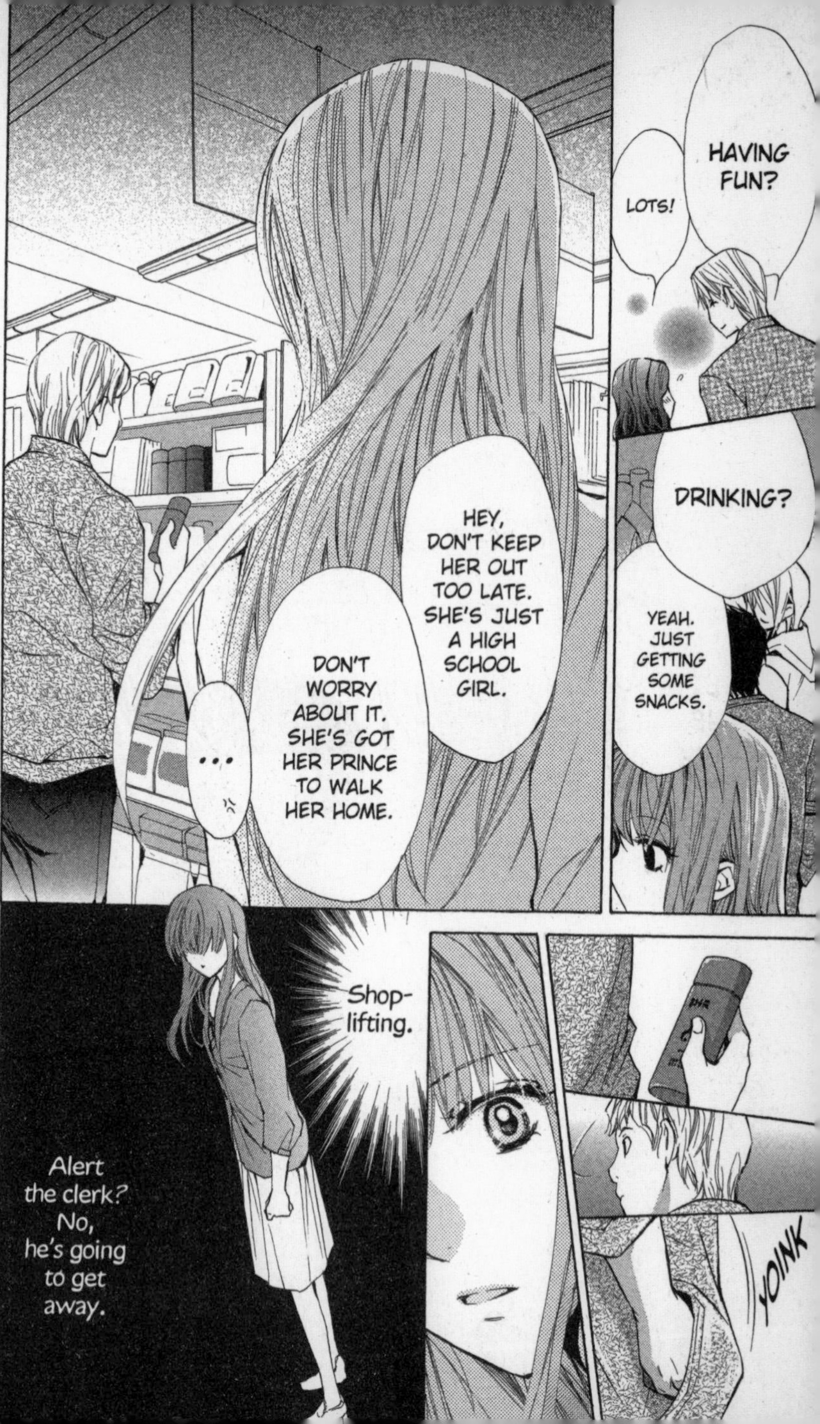
HAVING FUN?
LOTS!
DRINKING?
YEAH. JUST GETTING SOME SNACKS.
HEY, DON'T KEEP HER OUT TOO LATE. SHE'S JUST A HIGH SCHOOL GIRL.
DON'T WORRY ABOUT IT. SHE'S GOT HER PRINCE TO WALK HER HOME.
...
YOINK
Shop-lifting.
Alert the clerk? No, he's going to get away.

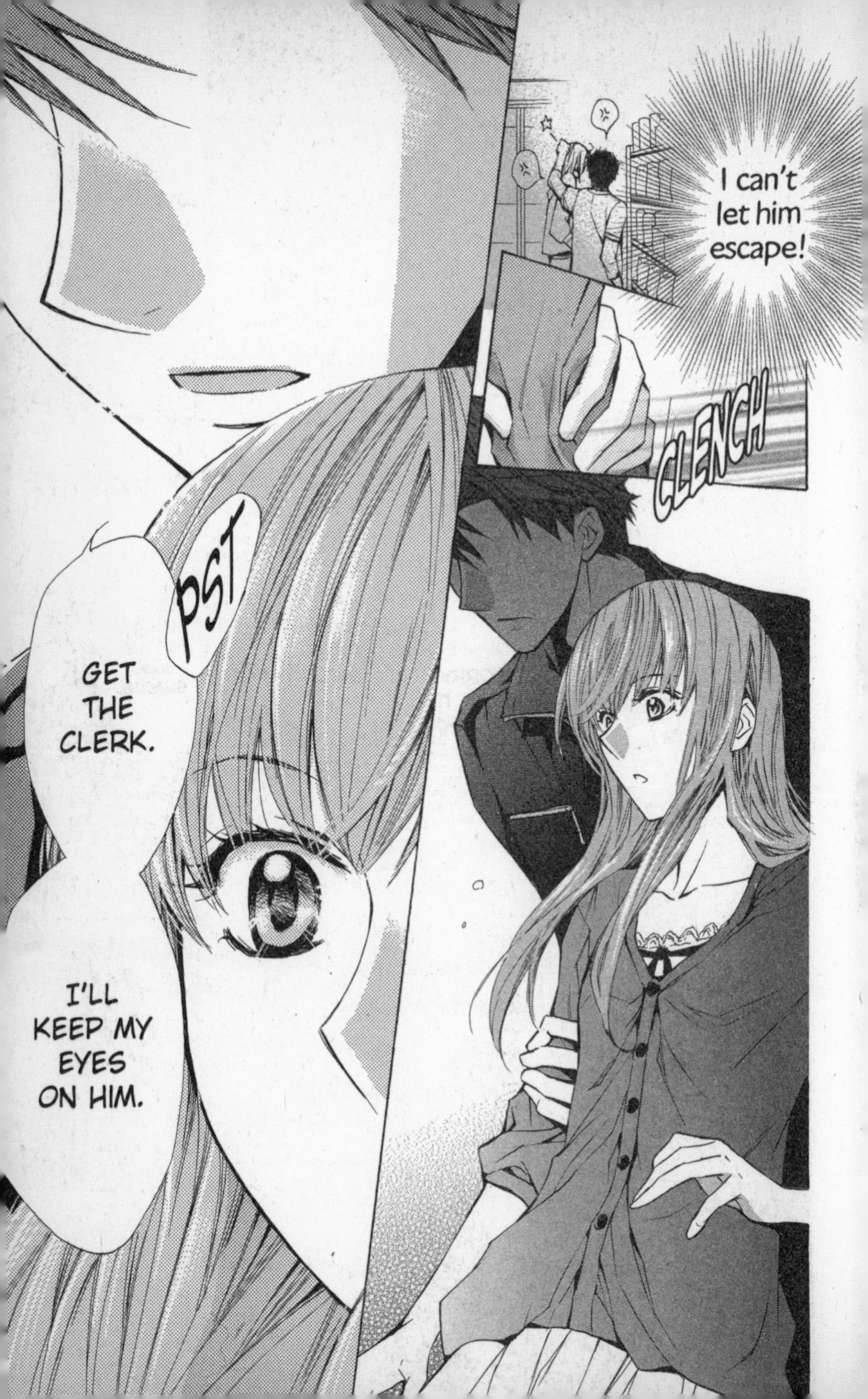
I can't let him escape!
CLENCH
PST
GET THE CLERK.
I'LL KEEP MY EYES ON HIM.

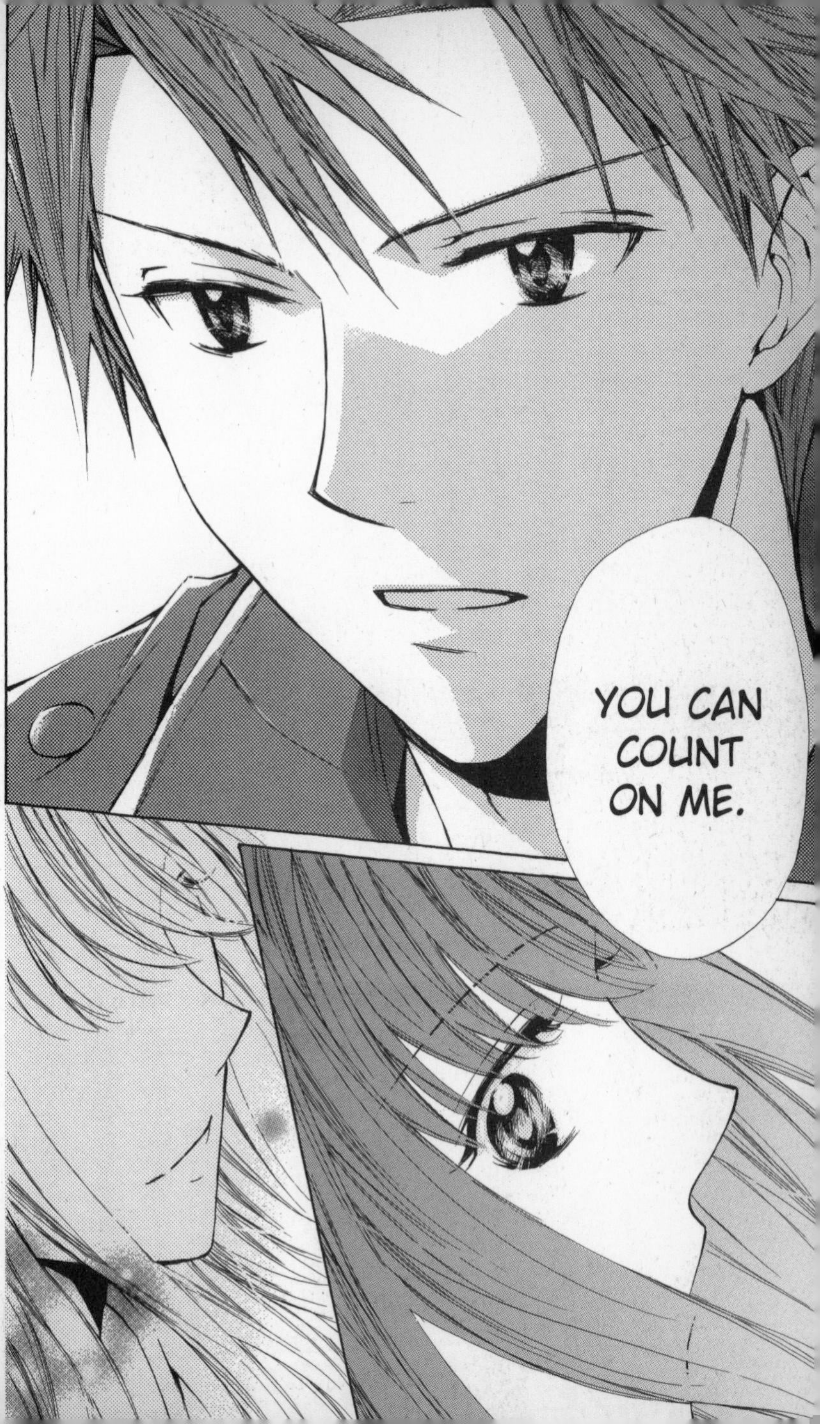
YOU CAN COUNT ON ME.

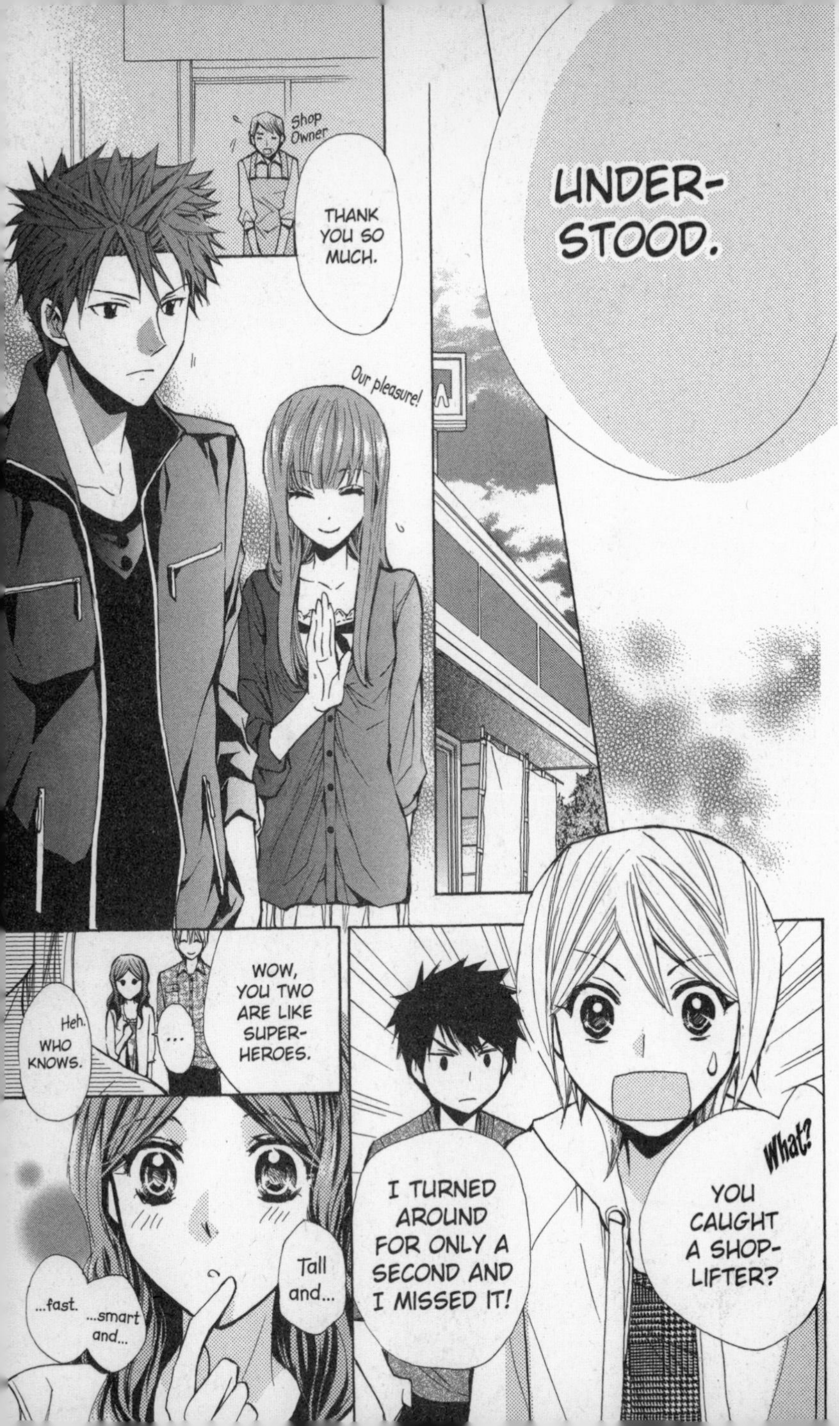
UNDER-STOOD.
Shop Owner
THANK YOU SO MUCH.
Our pleasure!
What?
YOU CAUGHT A SHOP-LIFTER?
I TURNED AROUND FOR ONLY A SECOND AND I MISSED IT!
WOW, YOU TWO ARE LIKE SUPER-HEROES.
...
Heh. WHO KNOWS.
Tall and...
...smart and...
...fast.

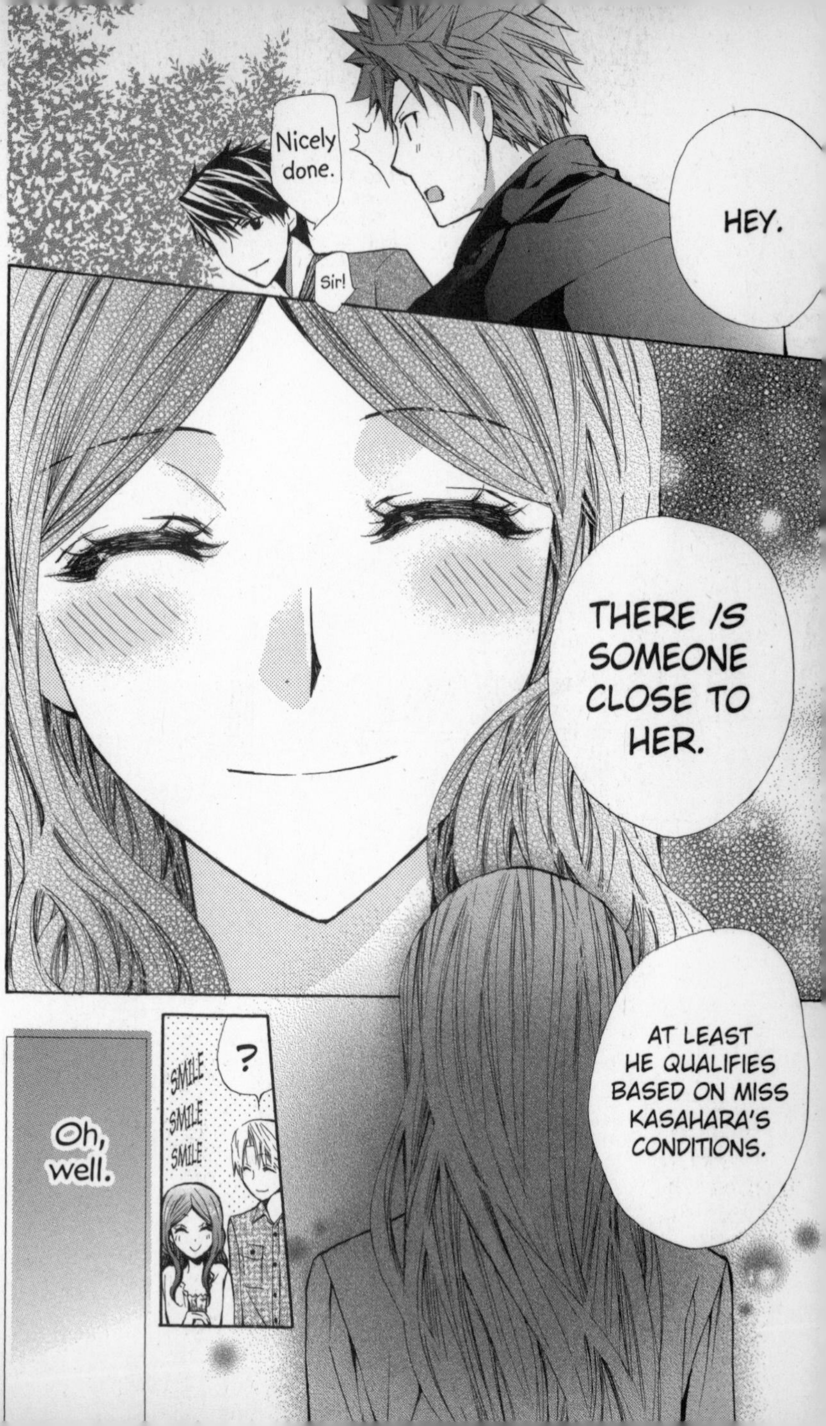
HEY.
Nicely done.
Sir!
THERE IS SOMEONE CLOSE TO HER.
AT LEAST HE QUALIFIES BASED ON MISS KASAHARA'S CONDITIONS.
?
SMILE SMILE SMILE
Oh, well.

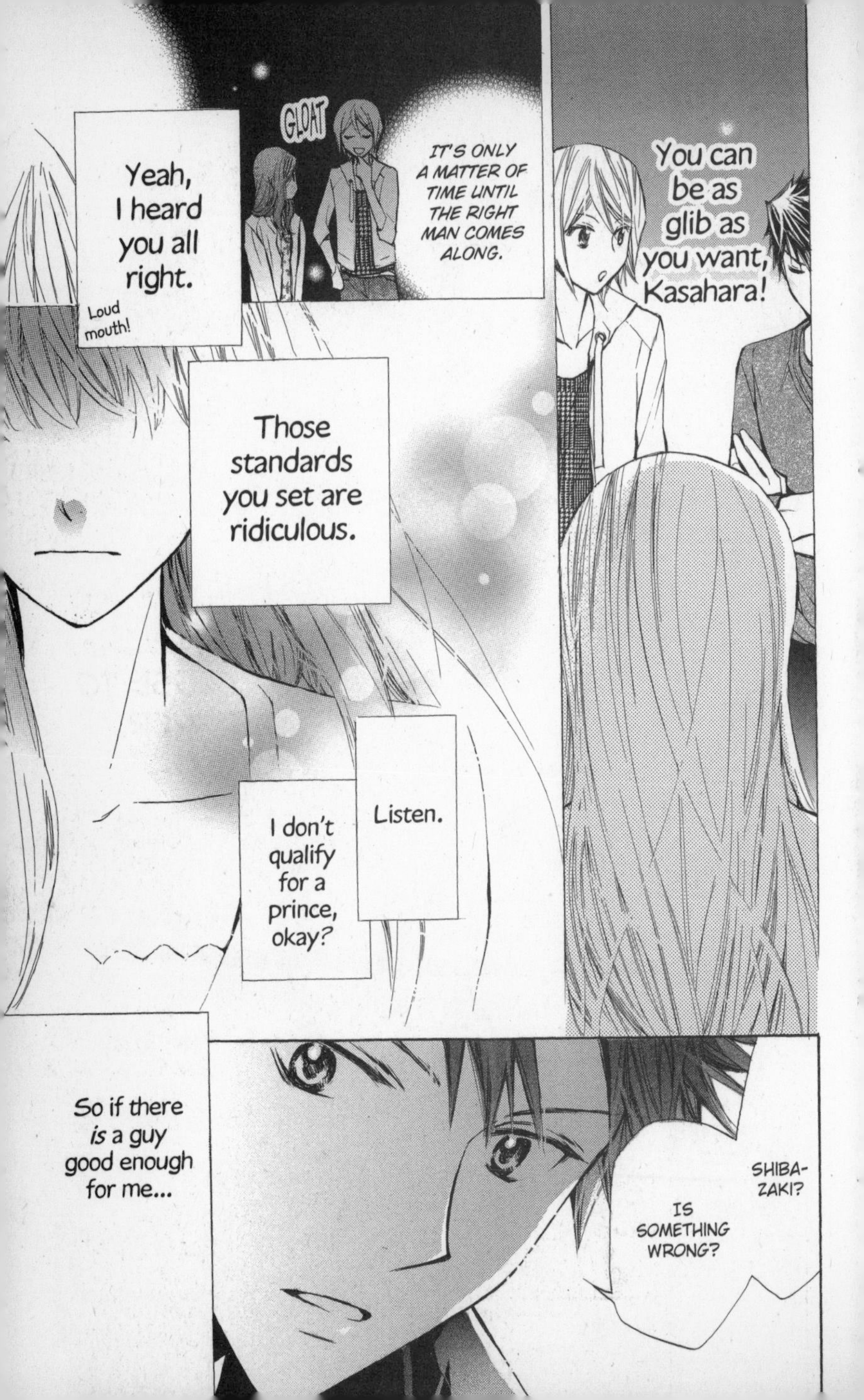
You can be as glib as you want, Kasahara!
GLOAT
IT'S ONLY A MATTER OF TIME UNTIL THE RIGHT MAN COMES ALONG.
Yeah, I heard you all right.
Loud mouth!
Those standards you set are ridiculous.
Listen.
I don't qualify for a prince, okay?
SHIBA-ZAKI?
IS SOMETHING WRONG?
So if there *is* a guy good enough for me...

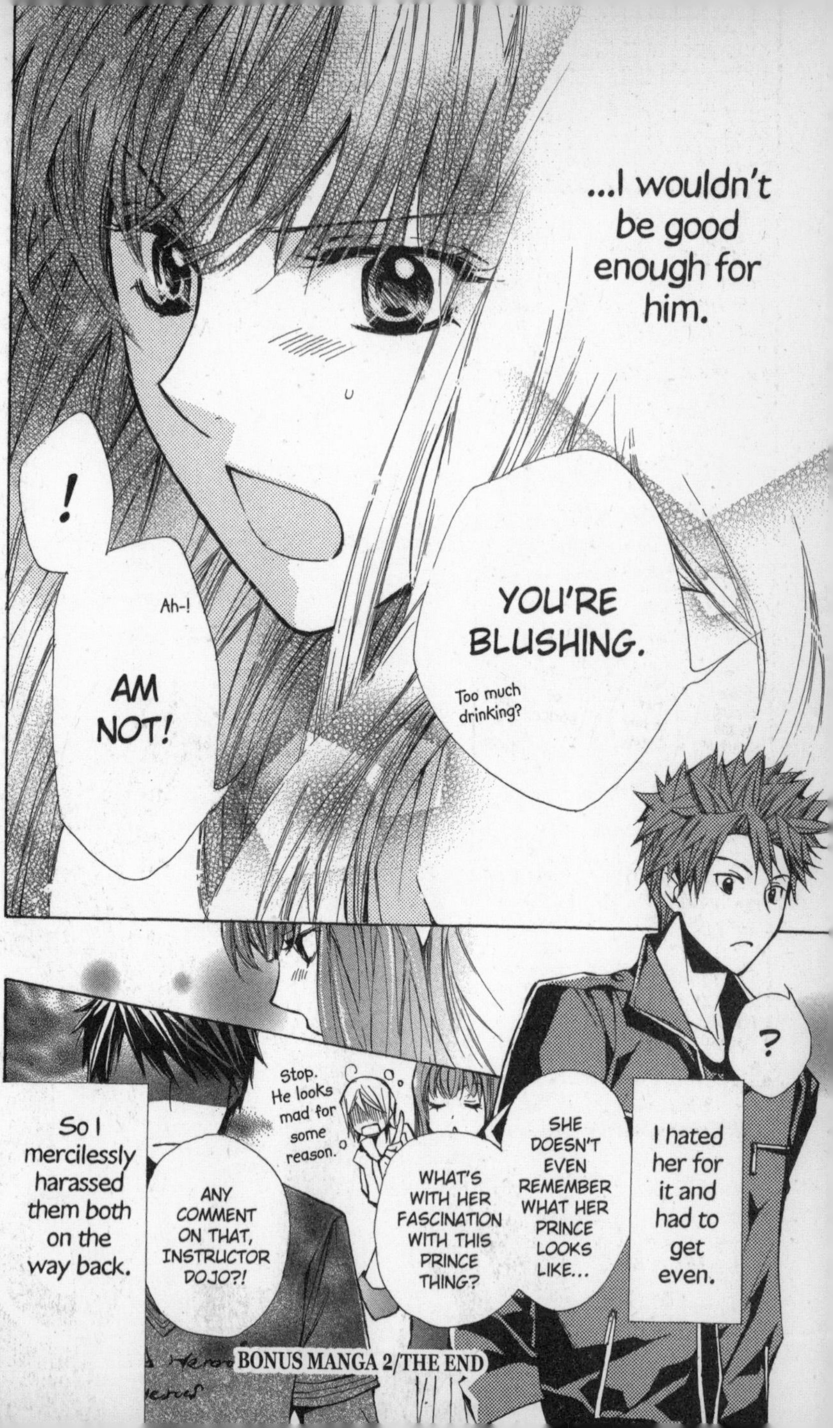
...I wouldn't be good enough for him.
YOU'RE BLUSHING.
Too much drinking?
!
Ah-!
AM NOT!
?
I hated her for it and had to get even.
SHE DOESN'T EVEN REMEMBER WHAT HER PRINCE LOOKS LIKE...
WHAT'S WITH HER FASCINATION WITH THIS PRINCE THING?
Stop. He looks mad for some reason.
ANY COMMENT ON THAT, INSTRUCTOR DOJO?!
So I mercilessly harassed them both on the way back.
BONUS MANGA 2/THE END

Special Thanks!!

Ms. Arikawa
Ms. Arikawa's editor (ASCII Media)
★
Mamada, Murakami, Aoki
★
My family
★
My editor, My former editor
★
Everyone who makes this series possible.
★★
Thanks so, so much!

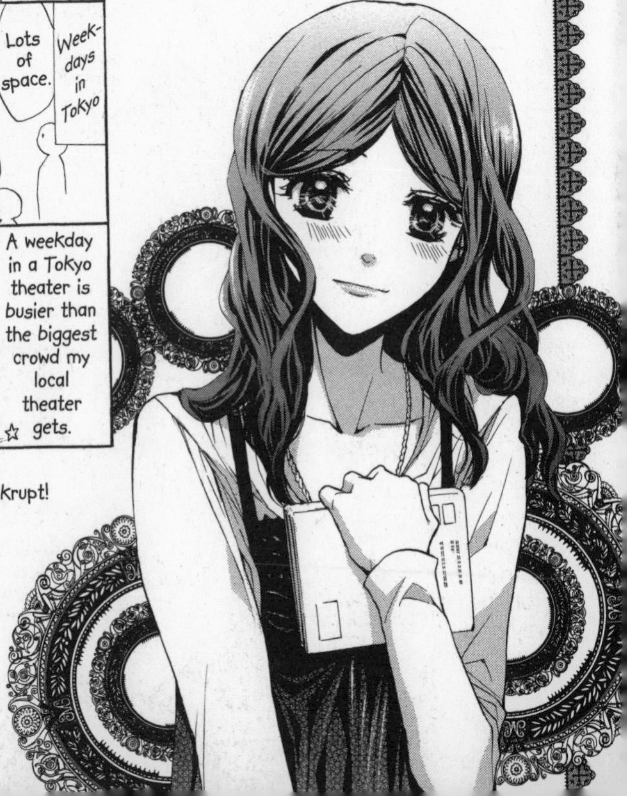

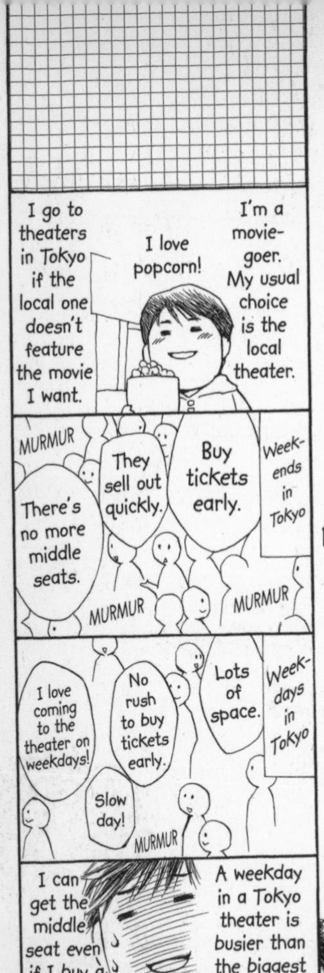
I'm a movie-goer. My usual choice is the local theater.
I love popcorn!
I go to theaters in Tokyo if the local one doesn't feature the movie I want.
Weekends in Tokyo
Buy tickets early.
They sell out quickly.
MURMUR
There's no more middle seats.
MURMUR
MURMUR
Weekdays in Tokyo
Lots of space.
No rush to buy tickets early.
I love coming to the theater on weekdays!
Slow day!
MURMUR
A weekday in a Tokyo theater is busier than the biggest crowd my local theater gets. ☆
I can get the middle seat even if I buy a ticket one minute before the movie.
PLING

I don't want the local theater to go bankrupt!

Hope to see you in the next volume.

Kiiro Yumi
弓きいろ

Kiiro Yumi won the 42nd *LaLa* Manga Grand Prix Fresh Debut award for her manga *Billy Bocchan no Yuutsu* (Little Billy's Depression). Her latest series is *Toshokan Senso Love&War* (*Library Wars: Love & War*), which runs in *LaLa* magazine in Japan and is published in English by VIZ Media.

Hiro Arikawa won the 10th Dengeki Novel Prize for her work *Shio no Machi: Wish on My Precious* in 2003 and debuted with the same novel in 2004. Of her many works, Arikawa is best known for the *Library Wars* series and her *Jieitai Sanbusaku* trilogy, which consists of *Sora no Naka* (In the Sky), *Umi no Soko* (The Bottom of the Sea) and *Shio no Machi* (City of Salt).

library wars

Volume 8
Shojo Beat Edition

Story & Art by **Kiiro Yumi**
Original Concept by **Hiro Arikawa**

ENGLISH TRANSLATION Kinami Watabe
ADAPTATION & LETTERING Sean McCoy
DESIGN Amy Martin
EDITOR Megan Bates

Toshokan Sensou LOVE&WAR by Kiiro Yumi and Hiro Arikawa
© Kiiro Yumi 2011
© Hiro Arikawa 2011
All rights reserved.
First published in Japan in 2011 by HAKUSENSHA, Inc., Tokyo.
English language translation rights arranged with HAKUSENSHA,
Inc., Tokyo.

The stories, characters and incidents mentioned in this publication
are entirely fictional.

Printed in Canada

Published by VIZ Media, LLC
P.O. Box 77010
San Francisco, CA 94107

10 9 8 7 6 5 4 3 2 1
First printing, September 2012

www.shojobeat.com   www.viz.com

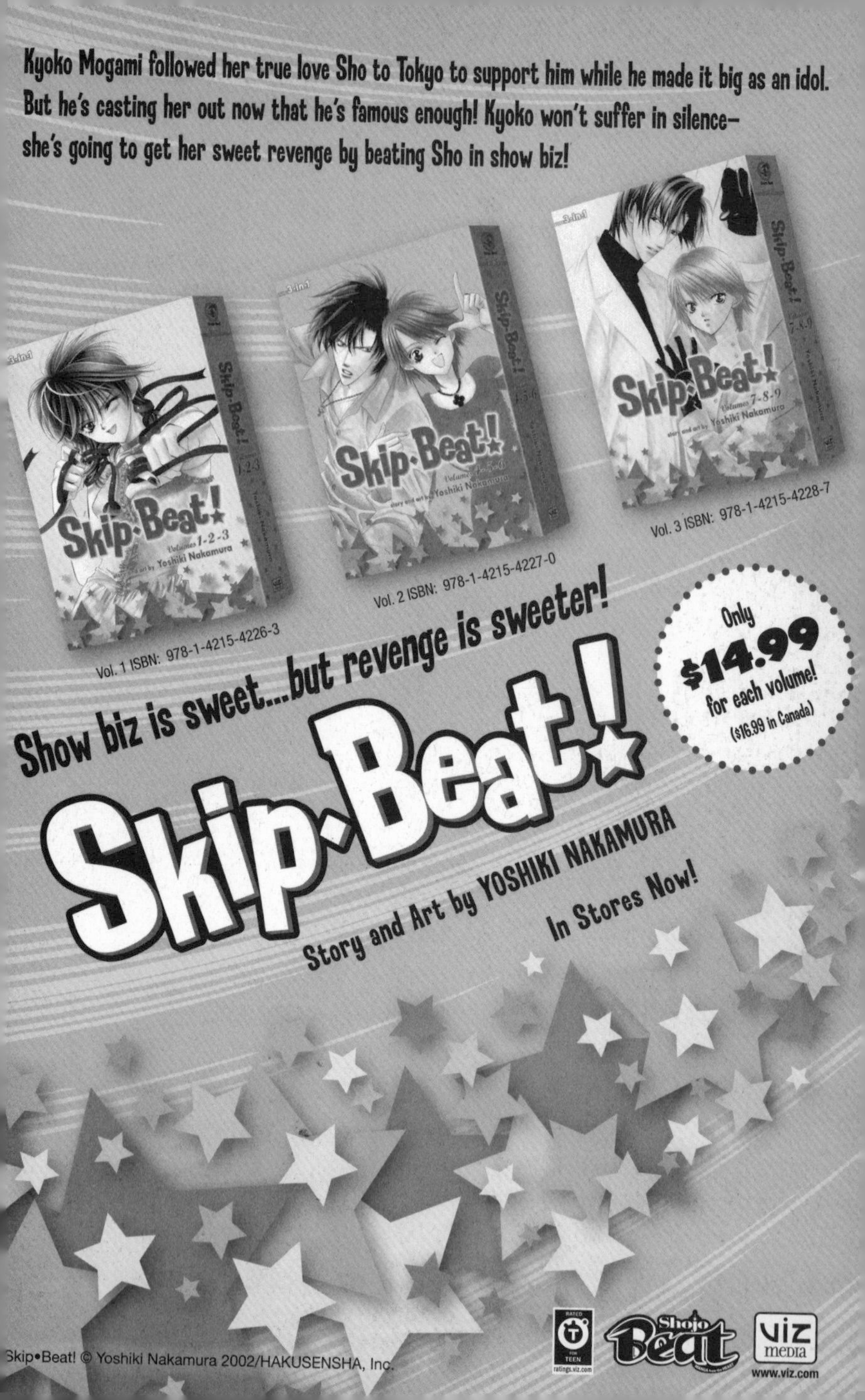
Kyoko Mogami followed her true love Sho to Tokyo to support him while he made it big as an idol.
But he's casting her out now that he's famous enough! Kyoko won't suffer in silence—
she's going to get her sweet revenge by beating Sho in show biz!
Vol. 1 ISBN: 978-1-4215-4226-3
Vol. 2 ISBN: 978-1-4215-4227-0
Vol. 3 ISBN: 978-1-4215-4228-7
Only $14.99 for each volume! ($16.99 in Canada)
Show biz is sweet...but revenge is sweeter!
Skip·Beat!
Story and Art by YOSHIKI NAKAMURA
In Stores Now!
Skip•Beat! © Yoshiki Nakamura 2002/HAKUSENSHA, Inc.
www.viz.com

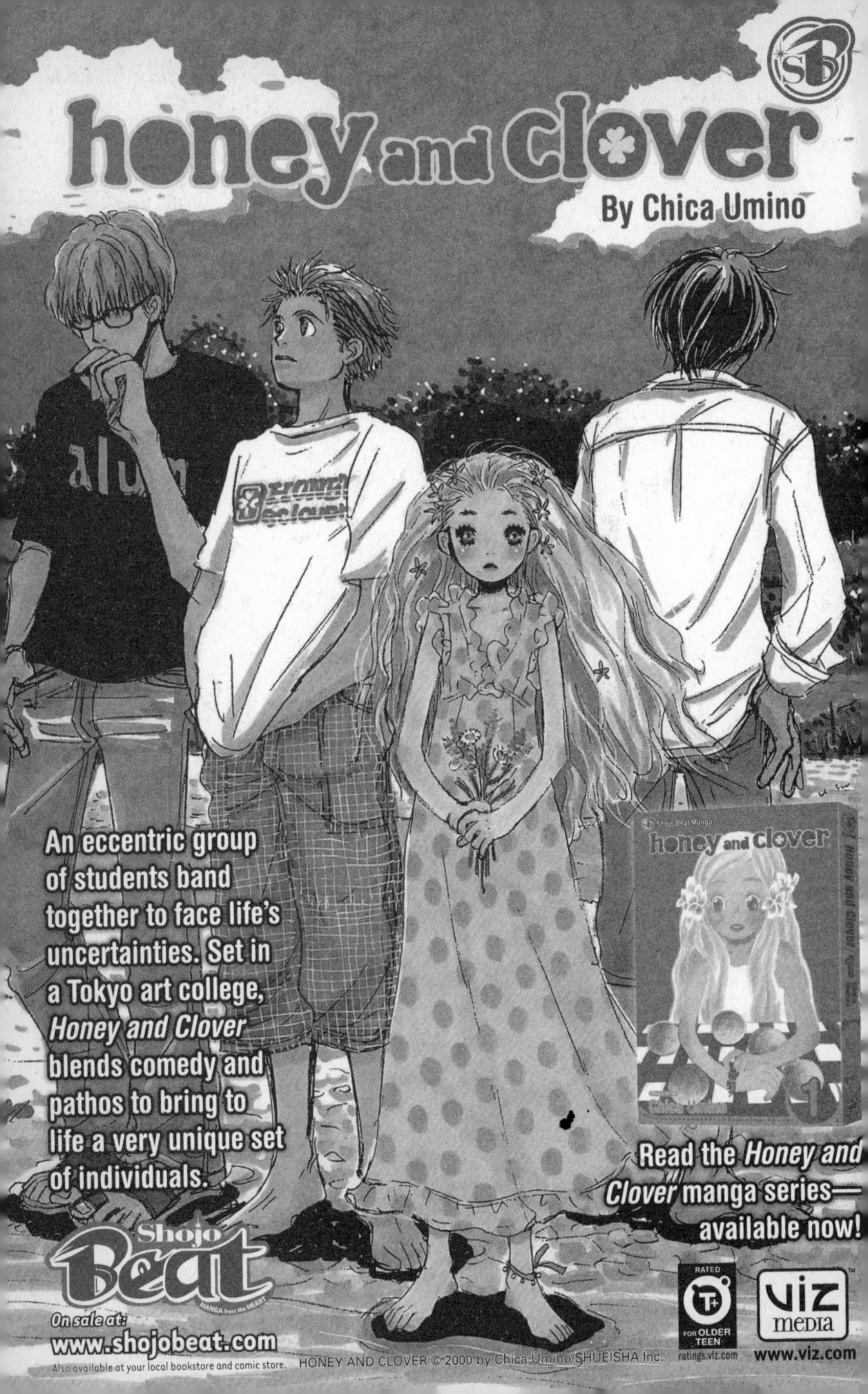
honey and clover
By Chica Umino
An eccentric group of students band together to face life's uncertainties. Set in a Tokyo art college, *Honey and Clover* blends comedy and pathos to bring to life a very unique set of individuals.
Shojo Beat Manga
honey and clover
Chica Umino
1
Read the *Honey and Clover* manga series—available now!
Shojo Beat
MANGA from the HEART
On sale at:
www.shojobeat.com
Also available at your local bookstore and comic store.
HONEY AND CLOVER © 2000 by Chica Umino/SHUEISHA Inc.
RATED
T+
FOR OLDER TEEN
ratings.viz.com
VIZ media
www.viz.com

This is the last page.

In keeping with the original Japanese
comic format, this book reads from right
to left—so action, sound effects, and
word balloons are completely reversed.
This preserves the orientation of the
original artwork—plus, it's fun! Check
out the diagram shown here to get the
hang of things, and then turn to the
other side of the book to get started!